Landscapes

compiled by

Sarah Johnson

Themes in Environmental History, 2

'Themes in Environmental History' is a series of readers for students and researchers. Each volume aims to cover a prominent subject in the discipline, combining theoretical chapters and case studies. All chapters have been previously published in the White Horse Press journals *Environment and History* and *Environmental Values*.

1. *Bioinvaders* (2010) ISBN 978-1-874267-55-3
2. *Landscapes* (2010) ISBN 978-1-874267-60-7

Further volumes forthcoming.

First published 2010 by
The White Horse Press, 10 High Street, Knapwell, Cambridge, CB23 4NR, UK

Set in 10 point Times

British Library Cataloguing in Publication Data
A catalogue record for this book is available from the British Library

ISBN 978-1-874267-60-7 (PB)

Contents

Publisher's Introduction

Sarah Johnson

William Cowper wrote in his famous pre-Romantic poem *The Task*, that

> The Love of Nature's works
> Is an ingredient in the compound, man (IV, 731–2)

This sense of the innateness of landscape appreciation[1] co-exists in long literary and philosophical tradition with intersecting sets of (often programmatic) discourses about how, precisely, human beings might formulate, communicate and respond to their apprehensions of landscape's aesthetic value. The present volume offers a dialogue between philosophical explorations of landscape aesthetics and historical case studies in which definitions of and responses to what is understood as 'landscape' are enacted upon the natural environment, shaping both Nature and the viewing subject.

Setting the Scene

The title *Landscapes* has quite deliberately been chosen, despite Benson's contention that the 'the terms "country", "countryside" or "land"' are preferable to '"landscape" with its implicit reference to the representation in painting of a view from a particular standpoint' (n.2, p.45). The picturesque tradition of landscape connoisseurship to which this objection refers will often be felt between the lines of the essays that follow. However, the term, as Olwig makes clear, has a highly suggestive evolution – originating in a Germanic word for a place of 'felt, cultural identity' (as opposed to either a topographical or political unit), the place to which an individual would proclaim affinity, the place shaped by but also shaping a people. The notion of 'shaping' remains in the word's next incarnation – as a piece of natural topography translated into the shape of a picture. It was from this pictorial sense that the term returned, newly inflected, to be applied to the physical land, in the sense of a natural view that recalled a landscape painting, firstly in a 'landskip garden' and then, in the later eighteenth century (after garden designer William Kent 'leaped the fence and saw that all Nature was a garden'[2]), in the countryside at large. Landscape therefore became 'a scene perceived, as in a theatre, from a particular point by an individual' (definition of landscape cited by Olwig, p.180, from Webster 1963).

The theatrical reference, whose ancestry can be traced back at least as far as Pliny the Younger's praise of the vista from his Tuscan villa as 'a vast amphitheatre such as could only be a work of nature',[3] has useful resonances. The amphitheatres of Ancient Greece were commonly designed around the local topography and tended to be sited on hillsides, the rows of seats echoing the gradient of the surrounding terrain. Indeed when visiting one of the unrenovated minor archaeological sites in Turkey, it is often hard to discern the boundary between theatre and hillside, so perfectly was the architectural style fitted to the topography. Moreover, Greek theatres commonly faced the sea, which would have provided a backdrop to the performance; nature, then, was called in to the theatre space. European travellers to exotic lands during the Enlightenment frequently invoked the 'amphitheatre' as a metaphor for the landscapes they saw, and fittingly so as it calls to mind not only a physical form but certain connotations that should be borne in mind in any discussion of landscape aesthetics. The Europeans were play-actors in a drama of discovery, as well as spectators of nature's scenes, an ambivalent role that encapsulates well the dynamics of landscape appreciation.[4] In construing a 'landscape', one does more than simply look; one acts, by interpreting and thus in some sense altering what is seen. The observer creates the 'amphitheatre', by mentally supplying the boundaries.

This chimes with Leo Marx's view that, broadly, landscape is shaped land, not raw matter. It involves contrivance and premeditation, and the ordering and shaping may be physical (as in agriculture or gardening) or metaphorical, 'accomplished by an act of mind or imagination'[5] that may be verbal or visual. Peter de Bolla reminds us that 'landscape only looks the way it does on account of an interactive relation among viewer, physical land and cultural imaginary', going on to state that 'we only ever see what we have learned to see'.[6] Whilst the viewer's culture will not wholly obscure the reality of what is seen, the viewing subject is constantly shaping and being shaped, learning by looking how to see landscape. Landscape is never, then, a static given. As Hepburn here observes, in viewing a landscape, 'the purely sensory component – colours, shapes, sounds, tactile sensations, smells' of landscape appreciation does not exist in isolation: we apply pre-conceived ideas to it; 'we conceptualise, we recognise, we add context, background, seek out formal relationships – reflectively' (p.1).

'The colour of the glass'[7]

The papers in the first section of this volume all deal with the impact of acquired ideas on the apprehension of landscape. This is both various (the range of such ideas covers philosophical aesthetics, religion, literature, biology, geology, agriculture, ecology and economics among many others) and variable, in that individual taste partly depends on the ideas that have primacy in the individual consciousness – though, as Brady argues, 'possessing an intersubjective grounding' and developed in a public context (p.16). Acquired ideas intervene between the viewer and the viewed. Hepburn observes that whether one's religious bent is toward seeing in Nature the 'divine archetype' of the perfect Creation or a deeply flawed remnant of the Fall will inevitably colour one's response to it (p.6). Benson notes that tracing a landscape's history 'on the ground ... may constitute an aesthetic experience ... even though, viewed ahistorically, the landscape is a dreary decaying one' (p.39). Brady points out that scientific knowledge can influence aesthetic valuing, positively and negatively': appreciation of 'the unscenic – even of the creepy-crawly – may be possible through immediate, sensuous appreciation anchored in scientific understanding which provides a background ecological story to what might otherwise appear, superficially, as ugly' (p.18); but, conversely, we may moderate our apprehension of beauty in the light of knowledge about detrimental effects on the environment, humans or biodiversity, as in the 'cases of beautiful non-native species crowding out, damaging or even causing the extinction of other species' (p.19).

Both philosophical essays and case studies interrogate the interactions of ideas and land. Douglas describes how scientific knowledge about the 'deep past' in South Australia can confer public value on otherwise unremarkable landscapes; at Lake Callabonna, for example, with its remarkable Pleistocene fossils, she writes that 'geological heritage [is] harnessed in the development of a landscape aesthetic appropriate to the "arid", "flat", "monotonous", "barren" country of north-eastern South Australia' (p.210). As Benson points out, when the eye takes in, say, a hedged field with grazing cattle, functional concepts are inevitably entangled with the textbook picturesque consciousness of variety of forms and pleasingness of composition. The 'purely practical' and the 'purely aesthetic' point of view commonly reside in the same consciousness. And when it comes to a landscape whose contours do not resemble a painting by Claude, an eye to other 'non-instrumental' knowledge systems may 'reveal qualities worthy of appreciation in landscapes that would otherwise appear aesthetically neutral or even ugly' (p.36). The same also applies to other knowledge systems: the scenes of greatest surface beauty may have considerably less ecological value than, say, 'Flat, fetid, dank, and visually unaesthetic swamps' (Olwig, p.193) but knowing this can inflect our view in favour of the latter.

While the yoking of acquired knowledge systems to the aesthetic impulse is often argued in this volume's chapters to enhance aesthetic appreciation, even if partially or delusively, the viewer of landscape is also frequently predisposed to regard a scene as distasteful, as in Dr Johnson's famous judgment of the Highlands, a modern paradigm of valued landscape. He loftily told Boswell's wife before embarking on his tour, 'Madam, we do not go there as to a paradise. We go to see something different from what we are accustomed to see.'[8] But inevitably he could not, in fact, leave behind his accustomed ideas – and his taste in landscape was for the Augustan Georgic, not the yet-to-be-fashionable sublime:

> An eye accustomed to flowery pastures and waving harvests is astonished and repelled by this wide extent of hopeless sterility. The appearance is that of matter incapable of form or usefulness, dismissed by nature from her care and disinherited of her favours, left in its original elemental state, or quickened only with one sullen power of useless vegetation. It will very readily occur, that this uniformity of barrenness can afford little amusement to the traveller; that it is easy to sit at home and conceive rocks and heath, and waterfalls; and that these journeys are useless labours, which neither impregnate the imagination, nor enlarge the understanding[9].

Wills' challenging account of America's 'nuclear parks' demonstrates that contemporary cultural assumptions can also impede appreciation: 'a bunch of coyotes hanging out at ground zero' (p.239) was not what the public was conditioned to expect of a post-nuclear landscape and it is thus a rare commentator who ventures with Rebecca Solnit to find the 'unpopulated zones of Nevada Test Site preferable to the claustrophobic Yosemite, shocked to discover "this country's national Eden so full of disturbing surprises and its Armageddon so comparatively pleasant"' (cited by Wills, p.236). The 'pure' aesthetic response to landscape – though heavily theorised by Enlightenment philosophers – is, in practice, impossible.

Defining and Defending

We shall return to the ways in which the interposing of ideas between the mind and the landscape is tied to dynamics of domination – of human over Nature and human over human. First, though, it is worth pondering, with Haldane, how it has come to pass that we think (despite the objectivist, utilitarian modes of thinking prevalent in policy circles, lamented by Brady, Douglas and others) that to appreciate landscape aesthetically is 'a mark of a refined sensibility and ... something to be approved of and cultivated' (Haldane, p.47). Furthermore, the kinds of landscapes appreciated and the relationship expected between the viewing subject and the viewed object, are by no means necessary givens. Haldane even problematises the reflex of construing landscapes as scenes – in paintings, photographs and in the mind. While the individual artwork in a gallery is fairly obviously delimited, 'it seems in principle impossible to say where one work of nature begins and another ends'; thus scenes in Nature – landscapes – derive only from 'the selective attention of spectators to aspects of a continuous realm', that selection at least in part being 'influenced by the experience of actual art-works' (p.52). As the mind of the viewer supplies the qualities that allow 'a landscape' to be isolated, we return to the idea that 'natural beauty is *constitutively* tied to human experience' (p.53) and cannot be pinned down in any other terms. However, the boundaries of the 'landscape' need not simply be the surface frames of the Claude-glass; other sorts of experience than surface appearances may shape aesthetic consciousness. Haldane instances Aldo Leopold's 'Marshland Elegy' as a paradigmatic example of this more holistic sort of nature aesthetic, which encompasses ecological history and Romantic empathy:

> our appreciation of the crane grows with the slow unravelling of earthly history[...] When we hear his call we hear no mere bird. We hear the trumpet in the orchestra of evolution. He is the symbol of our untamable past, of that incredible sweep of millennia which underlies and conditions the daily affairs of birds and men.

Every era has fashioned its own symbols from Nature, but there is a good case for arguing that the modern valuing of certain types of 'wild' landscape and sense of their spiritual impact is rooted in late eighteenth and early nineteenth century Romanticism[10]. Haldane quotes Dr Johnson's judgment of the Highlands in order to show that there is 'nothing perennially obvious about the present-day reverence for nature and the elevation of its appreciation to the higher categories of human consciousness' (p.48). Indeed, as he observes, St Augustine took his own admiration of the 'high mountains' as a culpable character failing, turning the mind away from contemplation of the self and its relationship with god towards mere external objects. It was only in the Romantic period that the sense developed of Nature and human appreciation of Nature as embodying the divine and the divine-in-human, the 'one life within us and abroad' as Coleridge put it.[11] Several chapters in this volume trace the evolution of that sensibility, by which external objects came to be valued for the beneficial, perhaps transcendent, possibilities they offered the viewing subject. As Hinchman and Hinchman observe, 'it is from the [Romantic] conviction that external landscapes shape the inner person that the modern enthusiasm for wilderness derives' (p.65). They argue that the Romantics 'believed that people exiled from or insensitive to nature's deeper rhythms and patterns forfeit an essential aspect of their humanity' (p.57), and trace this belief down to modern ecologists, such as Aldo Leopold or John Muir, albeit acknowledging that the 'primary impetus' of Romanticism 'was the all-sided development of the individual rather than the investigation and preservation of the natural world' (p.57). Hepburn notes a convergence of the two in the Wordsworthian vision whereby 'subject-object distinction is overcome, and the God-world distinction no less annulled' (p.8):

> ...sense sublime
> Of something far more deeply interfused,
> Whose dwelling is the light of setting suns,
> And the round ocean and the living air,
> And the blue sky, and in the mind of man
> ('Lines Written a Few Miles above Tintern Abbey', 95–9)

Brady's analysis of the intersection of the aesthetic and the ethical necessitates pluralising the mind and the man here and embeds the Romantic aspiration in modern thinking about nature's beneficial effects. She argues that the 'perceptual sensitivity, imaginative freedom, creativity and emotional expression' (p.17) required in aesthetic appreciation, whether of art or nature, have an important bearing on human relationships and empathy and that, furthermore, 'there is at least intuitive strength in the idea' that aesthetic valuation might lead to greater emotional attachment to a given landscape (p.18). The Romantic recognition of the 'restorative power' of Nature has a practical and two-way result, she claims: people are inclined to protect cherished environments and, in engaging with them, 'through activities more and less aesthetically motivated', such as gardening or recreation, people discover the 'potential of care for nature as well as caring for ourselves' (p.26).

A number of authors here are interested in what causes a certain landscape to be 'cared for'. Wills provocatively argues that to a very real extent America's yearning for 'human-less "frozen" wilderness' is supplied more by her nuclear no man's lands than by her national parks, though the same wilderness characteristics of both led to their initial selection for development or conservation. In the face of evidence that suggests natural degradation in national parks and unexpected thriving in nuclear test sites, Wills suggests that 'the vigour with which nuclear lands have been derided, and nature parks exalted, owes more to entrenched social values than to any extensive consideration of the places involved' (p.224). Guilt about technological domination of land, whether by building, resource-extraction or other development, is naturally more prevalent than concern over conservation efforts, however problematic or false their premises may be, and Hepburn links this strongly to the aesthetic as well as the moral: 'where technology threatens to modify or to dominate nature, we sense that we are so much the less likely to discern in that landscape the fundamental properties (whether comfortable, exhilarating or desolate) of actual nature' (p.3). The sense of personal unity with landscape being threatened is a natural spur to outrage which the Hinchmans root in the Romantic concept of the 'life-world' (where nature and humans are linked temporally as well as spatially) which gives natural objects 'a human significance that transcends their mere physical properties. That is why people often fight to save a threatened lake, meadow or mountain from development' (p.73). They go so far as to suggest that 'nature only becomes a matter for ethical concern, inspiration, love and protection once certain complex shifts have occurred in the sensibility of the subject' (p.57). Haldane's conundrum about the individuation of a landscape is here allied to individual memory and desire, positing Romantic antecedents for the environmentalist thought that acknowledges ecosystems to be temporal as well as spatial, and prizes integrity over time.

The Rhetoric of Unravished Quietness

While the Romantics' appreciation of landscape did not directly demand its protection, they believed that in the immemorial could be found humanity's most profound relationship with the landscape – in places where natural processes and phenomena are unscathed and where 'the fabric of human time and memories remain intact, where place has not yielded to abstract space, and where the mind and imagination still resonate with the forms of nature' (the Hinchmans, p.73). They felt, and bequeathed the feeling to twentieth-century ecologists, that 'there really is something in rural and wilderness landscapes that might transform us' (p.65), and that this quality is more present in less 'used and abused landscapes', the wild or the primitive, where human life and Nature are in harmony (p.71). Numerous commentators have derided as fallaciously nostalgic their idealisation of 'the good, simple, wholesome rural life' (Benson, p.42); and Goddard's chapter in the present volume offers a slightly queasy view of the foundations of affluent American 'penurbia' on continuing myths about idyllic rurality. Benson sides with Ruskin in castigating the aesthetic consumer of the rural ('Fallen cottage – desolate villa – deserted village – blasted heath – mouldering castle – to him, so that they do but show jagged angles of stone and timber, all are sights equally joyful', cited p. 33), arguing that it is 'heedless' at best to ignore the history of use that has shaped a seemingly 'wild' landscape like the Lakeland fells. While the Romantic-influenced view demands change to be arrested in even historically human-modified landscapes Benson argues that there is, of necessity, no 'reason to think that the aesthetic character of a landscape at any particular point in time has a privileged status' (p.42), and that, from aesthetic motivations,

> to preserve the appearance of a landscape when the function which produced that appearance has lapsed is to bring about radical change, even though the landscape bears no sign of that change on its face. (p.44)

Olwig shows how with Romanticism, the formerly despised people of Jutland Heath 'came to be seen as natural Arcadian shepherds who expressed, in their culture, the nature of the unspoiled landscapes which they inhabited' (p.182). Yet vigorous nineteenth-century efforts to afforest and cultivate the heath radically altered its character in the name of progress even while it was celebrated as the Danish Romantic landscape *par excellence*. Modern attempts at 'restoration' pay lip-service to the Romantic aesthetic but, Olwig argues, since the human-Nature interactions that formed the 'original' landscape are now consigned to history, what is left is a superficial pastiche, divorced from what the Hinchmans call the 'life-world'.

What is original and unspoilt, and to what point restoration (if restoration is valid) ought to return a landscape are fraught questions, especially when several cultural perspectives are involved. Douglas, describing a conservation battle to preserve Hallett Cove in South Australia notes a rhetoric of unspoiltness that is the direct descendant of Romantic delight in solitude and wilderness: the cove was described as being 'close to its natural condition' and 'nature in its untamed state', phrases that were 'patently at odds with the reality of a landscape which had been grazed, mined and farmed for well over one hundred years [... and] disingenuously heedless of evidence for pre-European modification of the landscape in the form of Aboriginal "tool factories" and fires' (p.205). The 'high-Romantic solitude' (Shaw, p.107) celebrated by Thomas Pringle in the South African desert – 'the blank horizon round and round / Without a living sight or sound' – obscures from view the indigenous tribes whose activities he describes in other poems. Equally relevant to the Kalahari is Douglas's warning: 'when dealing with material that might have informed Aboriginal understanding of their own pasts' one must ask: 'is there such a thing as non-cultural heritage in country as saturated with meaning as Australia?' (p.204) Early 'discoverers' routinely missed, ignored or misinterpreted the signs of earlier human presence on 'virgin' landscapes, (wishfully) thinking the stage clear for their colonial performances.

'Spirits ... from their confines call'd to enact / My present fancies.'[12] *Stage-Managing the Scene.*

Romanticism warned against making landscape a 'static backdrop for human dramas' (the Hinchmans, p.62), a view in keeping with the modern environmental consciousness, but Olwig points to a troubling effect in Romantic writing and Romantically inspired environmental restoration of viewing a place 'aesthetically as landscape scenery', as just such a 'backdrop': 'the people of the area become reduced to just another expression of that landscape scene – just so much ornament to be blotted out with the flick of a brush, so much stage scenery, to be changed at the close of a scene' (p.185). Goddard's 'penurbia' similarly elides previous historical or indigenous meanings: its 'new country types saw land as a setting', not as habitat but as a backdrop to be ornamented with 'horse pasturage, riding schools, vineyards, vineries and the like' (p.266).

The meanings ascribed to landscapes, who imposes them and to serve what agenda, are at the heart of this book's historical cases. From the falsely glowing reports 'representing the Zuureveld, as a fair and fertile region of unrivalled beauty and fecundity' sent home by colonists keen to entice settlers' (Pringle, cited by Shaw, p.100) to the religious meanings imposed by monks on the medieval Ardennes (Arnold); the conflicting definitions of Zimbabwean forest described by Schmidt; and the battles of definition between conservation bodies and nuclear agencies in the USA (Wills), interpretations of landscapes have often been far from disinterested. As Addison put it in 1712, 'a man of polite imagination' feels in surveying the countryside, 'a kind of property in every thing he sees'; the very act of visually framing a prospect, before he has even expressed any view as to its meaning, 'makes the most rude uncultivated parts of nature administer to his pleasures'.[13]

The position of aesthetic appreciation is generally one of dominance even when awe is protested – the 'prospect' of the eighteenth century connoisseur is inflected with Appleton's sense of socio-biological advantage. Thus, the urban émigrés in penurbia had the advantage of the 'wherewithal from metropolitan incomes, jobs and house sales' to 'take a vision from their mind's eye and project it across a plot of land' in the shape of 'toy' farms supported by city incomes. Bonyhady's thought-provoking essay on nineteenth-century Australian landscape photography shows how human domination could be physically inscribed on the landscape, in the name of 'compositional improvement', even without ownership. The idea of the photographer as the peaceful recorder of what nature has serendipitously composed into scenes is challenged by figures like John Watt Beattie who 'always carried an axe' so that he could 'soon remedy any faulty composition' (p.84) and Bonyhady examines photographs that boast foregrounds of 'stumps and felled tree trunks', intended to expose a panoramic view. What a landscape artist could do in imagination involved photographers in wilful destruction, perhaps only of relatively insignificant trees but, as Bonyhady points out, 'the destructiveness matters a great deal ... if we start from the premise that celebration of nature rests on appreciation and hence respect' (p.93); here the celebration is rooted in destruction.

It is in terms of interpretations jostling for primacy, though, that most of our cases approach power politics. Landscape is reconfigured in discourse as much as in fact. In Arnold's account of Benedictine monks in the medieval Ardennes, the economic fact of the wealthy monasteries' control and configuration of water resources is shown to have been rewritten as God-given power, in stories such as Saint Remacle's revival of a dried up spring, a miracle enshrined in the physical landscape by the channelling of the spring through a lead pipe ('converting the wild spring into a managed resource', p.152) and the erection of a cross. As Arnold observes, despite the reputation of medieval monasteries for seeking out deserted wildernesses, the reality was often one of 'controlling and taming nature for economic power', in turn increasing religious power:

> By claiming saintly approval of waterworks, irrigation canals and similar parts of the agricultural infrastructure, the monks of the Ardennes used their religious identity to justify and reinforce their social and economic power. (p.165)

Schmidt explores attitudes to East Zimbabwean rainforest, with colonial incursions being interpreted as the 'transformation' of 'wilderness' into 'known space', ignoring the reality of established indigenous understanding of the landscape. This is illustrated in the palpable absurdity of 'a Native Commissioner ordering a road gang of local people who know the area perfectly well to build a road which he can follow in order to find out where it leads to' (p.129). Schmidt argues that the employment of sexual metaphors of virgin territory 'enabled the construction of landscape as wilderness ... and thus legitimated penetration' (p.130). She juxtaposes this discourse with native Zindi stories of the rainforest which also gender it female but 'construct male human sexuality as being endangered by feminised landscape' (p.131). Thus, using similar metaphors, Europeans and Africans arrived at conflicting ideas about 'penetrating' forests: local Africans' sense that 'penetration meant danger' 'arguably prevented forests from being turned into agricultural production areas' (p.132), while European colonialists saw them as virgin territory, ripe for the taking. Schmidt's paper traces how these conflicting views led to 'real contestations over resources and informed the strategies employed by the parties involved' (p.140).

Binder and Burnett use the novels of Kenyan Ngugi Wa Thiong'o to show how conflicts between colonial and indigenous interpretations of landscape might give rise ultimately – if the former prevail – to widespread local alienation from the land. Ngugi's approach, they argue, 'questions the Western presumption that it is possible to manage a landscape separately from the society that depends on and shapes that landscape' (p.111) and shows how the imposition of western systems can damage local relationships with the land. It is argued that, as landscape 'contains the material symbols of culture', its people ought to maintain responsibility for it; 'to destroy a landscape is to destroy society and to control the landscape is to control society' (p. 113). Thus, in Ngugi's novels the imposition of British '"order" on the local jumble' (p.114) in the shape of colonial officers' neat gardens – seen by one local as 'so much energy and brains wasted on beautifying trees' (*Petals of Blood*, p.146, cited by Binder and Burnett, p.115) – becomes a symbol of social control. Ngugi's novels are concerned with loss of land and power to foreigners and, in *A Grain of Wheat*, with the problem of nostalgia; there is an unfulfilled hope 'that, with the departure of the foreign power, the landscape, like some ancestor of long-ago, will return and all will be right with the world' (p.116). *Petals of Blood* goes further, seeing the people's alienation from their land because of new commercial, capitalistic systems as so thorough as to make the landscape 'corrupted and unproductive as if man, alienated from his labour, his fellow man, and himself, is now alienated from nature too' (p.117). Binder and Burnett suggest that:

> This alienation from the land, rather than the economics of subsistence agriculture and excessive population growth alone, may explain much of the decline in Africa's environmental condition. The *wananchi* can hardly be expected to feel responsibility for things, including the land, over which they have little control. (p.121)

The altering or destruction of the culture embedded in landscape is an important act of domination, already alluded to in the case of Jutland heath. The elision of the existing cultural reality in the service of some vision – whether of Romantic solitude, progress or the desire for gain – is a recurring issue in discussions of historical landscape. Wills, for example, notes that in the establishment of both American National Parks and nuclear sites indigenous places and customs were disregarded as planners 'superimposed their desires for vacant spaces onto the physical landscape' (p.226).

From Prospect to Refuge, Scenery to Environment

A well-meaning wish to avoid this tendency to impose culturally contingent definitions on landscape has perhaps influenced the drive to what Binder and Burnett call 'an aesthetic free of individual and culturally sensitive standards of beauty' (p.112). Both they and Brady observe that 'mere' aesthetic judgment is often dismissed as individual and relative, as 'lying in the realm of the decorative' (Brady, p.16) and thus as 'trivial' compared to functional aspects or even concepts such as 'scientific value'. While Benson rightly argues that 'the aesthetic character of a landscape is logically independent of its having characteristics that make it scientifically or historically interesting, or of its being connected to oneself or one's people' (p.40), the experiential and pragmatic reality may be different: landscape appreciations that proclaim indifference to beauty and instead elevate ecology, cultural identity or even pecuniary value have tried to construct a 'responsible' landscape aesthetic that is far from Romantic numinousness and can be defended in a world where, as Douglas puts it:

> Value in a landscape is negotiated at the boundaries of the sometimes incompatible sacralisations of science versus heritage, education and training versus preservation, indigenous and other patrimonies and the requirements of tourism or industry. (p.197)

Several authors lay bare 'irresponsible' attitudes to landscape aesthetics – Goddard's play-farming in penurbia, Benson's castigation of tourism activities that mummify landscapes evolved from uses now obsolete, and, strikingly, Olwig's linking of the theatrical metaphor that was introduced so lightly at the start of this essay with ecological havoc:

> While the public stands hypnotised, distracted by a vision of landscape as scene, the landscape, in its original sense as an expression of the creative activities of its natives, is destroyed. Nature, as a generative physical force, is transformed into a scenic illusion. (p.191)

Benson asks a burning question: what is the 'proper relationship between the practical and the aesthetic'? (p.41)

Though a number of authors here consider the ways in which, knowingly or not, aesthetic appreciation is constructed and fed by cultural value systems and agendas, and argue that the aesthetic – to avoid ethical culpability – should not be detached from other structures of meaning, Brady makes an important point whose significance should not be underestimated for its coming so late in this essay: 'aesthetic experience is sometimes the most visceral, felt experience we can have of nature' (p.18). The awe or even simple pleasure we feel in the face of certain landscapes has stirred endless philosophical speculation, of which the volumes of text anatomising the sublime in the eighteenth century represent perhaps the most extreme example. Hepburn argues that the rational need not be the approved way of approaching the aesthetic, that perhaps 'the aesthetic experience may keep alive some view of the world that the concepts of systematic metaphysical thought cannot precisely articulate, nor its arguments support' (p.10). While the 'solemnly enlivening' sense of 'spiritual ascendancy' (p.12) we encounter in the face of the sublime is an undoubted pleasure of human existence, attempts to explain it – it has always been suspected – are perhaps inimical to the nature of the experience. Hepburn asserts that the knowledge-based perspective on landscape is not intrinsically more valuable than the metaphysical, the emotional, the subjective: 'we are under no rational imperative to allow the scientific to displace the human perspective or to play down the centrality of that perspective to any experience that can be called aesthetic' (p.4); various views can easily coexist, not least because 'the questions of metaphysics arise on and beyond the boundary of science' (p.4). He offers a corrective, however, to the claim reiterated by several authors in this book that scientific agendas seek to devalue aesthetic sensibility, arguing that we 'need to acknowledge that the opposite mistake can also be made, that of attributing excessive authority and revelatory power to metaphysical imagination' (p.1).

This volume's project is to take the authority of the metaphysical for granted and to ground it in the material. Appleton's socio-biological axiom of innate human cravings for 'prospect and refuge' deepens the widely held surface aesthetic preference for scenic variety by linking this to 'the landscape's ability to meet the need to see without being seen' (Binder and Burnett, p.112). Picturesque and Romantic accounts of pleasure in landscape emphasise the need for variety or even paradox – Wordsworth's 'stationary blasts of waterfalls', and Alpine 'tumult and peace' (*The Prelude*, VI), which Hepburn offers as exemplars of the aesthetically prized 'co-presence of ... opposites, life and stillness' (p.9). Brady points out that, 'in common usage, "diversity" and "variety" suggest richness and are contrasted with monotony, dullness, lack of interest – a kind of impoverished sameness' and that these concepts are shared by aesthetic theory and ecology (p.22). Traditionally farmed areas with hedgerows, for example, she argues, manifest both desirable diversity of species and aesthetically attractive variety of appearance.

Olwig is not the only author in this volume to suggest the need for a multiple perspective on landscape, one 'less visual, and more keyed to the totality of our senses, and the organic needs to which they are tied' (p.193). Perhaps, he argues, the pictorial, 'scenic' sense of landscape should overlay one more linked to the term's earliest meaning: perhaps we should return 'to the original concept of landscape, conceived of as a locus of dwelling' (p.193). If Appleton's 'prospect' implies domination, his 'refuge' resonates with the emphasis of several authors on 'home'. One of the chief 'non-instrumental' interests in landscape identified by Benson is 'the interest arising from a person's attachment as an individual to a local landscape which is home, the place where one belongs and knows one's way about' (p.37). It is the rupturing of this knowledge that, according to Binder and Burnett, leads to the corrosively ineffectual nostalgia traced in Ngugi's novels. Benson, though, notes that nostalgia may be an intensifier of meaning rather than a facile substitute: 'response to the beauty of the landscape is more intense because of the sense of connectedness, and may be further intensified by an accompanying sense of a connection lost' (p.40). The sense of connection lost is at the heart of environmentalism, whether scientific, mystical or anywhere in between. Indeed, Malcolm Andrews goes so far as to propose that:

> Landscape as a way of seeing from a distance is incompatible with this heightened sense of our relationship to Nature as a living (or dying) environment. As a phase in the cultural life of the West, landscape may already be over.[14]

NOTES

[1] Pithily summarised by Shaftesbury in proclaiming, 'the Wildness Pleases'. A.A. Cooper, Lord Shaftesbury, 1999, p.315
[2] H. Walpole, 1995, p.43.
[3] Pliny the Younger, 1969, p.139
[4] Of course the theatre trope here has ambiguous connotations – if acting, scenery and the theatre edifice itself are but an 'insubstantial pageant', figuring explorers and their actions in terms of theatrics awakens haunting questions about the validity of their enterprise, the truth of their tales and the solidity of their landfalls. In a sense, the frequent resort to the theatre trope betrays self-doubt, a recognition of an uncertain, perhaps fanciful position. Interestingly, amphitheatre images are never formed around native people or objects, perhaps implying that their relationship to the landscape is more substantial.
[5] L. Marx, 1989, p.xix.
[6] P. de Bolla, 2003, p.106.
[7] G. Forster, 1777, I, xiii, regarding the impossibility of complete objectivity.
[8] P. Levi, 1984, p.19.
[9] S. Johnson, 1984, p.60.
[10] Kenneth Clark argued in his seminal *Landscape into Art* that the medieval sensibility made symbols of Nature precisely because if, according to Christian theology of the period, 'ideas are godlike and sensations debased, then our rendering of appearances must as far as possible be symbolic'. K. Clark, 1956, p.18.
[11] S. T. Coleridge, 'The Aeolian Harp' 1.26.
[12] W. Shakespeare, *The Tempest*, Act IV, Sc1. 1.120–2
[13] J. Addison, p.369.
[14] M. Andrews, p.22.

REFERENCES

Andrews, M. 1999, *Landscape and Western Art*. Oxford University Press.

Addison, J. 'Pleasures of the Imagination', in *Selections from the Tatler and Spectator*, edited by Angus Ross, Harmondsworth, Penguin.

Clark, K. 1956 (1949) *Landscape into Art*, Harmondsworth, Pelican.

Cooper, A.A. Lord Shaftesbury, 1999 (1711) 'The Moralists', in *Characteristics of Men, Manners, Opinions, Times*, edited by Lawrence Klein, Cambridge University Press.

De Bolla, P. 2003 *The Education of the Eye* Stanford University Press.

Forster, G. *A Voyage Round the World in his Britannic Majesty's Sloop Resolution... 1772–1775*, 2 vols. London

Johnson, S. 1984 (1775) *A Journey to the Western Islands of Scotland*, edited by Peter Levi. Harmondsworth, Penguin.

Levi, P. 1984, introduction to edition of S. Johnson, 1984.

Marx, L. 1989, foreword to *Views of American Landscapes*, edited by Mick Gidley and Robert Lawson-Peebles, Cambridge University Press.

Pliny the Younger, 1969 (1st c. A.D.) *Letters*, translated and edited by Betty Radice, Harmondsworth, Penguin.

Walpole, H. 1995 (1785) *The History of the Modern Taste in Gardening*, New York, Ursus Press.

Landscape and the Metaphysical Imagination

Ronald W. Hepburn

I.

What is it to appreciate a landscape aesthetically? As several recent writers have claimed, it may be an experience within which many layers can be distinguished. The purely sensory component – colours, shapes, sounds, tactile sensations, smells – seldom if ever exists on its own; for we know that area of blue to be the blue of the sky, that broken disc to be a reflection, in nearly still water, of the moon, that object by the dried up lake to be the skull of a sheep or goat. We conceptualise, we recognise, we add context, background, seek out formal relationships – reflectively (Levinson 1992). Furthermore, we may see not simply a large and very dark cloud, just above the horizon, but see it as an ominous harbinger of a severe storm, threatening the still bright but fragile scene in the middle distance. There we have expressive properties, and the thought of changes over time – even a kind of drama. One layer more: we may experience a polar scene of ice and snow as revealing something fundamental (and no doubt grim) about how things really, or ultimately, are: something concealed from us in more familiar, temperate, farmed countryside. Or, in sharpest contrast, we may experience a nature whose poignant beauty on some occasion seems to speak of a transcendent Source for which we lack words and clear concepts.

In these last two instances, we have what I want to call 'metaphysical imagination'. We see the landscape *as* ominous, cosmically ominous, or as revealing-concealing a still greater beauty than its own. In a word, then, the many-levelled structure of aesthetic experience of nature can include great diversity of constituents: from the most particular – rocks, stones, leaves, clouds, shadows – to the most abstract and general ways we apprehend the world – the world as a whole.

In what follows, I shall try first of all to clarify and develop the central concept of metaphysical imagination and its place in aesthetic experience of nature; and secondly, to draw attention to a tendency among a number of philosophers today to underestimate the interest, importance and the diversity of the contributions of metaphysical imagination to the aesthetic experience of landscape. Next, we need to acknowledge that the opposite mistake can also be made, that of attributing excessive authority and revelatory power to metaphysical imagination; so thirdly, keeping, I hope, between these extremes of deficiency and excess, I shall try to explore the range of metaphysical imagining in relation to landscape appreciation. Last of all, we shall look briefly at a sample of difficult but fasci-

Environmental Values **5** (1996): 191-204

nating cases, where it is hard to discern what *are* the metaphysical-imaginative components of a particular experience, and whether they are, or ever could be, articulated in coherent philosophical theory.

First, then, to fill out the concept of metaphysical imagination: I shall take it to be an element of interpretation that helps to determine the overall experience of a scene in nature. It will be construed as a 'seeing as ...' or 'interpreting as ...' that has metaphysical character, in the sense of relevance to the whole of experience and not only to what is experienced at the present moment. Metaphysical imagination connects with, looks to, the 'spelled out' systematic metaphysical theorising which is its support and ultimate justification. But also it is no less an element of the concrete present landscape-experience: it is fused with the sensory components, not a meditation aroused by these.

Of course the total experience may *prompt* meditation. In particular, it may prompt one to ask whether this 'vision' of nature can be argued for systematically, and 'inhabited' as one's settled view of the world. Or, we ask, is it no more than one way that nature can, on occasion, present itself to us; but a fanciful, not a sustainable vision? Indeed the Coleridgean distinction between imagination and fancy can be put to use here, precisely to distinguish an instance of metaphysical imagination that connects with theory which is sustainable and which permits of coherent and convincing development, from the fugitive and (it may be) ultimately incoherent interpretation of 'fancy'. That is to say, it looks as if we may value the sustainable, not only as the dependably enjoyable, but as having the best claim to be true.

We want our experience to be of *nature as it really is*, not merely to consist of agreeable sensory stimuli or reverie. It often does matter to us that nature actually presents itself with the features to which we are responding. When I mistake a massive cumulus cloud on the horizon for a distant, immense snowy mountain range, I feel an inner obligation to downgrade the experience which my misperception has momentarily evoked. That is not simply because the experience was fleeting and, once re-interpreted, can no longer be recovered. Many highly valued aesthetic experiences of nature are fleeting and unrepeatable, but are not on that account downgraded.

I seem to discern a relevant difference here between attitudes to art and to aesthetic appreciation of nature. In the case of art, we accept that the artist may see part of his task in a landscape-painting as the aesthetic assimilating of human artefacts, industrial objects like pipe-lines, or a power-station on an estuary, or a 'wind-farm' on a hill-top – drawing these into the world of his painting. Why is it quite different (for many people) with aesthetic appreciation of nature – revulsion at the slicing of a Down, let us say, by a motorway cutting? There may be more than one reason. It may be the intrusion of the manipulatory, the wilful, the commercial, into what one had hoped would be a meditative release from all instrumentality, or, in Schopenhauerian terms, from all will and willing. A small intrusion can be enough to evoke the dejected – if exaggerated – sense that *there is no escape from the technological*. But there may often be also another factor: that where technology threatens to modify or to dominate nature, we sense that we are so much the less likely to discern in that landscape the fundamental properties (whether comfortable, exhilarating or desolate) of *actual* nature, and that, here at least, we shall be frustrated in that cognitive, sometimes metaphysical, endeavour.

Of course, I acknowledge that not by any means all aesthetic enjoyment of nature has this 'realist', cognitivist orientation. The emphasis may fall much more heavily on 'immediacy', on the impact of sensory elements and their enjoyment; and that can be a splendid source of delight, though it is not my present topic.

II.

Why should metaphysical imagination be under-acknowledged today? I suspect that some of the undervaluers may wish to keep their own account of aesthetic engagement with nature well free of the embarrassment of what they see as the paradigm case of metaphysics in landscape. I mean Wordsworthian romanticism, with its

> ...sense sublime
> Of something far more deeply interfused,
> Whose dwelling is the light of setting suns,
> And the round ocean and the living air,
> And the blue sky, and in the mind of man: (*Tintern Abbey*)

Embarrassment, because this is taken to express a religious experience whose object is very indeterminate, whose description virtually fails of distinct reference, and which may lack adequate rational support. Also the experience alluded to may have only a fugitive and tenuous hold on the person who has it. (Diffey 1993: 59) But my response to that is not to urge an aesthetic experience of nature *free* of metaphysics, for that would be grossly self-impoverishing, but rather to encourage a recognition of its endless *variety*. What comes to replace a theistic or pantheist vision of nature may well itself have the status of metaphysics – naturalistic, materialistic, or whatever: and may have its own metaphysical-imaginative correlatives.

There are other strands to this underplaying of the role of metaphysical imagination. A person may indeed acknowledge a thought-component in aesthetic experience of nature; and may see that as seriously concerned with the disclosure of truth. Truth may be taken to lie – predominantly or exclusively – in the *scientific* understanding of nature; and in landscape-appreciation that will be the imagining of evolutionary, geological, meteorological... settings and bringings-about of the visible scene.[1] Now, I can only agree that these factors may be relevant and may enter and enhance appreciation: but I cannot agree that they have an authority such that they ought (in our contemporary climate of thought) to *supplant* other elements. For science does not *oust* metaphysics: the questions of metaphysics arise on and beyond the boundary of science. They may receive naturalistic answers, or speculative answers centring, for instance, on the 'anthropic principle', the 'fine tuning' of the universe which alone could have yielded the conditions for life and consciousness to emerge, or answers that bring out the incompleteness of all scientific explanation and the *nisus* towards a completion or fulfilment of the world's processes in an Absolute or in God. Such metaphysical theorizing is not *in lieu* of science, but seeks to delineate the wider context in which science itself has its place.

I would argue against a one-sidedly science-dominated appreciation of nature on other grounds also. Science, rightly and necessarily, gives precedence to *objectivising* movements of mind; probes behind the human perspective with its phenomenal properties; abstracts from our emotion- and value-suffused, perceptually selective, view of the world, and works ultimately towards a mathematically quantifiable and imperceptible reality. In the course of that abstraction, most or all of the features of the world that are of human concern are eliminated. Yet the very pursuit of that scientific enterprise has dynamics that belong only within the human life-world, the world of perception and feeling, curiosity and striving to know, and vanish in the objective view. The *aesthetic* mode of experience, the development of which is a very different enterprise indeed from that of science, far from admitting a *nisus* to leave the subjective, human perceptual, evaluative and emotional experience, seeks to explore it and intensify it. And, crucially, the aesthetic experience of nature – notably of landscape – is a prime means of enriching, enhancing, increasing our powers of discrimination, as members of that life-world: a world which has as great a claim to reality as the objective world of the physicist. Some thought-elements concerning the geological past of the region we contemplate, some thought of the ecological unity of its plants and animals, may well enter and enhance our experience. But we are under no rational imperative to allow the scientific to displace the human perspective or to play down the centrality of that perspective to any experience that can be called aesthetic.

III.

I turn now (and more briefly) to the dangers of the opposite extreme: the *over*-valuing of the metaphysical imagination, the exaggeration of its authority. The possibility of such over-valuing is easily established. Just as occasionally the images of our dreams may have a strongly and puzzlingly 'revelatory' quality to the dreamer, so too some experiences of landscape may seem peculiarly revealing about the nature of reality as a whole. A useful term for such a felt revelatory character is 'noetic quality' (used, in aesthetics, by Harold Osborne, for example). But it is a quality which, though phenomenologically vivid, cannot be allowed infallibility. It can attach to contradictory 'revelations'. Idyllic, formally magnificent nature now seems to witness to a benign, intelligible source of its ordered beauty; but then desert- or wilderness-nature seems, no less strikingly, to proclaim its unconcern for any value.

Mary Warnock has discussed theories of imagination in its many forms and manifestations (Warnock 1992, ch.12). While not unaware of its limitations, she accepts an essentially Romantic conception of imagination and its products as 'in some sense' true. Imagination is 'that by which, as far as we can, we see into the life of things'; or, it is 'ability to see through objects ... to what lies behind them'. It is through the power of imagination that we have 'intuition of the infinite and inexpressible significance of the ordinary world'.

These remarks, intriguing though they are, leave me uneasy, since they do seem to invite us to give metaphysical-religious imagination too much independent authority, and they carry a risk of losing from sight its ability to render equally vivid quite incompatible views of the world. If, for instance, the theistic metaphysical imagination is to be taken as true, may we not also require, as a condition of our confidence in it, a background of sound theistic metaphysical argument and theory? Can anything less than that justify the move from noetic quality to noesis in the full sense – a knowledge-claim about how the world ultimately is?

IV.

I stand before a landscape in early summer. I see everywhere the fresh green of new leaves, the pink and white of blossom; there is bird-song, insect-life teeming, a warming sun and a scatter of innocent clouds. Resurgence, lushness, fecundity. My only thought-component (if it can be called that) is '*Enjoy this, here, now!*'

A friend standing beside me, contemplating the same landscape, modifies her experience with a differently-toned thought-component. '*Brilliant: but it is no more than a short interlude between the inertness of winter and the decay of autumn.*' It is easy to suppose this latter thought-component modulating and intensifying into a related and more clearly metaphysical-imaginative one. '*Brilliant indeed: but deceptive! Set this landscape in the wider context of space and of time, and the reality shows itself – life's resurgence as ephemeral and fragile: the wider cosmic context as one in which life cannot be sustained save in conditions of the utmost rarity.*' So a poignance – and a threatened, even doomed quality – is imparted to the present aesthetic experience of a landscape in early summer.

Suppose now that my own experience becomes increasingly metaphysical-imaginative. If spelled out, my (more optimistic) thought-component might amount to something like this: '*Here indeed is nature showing its real self – always, and fundamentally, fecund. Its wintry inertness is no more than quiescence – the condition for ever more resurgence. Even the vastnesses of circumambient space and its hugely dispersed occupants are the necessary and therefore benign conditions of the life we now enjoy and contemplate here in this landscape. Here and now these conditions are concretely and gloriously fulfilled.*' Of course, and once again, what I am thus 'spelling out' is ingredient in my experience, not as propositions of scientific cosmology or metaphysical theory, but as the 'posture of consciousness' (*Bewusstseinslage*), to which they condense. That is present and is a determinant of my total exultant experience (Cf. Findlay 1961).

I have taken the examples of fecundity, regeneration, vitality and their opposites, partly because they connect, illuminatingly, with an earlier opposition in the history of ideas – ideas philosophical and theological. Going back to the biblical sources: I am thinking of that strand in Christian thinking which posited a falling away not just of mankind but of nature more broadly from its first unspoiled state. After man's Fall, the entire world is inclement, hard to cultivate, inhospitable. There has been *cosmic* damage, *Cosmic* Fall. Even if it was agreed that in some way the visible world was an image of eternity, there could be deep division between those who declared it too deeply flawed to be properly enjoyed, and those in the same tradition who had no difficulty in seeing past the flaws – to the divine archetype.

Clearly there is a spectrum here between two poles of aesthetic response to landscape. At the one pole, the subject is content with discerning expressive quality at an instant, and at the other, he applies the imaginative schema of a presupposed metaphysical theory, characterising the world on a huge spatial and temporal scale. Between them, we are seeing, lies a variety of intermediate possibilities. They may involve visions that *foreshadow* a later theoretical elaboration, perhaps furnishing its first vivid and germinal coming-to-consciousness. The packed plenum of plant and animal life (say, in a tropical rain-forest) may be taken as a fecundity to be rejoiced in, or (more in the spirit of J-P. Sartre than of G.M. Hopkins) as a display of suffocating, 'absurd', over-abundance. Or the mutual predatoriness of the species before us may seem to intimate what Hume's 'Philo' characterised as a 'blind nature, impregnated by a great vivifying principle, and pouring forth from her lap, without discernment or parental care, her maimed and abortive children' (Hume 1779). Imaginative foreshadowings of such cosmologies – theistic, absurdist, Dionysian – we can think of as expressions we read on the 'face of nature': expressions we can both aesthetically enjoy, and seek – as a different task – to decipher.

Now, cases like those we have just instanced involve the importing into aesthetic experience of metaphysical-imaginative components quite distinct from anything actually present in the scene itself. These were components ('accounts') derived, e.g., from the belief that man's disobedience brought about cosmic cataclysm. We could say that such an added metaphysical thought-component is *externally related* to whatever scene is being contemplated. In other cases, the metaphysical imaginative schema is better described as *internal* to the appreciative experience itself, since it is concerned, perhaps, with the relation between subject and object, the relation between appreciator and landscape, or it may be with some high-level significance that is read off particular *formal* features of the scene. Either we do not have an account (story, doctrine, theory) to import schematically into the experience, or the experience itself generates what may *become* an account.

A related distinction can be made immediately. The last set of examples focused on perception of *concrete* features of landscape – regeneration, fecundity, or desolation and decay. Other exercises of metaphysical imagination, in contrast, can have a much more *abstract* focus, and could be described as the instantiation in experience of what may be *formal* and certainly will be *fundamental* metaphysical notions.

For an example of what I have in mind, consider the sense of being 'one with nature'. That clearly does focus on the relationship itself, between appreciator and landscape appreciated. And from the point of view of the second distinction just made (i.e., concrete / abstract), oneness is or can be as good an example of an abstract metaphysical concept as one could wish! Recent discussions have acknowledged the importance of this theme, but have seldom (I think) done justice to it.

What, then, can it mean to be one with nature? Well, when we speak of oneness with nature we may simply be meditating on the numerous common properties that we share with the nature we contemplate: we are ourselves *in* the scene and bodily continuous with it. Its life is our own life: we breathe its air; we are warmed, sustained by a common sun.

A distinguishable, and more distinctively aesthetic, variant is the contemplating of perceptible analogies between our life and that of the scene before us: branching stem- and leaf-patterns and the branching of our blood-vessels; gentle rhythm of calm waves up the beach and the rhythm of calm breathing. Here, oneness with nature *is* the aesthetic enjoyment of such chiming, resonating, reconciling, rhyming forms: much more than an intellectual recognition of them.

An emotionally intense form of oneness with nature can centre upon a heightened sense of our limited life-span through the vivid realising of our integration with the continuum of living forms. The emotional quality may be of an enhanced acceptance and resignation – nature and the observer united in a single manifestation of life-and-inevitable-death.

Yet another way of being 'one' with nature is to experience a sense of *equilibrium*: a suspension of conflict with nature, of threat, even of causal engagement.

Metaphysical imagination may see these occasions as, once more, poignant brief realisations of an equilibrium that cannot be read as a goal, a *telos*, of the world's processes. Maybe it is seen as an equilibrium achieved *in spite of* the blind and non-rational powers that determine the way the world goes.

A still more intense realisation of the metaphysical-imaginative annexing of 'oneness' is the nature mystic's, when it seems to him or her that the subject-object distinction is overcome, and the God-world distinction no less annulled. Oneness here can be the oneness of monistic metaphysics, or of panentheism – all is in God. So, for instance, Wordsworth wrote of the

> ...one interior life
> That lives in all things ...
> In which all beings live with God, themselves
> Are God, existing in the mighty Whole,
> As indistinguishable as the cloudless East
> At noon is from the cloudless West, when all
> The hemisphere is one cerulean blue. (Lines intended for *The Prelude*)

In this illustration of 'oneness' – with its several variants – I have been implicitly introducing yet a third distinction, of degrees of intensity, at the pole of which an experience *centres upon* the metaphysical-imaginative component, is dominated by it, as happens most thoroughly in the nature-mystical experiences. Although, obviously, each level of intensity may sustain an aesthetic experience of distinct and individual value to its subject, I suspect that (on occasion) some of the value attached to less explicitly mystical versions is derived from the *more* metaphysical-religious forms. There are cases in recent (and secular) literature, where it is difficult, otherwise, to account for the awed solemnity that clearly attaches, for the writer, to the experience he or she describes as unity with nature. Among these, there may well be a number in which the writer would not confidently assent to the underlying implied metaphysics of mysticism. This is an instance of a particularly perplexing and intriguing set of questions – questions about a person's 'entitlement', as it were, to aesthetic experiences of nature whose metaphysical-imaginative component rests on theoretical presuppositions which cannot perhaps be met.

My next example also illustrates that spectrum from less to greater centrality of metaphysical-imaginative components in aesthetic experience. It is also an example of what I called 'high-level significance' read into the *formal* features of a scene, where that contribution is potentially a thoroughly abstract metaphysical notion. Nevertheless, if the experience is to be aesthetic, it too must be anchored in the concrete, perceptually 'given'. (We could take this to illustrate a further kind of 'equilibrium'.)

In a book called *The Making of Landscape Photographs*, the author describes a scene and reproduces a photograph of it, a scene with bright yellow autumn larch trees in a valley with hills on both sides and in the misty far distance. The brightness of the yellow trees suggests that they are directly and vividly sun-lit: but the light in fact is 'flat and diffused'. The effect is *'full of two contradictory things: calm and excitement ... drama and ease'*. This 'must be the source of the pleasure' given by the scene (Waite 1992, p.91).

'Calm and excitement' – a paradoxical union. Tranquillity-with-vitality, unchanging form sustained by intense manifestation of energy: there are many variants. I think of Wordsworth on the 'stationary blasts of waterfalls', and of the 'tumult and peace' he saw in a single Alpine landscape (*The Prelude* , VI). I think of Ruskin on the part played in natural beauty by what he described as 'the connection of vitality with repose'. 'Repose,' he claimed, 'demands for its expression the implied capability of its opposite, Energy'. 'Repose proper, the *rest* of things in which there is *vitality* or capability of motion...', for example, a 'great rock come down a mountain side, ... now bedded immovably among the fern'. Its 'stability' is 'great in proportion' to the 'power and fearfulness of its motion' (Ruskin IV: 115). In my own view, the co-presence of these opposites, life and stillness, constitutes a fundamental, and too little recognised, key concept for aesthetic theory.

Again, we can place such cases on a spectrum from near-absorption in the concrete particularities of a scene (the motionless yet intensely alive individual tree branch) to awareness of the full metaphysical extrapolation to which the schema of 'calm and vital', 'intensely still and intensely alive' lends itself. At the extreme point, those near-opposites appear in some memorable accounts of metaphysical perfection: God as the being who is unmoved, all-sufficient, in eternal repose and who is yet at the same time *life* at its infinite intensity (Ruskin IV: 113ff). As a commentator on Aquinas put it: 'The divine stillness is the immobility of perfection, not imperfection: of full activity, not inertia' (Gilby 1951: 89). Or looking back to the sixth-century Pseudo-Dionysius: 'In his eternal motion, God remains at rest'. (Dionysius 1920 ed.: 100ff, 106, 168) Our normal expectation is that increasing stillness means decreasing vitality, and that what enhances life will do so at the expense of tranquillity. But these are cases where both those highly valued modes of experience are in some measure simultaneously secured, and the thought of their complete, full conjunction in deity can be taken either as true of an *actual* God, or at the least as marking an *ideal focus*.[2] Which of these options we take to be the truth will, without doubt, make a real difference to the metaphysical-imaginative component available to us in relevant aesthetic experiences. And a third distinct possibility is that we cannot determine which is the case – whether the focus is actual or ideal.

V.

That thought again anticipates my final topic. It is by no means always obvious exactly what presuppositions are being hinted at by the metaphysical imagination: and sometimes hard to tell whether a presupposed metaphysical view, if elaborated, would be fully coherent. Yet again we may wonder whether the spectator is entitled in consistency to draw upon certain presuppositions that clearly are being imported, imaginatively, into his or her experience. We also have to distinguish two importantly different possibilities:

(i) There are cases where a particular metaphysical-imaginative 'slant' can do its work of enhancing our total aesthetic experience of landscape – even though the systematic metaphysical or theological theory it presupposes (of which it is a 'schema') is not in fact rationally justifiable or fully coherent as an account of reality. As I have said, 'vitality-and-stillness' could be such a principle: signalling various approaches or approximations to an ideal, but an ideal that may be nowhere and never fully actualised.

(ii) In a second group of cases, failure at the theoretical, metaphysical level does threaten to undermine the associated metaphysical-imaginative component. The confident invalidating of all cosmological argumentation from the world to God, and a view of a world/God relation as incoherent, would surely be incompatible with a vision of landscape as depending wholly, moment-to-moment, on a divine sustaining, an incessant checking of what otherwise would be its lapse into non-being.

On the other hand, the fact that there are good reasons for rejecting a dogmatic metaphysical scepticism leaves open the fascinating alternative possibility, namely that the aesthetic experience may keep alive some view of the world that the concepts of systematic metaphysical thought cannot precisely articulate, nor its arguments support. (The fact that we have no satisfactory account of the relation between body and mind may mean that we lack the necessary concepts to make it intelligible; but certainly does not compel us to deny our experience of both!) Similar alternatives confront us in seeking to interpret our experience of *awe*. If we acknowledge that awe is 'dread mingled with veneration', 'reverential wonder' (*OED*), do we have somehow to negate our experience of awe (or downgrade it from the domain of imagination to that of fancy), if our reflectively endorsed inventory of the world includes no objects in external nature fitting to venerate, though doubtless plenty to dread? Could the continuing experience of awe itself call in question that inventory, or would it merely display a vestigial and no longer appropriate religio-aesthetic response?

Nowhere are these kinds of uncertainty and ambiguity more dramatically displayed than in the extraordinary history of the concept of *sublimity*. Mention of 'awe' has brought us close to it.

The concept of sublimity was fashioned in response to a need – a need to name a memorable, powerful and perplexing experience (or range of experiences) of undoubted aesthetic value, yet not experiences of beauty as understood in neoclassical aesthetic theory. It combined, or fused, dread at the overwhelming energies of nature and the vastnesses of space and time with a solemn delight or exhilaration. Landscapes, notably, could evoke the experience – and Alpine travellers were among the first to struggle to describe it. The exhilaration was hard to account for, and was explained in very different ways, many of which involved an essentially metaphysical-imaginative component. Kant's version balanced the fearful, imagination-boggling element with the thought of the subject's own rational, free moral selfhood, distinct from (and incommensurable with) the mere spreadoutness and brute force of physical nature. In other versions, the dreadful was checked by the spectator's awareness of his or her own – at least temporary – safety, or by the exhilarating realisation that we are able to take up a contemplative attitude to the menacing and the hostile. Other theorists again were even more speculatively buoyant, rejoicing in the capacity of the mind or soul to 'be present' (in some necessarily undefined sense!) to the remotest parts of the universe, or equating our perception of the cosmos with an interiorising of its vastnesses. Some of these materials continue to be reworked in our own day, though in ways often very remote from their first deployment – and even more remote from our present concern in this article (Monk 1935).[3]

It is reasonable, and tempting, to see the history of theories of the sublime as no more than a story of successive attempts to categorise, in different philosophical idioms, experiences of overlapping but not at all unified or converging kinds: moreover, the eventual popularity – even cult – of the sublime ensured that it was generalised and vulgarised. Nevertheless, the historian of the sublime, Samuel Monk, could speak of sublimity as a 'rare' experience, and I think myself that it is still seriously possible to look on a substantial set of recorded experiences of the sublime as having a phenomenological centre – approached but maybe never captured by aesthetic theorising in all its variety.

That would be to see the sublime as naming an elusive but momentous core experience (a close neighbour of Rudolf Otto's 'numinous' experience – as Otto acknowledged at one stage of his thinking), defying efforts to pin it down philosophically. All the accounts distort or 'hijack' the developing experience so as to make of it something other than it 'wants' to become: or they fail to 'tune' it in a way that seems authentic or faithful.

As critical philosophers, we may see ourselves as under an intellectual obligation to turn away from such experience, – it is strictly 'unavailable', since its history is no more than the history of failed attempts to make philosophical sense of it. Alternatively, we may judge ourselves obliged, rather, to remain open to the experience, and to see it as continuing to challenge us to make sense of its presuppositions – elusive as they are: we are obliged, that is, to be both open *and* critical.

In any case, it is not impossible to indicate in what respects a given theory *fails* to capture, or distorts, the central experience: critical reason is not wholly at a loss. We may criticise Burke, for example, for understanding sublimity too much in terms of fear – ordinary and untransmuted; or criticise Kant, for downgrading *nature's* contribution in favour of the onesided exalting of the rational subject-self. One or other of the rough approximations may suffice, for the susceptible, to evoke or trigger the experience, in vivid memory.

Undoubtedly, one way of making (partial) sense of it is theistic. The overwhelming magnitudes and energies defeat assimilation at the level of sensory stimulus and imaginative synthesis, but they are taken as 'pointing' to a yet greater Reality – something of whose mystery and splendour is glimpsed in the experience. The duality is essentially that of St Augustine's: '*et inhorresco et inardesco...*', 'I shudder to think how different I am from it; yet insofar as I am like it, I am aglow with its fire' (*Confessions*, XI, ch.9).

But of course we can make alternative, if again partial, sense of it on secular lines. It is only by way of sudden perceptual overloading that the resurgent, exhilarating moment can be evoked. We are aware not merely of sensory and conceptual *defeat*, but of the possibility of reading aesthetic – expressive – character in those very aspects of nature that display overwhelming energies and magnitudes, or mystery. And that is sufficient to exhilarate us. We are aware, too, in a solemnly enlivening way, of our own spiritual ascendancy in finding the resources to attempt that aesthetic assimilation of the daunting.

For a final, closely-related example of the crucial (and problematic) part metaphysical imagination can play in aesthetic experience of nature, consider the varying role of the thought of *infinity* in relation to the appreciation of a landscape.

An 'endlessly' receding, sunlit landscape, or a calm night-sky, may both readily suggest tranquil, benign continuations beyond nature as perceived – serene unbounded extrapolations. There have been writers, particularly among the Romantics, to whom the idea of infinity was a uniquely powerful source of good energy, life-enhancement. Wordsworth again: 'By the imagination the mere fact is ... connected with that infinity without which there is no poetry'.[4] In poetry '... it is *the imaginative* only, *[viz,] that which is conversant with or turns upon infinity*, that powerfully affects me'. And that occurs, notably, in 'passages where things are lost in each other, and limits vanish, and aspirations are raised'.[5] Although a poet of a very different metaphysical conviction, Leopardi, even while confessing that the idea of infinity 'shipwrecked' the mind, could yet find it '*dolce*' ('L'Infinito', in *Canti*). Hegel is lyrical: 'At the name of the infinite, the heart and the mind light up' (Hegel 1969 ed.).

But it is far from *dolce* in other contexts, and against other backgrounds of ideas. The thought and part-perception can be of a 'nightmare infinite', infinity as the never-completable, the demonically unreachable goal, the mockingly unfulfillable task. The difference in 'metaphysical pathos', in Lovejoy's phrase, between benign and nightmare infinites is indeed a function of the varying contribution to experience of metaphysical imagination; and there have been fascinating examples in literature of attempts to transform the malign versions of infinity – or, as Coleridge called them, following Cudworth, 'counterfeit infinity' – to the good infinity that exhilarates and energises (Cudworth 1673,

II: 647f). In *The Ancient Mariner*, the demonic vision of a 'thousand thousand slimy things', an uncountable overabundance of an insupportably alien kind, is transmuted to that of a world which – water-snakes and all – could be the object of blessing and love.

In *Modern Painters*, Volume IV, Ruskin saw infinity as a clear and powerful symbol of deity, and not only in the seemingly boundless distance of landscapes, but even in the infinite gradation of nature's curved forms (Ruskin, IV: 83). One short passage cries out for a final comment, for it may bring home to us the subtle and variable interconnection between the perceptual component and the metaphysical thought-component in aesthetic appreciation of nature. Ruskin writes:

> ...the sky at night, though we may know it boundless, is dark; it is a studded vault, a roof that seems to shut us in and down; but the bright distance has no limit, we feel its infinity, as we rejoice in its purity of light (Ruskin IV, III, Sect I, Ch 5, p.81).

Objectively-scientifically speaking, we of course glimpse more distant regions by night than by day; but Ruskin is seeking the most aesthetically effective bonding between the sensorily given and the metaphysical – seeking not simply to 'know' but rather to 'feel' infinity.[6]

NOTES

[1] See, for instance, Allen Carlson: 'Science is the paradigm of that which reveals objects for what they are ...' (Carlson 1993, ch. 10).

[2] One could argue that, when we extrapolate to the idea of deity, we do not, in thought, reach a marvellous coincidence of opposites: we are left, rather, with an irreducible set of contradictions. Compare Sartre on the contradictoriness of God conceived as *l'en-soi-pour-soi* (Sartre 1943: 653).

[3] I discussed some of these historical and current questions about sublimity in 'The Concept of the Sublime: Has it any Relevance for Philosophy Today?': *Dialectics and Humanism*, **XV**(1-2), 1988, pp.137-155.

[4] Reported in Crabb Robinson's Diary (London: Macmillan, 1869).

[5] Letter to W.S.Landor, 21/1/1824; emphases mine. *Letters*, ed. E.de Selincourt, revised A.G.Hill (Oxford: Clarendon Press, 1978).

[6] This essay was first given as a lecture at the First International Conference on Environmental Aesthetics, Koli, Finland, 1994.

REFERENCES

Carlson, Allen 1993 'Appreciating Art and Appreciating Nature', in *Landscape, Natural Beauty and the Arts*, edited by S.Kemal and I.Gaskell, Chapter 10. Cambridge University Press.

Cudworth, R. 1673 *The True Intellectual System of the Universe*.

Diffey, T.J. 1993 'Natural Beauty without Metaphysics', in *Landscape, Natural Beauty and the Arts*, edited by S.Kemal and I.Gaskell, pp.43-64. Cambridge University Press.

Dionysius (Pseudo-Dionysius, 'the Areopagite') c.500AD *The Divine Names*, trans C.E.Holt, 1920. London: SPCK.

Findlay, J.N. 1961 'The Logic of *Bewusstseinslagen*', in *Language, Mind and Value*. London: Allen and Unwin.

Gilby, T. 1951 *St Thomas Aquinas, Philosophical Texts*. Oxford University Press.

Hegel, G.W.F. 1969 ed. *Science of Logic*, (trans. A.V.Miller). London: Allen and Unwin.

Hume, David 1779 *Dialogues concerning Natural Religion*, Part XI.

Leopardi, G. 1965 ed. *L'Infinito*, in *Canti*. (*Tutte le opere di G.Leopardi*. Milan: Mondadori).

Levinson, J. 1992 'Pleasure, aesthetic', in *A Companion to Aesthetics*, edited by D.E. Cooper, pp.330-335. Oxford: Blackwell.

Monk, Samuel 1935 *The Sublime*. University of Michigan (Ann Arbor Paperback, 1960).

Ruskin, J. 1843-60 *Modern Painters*. Library Edition.

Sartre, J.-P., 1943 *L'être et le néant*. Paris: Editions Gallimard.

Waite, C. 1992 *The Making of Landscape Photographs*. Collins and Brown.

Warnock, Mary 1992 *The Uses of Philosophy*. Oxford: Blackwell.

Aesthetics in Practice: Valuing the Natural World

Emily Brady

1. INTRODUCTION

I have titled this paper 'Aesthetics in Practice' to convey how deeply aesthetic value permeates human practice, from engagement with everyday environments, to enjoying wild places, to making moral choices, to scientific study of nature. The aesthetic is not reserved for the art museum, concert hall or scenic viewpoint. While a distinctive kind of valuing, it is not separate or cut off but rather integrated into the relationships we develop with the natural world through a variety of human activities. Although I will not spend time discussing it here, a theoretical basis for this approach to aesthetics may be found in John Dewey's philosophy. True to his philosophical pragmatism, he argues that the aesthetic response is continuous with practical and intellectual experience. Dewey was critical of the elitism of aesthetic theories which raised the aesthetic out of the vital stream of human experience (Dewey 1980: 252–62). Put simply, he replaced an aesthetics of the rarified with an aesthetics of the everyday.

The aim of this paper is to show why aesthetic value of nature is important to environmental policy debates. Aesthetic value is a serious rather than trivial environmental value and ought not to be overlooked. It is not my strategy here to argue for aesthetic value as an intrinsic value of nature and how this might support valuing nature for its own sake (an approach that ought to hold sway in decision-making and policy). Rather than get tangled up in metaphysical arguments, I want to consider how aesthetic value finds its way into human practice in a pragmatic sense. My strategy will be to explain how aesthetic valuing is involved or embedded already in our relationships with nature, and following that, how it underpins many of our attitudes toward the environment. If this can be established, it will go a long way in showing how central, and serious, a value it is.

In line with this, section 3 of the paper tackles the complex area where aesthetics and ethics meet, as I point to some of the ways it has been claimed that aesthetic value supports moral value. The fourth section considers where aesthetics and science meet; in particular, how some ecological values are underpinned by aesthetic qualities such as variety, diversity and harmony. In the fifth section, I turn to aesthetic value as an instrumental environmental value, in so far as aesthetic experience of nature has restorative benefits for humans. But at the risk of glossing over the importance of aesthetic value in its own right, in

Environmental Values **15** (2006): 277–91

section 2 I begin by sketching out some of the reasons – misplaced I think – why aesthetics has not been given the attention it deserves in policy debates.

2. THE SERIOUSNESS OF AESTHETIC VALUE

Just as we find that funding for the arts in the public domain, in schools and so on, takes the back seat to other kinds of activities, this is also the case in environmental planning and policy. Although aesthetic value (sometimes seen as overlapping with 'landscape value') is mentioned, it is given low priority, and more often scientific considerations on the one hand or economic ones on the other hold more sway. Why is this so? There are at least two interconnected reasons. Aesthetic concerns are viewed as lying in the realm of the decorative. They belong to the area of human concerns that are attended to only after we have secured the fundamental necessities of life, e.g., food and shelter (Porteous 1996: 7). Aesthetic value is considered less important, even trivial, compared to other more 'serious' environmental values such as scientific value.

A second reason is tied to the common sense view that 'beauty is in the eye of the beholder', a highly contentious position in philosophical aesthetics. Much critical work on aesthetic judgment attempts to show the objectivity or intersubjectivity of our aesthetic judgments. This kind of argument has been seen as especially important in environmental aesthetics, for if it can be shown that aesthetic value is objective, this type of value is more likely to be given a voice in environmental policy debates. It is the perception of aesthetic value as subjective preference that has lead to its weak voice in such debates (Brady 2003: 224–5). Values which are underpinned by scientific or quantitative support, values which are assumed to be objective, are more commonly taken seriously. An unfortunate result of identifying aesthetic judgments with subjective preferences is that, for example, a community's aesthetic experience of an urban green space is left out of the equation as merely a matter of opinion. Instead, evidence which is deemed to be more objective, such as the economic or housing benefits of that space, is given more consideration.

In keeping with the broader aims of this paper, I cannot enter into the complex arguments against the subjectivity of aesthetic judgment. I have argued elsewhere that aesthetic judgments have an intersubjective grounding (Brady 2003: 191–223). Rather than being private expressions of individual taste, aesthetic judgements are based upon a set of critical activities that are practised and developed in a public context. Through aesthetic communication, we share our aesthetic responses, the reasons underlying them, and pin down reasons for disagreement. It is certainly possible to arrive at agreement in aesthetic matters, even if some disputes inevitably remain. Allen Carlson has argued more strongly for aesthetic objectivity in the environmental context by grounding aesthetic judgments through scientific cognitivism, where appropriate or correct aesthetic judgments are grounded in knowledge of the natural sciences. (Carlson 2000: 54–71). Outside environmental aesthetics, philosophers considering aesthetic properties and judgement have argued for aesthetic objectivism. For example, Jerrold Levinson argues that although aesthetic properties are relational, they supervene on non-aesthetic objective properties (Levinson 1990: 134–58). David Hume's concept of ideal judges provides an alternative strategy for establishing objectivity. Aesthetic judgments are justified by an appeal to competent judges, people with adequate experience and developed aesthetic sensibilities (see Hume 1985; Goldman 1995). So, although there is considerable ongoing debate, there are various established arguments against the common sense view that beauty is simply in the eye of the beholder.

I do not underestimate the difficult battles fought to protect the environment from harm and development, and it is not my view that aesthetic value should have priority over other environmental values. Rather, I want to suggest that through a critical understanding of aesthetic value we may better grasp why it deserves serious treatment in policy debates.

3. AESTHETICS AND ETHICS

Locating a link between aesthetic and moral value is not a new idea. There is a range of arguments from various thinkers, past and present, which claim that aesthetics is fundamental to ethics (Eaton 2001: 81–94). The complex and multi-faceted nature of the relationship between these two realms of value makes the topic difficult to address in detail here, but I would like to highlight one especially persuasive strand in the arguments. This view, developed by philosophers such as Kant, Schiller and, more recently, Marcia Eaton, argues that human capacities which contribute to the development of moral character and to making skilled moral decisions are capacities practised in a focused and deep way through aesthetic engagement. These may include capacities such as perceptual sensitivity, imaginative freedom, creativity and emotional expression (Eaton 2001: 83–8; Brady 2003: 256–8). The careful perceptual attention required and exercised in the experience of art may enable one to more carefully observe important features and detail in a complex moral problem. A well developed imagination may facilitate greater empathy with another being, and in this way help to motivate appropriate moral action. This approach is promising for supporting the aesthetic-moral connection, even if it has to be kept in mind that aesthetically sensitive beings are not always morally sensitive. As Eaton points out, there are a 'plethora of counterexamples to the claim that aesthetic experiences make people morally good in general' (Eaton 2001: 83).

Some environmental philosophers have suggested that developing a relationship with nature through aesthetic experiences, that is, first-hand, multi-sensory, emotional and imaginative engagement, can encourage or contribute to a moral attitude toward nature (Rolston 2002: 127–41; Elliot 1997: 61–73). In his 'Land Ethic', Aldo Leopold encourages us to develop our aesthetic sensibility for nature in order to judge what is 'esthetically right', thus suggesting a link between aesthetics and ethics (Leopold 2000: 189). These views grasp how fundamental the aesthetic response is to valuing nature, and they seek to build upon a foundation that is also fairly democratic in terms of the range of people and communities who may have aesthetic access to natural environments, whether that is wild nature or the modified environments of urban parks and gardens. This approach recognises that aesthetic experience is sometimes the most visceral, felt experience we can have of nature. In that sense it can be very penetrating, have a strong impact and just *stay with us*.

Care is needed though in how far one takes this suggestion. There is no necessary connection between positive aesthetic valuing of nature and ethical treatment of environments. However, there is at least intuitive strength in the idea. At least in cases of environments one knows and loves, or natural places one visits over and over again, one is more likely to treat them with respect, for aesthetic and other reasons (for example if a mountain is enjoyed not just for its sublimity but also for its recreational opportunities). The saying, 'not in my backyard' speaks volumes here in so far as it pins down our tendency to protect the environments we cherish because they are in fact our backyards – or places close to our backyards. But this also points to some of the problems in aesthetics underpinning an environmental ethic. If the most reliable connection between 'beauty and duty', as Holmes Rolston has put it (2002: 127), is generated by relationships between humans and cherished environments, what happens to those places that are strange, unfamiliar, and ugly? How will valuing based in aesthetic experience motivate care and respect towards environments with which we have not developed relationships?

It is not clear that it can, if what is important in engendering significant relationships is either the first-hand immediacy and impact of aesthetic qualities on us – rolling countryside, meadows of wildflowers, blue-green mountains, fragrant pine forests or the invigorating, crashing surf of the ocean – or the frequency of such encounters. Can we develop a caring attitude toward so-called 'unscenic nature', toward things we find just ugly, even if we know we ought to know better? Marshes and bogs are not obviously attractive places, yet a more intimate encounter with them reveals aesthetic as well as ecological interest. Like other recent philosophers writing on aesthetics of nature, Yuriko Saito argues persuasively that aesthetic appreciation must move beyond the legacy of the picturesque, beyond the enjoyment of scenery and towards a wider appreciation which includes 'unscenic nature' (Saito 1998). Positive aesthetic valuing of the unscenic – even of the creepy-crawly – may be possible through immediate, sensuous appreciation anchored in scientific understanding which provides a background ecological story to what might otherwise appear, superficially, as ugly (Saito 1998: 103–5).

In terms of the as yet unexperienced, it may be possible to aesthetically value things with which we have not developed a close relationship. I have never visited the Sistine Chapel or the Grand Canyon, but I have seen photographs and other representations of them, and I know there is wide agreement on their beauty and sublimity. But this doesn't take care of the problem altogether. These places are familiar and well known to many people, whereas the distant and unfamiliar may still be out of aesthetic-moral reach. It could be argued that if I care about a particular environment because I have often found it beautiful, I may be able to extend my attitude of care to other environments, based on the assumption that other beautiful places are also worth protecting, even if I have not judged their beauty through first-hand experience. Two more vexing questions present themselves: what about environments that for one reason or another are unavailable to the senses, or, worse, environments which have given people very bad experiences? The answer here is probably that we need to go beyond aesthetic experience to extend our understanding and grasp of environments we wish to protect. This may involve ecological understanding, as Leopold, Saito and others have urged, or simply going beyond caring relationships and toward some other kind of environmental ethic (Leopold 2000; Saito 1998: 103–5). Indeed, it may simply not be possible to positively value some natural objects, processes or events (Saito, 1998: 105–109).

One final worry about grounding ethics in aesthetics is the fact that moral and aesthetic values often conflict. What we find beautiful in nature may actually damage the environment in some way. For example, there are cases of beautiful non-native species crowding out, damaging or even causing the extinction of other species. The bright, attractive flowering plant, *rhododendron ponticum,* a non-native species in the UK, is known for creating a toxic environment around it which kills plant and insect life (Lawson, Rawles and Gritten, 1998: 38–40). However, many other environmental values that are generally seen as harmonious conflict from time to time, and in these situations one has to examine each case carefully to determine a solution. That the conflict exists in one situation does not mean that aesthetic value cannot support moral valuing of nature in other cases. Also, there are many cases of environmental degradation that coincide with aesthetic disvalue. The monotonous expanses of industrial agriculture are produced with harmful fertilisers and pesticides and cause severe erosion among other problems. The decrease of animal populations from destruction of habitat, especially birdlife, means that a key element in the aesthetic appeal of such landscapes is lost: the presence of birds and the rich soundscape of birdsong.

Aesthetic value and ethical value frequently overlap, intertwine, harmonise and conflict in human experience. I have shown that aesthetic value and experience have some recognisable role in shaping our moral attitudes toward the environment, if not always a positive one. Although not all intimate relationships are caring ones, it is worth encouraging direct experiences of nature, aesthetic and otherwise, in an effort to develop feelings of care toward environments, even if this just means making the effort to get past prejudices and ignorance. This is presumably an underlying assumption of environmental education. My suggestion is inspired also by recent philosophical arguments which claim that actively engaging in (benevolent) environmental restoration practices can enable an experiential involvement that may help to restore a positive relationship with nature. Andrew Light argues that

> Restorationists get firsthand (rather than anecdotal and textbook) exposure to the actual consequences of human domination of nature. A better understanding of the problems of bioactivating the soil, for example, gives us a better idea of the complexity of the harm we have caused to natural processes ... Restoration is an obligation exercised in the interests of forming a positive community with nature ... (Light 2000: 108).

I want to suggest that this relationship is not one-sided, merely from human to nature. It may work the other way too: from nature to humans. Intimate engagement with nature may enable a caring attitude, but likewise, it may be that practices such as ecological restoration, gardening, art in the environment and recreational activities like swimming and walking, enable active participation with a range of environments and contribute to human flourishing. I discuss this idea in more detail in section 5, below.

4. AESTHETIC VALUE AND SCIENCE

Another way aesthetic values permeate human practice is found in the use of various aesthetic concepts in the sciences and mathematics. Sometimes these are obviously aesthetic, when a proof or theory is described as beautiful. More often they are concepts that have a dominant aesthetic meaning and use but have been used in various non-aesthetic contexts so that their connection to the aesthetic has become more distant, although even in these cases the association with the aesthetic is understood within scientific discourse. The most commonly discussed examples of these concepts are harmony, symmetry and integrity. Harmony and integrity are key qualities of beauty in classical and medieval philosophy (especially Aquinas), and are closely connected to qualities such as order, balance and symmetry (Eco 1986).

Arkady Plotnitsky points to the role of harmony in mathematics in Kepler's work, which was influenced by Pythagoras:

> As a – or even *the* – paradigmatic example of this ideology of mathematical aesthetics, one might consider Kepler's famous 'longing for harmonies' and 'noble proportions', and his grand vision of the 'harmony of the world' ... Kepler's aesthetics and aesthetic ideology have been decisive for developing modern mathematics, physics, and astronomy, no less – and sometimes more – than the scientific or explanatory aspects of his discoveries (1998: 251).

James McAllister discusses how scientists, more recently, use aesthetic criteria to evaluate their theories. Scientists 'perform two sorts of evaluations of theories: one is directed at ascertaining the theories' likely empirical performance, whereas the other employs terms of aesthetic appreciation' (McAllister 1996: 3). Aesthetic appreciation has a role in the development of scientific theory through 'aesthetic induction', as he puts it:

> a scientific community's aesthetic preferences are reached by an induction over the empirical track record of theories: a community attaches to each property of theories a degree of aesthetic value proportional to the degree of empirical success of the theories that have exhibited that property (McAllister 1996: 4).

Scientists' aesthetic preferences are specified according to various aesthetic concepts, especially to different forms of symmetry (McAllister 1996: 39–40). Using examples from Einstein's theory of relativity and others, McAllister shows how forms of symmetry attach to different aesthetic properties of theories. Certain forms of symmetry will be deemed to make a successful theory, depending on the theory in question and other factors (1996: 42–3).

By attempting to show how aesthetic concepts such as symmetry and harmony are important to scientific theory, I do not intend to underplay the critical problems that surround theories of beauty. The concepts discussed here have a long history in theories of beauty (see for example, Burke 1958), but there are divisive arguments between realist and subjectivist accounts. One key argument against the view that beauty is identified with properties such as order and coherence shows that an art work, for example, may exhibit coherence without eliciting the response of pleasure normally associated with beauty. In other words, the claim is that there are no principles of beauty (McMahon 2001: 229–31). It might also be disputed that the concepts I have identified as aesthetic are in fact mathematical, so that it is not the case that specifically aesthetic concepts have migrated into science, but that it is the other way round. But given some of the examples discussed above (and below) there is little question that however we label harmony, symmetry, integrity, etc., their relationship to aesthetic value has historically always been close, and they have moved easily between the space of aesthetics and science. So, despite problems associated with the difficult notion of beauty, concepts typically associated with it and with aesthetic concerns, appear to be key to some forms of scientific thinking.

In the biological sciences, 'harmony', 'integrity', 'coherence', 'variety' and 'diversity' appear to have a role in identifying desirable natural states. For example, 'biological integrity' has been defined in this way:

> *Integrity* implies an unimpaired condition or the quality or state of being complete or undivided; it implies correspondence with some original condition. The term most appropriately refers to the condition at sites with little or no influence from human actions; the organisms living there are products of the evolutionary and biogeographic processes influencing that site. Biological integrity ... refers to

> the capacity to support and maintain a balanced, integrated, adaptive biological system having the full range of elements (genes, species, assemblages) and processes (mutation, demography, biotic interactions, nutrient and energy dynamics, and metapopulation processes) expected in the natural habitat of a region (Karr and Chu 1995: 40–41).

When Leopold said that, 'A thing is right when it tends to preserve the integrity, stability, and beauty of the biotic community, wrong when it tends otherwise', he may well have intended for 'integrity', 'stability' and 'beauty' to have entailed each other rather than to be sharply distinguished (2000: 189). Variety and diversity are central concepts to understanding biodiversity, which in broad terms refers to the number, variety and variability of living things. Biodiversity is considered desirable for healthy ecosystems and more diverse species often contribute to the aesthetic appeal of an environment. But I want to get deeper here; to understand how biodiversity as a scientific concept entails the aesthetic concepts of diversity and variety. 'Biodiversity' comes from 'biological diversity', where 'biological' specifies the kind of diversity in question. Although one might claim that diversity is being used here differently than in aesthetics, I would argue that diversity (and variety) in itself has an aesthetic meaning, and that this meaning is carried into the biological use of the term. In common usage, 'diversity' and 'variety' suggest richness and are contrasted with monotony, dullness, lack of interest – a kind of impoverished sameness. Variety and intricacy are named as central qualities of the eighteenth-century aesthetic theory and landscape taste of the 'picturesque', where garden design and scenery were valued for a diversity of elements and variety of forms and colours (Ross 1998: 133).

There is also psychological evidence for preferences for variety and richness alongside coherence in landscape elements (Porteous 1996: 132–3). Studies in evolutionary psychology show a marked preference for savannahs with trees, and landscapes 'with water; a variety of open and wooded space...trees that fork near the ground...vistas that recede in the distance, including path or river that bends out of view but invites exploration...and variegated cloud patterns' (Dutton 2003: 697). A biological basis for the human aesthetic preference for savannahs (and landscapes like them recreated in gardens and parks) is put forward by the Jay Appleton's prospect-refuge theory (Appleton 1975). Although Appleton's theory has been disputed, various studies confirm some of its claims (Ulrich 1993). Komar and Melamid found a surprising cross-cultural agreement in preferences for scenic paintings with varied open spaces combined with landscape elements of water, trees, domestic and wild animals and human beings (Dutton 2003: 698).

Other aesthetic concepts and values come into play in the biological context, especially in the conservation of plants and animals. For example, we find that aesthetic concepts and values have a role in the selection of particular species for conservation. Matthew Chew has argued that 'ecological nativists employ aesthetically repugnant and troubling archetypes to reinforce intra-disciplinary cohesion as well as to recruit public support for the anti-alien species project' (2005: 1). In relation to positive aesthetic values, terms such as 'cute', 'beautiful' and 'charismatic' have found their way into species conservation (and form part of anthropomorphic responses), where the attractiveness of a particular species will influence decisions and policy concerning its protection (Chapman 2005: 4; Serpell 2003: 83–90; see also Rolston 1986; Kellert 1993). It is also common to highlight the aesthetic appeal of various plants and animals through photographs and other means in conservation campaigns and literature. In these respects, scientists interested in protecting various species appear to recognise the important role aesthetics plays in motivating interest and persuading the public to care. I am not suggesting that conservation biologists and others seek to protect only aesthetically appealing species, but just that they recognise the centrality of aesthetics – for better or for worse – in the appeal of animals and plants to fellow conservationists and the public. Furthermore, this is not to say that ugliness in nature is ignored; although some philosophers have argued that there is no such thing as ugliness in wild nature (see Allen Carlson's 'positive aesthetics', 2000: 72–101, and Saito's refutation of the thesis, 1998: 105–9).

Finally, let me conclude this section with a brief look at 'wonder', which is often cited as fundamental to motivating the pursuit of scientific knowledge, as well as our interest in protecting the natural world. Wonder may be understood as a quasi-aesthetic concept, and it at least overlaps with aesthetic, spiritual and intellectual experience. It shares with aesthetics both appreciative and contemplative aspects, and both wonder and the aesthetic response describe experiences which are 'concentrated', 'rapt' and which tend to be 'heightened' and 'expanded' (Hepburn 1984: 147). Ronald Hepburn observes that 'wonder aroused by the discerning of intelligible patterns of nature' acts as a motivation in scientific enquiry (1984: 134), and for support he refers to Arthur Koestler's discussion of the role of wonder in the work of notable scientists in *The Act of Creation* (1964).

Aesthetic concepts and values underpin or play a role in the development of some scientific theories, as well as shaping some key scientific concepts and values, such as biodiversity and conservation. In these ways, one might argue, the aesthetic is already brought into important environmental values, albeit through the kitchen door.

5. AESTHETICS AND WELL-BEING

Earlier I pointed out that aesthetic value is given low priority in environmental debates at least because it is perceived as a luxury, something we attend to only after vital needs – physiological and social – have been met. Aesthetic experience has been associated with self-fulfilment rather than self-preservation (Porteous

1996: 6–8). But what if it can be shown that aesthetic and other experiences of the natural environment promote well-being, that without them we are essentially deprived? Many accounts of aesthetic value locate it as a non-instrumental value, Kant's aesthetic theory being one of the most important and influential in this respect. One reason for this strategy is to distinguish aesthetic value from hedonism, and to specify the distinctive kind of pleasure or 'liking', associated with the aesthetic response, namely, disinterested pleasure (Kant 2001: 90–91). But whether one holds a Kantian view or a more pragmatic one such as Dewey's, which tries to more obviously incorporate the aesthetic into the fabric of everyday life, both views recognise the beneficial effects of aesthetic experience. Dewey, for instance, argues that aesthetic experience is a life-enhancing, invigorating and vital human activity, although his theory is focused more on the aesthetic response to art (Dewey 1980: 1–19). Kant, who focused more on natural beauty and the sublime in nature than art, intimates how aesthetic engagement enlivens and expands the imagination in various ways and furthers our feeling of life (Kant 2001: 90; Hepburn 2001: 66–7; Schiller 1994: 60–84). Hepburn draws on Kant's views in particular to point up the element of reflexivity in the aesthetic response, where engagement with art and nature may lead to self-discovery or enhanced self-understanding (2001: 66–7; 2005).

In connection with these ideas, there is an established tradition in literature and poetry which celebrates the restorative value of nature through experiences which may be described as aesthetic. Romanticism is replete with humanistic reverence for natural beauty and sublimity, and the uplifting effects of nature on human emotions and imagination. Wordsworth's poetry is infused with ideas about the healing power of nature (see, for example, 'Tintern Abbey'; 'The Excursion'). These lines are from his autobiographical poem, 'The Prelude' (1850):

> O there is blessing in this gentle breeze,
> A visitant that while it fans my cheek
> Doth seem half-conscious of the joy it brings
> From the green fields, and from yon azure sky.
> Whate'er its mission, the soft breeze can come
> To none more grateful than to me; escaped
> From the vast city, where I long had pined
> A discontented sojourner: now free,
> Free as a bird to settle where I will.
> What dwelling shall receive me? in what vale
> Shall be my harbour? underneath what grove
> Shall I take up my home? and what clear stream
> Shall with its murmur lull me into rest?
> The earth is all before me. With a heart
> Joyous, nor scared at its own liberty,
> I look about; and should the chosen guide

> Be nothing better than a wandering cloud,
> I cannot miss my way. I breathe again!

Here we find nature as not only restorative, but also as a guide to shaping the self; directing one's life in positive ways. Thoreau is also well known for his reflections – based on first-hand experience – of the uplifting qualities of contact with wild nature:

> My spirits rise in proportion to the outward dreariness. Give me the ocean, the desert, or the wilderness! ... When I would recreate myself, I seek the darkest wood, the thickest and most terminable ... the most dismal swamp ... The wild-wood covers the virgin mould and the same soil is good for men and for trees. A man's health requires as many acres of meadow to his prospect as his farm does loads of muck (Thoreau 1993: 111).

Wild nature has long been valued as a tranquil haven from the chaos, noise and pollution of the city and a cure for the stresses of modern life, but rural nature may also have a healing effect. In a new book, *Nature Cure*, British naturalist, conservationist and writer, Richard Mabey, gives a deeply moving account of his gradual recovery from serious depression through the restorative effects of his explorations and discoveries in rural England: 'What healed me, I think, was ... a sense of being not taken out of myself, but back in, of nature entering me, firing up the wild bits of my imagination' (Mabey 2005: 224).

Evolutionary and psychological research supports many of these reflections. In relation to wild nature, Edward O. Wilson's 'biophila hypothesis', defined as the 'innate tendency to focus on life and life-like processes' (and involving aesthetic engagement with nature) argues that 'to explore and affiliate with life is a deep and complicated process of mental development ... To an extent still undervalued in philosophy and religion, our existence depends on this propensity, our spirit is woven from it, hope rises on its currents' (1986: 1). Douglas Porteous cites a range of psychological studies which show how both passive contemplation of nature and more active engagement through gardening and recreational activities promote human well-being (Porteous 1996: 134–8; Ottosson and Grahn 2005). These studies support the long-standing 'nature tranquillity hypothesis', which recognises the benefits of nature for humans and has had an important role in urban planning and landscape design, including the work of Frederick Law Olmstead, who designed Central Park and Prospect Park in New York, among other green urban spaces (Porteous 1996: 135).

Some of the most interesting support for the restorative value of nature is found in discussions of people-plant relations. The activity of gardening creates feelings of peacefulness and tranquillity and may have physical and mental health benefits (Parr, forthcoming; Cooper 2006: 73–6; 91). Community gardens are widely believed to 'promote sociability, reduce vandalism, and generate neighbourhood revitalization' (Porteous 1996: 134). Besides contributing to positive community and family relations, community gardens may also offer opportunities for developing caring relationships betweens humans and nature within an urban context (Light 2003). Isis Brook has shown how the 'person-plant-place relationship' develops into a caring attitude toward place, and grounds place-attachment: 'the most powerful way of establishing co-nurturing relationships is by engaging with plants first-hand: planting seeds, nurturing growth, learning about their needs and shaping their and our environment through such interaction' (Brook 2003: 232).

The benefits of wild and cultivated nature for human well-being are clear. Leisure activities such as gardening and spending time outdoors engage us more intimately, more concretely, with a range of environments, and aesthetic experience lies at the heart of many of these experiences. Qualities such as tranquillity and beauty are appreciated for themselves but also for their relaxing and emotionally uplifting effects. These are strong reasons to protect both wild and other green spaces, and some conservationists are already using these reasons to argue for new management policies. For example the 'Wild Ennerdale' initiative in the English Lake District seeks to 'join urban need with rural opportunity and articulate the restorative and spiritual qualities of the wild' (Evans 2005). As Brook points out, the relationships we may develop are 'co-nurturing', in other words, as we nurture ourselves we may in turn nurture nature. Along with Brook, I want to emphasise the possibility of reciprocal nature-human relationships. Deeper engagement with the natural environment through activities more and less aesthetically motivated offer the potential of care for nature as well as caring for ourselves. However, it would be mistaken to put too much emphasis on positive experiences of nature, since many encounters with nature's power and cruelty can be frightening and devastating for humans. Nonetheless, cultivating positive experiences and attempting to overcome the effects of negative ones ought to have benefits overall.

6. CONCLUSION

To conclude, I should point out that I have said little about how aesthetic value might underpin a non-instrumental valuing of nature or how aesthetic valuing is a route to valuing nature for its own sake rather than any benefits it has for humans. This strategy could support a non-anthropocentric environmental ethic. But this is the topic of another paper, so I merely suggest it here as a possible direction (see Brady 2003: 128–42). Rather than pursuing arguments in relation to the intrinsic value of nature, I have wanted to show other, more pragmatic avenues for understanding how aesthetic valuing of nature might support environmental protection, namely by showing how it is already a given in many other environmental values. I have done this quite apart from arguing for or showing the obvious and explicit ways we already value nature from a rich aesthetic perspective. If aesthetic value is embedded in the practices I have outlined above – moral, scientific, leisure and otherwise, it has a key place which needs proper recognition. Perhaps in this way the fundamental importance of aesthetic experience will become plain.

ACKNOWLEDGEMENTS

I would like to thank two anonymous referees, Dale Jamieson, Clare Palmer and Alison Stone for their helpful comments on earlier versions of this paper.

REFERENCES

Appleton, J. 1975. *The Experience of Landscape*. New York: Wiley.

Brady, E. 2003. *Aesthetics of the Natural Environment*. Edinburgh: Edinburgh University Press.

Brook, I. 2003. 'Making Here Like There: Place Attachment, Displacement and the Urge to Garden', *Ethics, Place and Environment*, **6**(3): 227–34.

Burke, E. [1757] 1958. *A Philosophical Inquiry into the Origin of Our Ideas of the Sublime and the Beautiful*, ed. J.T. Boulton. London: Basil Blackwell.

Carlson, A. 2000. *Aesthetics and the Environment: The Appreciation of Nature, Art and Architecture*. New York and London: Routledge.

Chapman, M. 2005. 'Anthropomorphism in Nature Conservation: New Thoughts from Animal Geographies', paper presented to 4th International Conference of Critical Geography, Mexico City, January 2005.

Chew, M. 2005. 'The (Anti-?) Aesthetics of Invasion Biology', paper presented to International Society for the History, Philosophy, and Social Studies of Biology conference, Guelph, Ontario.

Cooper, D. 2006. *A Philosophy of Gardens*. Oxford: Clarendon Press.

Dewey, J. [1934] 1980. *Art as Experience*. New York: Perigee.

Dutton, D. 2003. 'Evolutionary Aesthetics'. In J. Levinson (ed.), *The Oxford Handbook of Aesthetics*. New York and Oxford: Oxford University Press.

Eaton, M. 2001. *Merit, Aesthetic and Ethical*. Oxford and New York: Oxford University Press.

Eco, U. 1986. *Art and Beauty in the Middle Ages*. New Haven and London: Yale University Press.

Elliot, R. 1997. *Faking Nature*. New York: Routledge.

Evans, P. 'Winds of Change'. *The Guardian*, 26 January 2005.

Goldman, A. 1995. *Aesthetic Value*. Boulder: Westview Press.

Hepburn, R.W. 1984. *Wonder and Other Essays*. Edinburgh: Edinburgh University Press.

Hepburn, R.W. 2005. Personal communication.

Hume, D. [1757] 1985. 'Of the Standard of Taste'. *Essays Moral, and Political, and Literary*, ed. E. Miller. Indianapolis: Liberty Classics.

Kant, I. [1790] 2001. *Critique of the Power of Judgment*, ed. P. Guyer, trans. P. Guyer and E. Matthews. Cambridge: Cambridge University Press.

Karr, J. and Chu, E. 1995. 'Ecological Integrity: Reclaiming Lost Connections'. In L. Westra and J. Lemons (eds), *Perspectives on Ecological Integrity*. Dordrecht: Kluwer.

Kellert, S. 1993. 'The Biological Basis for Human Values of Nature'. In S. Kellert and E.O. Wilson (eds), *The Biophilia Hypothesis*. Washington, D.C./Covelo, CA: Island Press/Shearwater Books.

Koestler, A. 1964. *The Act of Creation*. London: Hutchinson.

Lawson, T., K. Rawles and R. Gritten. 1998. 'Alien Invasion', *BBC Wildlife Magazine*, **16**(9): 38–40.

Leopold, A. [1949] 2000. 'The Land Ethic', *A Sand County Almanac, with Essays on Conservation*. New York: Oxford.

Levinson, J. 1990. *Music, Art and Metaphysics*. Ithaca: Cornell University Press.

Light, A. 2000. 'Restoration or Domination?' In W. Throop (ed.), *Environmental Restoration: Ethics, Theory, and Practice*. Amherst: Humanity Books.

Light, A. 2003. 'Elegy for a Garden', *Terrain.org: A Journal of the Built and Natural Environment*, 13. http://www.terrain.org. Accessed 21/2/06.

Mabey, R. 2005. *Nature Cure*. London: Chatto and Windus.

McAllister, J. 1996. *Beauty and Revolution in Science*. Ithaca: Cornell University Press.

McMahon, J.A. 2001. 'Beauty'. In B. Gaut and D. McIver Lopes (eds), *Routledge Companion to Aesthetics*. London and New York: Routledge, pp. 227–38.

Ottosson J. and P. Grahn. 2005. 'A Comparison of Leisure Time Spent in a Garden with Leisure Time Spent Indoors: On Measures of Restoration in Residents in Geriatric Care', *Landscape Research*, **30**(1): 23–55.

Parr, H. Forthcoming 2006. 'Mental Health, Nature Work and Social Inclusion'. *Environment and Planning D: Society and Space*.

Plotnitsky, A. 1998. 'Science and Aesthetics'. In M. Kelly (ed.), *Encyclopedia of Aesthetics*, vol. 4. New York and Oxford: Oxford University Press, pp. 250–52.

Porteous, J.D. 1996. *Environmental Aesthetics: Ideas, Politics, Planning*. New York and London: Routledge.

Rolston, H., III. 1986. 'Beauty and the Beast: Aesthetic Experience of Wildlife'. In D. Decker and G. Goff (eds), *Economic and Social Values of Wildlife*. Boulder: Westview Press.

Rolston, H., III. 2002. 'From Beauty to Duty: Aesthetics of Nature and Environmental Ethics'. In A. Berleant (ed.), *Environment and the Arts: Perspectives on Environmental Aesthetics*. Aldershot and Burlington: Ashgate, pp. 127–42.

Ross. S. 1998. *What Gardens Mean*. Chicago: Chicago University Press.

Saito, Y. 1998. 'The Aesthetics of Unscenic Nature', *Journal of Aesthetics and Art Criticism*, **56**(2): 101–11.

Schiller, F. [1795] 1994. *On the Aesthetic Education of Man*, trans. R. Snell. Bristol: Thoemmes Press.

Serpell, J.A. 2003. 'Anthropomorphism and Anthropomorphic Selection: Beyond the "Cute Response"', *Society and Animals*, **11**(1): 83–100.

Thoreau, H. D. [1862] 1993. 'Walking', reprinted in S.J. Armstrong and R.G. Botzler (eds), *Environmental Ethics: Divergence and Convergence*. New York: McGraw-Hill.

Ulrich, R. 1993. 'Biophilia, Biophobia, and Natural Landscapes'. In S. Kellert and E.O. Wilson (eds), *The Biophilia Hypothesis*. Washington, D.C./Covelo, CA: Island Press/Shearwater Books.

Wilson, E.O. 1986. *Biophilia*. Cambridge, MA: Harvard University Press.

Wordsworth, W. 1896. 'The Prelude, Book First: Childhood and School Time'. *Poetical Works, Volume 3*, ed. W. Knight. http://www.gutenberg.org. Accessed 22/9/05.

Aesthetic and Other Values in the Rural Landscape

John Benson

INTRODUCTION

Rural scene, a rural scene,
Sweet especial rural scene.

In this paper I shall be concerned with the aesthetic significance or interest of rural landscape,[1] meaning by that land which is populated by human beings and worked on by them, exploiting its natural resources, especially by agriculture, aquaculture and silviculture; but excluding areas densely built over and housing human beings living and working in close proximity.[2] Rural landscape is an important object of aesthetic interest and enjoyment; aesthetic reasons are among the reasons people have for valuing rural landscape. But they are only one kind of reason for valuing rural landscape. The object of this paper is to distinguish aesthetic reasons from reasons of other kinds and to examine some important relationships between aesthetic and non-aesthetic reasons in this context. I discuss first the relationship between aesthetic reasons and reasons of utility; then I distinguish, and consider the often subtle relationships between, different non-instrumental kinds of interest in rural landscape. Finally I suggest the bearing on the problem of landscape preservation of the preceding discussion of aesthetic and non-aesthetic reasons for valuing rural landscape.

BEAUTY AND UTILITY: THEIR RELATIONSHIP IN LANDSCAPE APPRECIATION

Rural landscape is to a greater or lesser extent artefactual.[3] Most of it is not designed to reward aesthetic contemplation, though some is. In England the extensive parks surrounding the great houses of the aristocracy were designed in accordance with conscious aesthetic principles. The landscapes thus created may be regarded as large scale works of art. Utilitarian elements, such as farms and their buildings were either hidden or incorporated into the design. But however extensive such estates they are not typical of rural landscape. Most land that has been cultivated has been shaped by predominantly non-aesthetic purposes, even if aesthetic notions have played a minor role. Land that has been shaped for purposes of utility, as farm land or woodland, has aesthetic

Environmental Values **17** (2008): 221–238.

character, features that can be viewed aesthetically, found beautiful, ugly etc.; but – a crucial difference – these aesthetic features are consequences of the use for which the land has been primarily designed. It is in this kind of case, rather than in the artistic landscape, that the relationship between the aesthetic and the utilitarian or practical is especially problematic.

It is certainly possible for the aesthetic and the practical points of view to come apart. They may compete in a practical way, and either may be subordinated to the other. When farmers plant large fields of rape, producing huge areas of bright yellow in the landscape, or clear hedgerows to make the best use of machines, there is a marked change in the aesthetic character of the landscape, and, in the opinion of many, a loss of aesthetic value. On the other hand when farmers are paid to replace hedges, or to maintain them, to compensate them for the loss of income from intensive cultivation, reasons that are in part aesthetic – wildlife conservation is also commonly invoked – are used to displace reasons of farming utility.

It is possible in theory to make a distinction between a purely practical point of view, that of the farmer *qua* farmer for instance, and a purely aesthetic point of view, that of the connoisseur of landscape beauty. In practice of course the two points of view commonly coexist in the same person and interact in various ways. For one thing the practical viewpoint has its own aesthetic: many, perhaps most, craftsmen and women believe that if some article of use, such as a teapot or a chair, is well made it is aesthetically pleasing, at least that being well made is a necessary condition of aesthetic worth, and a positive contributing factor. An example relevant to the aesthetics of landscape appreciation is the attitude of farmers who regard tidiness as a sign of good farming, and whose aesthetic sense is offended by the sight of untidy fields. In a survey by the British Countryside Commission of post WW2 changes in agricultural landscapes it was noted:

> ... that a farmer's view of amenity is very much conditioned by his role as a food producer. This results in the frequently expressed view 'if it's farmed well, it looks good'. Thus many farmers do not object at all to bare landscapes provided that the farming is technically efficient. Conversely, an area, which is liberally supplied with overgrown hedges, copses and wet places, although of delight to the naturalist [and to the connoisseur of landscape], will usually generate a strong desire to 'tidy it up'. Indeed it was not unusual to find 'visual improvement' expressed as a major reason for hedge removal by farmers in the study areas, particularly if the hedges had begun to look weak and ragged.[4]

The implicit aesthetic may be criticised as inadequate. Being well farmed is too indeterminate, indeed too contested a notion to provide a criterion of aesthetic quality. A specification of good farming that itself lacked any aesthetic requirement would surely fail as a sufficient condition of aesthetic worth. The cited example of hedge removal illustrates this point. Although there may be aesthetic compensations for their removal it is implausible to suggest that changes in the landscape dictated by agricultural need will automatically result in aesthetic improvement. It is hard to suppress the suspicion that economic interest may produce a false aesthetic sensibility. An aesthetic wholly determined by practical concerns is one-eyed.

An aesthetic wholly detached from practical concerns is however equally one-eyed. There is no doubt that many of us find aesthetically pleasing the traditional enclosed landscape characteristic of the agrarian practices of the three or so centuries preceding the recent growth of mechanisation. Many of the aesthetic qualities that are valued are consequences of particular methods of cultivation. But it is possible to view a pattern of small fields divided by hedges in abstraction from the farming needs to which its appearance is indebted. What objection can there be to a form of aesthetic appreciation that disregards the utilitarian aspect of the object it contemplates? Why should the connoisseur of landscape not say that the aesthetic qualities are what he or she is interested in; how they come to be is immaterial?

A reply might be not that such an approach is inadequate from an aesthetic point of view, but that a purely aesthetic response to landscape, at least if that means a response to its formal and sensory qualities alone, is inadequate just because it is purely aesthetic. At best an appreciation of countryside that dwells on such qualities is likely to be limited and superficial; at worst it may be grotesquely insensitive to facts that it is not decent to ignore. This objection may be developed by considering John Ruskin's critique, in *Modern Painters,* of the contemporary school of picturesque painting. Ruskin distinguishes between the lower and the higher or noble picturesque (Turner being of course the outstanding exponent of the higher).

To illustrate the difference he compares two pictures of windmills, one by Clarkson Stansfield, the other by Turner. Stansfield's mill is a romantically dilapidated object in the landscape: its roof is 'nearly as interesting in its ruggedness as a piece of the stony peak of a mountain'; the clay wall is 'as beautiful as a piece of chalk cliff, all worn into furrows by the rain'. These signs of decrepitude, which contribute to its 'merely outward delightfulness', are not essential to it, indeed are detrimental to it, as a mill. Turner's mill on the other hand conveys accurate information about structure and function; it depicts what a windmill *is*, which is inseparable from what it *does*.

The objection to depicting it as just an interesting rustic feature, ignoring its function as a *mill,* is not only that this is to withhold information, but that in so doing it ignores the human beings whose way of life depends upon it, who work it, supply it, and eat its products. To depict objects for the sake of variety of form and colour, 'without any regard for the real nature of the thing, and without any comprehension of the pathos of character hidden beneath' constitutes the lower or 'surface' picturesque. The distinction between the higher and lower forms, then, rests on whether the painter has 'communion of heart' with the things he depicts:

> For, in a certain sense, the lower picturesque ideal is eminently a *heartless* one; the lover of it seems to go forth into the world in a temper as merciless as its rocks. All other men feel some regret at the sight of disorder and ruin. He alone delights in both; it matters not of what. Fallen cottage – desolate villa – deserted village – blasted heath – mouldering castle – to him, so that they do but show jagged angles of stone and timber, all are sights equally joyful. Poverty, and darkness, and guilt, bring in their several contributions to his treasury of pleasant thoughts. The shattered window, opening into black and ghastly rents of wall, the foul rag or straw wisp stopping them, the dangerous roof, decrepit floor and stair, ragged misery, or wasting age of the inhabitants, – all these conduce, each in due measure, to the fullness of his satisfaction. What is it to him that the old man has passed his seventy years in helpless darkness and untaught waste of soul? The old man has at last accomplished his destiny, and filled the corner of a sketch, where something of an unshapely nature was wanting.[5]

Ruskin is talking here about painting. But the point he is making is about the attitude to its *subjects* revealed in the painting. His point therefore applies more generally, not just to painters of landscape, but to anyone who looks at landscape with that attitude.[6] The conclusion of his critique of the lower picturesque is that the aesthetic standpoint, so far as cultural objects, including landscapes, are concerned, cannot legitimately be isolated from non-aesthetic considerations, certainly not from considerations about the quality of life of people and animals who use the objects or occupy the landscape.

The contemporary urban visitor to the countryside may not be *heartless*, but his enjoyment of the landscape may well be *heedless*. By heedlessness I mean either simple unawareness of significant facts about the landscape or deliberate disregard of such facts. The former produces an aesthetic appreciation that is uninformed and hence superficial, the latter one that is at worst perversely whimsical.

The most extreme form of unawareness is failure to recognise the part played by human activity in creating the character of the landscape. It is only relatively recently that it has been widely recognised that what were supposed to be wilderness areas in the New World owed their character, or important features of it, to the activities of people who were there when it was 'discovered'. Awareness of the extent to which the landscape has been formed by generations of human occupation, and of how it has been formed, is still probably quite limited on the part of the majority of lovers of rural landscape. One misapprehension then may be that the rural landscape is purely natural. Such comprehensive ignorance is hard to achieve in a country, such as the UK, most of whose land has been shaped by agriculture in ways that are quite obvious. But a detailed understanding of the forces, technological, social and economic, that conspire to determine the character of the landscape of a particular time and place is not automatically available on the mere survey. The changes in agriculture in recent decades have led to a widespread recognition that new methods of cultivation can transform a landscape, but without necessarily shifting, indeed perhaps reinforcing, the assumption that the preceding landscape was natural, the immemorial setting of an idyllic rural life. This, the Arcadian myth, may be barely conscious, the misty remnant of impressions gained from stories, poems and pictures.

The person I have termed the connoisseur of landscape beauty – perhaps a strawman – may be unimpressed by Ruskin's critique. He can agree that to be ignorant of the human significance of rural landscape is deplorable. But he may still contend that the aesthetic aspects of the landscape are in principle separable from and may be appreciated in abstraction from its utilitarian, and indeed from its moral and social, aspects. The aesthetic character of the landscape is a causal consequence of the land's having been formed for particular purposes. But once created that aesthetic character exists in its own right and is there to be perceived and appraised without awareness of why and how it came to be there.

The first response to make to the connoisseur is to concede that a possible mode of aesthetic response is to concentrate upon the sensory and formal qualities of a landscape or of particular objects within it in abstraction from their practical aspect. A rural landscape may be viewed as a rich tapestry of forms, colours and textures, sounds and smells, varying with the seasons and atmospheric changes. So viewed there are no fields, hedges, walls, gates, barns or sheepfolds, no pasture, ploughed fields, copses, haystacks or muckheaps. These are all functional concepts and we are supposing a mode of perception in which nothing is perceived as falling under such concepts. There is no need to deny that the aesthetic interest of rural landscape is in part, even in large part, due to elements that can be described in broadly sensory terms, and certainly in non-functional terms. That these elements are the consequence of particular methods of cultivation does not mean that they cannot be perceived and enjoyed without knowledge of their reason for being there. But they are not commonly perceived in isolation. It would be a difficult, though not an impossible, feat to describe a particular landscape without using functional concepts, and that indicates that such an abstract mode of perception is highly artificial. The experience yielded by it would be impoverished by comparison with the fuller composite experience which incorporates awareness of other, non-aesthetic aspects of the landscape. An analogy would be looking at a football match simply as a temporally extended pattern of swiftly evolving spatial configurations, in abstraction from its being a contest between two sets of more or less skilful human players, the spatial configurations being the result of the players' attempt to score. The act of abstraction may be worth doing from time to time, to heighten awareness of one aesthetic element in the total experience. But it is the total experience that matters.

But this response concedes too much if it implies that the abstracted formal and sensory aspects exhaust the aesthetic element in the total experience, for that is to concede that the aesthetic character of landscape is in principle separable from its character as, for example, farmland. That would be to ignore the existence of what Kant called dependent beauty, that is to say beauty that can be attributed to a thing only on account of its being a thing of a certain kind. I shall illustrate the notion by taking as example the product of a rural craft. Swill-baskets, traditionally used for many purposes on the farm and in the home, are woven from riven strips of coppiced oak, on bools (hoops) of hazel which form the basket rims. These baskets are to the uninstructed glance attractive enough, but their aesthetic interest is much enhanced by an understanding of how their shape is determined by the requirements of use, facilitated but also limited by the properties of the materials and the manipulative skill of the maker. Why have a basket this shape? How can these materials take this shape? What manipulations are necessary to form them? One will not have these items of information consciously in mind, but they inform the perceiving eye. The shapes are simple but graceful: the shallow or deep curves are the curves that riven oak naturally takes when bent. The strips are under stress, giving the basket liveliness and tension, but they are tough and substantial, giving it a robust and businesslike appearance. The basket is handsome and handy; its handsomeness is inseparable from its handiness, for it results from a cooperation of material and maker in the production of an artefact perfectly adapted to a practical use.[7]

It will not do in such cases to say that the abstract gaze can in principle separate the formal aesthetic qualities of the object from its character as a utensil. Admittedly it would be possible to place one of the baskets on a plinth in an art gallery, and a visitor ignorant of its use might admire its proportions, viewing it as a piece of abstract sculpture. As an abstract sculpture, however, it might seem rather crude, lacking in delicacy, too chunky to be really graceful and quite roughly finished. These qualities do not detract from its attractiveness as a basket. Greater refinement and delicacy would make it appear fragile and insubstantial, a bit flimsy. Viewed, and even more used, as a basket, it is satisfyingly tough, yet light and springy, balances comfortably on the hip, and the unstripped bark is agreeably rough to the touch.

I have been making use of Frank Sibley's illuminating treatment of the distinction between predicative and attributive uses of adjectives in aesthetic judgements.[8] To say, predicatively, that a basket is beautiful is to say that it is beautiful – for instance that it has a beautiful shape – and, as it happens, is a basket. In this case the judgement that the basket is beautiful does not require the knowledge that it is a basket. To say, attributively, that this is a beautiful *basket* is to imply some essential relationship between the object's being a basket and its being beautiful. Sibley's suggestion, which I follow, is that in attributive judgements the noun – 'basket' in my example – indicates standards of appropriateness for the application of the adjective. Thus, in my treatment of the example, I have argued that if and only if one knows what a swill basket is one knows what qualities are and what are not appropriate to it as the kind of utensil it is; one's assessment of a particular basket as a handsome one of its kind employs that knowledge. It is this essential connection between aesthetic judgement and an awareness of the uses of elements of the rural landscape that I wish to emphasise. It goes beyond the idea contained in my first response to the connoisseur, that the aesthetic aspect is but one element in a complex composite experience, and one that is in principle separable, if not often in practice separated, from the practical aspects of the composite. That aesthetic judgements of rural landscapes are mostly and most importantly attributive I have not by any means established. I set it down as a plausible claim. To support it I might suggest for consideration a few random examples: why the encroachment of bracken on fell grazing is aesthetically unpleasing; why well constructed drystone walls are immensely impressive, while picturesquely dilapidated ones are unsightly; why overgrown hedges, gappy at the bottom, unlike dense and neatly layered ones offend the eye; why a ploughed field with evenly spaced furrows in sweeping lines following the contours of the land is a magnificent sight. A full demonstration would require an examination of a variety of rural landscapes and would be a large undertaking.[9]

The case for an aesthetic approach to rural landscape that is informed by an understanding of the practical functions of that landscape does not require rejection of the abstracted, non-functional, view. The functional approach however greatly extends the range of qualities available for aesthetic appreciation, and may reveal qualities worthy of appreciation in landscapes that would otherwise appear aesthetically neutral or even ugly.[10]

Such an approach is, of course, a non-user's approach. An aesthetic interest in the practical aspect of a landscape is not a practical interest. The user is, strictly as such, not interested in the aesthetic qualities of the landscape at all.[11] The aesthetically engaged non-user is interested in the utilitarian features as bearers of the aesthetic qualities that she values. Practical reasons are one kind of instrumental reason. The farmer, *qua* farmer, is interested in the land as productive of crops; he values it as a means to a further end. Aesthetic reasons, on the other hand, are non-instrumental. To have an aesthetic interest in the land is to value it, not for the sake of some further end, but simply for its beauty.[12] That is still true when the beauty is specifically the kind of beauty that a landscape has *as* an agricultural one.

AESTHETIC AND OTHER FORMS OF NON-INSTRUMENTAL INTEREST IN RURAL LANDSCAPE

Aesthetic reasons are non-instrumental reasons, and aesthetic interest a form of non-instrumental interest. But there are other forms of non-instrumental interest in landscape, and it is worthwhile to consider the relationships between some of these on the one hand and aesthetic interest on the other. First I list four different varieties of non-instrumental interest in landscape, other than aesthetic, of which the first applies to landscape of any kind, the other three to cultural landscape specifically.

First is the non-instrumental interest of the geologist, the geographer, the natural historian or the ecologist (using these terms to include the professional and the serious amateur practitioner), when the aim of the scientist is simply to understand nature, not to control it or exploit its resources.

Second is the interest of the historian or the archeologist (again including the well-informed layperson as well as the professional) in the landscape as the product and record of human activity in the past.

Third is a more specialised and personally motivated kind of historical interest: a person's interest in the landscape of an area historically associated with his or her own people, nation, community or family, an interest typically shared with other members of the group.

Fourth and last (but not least) I put the interest arising from a person's attachment as an individual to a local landscape which is home, the place where one belongs and knows one's way about.

These are all cases of interest in knowing. In each case the reasons for acquiring knowledge may, by some persons and on some occasions, be instrumental. But I shall assume that in each case knowledge may also be pursued for its own sake, not for any further end that it may serve. It may seem needless to remark that the scientific, the historical and the aesthetic are different forms of non-instrumental interest, but there is a possibly influential view that would assimilate any disinterested activity or interest to the aesthetic just on account of its being disinterested, in the sense set out by Kant in his account of 'pure judgements of taste'.[13] The activities or kinds of interest I have mentioned have disinterestedness as a common feature, in so far as they are pursued without a further end in view, but their different objects, beauty and various forms of truth, distinguish them from one another. Nor is the aesthetic the prime exemplar of disinterestedness, so to use it as a broad category serves no useful purpose and obscures important differences.

If the connections and disconnections I discuss in what follows seem obvious, I can only plead that experience of philosophical discussion convinces me that what is obvious can differ disconcertingly from one person to another.

The non-aesthetic kinds of interest are themselves related to one another in various ways. For example, natural history may look at the way plant communities in a particular area, from a region to a field, have changed with changes in land use. Interest in the history of landscape in general may enhance one's sense of the past of one's native landscape. The relationships that I propose to look at, however, are between each of these four and the aesthetic interest in landscape.

First some remarks on the relation between the aesthetic and biological or ecological interest. Conservationists sometimes seem to assume a correlation between them, but naturally have more to say about the criteria for assessing biological value. There may be a relationship in that a landscape that is rich in species is likely to be visually as well as biologically diverse. The preference for hedgerows, for instance, can be justified in both ways. Much of the diversity of species, however, is only visible to the naturalist who knows about the insect life under the detritus of fallen and decaying matter in the hedge bottom. That is not to say that there is no beauty in the view that the naturalist gets crawling on all fours in the undergrowth. Nature reveals different aspects of its beauty at different focal distances. But when we speak of areas of natural beauty we mostly have in mind the broad view, and in that perspective biodiversity matters aesthetically only as it affects elements that contribute to that view: variety of species of tree, wild flowers and grasses, species of fauna, especially birds, butterflies, and dragonflies, the most visible and, in the case of birds, audible inhabitants of most temperate landscapes.

So there is a non-accidental association, but not an invariable one and certainly not a necessary one. Diversity of species does not necessarily imply aesthetic interest, nor does lack of diversity mean lack of aesthetic interest. An ecological change that is biologically an impoverishment may be an aesthetic enhancement, or simply a change in aesthetic character. A good example is the change in the landscape of Huntingdonshire described by N.W. Moore, one-time ecologist with the Nature Conservancy Council. Looking back to the 1940s from the late 1980s he writes of:

> a closed secret world of little grass fields surrounded by thick overgrown hedges ... It was rather a claustrophobic place. However, the lack of view was made good by the interest of things at one's feet: the meadow was full of conspicuous plants like cowslips and inconspicuous ones like Adder's Tongue ferns. Today Huntingdonshire has a totally different atmosphere. It is an open land with wide views – one can see the shape of the low rolling hills. They are now covered with wheat and barley ... It is a good county to drive through but a dull one to walk in.[14]

If there is a reason to prefer the earlier landscape it seems less likely to be an aesthetic than an ecological one.

There is some reason to think that aesthetic taste can follow ecological interests. Landscape architects contrast the aesthetic and the ecological style of associating different plants together, and there is a movement in the taste of practitioners towards preference for the association of plants grouped together because they are ecologically compatible: such groupings come to look better.[15] This kind of adaptation tempts one towards relativism about taste, but that may be too hasty. Once the eye is accustomed to the new kind of association one may become aware of more subtle harmonies of form and texture and colour. This then may be an example of the eye being trained to notice beauties of a less obvious kind. It is still not an example of an ecological value being itself an aesthetic value.

To turn to the relation between the aesthetic and the historical, I find another example of Moore's instructive. He discusses in his book the value of lowland heath, in particular the heathland of Dorsetshire. After giving some examples of rare species to be found there, which make the heath of great biological interest, he goes on without pause to give two further reasons for finding it interesting: 'When heather and gorse are in flower they are spectacularly beautiful. They have changed little for hundreds of years, except in extent, and thus they provide landscapes which we share with our forebears'.[16] Heathland has no economic value now, but it had once. It results from human activity in the distant past, and had, until comparatively recently, an economic function, as grazing and a source of bedding, fuel and fodder, as readers of Thomas Hardy's *The Return of the Native* know. So a historically aware viewer is likely to look at it not simply as visually beautiful but as the still visible testimony to a way of life with which she can feel continuous. The phrase 'landscapes that we share with our forebears' calls to mind Alan Holland's cogent argument for the importance of historical perspective in making judgements of the value of natural features: 'The value of these situations which we should be seeking to uphold lies in the way that the constituent items and the places which they occupy are intertwined with and embody the life-history of the community of which they form a part'.[17] What I wish to add, in relating this insight to the aesthetic dimension, is that the fact that a community's way of life has produced a beautiful landscape is one reason to be interested in and moved by that landscape's history. Conversely, to understand the history of the landscape enriches and adds poignancy to the enjoyment of its aesthetic features.

However much the experience of landscape may be enriched by their coexistence in consciousness, we can still distinguish between the historically interesting features of the landscape and the contingently related aesthetic quality of these features. They can be quite independent. In the first place we can clearly respond to a scene as pretty, lovely, beautiful, commonplace, bland, dreary and so on, without knowing anything about its history. Equally we can know the history of a landscape from a written account without having first hand experience of it. While the historical narrative may be moving or fascinating, so that following it is an aesthetic experience, I think we would hesitate to say that this would be enough to justify speaking of an aesthetic response *to the landscape*. For that one needs some first hand experience. If however one follows the narrative on the ground, perhaps with a guide who can point out the significance of its observable features, that may constitute an aesthetic experience, one which has a major intellectual component. It may be an engrossing one even though, viewed ahistorically, the landscape is a dreary decaying one.

The kind of aesthetic experience that is most intimately involved with history is that of the landscape associated with a person's own history, or with that of his or her family or community. The two may be the same, but urbanisation ensures that for most they are different. For the town dweller to visit the country is often to recover in imagination the sense of being part of a more natural environment. Our feeling for natural beauty is, in Collingwood's words, concentrated upon 'the spectacle of a rural society living in the pursuit of traditional arts and deeply rooted in a landscape which has in part created it and in part been created by it. Such a society is the pit whence we were digged; it is what we all were before the industrial revolution.'[18] The response to the beauty of the landscape is more intense because of the sense of connectedness, and may be further intensified by an accompanying sense of a connection lost. One can become attached to a landscape because of its beauty, quite independently of any personal connection with it. But it is perhaps more commonly the case that attachment to the beauty of a landscape results from, or is reinforced by, a different kind of attachment, either personal or ancestral.

That is especially so in the case of the landscape in which one's aesthetic sensibility was formed, and whose features are associated with significant events in one's early life. This is complicated, reinforced and enriched if that was also the landscape of one's ancestors. One's identity is then bound up with two intertwined histories, of the landscape and of the people who made it. The personal association functions in three ways. Firstly, one is likely to be fond of a place that one has known and received one's first impressions from, and being fond of a place, like being fond of a person, normally means liking the look of it, even though, viewed impersonally, it is not very beautiful. Secondly, knowing something well means being sensitive to those aspects of it in which beauty is to be found, but only by the discerning and accustomed eye. Thirdly, love of a place as home and love of its beauty are mutually reinforcing.

This last is an association that is brought out movingly in Gerard Manley Hopkins poem 'Binsey Poplars', which provides the epigraph to this paper.[19] The poem begins with a very personal lament for 'my aspens dear': 'All felled, felled, are all felled'. But personal regret for a particular loved scene prompts reflections of a more general kind about the fragility of country, and its transience: 'Aftercomers cannot guess the beauty been./ Ten or twelve, only ten or twelve/ Strokes of havoc unselve/ The sweet especial rural scene'. There is nothing inevitable about any of these associations. One can feel alienated from one's home landscape and indifferent to its beauty, or remember it as reassuringly familiar despite being ugly.

I conclude this discussion of the relation of aesthetic with other non-utilitarian sources of interest in landscape with a general comment. The aesthetic character of a landscape is logically independent of its having characteristics that make it scientifically or historically interesting, or of its being connected to oneself or one's people. In that sense its aesthetic character is a distinct feature, and I think it follows that, judged impersonally, the aesthetic value of a landscape is independent of other kinds of value. Viewed as aspects of an individual's experience, however, there are important ways in which aesthetic and non-aesthetic elements interact. The discussion has emphasised two in particular. First, acquiring knowledge, scientific or historical, of a landscape is revelatory; it makes the observer aware of attributes whose aesthetic significance would otherwise not be apparent. Secondly, there is a kind of osmotic process by which one kind of experience transfers intensity to another. As the student of ferns becomes adept at identifying different species, she becomes increasingly sensitive to their various aesthetic features, and susceptible to their aesthetic appeal. Such a case exemplifies both the revelatory and the osmotic: the opening up of a realm to be explored, and the transfer of feeling, from the passion for discovery to love of the beauty of the discovered.

AESTHETICS AND THE PRESERVATION OF RURAL LANDSCAPES

Agricultural land is valued for both instrumental and non-instrumental reasons. It is land that is cultivated to serve essential human needs. It is also valued for its beauty and for its scientific and historical interest. Changes in the use of land brought about for reasons of utility may threaten other values, aesthetic, ecological or historical. It may happen, for instance, that the lover of landscape values highly the aesthetic qualities of a landscape that is obsolete from the user's point of view. The appearance of the fell-country in the English Lakes, for instance, depends on a system of hill farming that is increasingly uneconomic.[20] Should it be maintained in order to preserve the familiar beautiful landscape, or does that invert the proper relationship between the practical and the aesthetic?

I shall assume that any kind of non-instrumental value provides a *prima facie* reason for wanting something that has it to continue in existence. This is of course not so with utility value, being a kind of instrumental value. That something has instrumental value means that it is valuable as a means to an end, and if the end ceases to be wanted the means, if *merely* a means, no longer has value. The problem about rural landscape is that its character is largely the product of its utility; if it no longer has utility it loses its prime reason for existence. Loss of utility, however, does not mean loss of non-instrumental values, so the problem is whether a landscape's surviving non-instrumental values are sufficient reason for preserving its character.

In particular, how important is it to conserve beautiful rural landscapes simply for their beauty? It may be helpful to consider how similar or different are the principles of art conservation and landscape conservation. If we assume that paintings are produced to have certain permanent characteristics, then conservation may reasonably aim to retain or restore those characteristics. The natural processes that change tonal relationships may result in a different aesthetic character that some art lovers prefer, but there are strong reasons to ignore those preferences. The situation is not the same with land. Growth and decay, climate change, geological change, even without different land use policies, effect changes in the landscape, with concomitant changes in aesthetic character;

there seems no reason to think that the aesthetic character of a landscape at any particular point in time has a privileged status.

Change often results in a different aesthetic character, but not necessarily an inferior one. The Huntingdonshire example is instructive. The hedgeless landscape favours the appreciation of the quick tour, but why, from a simply aesthetic point of view, is that a less valid kind of appreciation than that of the slow walker? For those who grew up among the little grass fields, accustomed to the interest at their feet, the change is a loss; but without accepting a wholly subjectivist view of natural beauty, it is possible to say that only familiarity stood in the way of people recognising that they were experiencing a change but not a loss, or a loss of one *kind* of beauty, compensated for by an equal beauty of another kind. Moore remarks that few people in Huntingdonshire, because they were too young to remember, were acutely conscious of the change.

The mere fact of familiarity, that we are used to our landscape having a certain character, is surely of little weight, and not obviously a reason for favouring one form of aesthetic quality over another, and attempting to halt change that is not demonstrably change for the worse.

Aesthetic considerations provide rather weak support for attempts to preserve landscapes and the activities that maintain them when social and economic change renders them no longer self-supporting. It might be objected that this is no different from the preservation of certain kinds of artistic activity, playing early music on authentic instruments for instance. But the analogy fails because this is not an activity whose primary function is a non-aesthetic one. The problem with obsolete farming methods is that their function was non-aesthetic, though they produced landscape with a particular aesthetic character, and involved activities and artefacts with a particular aesthetic character, as consequences of the primary function. These aesthetically pleasing things were the unintended result of activities engaged in for quite different reasons. Preservation of the methods for the sake of the aesthetic aspects is an inversion of the original and natural relationship between the utilitarian and the aesthetic.

The aesthetic preference for the landscape of labour intensive mixed farming is reinforced by dubious history. We find it pleasing partly because of associated ideas of the good, simple, wholesome rural life, ignoring the fact that the life of the farm was laborious in the extreme. There is a kind of charm in the fictional pastoral idyll. We no longer dress up as shepherds and shepherdesses for our country picnics, but to the extent that we think of the countryside as the setting of a happy peasant life, close to the earth and in harmony with the rhythm of the seasons, and so on, we are getting aesthetic pleasure based on an illusion. It would be priggish to be disapproving of harmless indulgence in a conscious fiction. But realism about the past, rather than nostalgia for an idealised past, is likely to induce a correct valuation of landscape as it now exists, and a more constructive approach to landscape change.

The argument just set out requires some important qualifications. First it gives no weight to the kind of intense personal attachment to a particular landscape and its beauty that were discussed in the second section of this paper. The thought that a new set of aesthetic qualities can compensate for the loss of an old presupposes a temporally and personally neutral standpoint. It is not at all obvious that such a standpoint is the only rational one from which to evaluate change. The sense of loss, of something uniquely precious having vanished, is not mere sentimentality. The cost to those for whom the loss is a personal one can be severe. The best that can be said for the neutral standpoint is that when change is inevitable it provides a wider view, the possibility of a more detached estimate of gains and losses. Within that view what is a reason for regret may not necessarily be a reason to oppose the cause of it.

Second, changes in land use may be undesirable for many reasons, the aesthetic being only one. Industrialised farming may be an unsustainable form of cultivation, may result in loss of biodiversity, may efface the record of human and animal occupation, and may at the same time replace a varied with a monotonous landscape. Aesthetic reasons then may quite legitimately contribute to rational opposition to some sorts of change. It is not part of my argument that any sort of economic reason for change is dominant over non-instrumental reasons for resisting it.

Third, despite the fact that the taste for country ways and products – the country itself and the artefacts displayed in folk museums and at craft fairs – may get some of its popularity from spurious history, that is not to deny that there are authentic, non-illusory, aesthetic qualities in many traditional countryside activities. Even though they may be kept going only by the efforts of heritage preservation bodies, a neatly laid hedge, a dry stone wall, a hazel hurdle, a handmade basket, a ploughed field, a coppice, may be beautiful and the record of beautiful work. One cannot help regretting the passing of activities with inherent grace and skill, and if they can be given a genuine role in the work or leisure of the region to which they belong their preservation or revival is a good thing. But there is increasingly a development in which tourism replaces the primary economic activities of rural areas, and those activities – methods of cultivation and associated crafts – are continued as part of the theatre laid on for visitors. Increasingly upland farming is maintained to preserve the landscape and its way of life. In an important sense, however, it is impossible to preserve the way of life when its primary motivation is so radically changed. The farmer becomes a museum curator, or a theatre director. The distinction I made at the beginning of the first section between rural landscape and the landscaped grounds of great houses disappears. Both are works of art, with the important difference that the former pretends to be something else.

In the paper from which I quoted earlier Holland and O'Neill contend that the question that should be asked when we are faced with the problem whether and how to conserve some feature is '*how best to continue the narrative …*

what would make the *most appropriate trajectory* from what has gone before?'[21] They do not offer a formula by which this question can be answered. Indeed they consider the attempt to produce some sort of value calculus to be fruitless. Instead they offer, in an Aristotelian spirit, two 'guiding considerations', in brief that the pace and scale of change should be moderate, and that change should preserve narrative integrity: 'above all is the thought of being 'true to' what has gone before'.

It might be thought that following these guiding thoughts should lead one to favour the preservation of the Fells just as they are. After all they look much as they have looked, except for changes due to, for example, over-grazing, for generations. Why is their continuing to look that way not an appropriate future trajectory? Holland and O'Neill however point out that too little change can be as disruptive as too much, and that conservation efforts can be disruptive in that they stifle change and transform 'the lived world into a museum piece'. I would amend this by submitting that such transformation cannot be called too little change. My argument in this section has been that to preserve the appearance of a landscape when the function which produced that appearance has lapsed is to bring about radical change, even though the landscape bears no sign of that change on its face. The overt aesthetic features remain, but an uneasy sense of artificiality may spoil one's appreciation of them.

CONCLUSION

I have not argued for a single thesis, but have tried to elucidate some relationships between aesthetic and other kinds of interest in rural landscape. The tentative conclusions I arrive at are these: first, that although there are important connections between aesthetic and other non-instrumental reasons for valuing rural landscapes, none is a necessary relationship, but the aesthetic is a logically independent form of non-instrumental value; secondly that on the contrary there are some aesthetic judgements of rural landscape that are necessarily dependent on its characterisation as land cultivated in a particular way for particular purposes; and thirdly that the *undesigned* aesthetic character of rural landscape puts in question the force of aesthetic reasons for preserving rural landscapes which have lost their primary traditional function.

ACKNOWLEDGMENTS

For useful comments at various stages in the writing of this paper I thank Penelope Benson, Bob Hale, Michael Mumford, Vernon Pratt, two anonymous readers for the journal, and Emily Brady in her editorial capacity.

NOTES

[1] I have to confess to worse than insularity, in that all my examples are of English rural landscape, the only one I know at all intimately. How far my remarks might apply more generally I cannot tell.

[2] Or, as the *Concise Oxford Dictionary* concisely puts it, 'the countryside rather than the town'. I prefer the terms 'country', 'countryside' or 'land' to 'landscape' with its implicit reference to the representation in painting of a view from a particular standpoint. I intend to use the term without this implication, as I take it do most of those who use the phrase 'cultural landscape'.

[3] Emily Brady has a good review of the gradations of artefactuality in humanly modified environments; see Brady, 2003: 55–60. In a recent paper (Brady, 2006) she analyses the varied dialectical relationships between natural processes and human activity at work in the production of traditional and modern agricultural landscapes.

[4] Westmacott and Worthington, 1974: 44. The parenthesis in square brackets is mine.

[5] Ruskin, 1904: Vol. 4, Part V, ch 1, 'Of the Turnerian Picturesque', §§ 7–12. The extended passage and all quoted phrases in the preceding two paragraphs are from these sections of Ruskin's work, which includes a plate of the two paintings.

[6] Poetry, just as much as painting, can provide examples of the noble picturesque. Wordsworth's description of the leech gatherer in 'Resolution and Independence' or of the thorn in the poem of that title could be taken as a paradigm of it. Neither is seen as enhancing a landscape by being picturesquely rugged.

[7] I owe my appreciation of these baskets to the work of Owen Jones, a fine Cumbrian maker. (email: owen.swills@virgin.net). See http://www.woodsmithstore.co.uk for pictures.

[8] Sibley, 2001: 176–89.

[9] Good examples of the kind of detailed work I have in mind are provided by Emily Brady's discussion of hedge-laying and stonewalling (Brady, 2006).

[10] This point is convincingly argued in relation to the landscapes of industrial farming by Allen Carlson (Carlson, 1985). Carlson has further elaborated his functional approach in a more recent paper (Carlson, 2001).

[11] The persons I call the 'user' and the 'non-user' are ideal types. I am not supposing that farmers, for instance, are without aesthetic appreciation of their own work and the land they work. Moreover, a non-user may admire some artefact, say a tool, and know what it is for, but only a user can fully appreciate its aesthetic qualities.

[12] Some philosophers contend that an aesthetic interest is instrumental in that the beautiful object is contemplated for the sake of the experience enjoyed by the subject, and hence is not valued for its own sake. This view is mistaken: see my *Environmental Ethics*, chapter 2 (Benson 2000).

[13] In an interesting paper, 'Nature connoisseurship', Allan Greenbaum (2005) suggests that those who hold nature to be intrinsically valuable, i.e value it for its own sake, do so by virtue of an 'aesthetic disposition', which he characterises by reference to Pierre Bourdieu's account of Kant. Kant however certainly did not assimilate the scientific understanding of nature to the aesthetic appreciation of it.

[14] Moore, 1987.

[15] I owe this observation to Isis Brook, in conversation.

[16] Moore, 1987: 35

[17] Holland and O'Neill, 1996: 4.

[18] Collingwood, 1964: 106. The quotation is from Collingwood's interesting discussion of the aesthetic appreciation of nature in his early *Outlines of a Philosophy of Art* (1925).

[19] Hopkins, 1948, poem 43.

[20] Uneconomic, that is, in a farming context as traditionally understood: farmers cannot make a living by selling their produce, viz. meat and wool. But as Michael Mumford has pointed out to me, economics is about the efficient use of resources, and within the context of the economy of the region it may well be an efficient use of resources to maintain sheep farming on the fells by subsidy. This does not alter the fact that farming has a new *raison d'être*, and the appearance of the land is no longer merely a consequence of farming it, but its purpose.

[21] Holland and O'Neill, 1996: 4.

REFERENCES

Benson, J. 2000. *Environmental Ethics: An Introduction with Readings*. London: Routledge.

Brady, E. 2003. *Aesthetics of the Natural Environment*. Edinburgh: Edinburgh University Press.

Brady, E. 2006. 'The aesthetics of agricultural landscapes and the relationship between humans and nature'. *Ethics, Place and Environment* **9**(1): 1–19, doi: 10.1080/13668790500518024.

Carlson, A. 1985. 'On appreciating agricultural landscapes'. *Journal of Aesthetics and Art Criticism* **43**: 3001–3012.

Carlson, A. 2001. 'On aesthetically appreciating human environments'. *Philosophy and Geography* **4**(1): 9–24, doi: 10.1080/10903770125625.

Collingwood, R.G. 1964. *Essays in the Philosophy of Art*, edited by Alan Donagan, Bloomington: Indiana University Press.

Greenbaum, A. 2005. 'Nature connoisseurship'. *Environmental Values* **14**: 389-407, doi: 10.3197/096327105774434477.

Holland, A. and J. O'Neill, 1996. 'The integrity of nature over time: some problems'. *Thingmount Working Paper* No. 8 (Philosophy Dept, Lancaster University, in association with BANC).

Hopkins, G.M, 1948. *Poems of Gerard Manley Hopkins,* 3rd edn. London: Oxford University Press.

Moore, N.W. 1987. *The Bird of Time: The Science and Politics of Nature Conservation*. Cambridge: Cambridge University Press.

Ruskin, J. 1904. *Modern Painters*. in The Library Edition, edited by E.T. Cook and Alexander Wedderburn. London: George Allen.

Sibley, F. 2001. 'Aesthetic judgements: pebbles, faces and fields of litter', in the author's *Approach to Aesthetics: Collected Papers on Philosophical Aesthetics* (Oxford: Clarendon Press).

Westmacott, R. and T. Worthington. c.1972. *New Agricultural Landscapes*, report of a study undertaken on behalf of the Countryside Commission during 1972. Cheltenham: Countryside Commission.

Admiring the High Mountains: The Aesthetics of Environment

John Haldane

EXPERIENCES OF LANDSCAPE AND ENVIRONMENTAL AESTHETICS

My main title is drawn from a passage in St Augustine's *Confessions* (x.8.15) as quoted by Petrarch in a famous letter addressed to Francesco Dionigi da Borgo San Sepolcro, an Augustinian professor of theology. Dated 26th April 1336, it recounts an ascent of Mont Ventoux (the 'Windy Peak') made that same day by Petrarch, his brother and two servants. After describing his preparations for the climb and its early stages he turns to religious matters, drawing parallels between the difficulties of the physical ascent and the process of spiritual formation. Having reached the highest summit he reflects on his recent past and then, as the sun begins to set he looks around again in all directions:

> I admired every detail, now relishing earthly enjoyment, now lifting up my mind to higher spheres after the example of my body, and I thought it fit to look into the volume of Augustine's *Confessions* ... Where I fixed my eyes first it was written: "And men go to admire the high mountains, the vast floods of the sea, the huge streams of the rivers, the circumference of the ocean, and the revolutions of the stars – and desert themselves." I was stunned, I confess. I bade my brother, who wanted to hear more, not to molest me, and close the book, angry with myself that I still admired earthly things. Long since I ought to have learned, even from pagan philosophers, that "nothing is admirable besides the mind; compared to its greatness nothing is great." [Seneca, *Epistle* 8. 5] I was completely satisfied with what I had seen of the mountain and turned my inner eye toward myself. From this hour nobody heard me say a word until we arrived at the bottom. [1]

This is a interesting passage and for more than one reason. It belongs within a corpus that bears the marks of the emerging renaissance humanism, and the letter itself has often been referred to as anticipating later European mountaineering interests; but what I think we should be struck by is the unironic willingness with which Petrarch sets aside his aesthetic delight as unworthy of the human mind. We have become accustomed to praising natural beauty and to thinking of its appreciation precisely as a mark of a refined sensibility and as something to be approved of and cultivated. Thus the implicit opposition of aesthetic and spiritual concerns is hard for us to accommodate. Consider how unexceptional (and congenial to modern environmentalism) seem the ideas, if not the form, of Hopkins' sonnet "God's Grandeur":[2]

The world is charged with the Grandeur of God.
It will flame out, like shining from shook foil;
It gathers to a greatness, like the ooze of oil
Crushed. Why do men then not now reck his rod?
Generations have trod, have trod, have trod;
And all is seared with trade; bleared, smeared with toil;
And wears man's smudge and shares man's smell: the soil
Is bare now, nor can foot feel, being shod.

And for all this, nature is never spent;
There lives the dearest freshness deep down things;
And though the last lights off the black West went
Oh morning, at the brown brink eastward, springs –
Because the Holy Ghost over the bent
World broods with warm breast and with ah! bright wings.

Of course Petrarch was writing over six hundred and fifty years ago, long before romantic quasi-panentheism, and addressing a theologian with whom he shared an admiration for Augustine. This large historical and intellectual gap helps to explain the otherwise puzzling deprecation of the aesthetic appreciation of nature. Yet even in more recent times sensitive and thoughtful authors have dismissed what are now canonised landscapes in terms which are at least striking and which some will regard as blasphemous. Consider, for example, the following description from the pen of Dr Johnson writing of Scottish scenery:

> [The hills] exhibit very little variety; being almost wholly covered with dark heath, and even that seems to be checked in its growth. What is not heath is nakedness, a little diversified by now and then a stream rushing down the steep. An eye accustomed to flowery pastures and waving harvests is astonished and repelled by this wide extent of hopeless sterility. The appearance is that of matter incapable of form or usefulness, dismissed by nature from her care and disinherited of her favours, left in its original elemental state, or quickened only with one sullen power of useless vegetation.
>
> It will very readily occur, that this uniformity of barrenness can afford little amusement to the traveller; that it is easy to sit at home and conceive rocks and heath, and waterfalls; and that these journeys are useless labours, which neither impregnate the imagination, nor enlarge the understanding.[3]

This text and Petrarch's letter should serve as reminders that there is nothing perennially obvious about the present-day reverence for nature and the elevation of its appreciation to the higher categories of human consciousness. The 'aesthetics of the environment' is like the 'politics of the home' a term of art invented to label a set of concerns and an associated field of academic study each developed over time and out of particular cultural histories. In what follows I first sketch something of the relevant philosophical background and then discuss an account of the aesthetics of beauty suggested by remarks of Aquinas.

Recent years have seen the rapid rise to prominence of a range of studies, policy directives and initiatives concerned with the environment. These are sometimes unphilosophical, pragmatic responses to perceived threats arising from, for example, heavy industrialisation and increasing levels of human activity. Very often, however, they are presented through patterns of judgment and justification that are avowedly moral, not to say moralistic. Those involved in such presentations are then liable to speak in terms of 'environmental *ethics*', or more likely of 'an environmental *ethic*'. Although there are reasons for doubting whether values can be thought of in compartmentalised isolation I want for present purposes, and so far as is possible, to place ethical concerns on one side and to focus on *aesthetic* considerations.[4] More precisely my interest is in whether, and if so how, philosophical aesthetics might be brought into contemporary thinking about the natural environment.

In advance one might suppose that the effect of introducing any kind of objective aesthetic element into the discussion of environmental values (what might be termed 'environmental axiology') would be to strengthen the case for 'deep' ecology. It is, after all, a common plea made by those concerned with protecting the natural environment from the effects of industry, say, that these deface the landscape, transforming what is naturally beautiful into something ugly. How then could an interest in the aesthetic qualities of nature be other than an instance of respect for the environment considered as something valuable in and of itself? In order to answer that question I need to say something about the general character of aesthetic theory.

SOME ELEMENTS OF AESTHETIC EXPERIENCE

From antiquity, through the middle ages, the renaissance and the enlightenment, to the present day, there has been a movement in philosophical discussions of beauty and other aesthetic values (such as the sublime – and in later periods the picturesque) from attention to the *objects* of aesthetic experience to the character of the *experience* itself, and of the modes of attention or *attitudes* it involves. Although there is no agreed inventory of the elements or aspects of aesthetic experience, and certainly there is no agreement on their inter-relationships, the following schema (Figure 1) sets out something of the broad range of favoured possiblities.

Aesthetic Object		*Aesthetic Value*		*Aesthetic Response*	*Aesthetic Attitude*
Anything at all	*Specific things* reality; emotion; form; etc.	*Intrinsic values* content; form; sensuous qualities; etc.	*Extrinsic values* satisfaction; release; under-standing; etc.	Pleasure; interest; universal validity; satisfaction; understanding; etc.	Detachment; disinterest; contemplation; isolation; physical distance; interpretation; etc.

FIGURE 1
The Elements of Aesthetic Experience

Again considered historically, the focus of interest has moved from left to right. Thus in *pre-modern aesthetics* (to the extent that one can reasonably speak in these terms of a subject that is often thought to have originated only in the eighteenth century[5]) aesthetic objects and values are generally taken to be prior, with aesthetic responses and attitudes being held to be posterior to and explicable in terms of these. So, for example, it might be argued that the 'objects' of aesthetic experience are the forms of natural entities, and that aesthetic value consists in the harmonious organisation of parts realised in such forms. An aesthetic experience will then be any experience in which these forms and values are attended to and appreciated, and an aesthetic attitude will be an (or perhaps *the*) attitude induced by such experiences.

Clearly any view of this sort, if it is to avoid explanatory circularity, must postulate certain objective features that are the basis for our experiences of beauty. The task of doing so is a challenging one and though there are still efforts to complete it many have come to think it is impossible. Such scepticism together with other factors led, in the *modern* and *enlightenment* periods, to the development of broadly subjectivist accounts of aesthetics. By 'subjectivist', here, I do not mean arbitrary or idiosyncratic. Rather, the unifying feature of such accounts is that the direction of explanation runs from the attitude or experience to the value or object. One might, for example, identify the aesthetic attitude as one of detachment from theoretical and practical concerns or of disinterested contemplation, thereby specifying the character of aesthetic experience as being that of expressing or being conditioned by such an attitude. Following this one might then say that an aesthetic object is any object attended to in that kind of experience, and an aesthetic value is any feature singled out in such an experience as rewarding of attention, or, and more likely, any feature of the experience itself which is found to be pleasant or beneficial. Once again explanatory circularity will only be avoided so long as one does not at this point appeal to aesthetic objects in order to specify the relevant class of attitudes and experiences.

Even if that can be done, however, it is tempting to suppose that a consequence of a subjectivist approach is that there can then be no question of correct or incorrect aesthetic judgements, or relatedly of better and worse judges; for without autonomous aesthetic objects surely there can be no aesthetic objectivity. One familiar reaction to this thought is to welcome it, arguing that one of the main reasons for favouring subject-based approaches is precisely that aesthetic judgements lack criteria by which to be assessed. However, a subtler response recognises that in giving explanatory priority to the aesthetic attitude and aesthetic experience one is not wholly precluded from having external criteria of greater or lesser, coarser and more refined aesthetic sensibility; for one may hold that there are *intersubjective* standards.[6]

Consider the case of table manners. At the level of serious reflection we should not be tempted to suppose that there are objectively offensive modes of eating. Rather we should say that manners are a function of culturally shared interests. A mode of eating is offensive for a given community if in normal circumstances it would be judged offensive by a competent member of that community. Competence here being explained not in terms of an ability to discern objectively offensive eating practices but by reference to mastery of certain social conventions governing public eating. Although these norms are *subjective,* in the sense of being rooted in the dispositions of *subjects*, none the less their existence allows for the idea that some member of that community can go wrong in his style of eating, and thereby correctly be described as ill-mannered.

It should be clear then that the resources of certain 'subjectivist' aesthetic theories are more considerable than might initially be supposed. Moreover, as Figure 1 indicates, there are many different elements and combinations that might be included in an aesthetic theory of either objectivist or subjectivist orientations. Rather than pursue these possibilities in detail, however, I want to consider next how the aesthetics of the environment is likely to fare when considered from these perspectives. An objectivist approach will look for certain features of environments which will serve as the basis for aesthetic experience and evaluation. Immediately, however, various difficulties suggest themselves. To the extent that we think of artworks as the paradigm class of objects involved in aesthetic experience we will see a problem in seeking for beauty in nature. If, like Hopkins, one were a creationist, holding that the universe is an artefact fashioned by God, then of course one could treat it formally in just the same way. But traditional theists are likely to be cautious of aestheticising Divine creation; and others will find the theistic assumption at least unwarranted and perhaps incoherent.

However, while denying that the natural world is the product of deliberate design one might nevertheless regard it *as if* designed, and maybe even speak of 'Nature' itself as the source of aesthetic order. This move, however, generates problems of its own. Consider the question of how many pictures there are in a given art gallery, or performances in a particular concert hall. Notwithstanding elements of the avantgarde this would, in principle, be a relatively easy matter to settle by reference to the form, content, matter and source of the works. However, if one eschews any claim of literal creation it seems in principle impossible to say where one work of nature begins and another ends. The category of the scenic view, for example, is all too obviously one of our own fashioning. If there is any element of art-making in nature it is surely present through the selective attention of spectators to aspects of a continuous realm. Furthermore, in deciding where to locate the boundaries of one scene our designs are influenced by the experience of actual artworks. In short, the effort to identify aesthetic objects in nature tends quickly to return one in the direction of the subject of experience and of his or her interests, cultural presuppositions and classifications.

Whether for these or other reasons, an objectivist might not choose to employ the artwork model but try instead the sort of approach I described as being characteristic of pre-modern thinking. That is to say, he or she might hold that the objects of environmental aesthetic experience are natural forms, by which I mean, primarily, the forms of organisms and derivatively those of non-organic entities. Something of this view is suggested by the fragmentary but very interesting remarks made by Aquinas in his discussions of beauty. He explicitly denies the claim that something is beautiful simply because we like it, insisting by contrast that our appreciation is directed towards the beauty of things, and that a thing is beautiful to the extent that it manifests its proper form or natural structure. He writes:

> Three things are required for beauty. First integrity or perfection (*integritas sive perfectio*), for what is defective is thereby ugly; second, proper proportion or consonance (*proportio sive consonantia*); and third clarity (*claritas*).[7]

The background assumption is that each substance or individual is possessed of a nature which, in the case of living things, is at once a principle of organic structure and a determinant of its characteristic activities. Integrity and proper proportion are directly related to this nature or form (*forma rei*) and the issue of clarity arises from them. *Integrity* consists in the possession of all that is required by the nature of the thing, such and such limbs and organs, active capacities and so on; while *proportion* includes both the compatibility of these elements and their being well-ordered. These two factors are then presupposed in the idea of *clarity*, for that concerns the way in which the form of a thing is manifest or unambiguously presented.

This neo-Aristotelian account has certain merits from the point of view of those interested in developing an objectivist environmental aesthetic. Forms are real, mind-independent entities, there to be discovered and contemplated. Thus the question of whether one member of a natural kind better realises the species' common nature is one that it makes sense to ask and one which informed attention can hope to answer. Also values and policies seem to be implicit or rootable in such facts. A 'good' specimen is *ontologically* better than a 'poor' one; and it is clear enough how industrial practices can be detrimental to these natural values by causing harm to individual organisms and injuring the species. Thus, unlikely as it might have been supposed given the tone of Petrarch's fourteenth century reflections, it may seem that in the thirteenth century writings of Aquinas there is a promising source for a deep ecological aesthetic, i.e., one in which the relevant values owe nothing to man's interests – save of course where the forms in question are human ones.

However, this conclusion would be a mistake and it is important to see why that is so. First, although Aquinas is insistent that beauty is not simply a function of subjective preference his account of its conditions indicates that there is a subtle form of subjectivity, in the sense of relativity-to-a-subject, in its very constitution. Recall that beauty requires perfection, proportion and clarity. The last of these I glossed as unambiguously presented or manifest form. The existence and character of a given form may be a wholly mind-independent affair, but to speak of its presentation implies actual or possible knowers. Furthermore whether something is unambiguous or clear is in part a function of the cognitive powers and accomplishments of the actual or imagined subject. So to say that something is beautiful if the perfection of its form is clearly presented indicates that, of necessity, beauty is something which involves a spectator. It is also apparent both from what Aquinas says and from the logic of his position that the spectators in question require the sort of intellectual capacity which there is little reason to think is possessed by any creature other than man. In short, natural beauty is *constitutively* tied to human experience.

Second, on Aquinas' view there is an equivalence between goodness and beauty – known as the 'convertibility of the transcendentals'. What this means is that in thinking or speaking of these attributes one is referring to the same feature of reality, *viz.*, the condition of the natural form that constitutes an item's essential nature. Thus a thing is good and beautiful to the extent that its form is perfected. This is an interesting thesis, and on reflection a plausible one with relevance for environmental philosophy. But it has a corollary that moves aesthetics deeper into the territory of humanistic ecology. If the referents of 'good' and 'beautiful' are one and the same how do the terms differ? Aquinas answers that each expresses a distinct kind of interest in, or concern with, the forms of things.

> The beautiful is the same as the good, and they differ in aspect only. For since good is what all seek, the notion of good is that which calms the desire; while the notion of the beautiful is that which calms the desire by being seen or known. Consequently those senses chiefly regard the beautiful which are the most cognitive, *viz.*, sight and hearing, as ministering to reason; for we speak of beautiful sights and beautiful sounds ... Thus it is evident that beauty adds to goodness a relation to the cognitive faculty: so that *good* means that which simply pleases the appetite; while the *beautiful* is something pleasant to apprehend.[8]

Thus although Aquinas roots his account of beauty in objective fact, the existence of aesthetic objects and values involves human subjects taking delight in perceptually and intellectually discernible structures. His view should be congenial to those concerned with environmental axiology in general and with aesthetic values in particular. It accords a major role to natural forms and can accommodate within this classification entities more extensive than individual organisms, such as species and even eco-systems. Further, unlike the aesthetics of the scenic it need not confine itself to the 'visible surface' of the world. It can, for example, allow the aesthetic relevance of ecological history and of the sorts of environmental structures to which Aldo Leopold's *A Sand County Almanac* did much to draw attention. In "Marshland Elegy" Leopold writes:

> Our ability to perceive quality in nature begins, as in art, with the pretty. It expands through successive stages of the beautiful to values as yet uncaptured by language. The quality of cranes, lies, I think, in this higher gamut, as yet beyond the reach of words.
>
> This much though can be said: our appreciation of the crane grows with the slow unravelling of earthly history. His tribe, we now know, stems out of the remote Ecocene. The other members of the fauna in which he originated are long since entombed within the hills. When we hear his call we hear no mere bird. We hear the trumpet in the orchestra of evolution. He is the symbol of our untamable past, of that incredible sweep of millennia which underlies and conditions the daily affairs of birds and men.[9]

It should be clear, however, that like the earlier attempt to conceive an aesthetics of the natural environment along the lines of a philosophy of art, an element of which is also present in Leopold's thinking, Aquinas' theory of natural beauty has an ineliminable subjective aspect.

CONCLUSION

We have come a long way from Petrarch's revulsion at his own delight, but we do not as yet have a clear and complete account of the nature and value of the aesthetics of environment. The task that remains, therefore, promises both theoretical and practical rewards. My general conclusion, however, is that whichever side of the diagram one starts from – focusing on the aesthetic attitude or the aesthetic object – one should be led to think that human experience plays a constitutive role in environmental aesthetics.

NOTES

[1] Petrarch, 1956 (1336), p. 44.
[2] Hopkins, 1970, p. 66.
[3] Johnson, 1944 (1773), pp. 34-5. It is interesting to compare these remarks with those of Thomas Gray: "I am returned from Scotland, charmed with my expedition: it is of the Highlands I speak: the Lowlands are worth seeing once, but the mountains are ecstatic and ought to be visited in pilgrimage once a year. None but those monstrous creatures of God know how to join so much beauty with so much horror. A fig for your poets, painters, gardeners and clergymen, that have not been among them, their imagination can be made up of nothing but bowling greens, flowering shrubs, horse ponds, Fleet ditches, shell grottoes and Chinese rails. Then I had so beautiful an Autumn. Italy could hardly produce a nobler scene, and this so sweetly contrasted with that perfection of nastiness and total want of accommodation that only Scotland can supply." Letter of 1765, Gray, 1935, p. 899. I am indebted to Christopher Smout for this quotation. He uses it to introduce a fascinating discussion of attitudes to Scottish landscape; see Smout, 1990.
[4] For a discussion of the way in which ethical concerns may constrain aesthetic appreciation see Foster, 1992.
[5] The first philosophical use of the term 'aesthetics' to identify a (more or less) autonomous field of experience is to be found in Baumgarten 1974 (1734). Baumgarten claims that the subject is the science of sensitive knowledge, "*scientia cognitionis sensitivae*".
[6] This in effect is the position advanced by Hume in his classic essay "Of the Standard of Taste", see Hume 1965 (1757).
[7] Aquinas, 1914 (c. 1270) Ia. q. 39. a. 8. For a brief account of Aquinas' view and of related ways of thinking see Haldane, 1993.
[8] Aquinas, 1914 (c.1270) Ia, IIae, q.17, a.1, ad. 3.
[9] Leopold, 1989 (1949), p. 96. For an account of the aesthetic dimension of Leopold's writings see Callicot, 1983.

REFERENCES

Aquinas, T. 1914 (c. 1270) *Summa Theologiae*, translated by Fathers of the English Dominican Province. London, Washbourne.

Baumgarten, Alexander 1974 (1734) *Reflections on Poetry*, translated by K. Aschenbrenner and W. Holther. Berkeley, University of California Press.

Callicot, J. Baird 1983 "Leopold's Land Aesthetic", *Journal of Soil and Water Conservation*, 1983; reprinted in J. Baird Callicot, *In Defense of the Land Ethic: Essays in Environmental Philosophy*. Albany, SUNY Press, 1989.

Foster, C. 1992 "Aesthetic Disillusionment: Environment, Ethics, Art", *Environmental Values* **1** (3): 205-15.

Gray, T. 1935 (1765) *Correspondence of Thomas Gray* edited by P. Toynbee and L. Whibley. Oxford, Clarendon Press, Vol II: 1756-65, p. 899

Haldane, J. 1987 "Aesthetic Naturalism and the Decline of Architecture, Part 1: Architecture and Aesthetic Perception", *International Journal of Moral and Social Studies* **2** (3): 210-24.

Haldane, J, 1988 "Aesthetic Naturalism and the Decline of Architecture Part 2: Form, Matter and Understanding", *International Journal of Moral and Social Studies* **3** (2): 173-90.

Haldane, J. 1990a "Philosophy and Environmental Issues", *International Journal of Moral and Social Studies* **5** (1): 79-91.

Haldane, J. 1990b "Architecture, Philosophy and the Public World", *British Journal of Aesthetics* **30**: 203-17.

Haldane, J. 1993 "Aquinas" and "Medieval and Renaissance Aesthetics" in *A Companion to Aesthetics*, edited by D. Cooper. Oxford, Blackwell.

Hopkins, G.M. 1970 *The Poems of Gerard Manley Hopkins*, edited by W.H. Gardner and N.H. MacKenzie. Oxford, Oxford University Press.

Hume, D. 1965 (1757) *Of the Standard of Taste and Other Essays* edited by John W. Lenz. Indianapolis, Bobbs-Merrill. pp. 3-24.

Johnson, S. 1944 (1773) *A Journey to the Western Islands* edited by R. W. Chapman. London, Oxford University Press.

Leopold, Aldo 1989 (1949) *A Sand County Almanac*. New York, Oxford University Press.

Petrarch, 1956 (1336) *The Ascent of Mont Ventoux*, in *The Renaissance Philosophy of Man* edited by E. Cassirer, P.O. Kristeller & J.H. Randall, pp. 36-46. Chicago, Chicago University Press.

Smout, C. 1990 "The Highlands and the Roots of Green Consciousness, 1750-1990", Raleigh Lecture, *Proceedings of the British Academy*.

What We Owe the Romantics

Lewis P. Hinchman and Sandra K. Hinchman

It has long been recognised that modern environmentalism emerged from the Romantic movement and associated currents of German idealism and American transcendentalism (Oelschlaeger 1991; Roszak 1972; Glacken 1976; Hargrove 1986; Nash 1982). The Romantics gave expression to a new sensibility that anticipated and even partly evoked that of contemporary nature writers and environmental crusaders. This elective affinity has been reinforced by the modern prejudice that the 'Enlightenment' and 'humanism' are arch-antagonists of a biocentric worldview (Ophuls 1997; Ehrenfeld 1978; Merchant 1980; Leiss 1972; Berman 1981). Since the Romantics, too, frequently looked at the Enlightenment with a jaundiced eye, denouncing its mechanistic or utilitarian accounts of nature, they appear to have been environmentalists *avant la lettre*. We shall argue that this genealogy is wrong in its approach and assumptions, but correct in its conclusions. The Romantic movement was still 'humanistic', for its primary impetus was the all-sided development of the individual rather than the investigation and preservation of the natural world. Yet the Romantics' scepticism about the Cartesian-Galilean image of nature led them down paths that anticipated both ecology and the theory of natural selection. More importantly, they believed that people exiled from or insensitive to nature's deeper rhythms and patterns forfeit an essential aspect of their humanity. In that sense Romantic humanism did indeed anticipate essential impulses of modern-day environmentalism.

We will characterise Romanticism as environmentalism's 'predecessor culture', one from which our contemporaries may still recover important insights. The ongoing shift in environmental ethics toward predominantly scientific-objectivising and/or economic justifications may obscure the Romantics' great discovery: that nature only becomes a matter for ethical concern, inspiration, love and protection once certain complex shifts have occurred in the sensibility of the subject. The Romantics understood that a deeper awareness of our connections to nature requires a new kind of symmetry or mutuality between subject and object and an appropriate set of descriptions to evince that mutuality. The language they fashioned to accomplish this differed *toto coelo* from the one devised by classical liberals and their heirs in political economy, a lesson Jack Turner would have us remember: 'By now, the language of economics (and law) exhaustively describes our world and hence becomes our world ... In accepting their descriptions we allow a set of experts to define our concerns in economic terms and predetermine the range of possible responses. Often we cannot even

Environmental Values **16** (2007): 333–354.

raise the issues important to us… Every vocabulary shapes the world to fit a paradigm' (Turner 1996: 58–62).

We begin from the conviction that the object language of such disciplines, however well-suited it might seem to express the insights and commitments of ecological philosophy, cannot support their full weight. We believe that the humanistic traditions associated with phenomenology and even (*mutatis mutandis*) hermeneutics provide a much firmer foundation for them, even though at first sight the cognitive interests of these traditions' founding thinkers, men like Dilthey and Husserl, seem remote from problems of ecological sustainability and nature preservation. The broader argument for the relevance of humanistic approaches and concerns to environmentalism surpasses the limits of this article. We have outlined it in other forums (Hinchman 1995; 2004; 2005) and it has been ably defended by eminent contemporary thinkers such as Erazim Kohák (1984), Albert Borgmann (1984) and David Abram (1996). But, to elucidate some of the points to follow, we would like to recall three of the crucial premises of phenomenology. First, the starting-point for phenomenological reflection is the world as we experience it, as it presents itself to us prior to all theorising. Second, we experience that world as making sense, or as 'a matrix of meaning' (Kohák 1978: 18). That is, prior to all scientific abstraction we inhabit a pre-theoretical, meaning-laden 'life-world'. As Bill McKibben (2004) has proposed, one may develop an environmentalist 'argument from meaning' in defence of that life-world. Finally, the life-world is thoroughly historical, since the meanings it evinces form lattices stretching far back into the past and extending into the future toward as-yet-incomplete projects. Thus, understanding our relationship with our physical environment, which is part of that life-world, presupposes an interpretative or hermeneutical effort to reconstruct the history of human experiences of it. In the case of the present essay, we shall have to investigate the ways that sensitive observers (here the Romantics) have described their own contact with and responses to the natural world in works of prose and poetry. These testimonies, as much as any scientific data, show what an intact natural world has meant – and still may mean – to us. We owe the Romantics not only the invention of a new sensibility, but the perennial possibility of reliving it and thus potentially relearning the reasons why the natural world was, and ought to be, a matter of such vital concern.

A word about defining Romanticism: some scholars regard it as an outgrowth of pastoral and Arcadian traditions reaching back to Roman times and still vibrant in eighteenth-century England (Williams 1973: 127; Buell 1995: 54). Others interpret it as a secularisation of inherited theological ideas (Abrams 1973), or as a subjectivist movement that portrayed the world as a stage for the display of poetic sensibility (Larmore 1996: 1–7; Taylor 1989: 368; Levere 1981). We shall leave these disputes to literary critics. We provisionally adopt the definition offered by Novalis, a self-described Romantic, that the adjective 'Romantic' means giving to the common a higher meaning, to the usual an unusual look, to the known the dignity of the unknown. In short, Romanticism concerns the 'recovery of the magic of everyday life' (Larmore 1966: 10). It involves both a discovery of what is already objectively present in the world around us and an active intervention by mind or imagination to bring it to light and reveal its true colors.

ANTICIPATIONS OF ECOLOGY

Some claim that Romanticism was the 'antithesis of everything scientific' (Pepper 1986: 77, 89). But careful scholars have come to recognise that such charges are false (Miller 2005: 298, 305). Many Romantic writers were scientists themselves, or at least enthusiastic amateurs bent on assimilating the latest research. In fact, much of nineteenth-century biology developed from early German Romanticism, which attracted not only poets and philosophers but scientists of the first rank, including Johann Friedrich Blumenbach and Alexander von Humboldt (Richards 2002: xiv, 216–229, 519–526). Goethe did considerable work on the origin of colours, optics and plant and animal morphology, and influenced Ernst Haeckel, the founder of ecology, by developing proto-evolutionary ideas of natural adaptation. Goethe stressed the way in which organisms were shaped 'from the outside' by the environments to which they had to adapt, and – though never accepting the complete indeterminacy of plant forms – rejected final causes as explanations for floral and faunal development (Miller 2005: 302). The following prescient observation helps us appreciate how scientific this Romantic writer was:

> 'The fish exists for the water' seems to me to say much less than 'the fish exists in and through the water'. For the latter expresses much more clearly that which is dimly concealed in the former: namely the idea that a creature we call a fish is only possible on the condition that there is an element that we call water in which it not only exists but becomes ... The decisive shape is, as it were, an inner core that is defined and shaped variously by the external element. (Goethe n.d.; L.H. translation)

Coleridge studied science in Germany, and in England maintained close ties to some of that nation's leading scientists (Levere 1981: 2, 18). He believed that the foremost task of philosophy was to reconcile moral autonomy with natural necessity. Thoreau read Humboldt and Lyell, as well as Darwin's *Voyage of the H.M.S. Beagle*, and published research on forest succession in New England. Even the less scientifically-inclined Wordsworth confessed that naturalists' precise descriptions enhanced the beauty of organisms by revealing more about their properties and powers than casual observation would disclose (Abrams 1971: 310).

How then did Romanticism get associated with an animus against science? What many Romantics opposed was not science *per se*, but the reductionist variety derived from Galileo, Descartes and their mechanistic acolytes. The Renaissance legacies of neo-Platonism, Hermeticism and historicism, which had gone underground for several centuries, made a startling comeback during the early Romantic period (Taylor 1989: 378; Robertson 1962: 193; Beiser 2003: 72; Hinchman 2005: *passim*). They were seen as a 'viable counter-metaphysics' capable of furnishing a competing paradigm to the mechanistic world view increasingly challenged by the rise of new sciences like geology, or advances in old ones like biology and chemistry (Abrams 1973: 171; Beiser 2003: 140; Barzun 1961: 54; Kroeber 1994: 90–91). The mechanical paradigm seemed unable satisfactorily to explain life, organic relationships and historical development – indeed, anything particular or unique.

The counter-metaphysics so attractive to Romantics had several components that anticipated contemporary ecology. Schelling distilled the ideas of Plotinus, Bruno and Spinoza as well as Kant and Fichte into a *Naturphilosophie* that attracted a circle of admirers in Germany as well as the more cerebral English Romantics, notably Coleridge. Against Kant, Schelling argued that mind and nature, subject and object, and other comparable dichotomies could be resolved into an absolute identity by tracing out each side of the polarity to the full development until it revealed its identity with its putative other. Above all, nature would begin to exhibit more and more spontaneity, self-initiated motion and organic complexity as one moved up the scale toward higher life forms or 'powers'. That is, nature would demonstrate 'emergent properties', including even freedom, for which mechanistic explanations could not fully account. As a result, mind and nature could be regarded as alternative aspects of a self-same reality, not radical antitheses. In short, Romantic nature philosophy was not a speculative deviation from mainstream empirical science, but was congruent with the most advanced thinking of its day (Beiser 2003: 156; Richards 2002: 115–116).

Furthermore, because they embraced an organic paradigm, the Romantics and their successors tended to notice the interdependencies that knitted together different species, as well as humans and their natural environment. Romanticism has in fact been defined as the quest for harmony within a higher, more encompassing order (Taylor 1989: 369; Marx 1964). Coleridge and Schelling held that no part of nature is fully intelligible until one has understood the whole (Levere 1981: 83; Beiser 2003: 169). It was convictions such as these that led Goethe to the threshold of the idea of natural selection, and inspired his successor, Haeckel, to launch the study of ecology. Schelling, too, moved closer to evolutionary thinking. He pointed out that we can explain organic beings through a gradual development of one and the same organisation, assuming we posit enough time for the transformations to take place: 'there would be no permanently existing entities; every product that seems now fixed in nature would exist only for a moment and, caught up in continual evolution, would be perpetually mutable'

(Schroter 1927: 19; L.H. translation). Thus, modern ecological and evolutionary sciences are rooted in certain tendencies of Romantic thought

The Romantics were wrong in their wholesale denunciations of mechanism. Coleridge and Goethe were misled into undertaking crusades against Newton in the hope that another, more organic version of science could save the values that they wished to preserve. Yet that does not mean they were wrong to worry that the Enlightenment-inspired scientific paradigm yielded a distorted picture of nature and of people's relationship with it. In fact, this was the case, but they could have made it more persuasively by framing a different image of human knowledge, psychology and experience. What had to be understood was that the scientific image of nature was a highly artificial product of abstraction and reduction, winnowed out from the intricate, multidimensional life-world. Rather than picking a fight with Newtonian science, they might have contented themselves with delineating the scope of that science and challenging its implicit claim to represent reality *tout court*, as Husserl, Dilthey and Gadamer would later do.

LIFE, FRESHNESS OF VISION AND SPONTANEITY

One critic has flatly asserted that 'the ground concept of Romanticism is life. Life is itself the highest good, the residence and measure of other goods' (Abrams 1973: 431). Accordingly, the organic, epitomised in the growing plant, became the Romantics' favourite metaphor. Coleridge, especially, associated life with the power of imagination that enables the genius to break through the encrustation of familiarity and produce 'freshness of sensation' and 'novelty' (Coleridge in Stauffer 1951: 155). In nature as well as in mind, the Romantics hoped to draw attention to the emergent properties (life, imagination, aesthetic appreciation) that hinted at powers of creativity.

The Romantics' discovery of life tended to coincide with the waning of the older mechanistic paradigm. Cutting-edge science in the 1790s seemed to be moving toward the conviction that nature possessed a self-formative, self-expressive power manifested in polarities of increasing complexity. The highest stage of nature's self-unfolding was manifested in activities of mind that revealed its deeper-lying structure (Richards 2002: 402, 405; Kluckhorn 1966: 27, 31; Beiser 2003: 21, 138). Poets and philosophers did not simply write *about* nature; they were nature writing about itself. That implied that the artistic depiction of nature would not necessarily count as inferior to its representation in scientific theory of the organicist stamp; the approaches were complementary and flowed from the same source. Schelling, for instance, thought that the biologist needed the poet's aesthetic judgment to penetrate nature's secrets (Richards 2002: 114). When the poets confessed their feeling of kinship with all life, they did not simply mean that animals' biological processes or genetic endowments resemble those in humans; rather, they refer to the self-directing, self-expressive impulses that appear in a meadow flower, a birdsong and a poem. Quite literally, insight into the life of nature was also insight into the self and its animating principles.

Wordsworth and Coleridge both gave poetic expression to vitalism. The latter's ancient mariner, having killed the symbol of life, the albatross, is becalmed in a sea in which nothing changes except the advance of decay, an image of the passivity and deadness of the mechanical universe. What releases him from this horror is the vision of sea snakes slithering through the putrefying ocean. The mariner loves them for being alive, and love for kindred life frees him from the static, mechanical trap; change resumes, the winds blow and eventually carry him back home. Yet – as though still in the grip of mechanical processes – he is compelled by mysterious forces to repeat his tale to every passing stranger.

The evanescence of spontaneous delight in nature occasioned some of Wordsworth's finest poems, such as 'Intimations of Immortality':

> – But there's a Tree, of many, one,
> A single Field which I have looked upon.
> Both of them speak of something that is gone:
> The Pansy at my feet
> Doth the same tale repeat:
> Whither is fled the visionary gleam?
> Where is it now, the glory and the dream?
> (Selincourt 1940, v. 4: 280, lines 51–57)

The poet's reply to his own question suggests that the poetic imagination, joined to mature understanding, may eventually recover a spark of youthful spontaneity at a higher level of reflection, enabling the poet to 'see into the life of things' (Selincourt 1940, v. 2: 260, line 49). But for most unpoetic souls, maturation and socialisation mean a long march into 'the light of common day' (Selincourt 1940, v. 4: 281, line 76).

> Full soon thy Soul shall have her earthly freight,
> And custom lie upon thee with a weight,
> Heavy as frost, and deep almost as life!
> (Selincourt 1940, v. 4: 282, lines 127–129)

Life as the Romantics conceive it does not connote automatic internal processes like circulation or digestion. In people, at least, it is the capacity to recover the magic of everyday life, to feel and think in ways not preordained by social convention, to become intensely aware of all that surrounds us, rather than converting it into a static backdrop for human dramas. 'Life' – for humans, anyway – is the power to break through the crust of convention and experience the world as though for the first time.

We hear similar refrains from environmental writers today. Wendell Berry (1986: 90) attacks efforts to impose 'scientific exactitude' on 'living' complexities or to use living things as though they were machines. Aldo Leopold (1949:

173) describes the supreme virtue of a naturalist as 'perception', or sensitivity to events and presences in the natural environment that most people ordinarily overlook, whether because the former are too subtle or simply deemed beneath our notice.

NATURAL LANDSCAPES AND HUMAN SENSIBILITY

In the 'Prelude' Wordsworth observes that urban life presents a kaleidoscope of sensations likely to excite curiosity, shock, revulsion and confusion. There is always something new to see; yet beneath the 'blank confusion' the mind can find nothing to sustain it: only 'the same perpetual whirl of trivial objects, melted and reduced to one identity, by differences that have no Law, no meaning, and no end' (Stillinger 1965: 288). One is struck by the sheer weight of difference, the multiplication of forms, costumes, modes of entertainment. But since those differences do not resonate with the deeper chords of human character, they leave the observer jaded. Wordsworth saw London as a terrestrial cave (à la Plato) in which 'shapes and forms and tendencies ... shift and vanish, change and interchange like spectres' (Stillinger 1965: 301). The physical setting of people's lives shapes their individual psychological development. Urban life, in particular, stimulates a hunger for excitement: 'gross and violent stimulants' (Selincourt, 1940, v.2: 389); yet the overload of sensory stimuli leaves little opportunity for a 'second look' at what we experience (Simpson 1987: 2). In sum, metropolitan living may impoverish our capacity for experience, numbing us to more subtle and slowly-developing forms.

The rural life and landscapes of Wales and the English Lake District assumed an almost mythic restorative and formative power in Wordsworth's career. They represent the antithesis of London, not least because their inhabitants are much freer and more self-reliant:

> Man free, man working for himself, his choice
> Of time, and place, and object... (Stillinger 1965: 291)

Second, the sparse population and quiet, settled life offer less direct stimulation to the senses, encouraging people to notice and reflect on the land itself. Natural landscape becomes a presence in their lives, apt to leave an imprint on their sensibility and character. Unlike the variegated, intense whirl of cities, the Lake District impressed on the mind just a few permanent objects, but ones that changed subtly with the weather, the seasons and the characteristic activities pursued at different times of year. Instead of meaningless differences, random variety and blank confusion, the setting of life in rural England conveyed a sense of order and permanence, of change within stable and predictable limits. In this sense Renaissance Platonism lived on in Wordsworth's poetry, with the Forms now drawn down from the transcendent realm and objectified in rocks, mountains, lakes and forests. Wordsworth's own verse expresses that idea gracefully and powerfully:

> Ye Presences of Nature in the sky
> And on earth! Ye Visions of the hills!
> And souls of lonely places! Can I think
> A vulgar hope was yours when ye employed
> Such ministry, when ye through many a year
> Haunting me thus among my boyish sports,
> On caves and trees, upon woods and hills,
> Impressed upon all forms the characters
> Of danger or desire; and thus did make
> The surface of the universal earth
> With triumph and delight, with hope and fear,
> Work like a sea? (Stillinger 1965: 203)

Wordsworth realised that his poetry embodied a novel conception of the way that nature affects human sensibility, and he defended it explicitly in his preface to *Lyrical Ballads*. In places like the Lake Country, 'the essential passions of the heart find a better soil in which they can attain their maturity ... [because they] are incorporated with the beautiful and permanent forms of nature' (Selincourt 1940, v. 2: 386–387). Thus, rural enclaves acted almost like cultural amber, preserving modes of speech, thought and feeling, that were fading elsewhere under the onslaught of modernisation. There, a poet could discover the 'image of man and nature' as it once had been when the forms of nature spoke more directly to people and affected their mental and emotional life more profoundly. Writing of the Alpine Swiss, Wordsworth noted that 'here the traces of primaeval Man appear ... Nature's child' (Birdsall 1984: 82).

The intuition that the land itself may mould our perceptions and sensibility unites many modern environmentalists with the Romantics. Edward Abbey echoes the poet in his description of the impression that Utah's Delicate Arch makes on the observer. For him, the natural world both presupposes and encourages a different view of oneself, an insight into a more elemental human reality easily lost sight of amid one's daily business. His comments also echo Novalis' definition of Romanticism as the recovery of the magic of everyday life.

> A weird, lovely, fantastic object like Delicate Arch has the curious ability to remind us – like rock and sunlight and wind and wilderness – that *out there* is a different world, older and greater and deeper by far than ours ... For a little while we are again able to see, as the child sees, a world of marvels ... For if this ring of stone is marvelous then all which shaped it is marvelous, and our journey here on earth, able to see and touch and hear in the midst of tangible and mysterious things in themselves, is the most strange and daring of all adventures. (Abbey 1968: 41–42)

It is from the conviction that external landscapes shape the inner person that the modern enthusiasm for wilderness derives (Nash 1982: 47). The English Romantics were inveterate hikers and explorers of the remote mountains and forests. Coleridge practically invented mountaineering as a form of recreation (Levere 1981: 18). Wordsworth claimed to have walked some 175,000 miles, and had his spiritual epiphany atop Mount Snowdon, memorialised in the 'Prelude' (Bate 1991: 49).

What set wild nature apart from its civilised counterpart was its remoteness from human use. As Emerson noted, the sky, the mountains, the wild animal 'give us delight *in and for themselves*' (Spiller 1954: 7). They evoke different feelings, thoughts and self-evaluations than a ploughed field or a barnyard, let alone a city. Wild places save people from the maze of mirrors in which a too self-reflexive culture can trap them. That notion of wilderness as a sphere that ought to remain exempt from utilitarian calculus has been taken up, of course, by modern environmentalists like Leopold (Gottlieb 1993: 33), Berry (1986: 29) and Turner (1996). For all of them wilderness helps establish a baseline sense of how the world would be if it were not subjected to the unrelenting pressure of human desires and resource-exploitation. Although the Romantics could not have foreseen that the natural environment would end up as besieged as it is today, they recognised the potential impact on it of what Abbey (1968: 45–67) called 'industrial tourism'. Wordsworth opposed a plan to bring a rail line to the Lake District, because he feared that day-tripping tourists on mass excursions would not really experience the land and its subtleties, while their presence would alter its rural, secluded ambience. The stance of these authors bespeaks more than elitism. They recognise that the natural world cannot be treated as a mere curiosity by gawking visitors without losing its power to stir and transform. So they recommend that tourists eschew mechanical conveyances in favour of walking. Wordsworth wrote a guidebook to the Lake District for that very purpose (Simpson 1987: 69–71). We must therefore take exception to the way that Pepper (1986: 79, 84) and others dismiss Romantic enthusiasm for wild, rural settings as a 'myth' and Arcadian/pastoral dream of a life and society that never existed. It is an indispensable tenet of both Romanticism and contemporary environmentalism that there really is something in rural and wilderness landscapes that might transform us, as long as they have not become mere tourist attractions or venues for 'extreme' sports.

What epitomised the Romantic sensibility was an overflowing sense that the religious promises of yore – an afterlife in which this 'vale of tears' would be left behind – do the earth an injustice. If we just look at the land around us, we will recognise that it is and always has been a paradise. Wordsworth intimated as much in the 'Prelude,' when he wrote of

> ... the very world, which is the world
> Of all of us, – the place where, in the end,
> We find our happiness or not at all. (Stillinger 1965: 333)

As one critic observed: 'In Wordsworth, man's ancient dream of felicity is brought down from a transcendent heaven and located in this very world' (Abrams 1973: 289). Thoreau's sojourn at Walden Pond taught him a similar lesson: anyone can become the 'new Adam' who inhabits a pristine garden, an Eden (Abrams 1973: 412). Abbey (1968: 190) echoes their discovery: 'But the love of wilderness is more than a hunger for what is always beyond reach; it is also an expression of loyalty to the earth, the earth which bore us and sustains us, the only home we shall ever know, the only paradise we ever need – if only we had the eyes to see.'

But that, of course, is precisely the rub. Too few of us have eyes to see. Romanticism's mission was to teach people to cultivate their power of seeing, whether through poetry, novels, painting, music or (eventually) ecological science. The emphasis on life as against dead mechanical processes in nature has its exact counterpart in the summons to awaken the life within, the power of vision, perception and receptivity that circumstances – especially those connected to modern urban life – conspire to stifle. As Charles Taylor (1989: 372) comments, Romanticism was a quest to disclose a new 'way of experiencing our lives ... and the larger natural order in which they are set.' Objective descriptions of landscape, organisms and natural interrelationships had the double task of revealing what nature was and creating or reviving the capacity to respond to it. This insight helps illuminate the paradox that Romanticism aspired simultaneously to represent artistically the inner truth of nature, and to express the self (Taylor 1989: 374). As Elaine Miller remarks, Goethe – as well as other Romantics – postulated a 'fundamental sympathy between the order of nature and the order of self-consciousness...' (Miller 2005: 303)

ROMANTIC RECONSTRUCTIONS OF TIME

The psychological theories propounded in the seventeenth and eighteenth centuries were appallingly unsuited to make sense of Romantic intuitions about nature and the self. In particular, these theories offered an impoverished depiction of time. They fashioned from the Galilean/Newtonian worldview an image of the individual as pushed and pulled by expectations of future pleasures and pains, or recollections of past ones. The future looms as an inscrutable, disquieting source of possible pleasures and pains, while the past is at best an unreliable guide to successful behaviour.

The most striking examples of anti-Romantic conceptions of time may be extracted from the writings of Hobbes and Bentham. Hobbes compares human beings, perpetually fearful about the future (especially the afterlife), to the suffering Prometheus, their 'heart all the day long gnawed on by fear of death, poverty or other calamity' (Hobbes 1958: 93–94). Hobbes does not regard happiness as a state of mind, character or emotion, but as a fleeting feeling of pleasure that accompanies the satisfaction of a desire (Hobbes 1958: 61). Having attained an object of desire, the trick is to acquire the power to hang onto it. So life degenerates into a 'perpetual and restless desire for power after power that ceases only in death' (Hobbes 1958: 86). Anxiety inevitably pervades the deepest layers of temporal experience and can never be extinguished even by the most cunning gambits of instrumental reason.

Bentham likewise places people under 'two sovereign masters, pain and pleasure,' that motivate all their action (Mack 1969: 85). And, like Hobbes, he worries about the tendency for fear to overwhelm society: not so much fear of the afterlife, in his case, but of crime. A theft in the neighbourhood stirs up painful feelings not only in the victim of the crime but in everybody else, the 'pain of apprehension' or 'alarm' caused by the fear that they might be next (Mack 1969: 118). As 'danger and alarm' spread throughout society, 'the pain is for a thousand, for ten thousand, for all'. Unless repressed, one theft could lead to 'universal and durable discouragement, a cessation of labour, and at last the dissolution of society' (Mack 1969: 119). As in Hobbes, anxiety about the future dominates the psyche, especially since the social bonds appeared so fragile to Bentham.

In both philosophers, the past has significance chiefly as the environment in which learning by association works and habits have therefore been acquired. Time resembles Newtonian space: an indifferent medium through which beings move along trajectories established in the past that are continually being modified by new forces active in the present or expected in the future. The chief task of wise legislators is prediction and control of the future. The tone, the language, the imagery here are so thoroughly instrumental, so wedded to a mechanistic or 'economic' paradigm of human behaviour, that they cannot disclose the complex interweaving of the tenses in actual human, lived time.

Indeed, because the entire temporal process is conceived so reductionistically, it is difficult to find language capable of evoking constitutive, meaningful ties to either past experiences or future possibilities. To the extent that people actually began to resemble the calculators of pain and pleasure that thinkers like Hobbes and Bentham supposed them to be, they would begin to lose those constitutive ties. Tocqueville, who often thought of America as the place where liberal psychology had 'come true', described its long-term consequences better than anyone else: 'In democratic peoples ... the fabric of time is torn at every moment and the trace of generations is effaced. You easily forget those who have preceded you, and you have no ideas of those who will follow you ... democracy... separates [man] from his contemporaries; it constantly leads him back toward himself alone and threatens finally to confine him wholly in the solitude of his own heart' (Tocqueville 2000: 481–482).

Romantic authors sought to craft a novel language for capturing our experiences in and of time. That experience features a much more complex relationship to the past than the one articulated in the commonplaces of Enlightenment-era and 'economic' psychology. For Goethe, 'the so-called Romantic aspect of a region is a quiet feeling of sublimity *under the form of the past* or, what is the same, a feeling of loneliness, absence, isolation' (Richards 2002: 21). By this he meant that we may experience a place as still suffused, or even haunted, by what it used to be or by experiences we once had of it. That form of experience also pervades environmental thought, which is sensitive to the integrity, beauty and stability of ecosystems and the disturbances that human activity may have imported into them. As Kroeber (1994: 55) notices, an ecosystem is temporal as well as spatial – an ongoing process made up of subordinate temporal processes. Immediate sensation is permeated by language that is both 'recollective and premonitory … '

It is Wordsworth, above all, who invented a new temporal structure meant to express the individual and collective experience of time as actually lived, not as abstracted by the pain–pleasure calculus. In that structure time draws us inexorably away from our immediate integration into the natural environment, yet also returns us to it at a higher, more reflective level, in which we can relive and reinterpret earlier events. So there is development and change in an individual life and sensibility, yet within that linear trajectory nests another, circular movement. In *Tintern Abbey* the mature Wordsworth, gazing down on the Wye Valley, thinks back to the hours he spent in the same spot during his youth, as well as the occasions when he recalled those times with relief and pleasure during his stay in the 'lonely rooms' of 'cities and towns'. Then, looking to the future, he adds:

> … here I stand not only with the sense
> Of present pleasure, but with pleasing thoughts
> That in this moment there is life and food
> For future years. (Selincourt 1940, v. 2: 261, lines 62–65)

Romantic time does not flow by at a constant rate; it eddies and swirls, densely present in certain defining experiences and moments that hold the tenses together. Each visit to the Wye Valley includes, recapitulates and anticipates the others; the later visits reconnect Wordsworth the man to the spontaneous, unself-conscious boy he once was. In such mediated experiences we encounter Wordsworth's renowned 'spots of time':

> There are in our existence spots of time,
> That with distinct pre-eminence retain
> A renovating virtue, whence, depressed
> By false opinion and contentious thought
> Or aught of heavier and more deadly weight,
> In trivial occupations, and the round
> Of ordinary intercourse, our minds
> Are nourished and invisibly repaired. (Stillinger 1965: 345)

Wordsworth's spots of time foreshadow modern environmental thought in several ways. First, people sometimes bond to a specific place that has been experienced repeatedly in the many seasons and phases of life. All of us who have lived in and with the natural world have our own equivalent of the Wye Valley and Lake District. We sense that our experiences anchor us against the fraying and snapping of temporal bonds depicted by Tocqueville. Long and thoughtful acquaintance with a place breeds both understanding of its subtleties and a sense of personal, psychological continuity that reflects the continuity of the place itself (Kemmis 1990). As Berry (1986: 45) remarks, a culture closely tied to the land will sustain 'ties across generations, sublimation of self-interest by bonds of loyalty, memory, and tradition'. But that requires – and helps foster – a more expansive sense of time, one stretching across generations with strong communal memories. Moreover, durable bonds across generations assuage the anxiety and alarm that Bentham and Hobbes associate with the human condition. Since our individual fates are so entwined with the destiny of our beloved places and their continuity through time, the only thing that can really turn one into a latter-day Prometheus is the fear that they will be destroyed by callous developers.

Second, to see time as circling back on oneself discourages the obsession with progress and technological mastery associated with the Cartesian/Baconian tradition. Meaning is sought not in what might be, but what already is or what may be slipping away. Indeed, as one critic notes, Romantic writing emphasises the way that an instant of consciousness, even an ordinary event, 'suddenly blazes up into revelation ... the intersection of time and eternity' (Abrams 1973: 385). The psychological theories of Hobbes and Bentham could make no sense of such an experience; in order to do so, a different and more subtle language had to be invented.

Third, Wordsworth's spots of time suggest a programme for ecological investigation. Thoreau, among the Romantics and Transcendentalists, inaugurated that method. As a historical ecologist and inveterate wanderer, he came to think of the environment around Concord as a book missing many pages, a 'maimed and imperfect nature' (Worster 1994: 66) Only if we understand what that environment once was, might it be possible for us to try to restore it. More broadly, Thoreau aimed at a 'retrieval' of small, homely, rustic things that tie the present to the ancient past (Buell 1995: 401). Only those who revisit a place and come to know it intimately will perceive the changes wrought by human intervention over many years. Perhaps more importantly, attention to the passages and transitions in the natural world alerts observers to their own affinity to deep time, far older than merely human history. Leopold's (1949: 97) famous elegy to the crane illustrates that point:

> Our appreciation of the crane grows with the slow unraveling of earthly history. His tribe, we now know, stems out of the remote Eocene. The other members of the fauna in which he originated are long since entombed within the hills. When

> we hear his call we hear no mere bird. We hear the trumpet in the orchestra of evolution. He is the symbol of our untamable past, of that incredible sweep of millennia, which underlies and conditions the daily affairs of birds and men.

Leopold's encounter with the crane qualifies as a Wordsworthian 'spot of time' in which the present moment fuses with others past and future, though now the past is far more ancient even than human memory can encompass. The crane lifts us out of the anxiety-ridden time experience of Hobbes and Bentham, and bestows a certain repose nourished by the reflection that our little lives intersect patterns far older and deeper than human civilisation. As Leopold (1949: 112) observes, 'to love what *was* is a new thing under the sun ... To see America as history, to see destiny as a becoming, to smell a hickory tree through the still lapse of ages.'

Finally, the Romantics inherited the fascination of many Renaissance figures with historically unique cultural artefacts and natural kinds, rather than laws or law-like generalisations. Here it was Herder who made the greatest advances, substituting organic for mechanical metaphors in attempting to account for cultural efflorescence. Just as plants thrive in certain soils and not in others, so every *Volk* has a unique stock of historical memories and stories out of which it fashions its own idiosyncratic cultural artefacts (Abrams 1971: 204–205). To impose a uniform artistic regimen or universal standards of value, taste, behaviour or knowledge on all peoples would undermine the very conditions that fostered artistic creation. It is not a long step from Herder's theory concerning a *Volksgeist's* artefacts to the recognition that the earth itself teems with unique and unrepeatable creations of nature, each as valuable in its own way as the legends, poems and songs of a nation. The common thread is a new way of looking at time. Instead of seeing time as an inessential husk to be peeled away to lay bare the constant, mathematical relationships and laws beneath it, Romantics began to interpret it as a creative protagonist, tossing off cultural and natural products that, once gone, will never return, and therefore should be protected against wear and destruction. Nor is it a long step from Herder to Berry's emphasis on the fragility of culture and the imperative of nurturing its continuity and keeping its collective memories alive. The only conceptual move that needs to be made is to shift the level of argument from the entire nation (a rather artificial unit anyway) to the local community. But in any case, the Romantic obsession with concrete, historical particulars easily segues into the hermeneutical position of Gadamer: 'historical research does not endeavour to grasp the concrete phenomenon as an instance of a universal rule...Its ideal is rather to understand the phenomenon itself in its unique and historical concreteness...to understand that something is so because it understands that it has come about so' (Gadamer 1993: 5) That position, in turn, perfectly captures the aims of ecologists like Leopold or Thoreau investigating the unique ecosystems of their localities.

ROMANTICISM AND THE SENSE OF PLACE

The reconstruction of time described above slides easily into a more intimate, nuanced sense of place. In the categories of economics and Enlightenment-era psychology, what matters is obtaining pleasure (or money, pleasure's placeholder in economics) and avoiding pain. But Romantic writers tried to articulate a different feeling for the physical and emotional setting of a life. We saw earlier that they understood certain landscapes – mountains, crags, lakes – as beneficent influences on human character. We may now add that their project fit into a more ambitious quest to rediscover the earth, including its harshest terrain, as humanity's proper home (Abrams 1973: 12). Formerly, that would have seemed a strange and vaguely blasphemous enterprise, since mountains, seas and deserts were regarded as evidence of the destruction of Paradise. In contrast, Romantic authors value places more highly when they have not been intensively used and abused.

It is perhaps Goethe who gives the most succinct and poignant expression to the ethic of place through his rendition of the Philemon and Baucis legend, adapted from Ovid, in *Faust II*. By this point in the story, Faust has become a land reclamation specialist and developer in the best capitalist spirit. His factotum, Mephistopheles, has dyked and channelled the ocean, reclaiming land for housing and farms. However, Philemon and Baucis have lived amid the beach dunes from time immemorial, ringing the bell of their little chapel and aiding travellers. By the time the scene unfolds, Faust's reclaimed tract has completely encircled their hut and plot of land, which he now seeks to purchase. But the kindly old couple refuses his offer. This drives Faust to distraction, as his words attest when he hears the ringing of their chapel bell:

> That cursed bell. It hurts me cruelly like a stab in the dark. Before my eyes my dominion is complete, but from behind vexation teases me, reminding me with taunting noise that my vast estate is not unblemished. I don't possess the linden trees, nor the brown cottage, nor the crumbling chapel … It's a thorn in the flesh, an offence to the sight. (Goethe 1970: 190)

He orders Mephistopheles to evict the couple, explaining: 'I want those lindens for my recreation. This handful of trees that are not my trees, wrecks everything … [T]he freedom of my mighty will is brought to nothing here in the sand' (Goethe 1970: 191). Mephistopheles sends his enforcers to do the job, but they end up killing Philemon and Baucis and burning down their cottage.

Although both Faust and the old couple want the same place, their attachments are entirely different. The personal histories of Philemon and Baucis are intertwined with this plot of land on which they had always lived so lightly and gently. They hold out against Faust's pressure because the land is so much a part of them that they cannot envision living anywhere else. Faust, however, only wants their cottage because it is not his; its mere existence reminds him that he does not exercise total control, that his will is limited. Of course, he has benevolent intentions and boasts about the human benefits of his land reclamation scheme, but at bottom it appeals to him primarily as confirmation of his power. 'Place' for him lacks personal associations; it is merely an objectification of will: something to own, not to inhabit. Goethe here anticipates a whole genre of environmental writing, in which the sense of place is central (e.g., Krutch 1971; Dillard 1975; Callenbach 1975; Meyer 2001, ch.6)).

Thoreau adds another dimension to the Romantics' sense of place by linking it more explicitly to exploration of the local environment. Unlike Wordsworth, who praised the noble simplicity of the dwellers in his home region, Thoreau criticised his neighbours for their obsession with unremitting toil, a self-imposed 'servitude' and the 'quiet desperation' it inflicted on them (Thoreau 1962: 5–6), which blinded them to the marvels in the forest around Concord. By contrast, Thoreau had time for daily walks, quiet reflection, close study of local ecology, and an appreciation for the myriad ways in which human life intertwined with nature. He realised that maintaining a lively sense of place required not only 'habitual familiarity with its phenomena', but also 'keeping alive a sense of strangeness', not becoming so absorbed in the trivia of everyday life that the natural environment would become mere wallpaper, losing its power to evoke surprise, curiosity and reverence (Thoreau 1962: 261, 264).

The Romantics' evocations of place were part of a much broader project: to discover an alternative language and imagery to the commonplaces of philosophers and psychologists from Bacon to Bentham. Just as their reconstruction of time had been intended to challenge the empty, undifferentiated medium pictured by the new physics, so too the space of the Romantics was defined by human and natural ties. The space of physics was an abstraction from space as experienced by real people in their life-worlds.

SUCCESSES AND FAILURES OF THE ROMANTICS

Despite its affinities with modern-day environmentalism, the Romantic worldview strikes us today as quaint, mainly because of its association with discredited scientific ideas. Too many Romantics fought a pointless battle against Galilean and Newtonian physics. Although their more holistic vision inspired – and still superficially resembles – ecological thinking, no scientist today takes seriously Schelling's *Naturphilosophie*. Romantic ideas may indeed have influenced the *origins* of ecology, but they are irrelevant to its *validity*, which is established by the scientific method.

The Romantics' commitment to obsolete scientific ideas tells a cautionary tale for contemporary environmentalism. Not long ago, many environmentalists thought they could deduce the features of an ecologically-correct society directly from the characteristics of a stable ecological order, especially in the climax phase (Sale 1991; Ophuls 1997; Commoner 1971; Goldsmith et al., 1972). That aspiration has been criticised not only for its logical difficulties, but also because ecology has abandoned or strongly modified its claims about stable ecosystems (Stevens 1990; Golly 1998; Botkin 1990). Others believe that an environmental ethic can be elicited from some version of Darwinian evolutionary theory (Wilson 1984; Callicott 1987). But Darwinism is equivocal; it can be made to support Herbert Spencer as easily as Aldo Leopold. At bottom, no natural scientific theory or set of facts, in and of itself, can form the foundation of such a complex moral, ethical and political doctrine as modern environmentalism, any more than Schellingian physics could sustain the edifice of Romanticism. Science lends an aura of objectivity to doctrines that are essentially non-scientific, and that might seem to be a good enough reason to invoke them. But one pays a heavy price when scientific foundations shift, or appear to justify drastically different conclusions than one would wish. Environmentalism should avoid the trap Romanticism fell into by not making its validity depend on any particular set of scientific theories or findings. For, if the scientific consensus changes, one is left with the unpalatable alternative of either abandoning one's ethical commitments or clinging to the discredited version of science that supported them. The latter is what helped Romanticism earn the reputation of being anti-scientific and anti-modern.

But in other ways, Romanticism succeeded. Its adherents developed an alternative language and psychology capable of explaining why a life entwined with natural landscapes and temporal rhythms offers deeper satisfactions than one addicted to intense sensory stimuli. Above all, they had an intuitive feel for the integrity of the life-world. Wordsworth and his contemporaries preferred rustic settings not so much because they were anti-modern, but because they sensed that the life-world was more intact there, permitting them more easily to identify the 'primary laws of our nature' (Selincourt 1940, v. 2: 386).

The life-world thrives where the fabric of human time and memories remain intact, where place has not yielded to abstract space, and where the mind and imagination still resonate with the forms of nature, not having been overwhelmed by 'gross and violent stimulants'. It is no coincidence that such a setting is one in which natural landscapes and processes *also* remain unscathed. Under those circumstances, sky and sun, rain and rock, mountain and valley insinuate themselves into a person's character, speech and thought almost as though they formed part of the life-world itself. One can poke fun at a Thoreau or Muir for 'anthropomorphising' trees and animals, but insofar as such natural entities enter into the life-world, they become tinged with a human significance that transcends their mere physical properties. That is why people often fight to save a threatened lake, meadow or mountain from development. It may resemble a hundred others to a developer, but to the person who has lived with it for many years, it acquires the semblance of individuality, and does not seem abstract and interchangeable like a machine part. The recovery of the magic of everyday life touches both the natural environment and the mind of its perceiver.

In short, the Romantics were right to think that a life in harmony with nature was inseparable from the effort to preserve the human world from being overwhelmed by industrialisation and technology as well as its intellectual cutting-edge, mechanistic, behaviourist and 'economic' philosophy. Those who decry 'humanism' as the root cause of environmental destruction simply do not know what they are saying: humanism is nothing but the commitment to preserve what is genuinely human (what the Romantics thought of as 'life') from reification, trivialisation and routinisation. And that is largely the same fight as the one against environmental despoliation. Part of that struggle involves a choice of language and metaphor, a decision about how to define what one wishes to preserve and endorse. Here again Romanticism provides a salutary lesson. Many environmentalists have fallen under the spell of ecological economics, which shows in extremely clever ways why mainstream economic theory blocks off the kinds of questions environmentalists want to ask (Daly 1996). It is attractive to think that the world will pay attention if we can measure ecosystem services and the like in scientifically acceptable ways, thereby 'proving' that environmental destruction is irrational. We can and should do this in the proper forums and settings (e.g., legislative committee hearings). But it would be a mistake to conclude that ecological economics – or any kind of economics – can provide a philosophical foundation for environmentalism. Its language is still that of Bentham and the mechanistic psychologists who preceded him. And that language is entirely unsuited to explain why anyone should care a bit about the natural world, except insofar as it serves that person's narrowly defined self-interest. The language of economics is a Trojan Horse that leaves no way to talk about the experiences of Wordsworth and Coleridge, Abbey and Muir without rendering them unrecognisable – *unless* one treats that language as provisional, an abstraction from the life-world in which the real significance of nature can be articulated and understood. In this sense the Romantics, despite their untenable scientific ideas, saw more deeply than we do.

BIBLIOGRAPHY

Abbey, Edward. 1968. *Desert Solitaire*. New York: Ballantine.

Abram, David. 1996. *The Spell of the Sensuous*. New York: Pantheon Books.

Abrams, M.H. 1971. *The Mirror and the Lamp*. New York: Oxford University Press.

Abrams, M.H. 1973. *Natural Supernaturalism*. New York: Norton.

Barzun, Jacques. 1961. *Classic, Romantic, and Modern*. New York: Doubleday.

Bate, Jonathan. 1991. *Romantic Ecology*. New York: Routledge.

Beiser, Frederick. 2003. *The Romantic Imperative*. Cambridge: Harvard University Press.

Berman, Marshall. 1981. *The Reenchantment of the World.* Ithaca, NY: Cornell University Press.

Berry, Wendell. 1986. *The Unsettling of America.* San Francisco: Sierra Club.

Birdsall, Eric, ed. 1984. *Descriptive Sketches.* Ithaca, N.Y.: Cornell University Press.

Borgmann, Albert. 1984. *Technology and the Character of Contemporary Life.* Chicago: University of Chicago Press.

Botkin, Daniel. 1990. *Discordant Harmonies.* New York: Oxford University Press.

Buell, Lawrence. 1995. *The Environmental Imagination.* Cambridge: Belknap Press.

Callenbach, Ernest. 1975. *Ecotopia.* Berkeley: Banyan Tree.

Callicott, J. Baird. 1987. *Companion to A Sand County Almanac.* Madison: University of Wisconsin Press.

Coates, Peter. 1998. *Nature.* Berkeley: University of California Press.

Commoner, Barry. 1971. *The Closing Circle.* New York: Knopf.

Daly, Herman. 1996. *Beyond Growth.* Boston: Beacon Press.

Devall, Bill, and Sessions, George, eds. 1985. *Deep Ecology.* New York: Peregrine Smith.

Dillard, Annie. 1975. *Pilgrim at Tinker Creek.* Toronto: Bantam.

Ehrenfeld, David. 1978. *The Arrogance of Humanism.* New York: Oxford University Press.

Gadamer, Hans-Georg. 1993. *Truth and Method.* New York: Continuum.

Glacken, Clarence. 1976. *Traces on the Rhodian Shore.* Berkeley: University of California Press.

Goethe, Johann Wolfgang, n.d. *Schriften zur Literatur, Kunst und Natur.* Munich: Wilhelm Goldmann.

Goethe, Johann Wolfgang. 1970. *Faust,* translated by Barker Fairley. Toronto: University of Toronto Press.

Goldsmith, Edward, et al.. 1972. *Blueprint for Survival.* New York: New American Library.

Golly, Fred. 1998. *A Primer for Ecological Literacy.* New Haven: Yale University Press.

Gottlieb, Robert. 1993. *Forcing the Spring.* Washington, D.C.: Island Press.

Hargrove, Eugene 1986. *Foundations of Environmental Ethics.* Denton, TX: Environmental Ethics Books.

Hobbes, Thomas. 1958. *Leviathan.* Indianapolis: Bobbs-Merrill.

Hermand, Jost. 1991. *Grune Utopien in Deutschland.* Franfurt am Main: Fisher.

Hinchman, Lewis P. 1995. 'Aldo Leopold's hermeneutic of nature'. *Review of Politics* **57**(2): 225–249.

Hinchman, Lewis and Sandra. 2004. 'Is environmentalism a humanism?' *Environmental Values* **13**: 3–29.

Hinchman, Lewis and Sandra. 2005. 'Scenic byways: from Renaissance humanism to modern nature preservation'. *International Humanities Journal,* http: //ijh.cgpublisher.com/product/pub.261/prod.420

Kant, Immanuel. 1930. *Kritik der Urteilskraft.* Leipzig: Philipp Reclam.

Kemmis, Donald. 1990. *Community and the Politics of Place*. Norman: University of Oklahoma Press.

Kluckhorn, Paul. 1966. *Das Ideengut der deutschen Romantik*. Tübingen: Max Niemeyer.

Kohák, Erazim. 1978. *Idea and Experience: Edmund Husserl's Project of Phenomenology and Ideas I*. Chigago: University of Chicago Press.

Kohák, Erazim. 1984. *The Embers and the Stars*. Chicago: University of Chicago Press.

Kroeber, Karl. 1994. *Ecological Literary Criticism*. New York: Columbia University Press.

Krutch, Joseph Wood. 1971. *The Best Nature Writings of Joseph Wood Krutch*. New York: Pocket.

Larmore, Charles. 1996. *The Romantic Legacy*. New York: Columbia University Press.

Leiss, William. 1972. *The Domination of Nature*. New York: George Braziller.

Leopold, Aldo. 1949. *A Sand County Almanac*. New York: Oxford University Press.

Levere, Trevor. 1981. *Poetry Realized in Nature*. New York: Cambridge University Press.

Mack, Mary Peter, ed. 1969. *A Bentham Reader*. New York: Pegasus.

Marx, Leo. 1964. *The Machine in the Garden*. New York: Oxford University Press.

McKibben, Bill. 2004. *Enough*. New York: Henry Holt.

Merchant, Carolyn. 1980. *The Death of Nature*. San Francisco: Harper & Row.

Meyer, John M. 2001. *Political Nature*. Cambridge, MA: MIT Press.

Miller, Elaine. 2005 '"The world must be romanticised...': The (environmental) ethical implications of Schelling's organic worldview'. *Environmental Values* **14**: 295–316.

Nash, Roderick. 1982. *Wilderness and the American Mind*. New Haven, CT: Yale University Press.

Oelschlaeger, Max. 1991. *The Idea of Wilderness*. New Haven: Yale University Press.

Ophuls, William. 1997. *Requiem for Modern Politics*. Boulder: Westview.

Pepper, David. 1986. *The Roots of Modern Environmentalism*. New York: Routledge.

Phillips, Adam, ed. 1998. Edmund Burke's *Enquiry into the Origin of our Ideas of the Sublime and the Beautiful*. Oxford: Oxford University Press.

Richards, Robert. 2002. *The Romantic Conception of Life*. Chicago: University of Chicago Press.

Robertson, J.G. 1962. *Studies in the Genesis of Romantic Theory in the 18th Century*. New York: Russell and Russell.

Roszak, Theodore. 1972. *Where the Wasteland Ends*. Garden City, N.Y.: Doubleday.

Sale, Kirkpatrick. 1991. *Dwellers in the Land*. Philadelphia: New Society.

Schroter, Manfred, ed. 1927. *Schellings Werke, Vol. II*. Munich: Beck & Oldenbourg.

Selincourt, E. de, ed. 1940. *The Poetical Works of William Wordsworth*, five volumes. Oxford, at the Clarendon Press.

Simpson, David. 1987. *Wordsworth's Historical Imagination*. New York: Methuen.

Spiller, Robert, ed. 1954. *Five Essays on Man and Nature: Emerson*. Arlington Heights, Ill.: Crofts.

Stauffer, Donald, ed. 1951. *Selected Poetry and Prose of Coleridge*. New York: Random House.

Stevens, William. 1990. 'New eye on nature'. *The New York Times,* Science section, 31 July.

Stillinger, Jack, ed. 1965. *Selected Poems and Prefaces by William Wordsworth*. Boston: Houghton Mifflin.

Taylor, Charles. 1989. *Sources of the Self*. Cambridge: Harvard University Press.

Thoreau, Henry David. 1962. *Walden*. New York: Time.

Tocqueville, Alexis de. 2000. *Democracy in America,* ed. Harvey Mansfield. Chicago: University of Chicago Press.

Turner, Jack. 1996. *The Abstract Wild*. Tucson: University of Arizona Press.

Williams, Raymond. 1973. *The Country and the City*. New York: Oxford University Press.

Wilson, E.O. 1984. *Biophilia*. Cambridge: Harvard University Press.

Worster, Donald. 1994. *Nature's Economy*. Cambridge: Cambridge University Press.

Artists with Axes*

Tim Bonyhady

> After fixing our points of view and holding a council of war in reference to the execution of some trees which obstructed the view in one or two directions, and which we decided should be lowered on the morrow, we returned to the camp, and the evening was devoted to a grand clothes drying match.
>
> (J.H. Harvey, *Australian Photographic Journal*, 1895)

The engraving shows 'Our Artist'. Charles Walter was a German from Mecklenberg who settled in Victoria in the 1850s. When not collecting new specimens for Ferdinand Mueller, Victoria's Government Botanist, Walter worked as a 'Country Photographic Artist'. Much of his market seems to have been local landholders to whom he offered 'Views of Residence Seats and Scenery ... in any parts of the colony, at Moderate Terms'. But Walter also contributed to the monthly *Illustrated Australian News* which made something of an identity of him – hence the engraving which the *News* published in 1873 as one of nine illustrations to an article by Walter about a trip to Cape Otway, south-west of Melbourne.[1]

The engraving shows Walter with a box on his back, a tent over his shoulder, a tomahawk in hand. The box and tent are easily explained as essential tools of Walter's trade. The box contained his photographic equipment – his camera, glass plates, processing trays and chemicals which he needed because wet-plates had to be processed immediately as the emulsion on them was sensitive to light only when wet. The tent was Walter's portable darkroom. But what of the tomahawk?

The only contemporary accounts of Walter's work as a photographer suggest that he used his tomahawk simply to clear his path as he made his way to places rarely, if ever, visited by his fellow colonists. On a trip to Mount Buller in 1868, he 'penetrated to places inaccessible to vehicle or horse, and only penetrable to human foot, after considerable clearances had been effected in the thickets by means of a tomahawk'. When he went to Cape Otway in 1873, he made his way 'through a dense undergrowth of scrub from six to eight feet high' with 'tomahawk in hand'. Even some of the tracks were so overgrown that 'saplings had to be cleared out of the way'.[2]

Walter's tomahawk also symbolised the larger difficulties he encountered on expeditions which the *Illustrated Australian News* liked to present as a public

*This article is a revised version of the Canberra School of Art's Annual Lecture for 1994

OUR ARTIST.

FIGURE 1
'Our Artist', *Illustrated Australian News* 31 December 1873

service. The *News's* image of Walter – like that developed around other colonial landscape painters and photographers who made similar expeditions – was that of the selfless artist who risked life and limb so that his fellow colonists could discover 'the romantic and the picturesque' which Nature had scattered 'so lavishly' around them. Out for two, even three months at a time, Walter travelled alone, sleeping 'at squatters stations, in shanties, or under a gum tree' and relying on such provisions as he could procure by the way. As the *News* put it, just to see Walter with his 'heavy and cumbersome apparatus' was to wonder 'how he managed to get there'.[3]

The pursuit of the romantic and the picturesque by photographers such as Walter did not, however, always involve a corresponding respect for nature, at least of the type we know today. Even some of the photographers most concerned for the protection of the environment did not carry tomahawks and axes simply to clear their paths. They – or sometimes their patrons or assistants – also used them for view-making in the most literal sense, for felling trees in order to expand the horizon.

One example is the artists' camp in the Grose Valley in the Blue Mountains organised by Eccleston du Faur, who played a key role in securing institutional support for both art and environmental protection in New South Wales in the late nineteenth century. While du Faur's day job was Chief Draughtsman in the Crown Lands Office, he also served as the honorary secretary of the New South Wales Academy of Art from 1872; the *de facto* director of the Art Gallery of New South Wales from 1876 until 1892, and President of its Trustees and the Gallery's chief policy-maker until his death in 1915. Du Faur was also the main advocate of the dedication of Ku-ring-gai Chase as a National Park for northern Sydney, just as Royal National Park served the city's south. When the Chase was gazetted in 1894, less than two years after du Faur first advocated its creation, he became its managing trustee and 'devoted the greater part of his time to it'. While one of his objects was to open the Chase as a recreation ground, du Faur also had 'a higher mission'. Exceptionally for his day he 'aimed above all at the fullest preservation of natural flora and at the establishment of an area over which marsupials and other Australian fauna might roam and breed in safety'.[4]

Du Faur organised his artists' camps in the Grose Valley in 1875 to show that it was at least the equal of the Yosemite Valley in California which had become a State park a decade before, partly through the agency of art. As part of campaigning for protection of Yosemite and the Mariposa Grove of great sequoia trees, a group of Californians led by the landscape architect, Frederic Olmstead, had sent photographs of Yosemite taken by Carleton Watkins to several influential senators. These mammoth plates – up to 18 by 22 inches – persuaded Senator John Conness to introduce the legislation that made Yosemite a park in 1864. The following year Olmstead turned to Watkins and the landscape painters, Virgil Williams and Thomas Hill, for advice on how the beauty of Yosemite could best be preserved.[5]

Yosemite was known to Australian colonists through both photographs and engravings as well as many published accounts. In 1871 the National Gallery of Victoria bought 20 of Watkins's giant plates including seven views of Yosemite. In 1872 one of the Batchelder brothers exhibited a panorama at the Sydney School of Arts which included the 'celebrated' Yosemite Valley where 'every natural object' was 'on the most colossal scale'. In 1873 the *Illustrated Australian News* and the *Illustrated Sydney News* both carried an engraving of Yosemite – possibly based on a photograph by Watkins – which, they declared, contained 'more scenes of grandeur and beauty' than could 'be found within an equal space in any other part of the world'. In the same year, the *Sydney Morning Herald* serialised 'A Holiday Tour Round the World' by John Smith – Professor of Chemistry at Sydney University and a significant amateur photographer – which included two chapters about his stay at Yosemite which he believed was unmatched for compressing 'so much varied grandeur and beauty ... into so small a scale'.[6]

Du Faur wanted to reveal the Grose Valley not just to his fellow colonists but also to the world at large. While both paintings and photographs of the Grose were shown in Sydney and Melbourne, he wanted photographs of the valley to be included in the New South Wales display at the Centennial Exhibition in Philadelphia in 1876. Inspired by the giant plates taken by Watkins, he persuaded the Commissioners responsible for the New South Wales exhibit to employ the Sydney photographer, Joseph Bischoff, to go to the Grose Valley. While Bischoff's 12 by 16 inch plates were almost half the size of Watkins's photographs, they still were twice the size of most Australian colonial photographs. Just to carry Bischoff's plates required five men.[7]

Du Faur also needed to get his artists to spots where they could record the 'stupendous size' of the 2,000 feet high cliffs. While surveyors had cut a track to the bottom of the valley in 1857, it was 'overgrown, encumbered by fallen trees, and obliterated in part by landslips'. Moreover, even if the artists were able to reach the valley floor, the 'density of the scrub and forest timber' meant that there were few spots from which 'the abruptness of the cliffs on either side and the narrowness of the gorge' could 'fairly be appreciated'.[8]

Du Faur's solution was to employ a work gang not only to re-open the old track into the valley but also to clear 'views to be taken by pencil and camera' at sites which he selected. The first artist to arrive was the Tasmanian landscape painter, W.C. Piguenit, who seems to have worked happily on his own without engaging in further clearing. But when most of the rest of the party arrived ten days later, they spent the entire afternoon creating new views at their second camp at the junction of the Grose River and Govett's Leap Creek. Three days later du Faur and five companions renewed their axe-work closer to Govett's Leap Falls.[9]

By the time the Sydney photographer, Ernest Docker, joined du Faur, 'a large number of trees' had been felled at the party's first camp. On his way to the second camp, Docker noticed 'several points cleared and marked for taking'. Du Faur proudly recorded that his party did not just 'clear', but 'properly cleared', views of the two main waterfalls in the gorge.[10]

The results of this axe-work are most obvious in a panorama by Joseph Bischoff taken from the first camp looking from the north-east through to the south towards Mount King Gorge. The foreground is all stumps and felled tree trunks – a strip several metres wide has been cleared across the full breadth of the panorama to obtain the view of the cliffs.[11]

While Docker recognised the benefits of this work in 'opening to view some grand crags with broken and picturesque skyline', he also emphasised its costs in 'unfortunately supplying a very inartistic foreground'.[12] This response was probably unusual. Contemporary descriptions of some of Nicholas Caire's 'Views in Victoria', which are similarly full of stumps, overlook these foregrounds for the 'beautiful and romantic' scenery behind.[13] Du Faur's one disappointment was that, notwithstanding 'a considerable amount of clearing' at the first camp, his party had opened only a partial panorama of the surrounding cliffs. As he regretfully informed a conversazione held by the New South Wales Academy of Art late in 1875, just 'a few days' more work would have opened up the sky ... all round the compass, forming a view of cliffs of 2000 feet high all round, not easily to be surpassed'. Four years later, du Faur was still lamenting that his party – although numbering 16 at its peak – was 'altogether inadequate for making the clearings in timber and scrub, without which many of the finest views could not be favourably reproduced by photography'.[14]

FIGURE 2

This appetite for view construction by axe-work was not unique to Australia. Take the Anglo-American photographer, Edward Muybridge. Although best known for his studies of human and animal locomotion, Muybridge made his name with a series of photographs of Yosemite which he took in 1872. By then, Yosemite and Mariposa Grove had been State Parks for eight years – committed by the Federal government to the State of California 'for their constant preservation, that they may be exposed to public view, and that they may be used and preserved for the benefit of mankind'.[15] But because California was yet to appoint a guardian to take care of Yosemite, Muybridge was able to disregard this injunction with impunity.

Muybridge took up his axe out of competiveness with Carleton Watkins – it was just one of his ways of obtaining new views which would distinguish him from his rival. As the San Francisco newspaper, the *Alta California* put it, Muybridge 'had himself lowered by ropes down precipices to establish his instruments in places where the full beauty of the object to be photographed could be transferred to the negative'; he went 'to points where his packers refused to follow him; and ... carried the apparatus himself rather than ... forego the picture on which he has set his mind'. Not least, he 'cut down trees by the score' that interfered with his cameras.[16]

Such destructiveness was not confined to professional photographers who at least had a commercial justification for their actions. Amateurs such as J.H. Harvey, the honorary secretary of the Victorian Amateur Photographic Association, were just as ready to use axes to open new views. When Harvey and

Joseph Bischoff, *The Grose Valley* 1875

another 'leading and pioneering' amateur visited Kanangara Walls in the Blue Mountains in 1894, the two men began by selecting views which they wanted to take when the weather cleared. As part of the larger sport of their trip, written up by Harvey as a kind of boy's own adventure, they decided on the 'execution' of some obstructive trees. After marking their victims that evening, they felled them the following morning and took their photographs.[17]

This axe-work is all the more noteworthy because Harvey was appalled, three days later, when he discovered that 'vandals' had destroyed Dante's Glen, a fern gully near Grenville which had been 'a real beauty spot' when he had first visited it in the early 1880s. Harvey declared it 'shameful' that the rough barricade of stakes, which had protected the Glen on his first visit, had been removed due to the opposition of tourists who 'wished to be free to roam about any portion of the gully' and had ruined its 'luxuriant vegetation' in the process. One explanation of this apparent inconsistency may be that Harvey valued fern gullies more than eucalypts – a common nineteenth century preference. However, it may also be that he put Art before Nature.[18]

Photographers found another use for their axes when, far from being obstructed, their foregrounds were empty and hence devoid of interest according to the conventions of the picturesque derived from eighteenth- and nineteenth-century landscape painting. For photographers who wanted to mimic this style of painting, the only remedy was to introduce some foreground vegetation to lead the eye into the view. But photographers also had their own reasons to fill their foregrounds, at least when taking stereographs, as the depth of field which made these photographs so popular could be established only if there was an immediate reference point in the foreground from which the middleground and background could be measured.[19]

This type of re-arrangement of nature was cheerfully admitted by John Watt Beattie who not only was Hobart's leading photographer from the 1880s to the 1910s but who also was one of the great advocates of scenery preservation and the dedication of national parks in Tasmania. In a lecture in Hobart in 1897, Beattie explained that he always carried an axe so that he could 'soon remedy any faulty composition'. His favourite targets were grass trees because they were 'so handy for foregrounds' – as one can see in his photographs of Lake Emily in the Hartz Mountains and Lake Marion and Mount Gould which lie to the north-west of Lake St Clair.[20]

The hunt for giant trees also brought out the photographers' axes when surrounding vegetation obstructed their views. Recording and destruction went together in 1888 when the Commissioners responsible for Melbourne's Centennial Exhibition employed the photographer, J. Duncan Peirce, to find Victoria's tallest tree. Peirce's assistants not only cleared his views but then posed proudly with their axes amidst their handiwork in a number of his photographs. Victoria's first Conservator of Forests, G.S. Perrin, was equally destructive when he joined this hunt in the Sassafras Valley in the Dandenong Ranges east of Melbourne in 1889. When Perrin 'saw that the trees were very tall, he set four men to work to clear the scrub and undergrowth away so as to allow both a theodolite and a camera to work on them'.[21]

If instructional essays and photographic manuals published in the late nineteenth century are any guide, such axe-work was far from a quirk of just a few photographers. In an essay on 'Landscape Photography' published in the *Philadelphia Photographer*, James Mullens recommended:

> The foreground being on of the main points in a picture ... if not naturally [attractive, can be made so] by a little labor in the way of rolling up an old log or stump in an effective position ... and let me advise you here to always have with you on your photographic trips a spade and a good axe: the latter particularly will often be found 'a friend in need', when it is desirable to cut a small tree or remove a branch that would otherwise obscure some important point of your view.

The British critic, Alfred Wall similarly advised that it was sometimes 'desirable to fill up a spot' which was 'too startingly conspicuous'. His solution was to plug the gap 'by moving a bush, the trunk of a felled tree, some broken or displaced boughs, some transplanted weeds ... in some naturally suggestive way'.[22]

All this evidence of artist-axemen means that when I look at a 'Bridge over the Delegate at Quedong', an engraving which the *Illustrated Australian News* published in 1871 after a photograph by Charles Walter, I suspect that Walter did not use his tomahawk just to clear his path. Even though Walter was an early member of the Field Naturalists Club of Victoria – the main Victorian organisation which campaigned for protection of the environment in the late nineteenth century – I think that Walter was happy to use his blade to construct his views. The double stump in left foreground, if not also the one behind, were probably his handiwork – left by him in opening his view of the river and the bridge.[23]

I am equally suspicious of the grass tree in Morton Allport's stereoscope, *Mount Ida (Lake St Clair)*, taken in Tasmania in 1862. It is not just that this grass tree looks as if it may be propped up by the log in front of it but also that this grass tree is so perfectly positioned to satisfy the conventions of the picturesque. Already in 1863 the Tasmanian monthly, *Walch's Literary Intelligencer*, declared this stereograph 'the most beautiful and artistic' of Allport's photographs.[24] More recently, Ann-Marie Willis recognised that it was one of Allport's few photographs to take 'full advantage of the stereoscopic effect because it has been defined with a clearly defined foreground (a large grass tree), middle distance (bushes and a man in a boat on the lake) and background (mountain)'.[25]

I have the same suspicions when I look at the work of Carleton Watkins and William Henry Jackson, two of the American photographers most often identified with the rise of environmental concerns because of the role played by their work in the protection of Yosemite and Yellowstone. Not only do a number of photographs by Watkins and Jackson include axes but the stumps, which occupy the foregrounds of several of their views, suggest that Watkins and Jackson, or at least their assistants, also used them to reveal new scenery.

Look, for example, at Watkins's photograph of Castle Rock on the Columbia River which he took during a four month trip to Oregon in 1867. Look at the felled trees in the foreground of the *Steamer Cascade at the Lower Landing, Columbia River*. Look, perhaps above all, at his photograph of Cape Horn where there is a real freshness about the stump in the left foreground.[26]

Other cases may be impossible to detect if photographers resorted to axes but – sharing Ernest Docker's aesthetics – did so in such a way that the stumps and felled trunks could not be seen in their photographs. One example may be Eadward Muybridge. None of his photographs of Yosemite which I have seen reveal any obvious signs of the dozens of trees which he felled.

Landscape painters did not have the same need as photographers to shape their views in this way. They could shift position – making a foreground sketch from one spot while sketching their middle ground and distance from another. They could invent their foregrounds, omitting obstructions and introducing trees to frame their views and figures or animals to enliven them. Comparison of preliminary drawings and finished paintings reveals that these practices were commonplace among Australian colonial artists. They were also the norm in the United States where, as Barbara Novak has put it, Thomas Cole thought it 'kinder to let the ancient trees stand, altering them at will in composition, or imposing Claudian pastorales on them when the mood demanded. The artist made the necessary changes on canvas. Nature remained intact.'[27]

Yet tomahawks were also part of the basic kit of landscape painters on sketching expeditions. When the Victorian artists, Eugene von Guerard and Nicholas Chevalier, accompanied Alfred Howitt on a trip from Ferntree Gully in the Dandenong Ranges to the Baw Baw plateau in 1858, Howitt recorded that von Guerard carried 'a big knapsack, in front a roll of blankets – a sketchbook in a leather case at his side – round his waist a hunting knife – a tomahawk – a tobacco pouch'. Chevalier carried an even greater armoury: 'shot and powder – knife and tomahawk in belt – gun on shoulder'.[28]

While the artists needed these tomahawks to clear their paths, they probably also sometimes put them to other uses. One example may be *Ferntree Gully in the Dandenong Ranges*, now in the National Gallery of Australia, which made von Guerard's reputation when he first exhibited it in Melbourne in 1857. When von Guerard first went to the Dandenongs in 1855, they were already one of Melbourne's main sources of palings and shingles so that timber-getters were hard at work, cutting tracks and searching out the tallest, straightest mountain ash. The site of von Guerard's painting was known as 'Dobson's Gully' after Thomas Dobson who had established a timber camp nearby in 1854.[29]

As was so often the case, what attracted the timber-getter attracted the landscape painter. While von Guerard focussed on the tree ferns in his painting, he made several drawings of the eucalypt forest and, in a subsequent discussion about Australia's big trees at the Royal Society of Victoria, observed that 'he had seen one 100 feet high, and 45 paces round, two miles from Ferntree Gully

FIGURE 3
Eugene von Guerard, *Ferntree Gully in the Dandenong Ranges* 1857

on the southern slope of the Dandenong Ranges'. That the Dandenongs were common ground for the timber-getter and the landscape painter was recognised by one contemporary account which described the area as visited only by 'the woodman, who repairs thither to fell their gigantic timber' and 'the adventurous artist, who visits them for the purpose of transferring to his canvas the marvels of their scenery'.[30]

The potential for conflict between the artist and the timber-getter is illustrated by a cartoon in *Melbourne Punch* in 1858, drawn most likely by Nicholas Chevalier who was just starting out as a landscape painter in Victoria. Titled 'The Picturesque and the Practical', it shows how the artist, 'Mr Cobalt having made a pleasing sketch of a picturesque gum tree, returns two days afterwards to complete the picture, but finds the aspect of his subject has materially changed in the interval.' The tree has become a stack of palings.[31]

There seems, however, to have been no such conflict between von Guerard and Dobson. The artist not only sketched Dobson's hut but stayed with him, possibly for an extended period (as one later account records that he was there six months). Von Guerard and Dobson also had an identity of interest so far as certain clearing was concerned. According to James Smith, Melbourne's foremost art critic in the mid-nineteenth century, it was only because of 'the felling of some timber' that von Guerard could 'obtain a fore-ground sufficiently clear of obstructive objects' to allow him to include 'the distance in his range of vision' in *Ferntree Gully in the Dandenong Ranges*.[32]

We do no know who was responsible for this felling. Von Guerard may have simply exploited a view already opened by Dobson as part of his ordinary timber-getting. But von Guerard may have asked Dobson to fell these trees for him. He may even have taken up an axe himself – drawing on his experience on the Ballarat goldfields where, as part of helping to sink several deep shafts in 1853, he spent days 'felling trees, sawing the trunks into lengths, and splitting these into planks'. While von Guerard had regretted the destruction of the environment around Ballarat – the 'stretches of fine forest transformed into desolate-looking bare spaces, worked over and abandoned' – his reason was not so much the devastation of the landscape but that, for all their toil, so many miners, including himself, had left the diggings no richer and sometimes even poorer than when they started.[33]

Whatever its origins, this axe-work did not trouble James Smith who, within a few years had become a powerful advocate of protection of Australia's forests. Possibly Smith remained unconcerned because the Gully continued to appear intact (even though the axe-work could not have been far off to allow von Guerard to get his view). Smith may also have thought the clearing in a good cause – assisting Art – and that, even if von Guerard had been involved, he had done no more than put in practice the prevailing theory that it was the job of the artist not just to record Nature but to improve on it.

Other colonial landscape painters were also beneficiaries of this type of clearing, even if they did not take up axes themselves. When Eccleston du Faur established his artists' camps in the Grose Valley, his main object was not to attract photographers from Sydney but to entice W.C. Piguenit from Tasmania. According to one of du Faur's companions, who helped with the axe-work in the valley, their object was 'to clear views for the photographer *and* the sketcher'.[34]

This nexus between axe-work, view-making and landscape painting was recognised by Francis Myers who, as 'Telemachus' in the Melbourne *Argus*, was one of the most influential writers about the Victorian countryside in the late nineteenth century. Like both du Faur and John Watt Beattie, Myers was a keen advocate of protection of the natural environment, who argued for the Dandenongs to be declared a 'people's park' and Wilson's Promontory to be declared a wildlife sanctuary.[35] But he also wanted more 'views', even if trees had to be felled to reveal them.

In writing about the Upper Yarra country between Marysville and the Black Spur, Myers commented

> A few judicious axe strokes are badly wanted here ... toppling two or three trees by the roadside right over into the gorge, where the scrub growth would speedily bury them. If three trees were so removed, an uninterrupted view would be obtained of a valley and mountain which were designed by nature to prompt and gratify the

painter's art. Just exactly suited to a moderate canvas ...

A little further on, Myers was again wanting 'a little judicious clearance'.[36]

While Myers lamented that this type of work was 'in the category of nobody's business', elsewhere views were opened by a combination of private and public action. The authorities responsible for Australia's first reserves and national parks seem to have been particularly active. One of the primary objects of the trustees responsible for Royal National Park south of Sydney was to open new roads and walks and clear old ones so that 'with ease and safety' all visitors 'including ladies and young children' could enjoy the 'excellent views', 'charming vistas' and 'additional beautiful scenery'.[37]

This role of the axe in view-making was probably equalled, if not surpassed, by that of the gun in natural history illustration. Before photography, the killing of specimens was generally a prerequisite to their documentation in paint. While some animals were trapped and then killed in the studio (either by suffocating them or piercing their hearts with a steel pin), most were shot in the field. When the natural history painter, John Lewin, sailed for New South Wales in 1799, his kit included 'A Long barreld gun 6 feet in the Barrel'.[38] The great trick of the zoological and ornithological illustrator was to restore life through art to what he had shot or had been killed on his behalf.

The embodiment of the marksman-artist was America's most famous bird man, J.J. Audubon, who was not only a remarkable watercolourist but also an accomplished hunter whose field equipment included a shotgun, pistol, Dakota Indian war club, pipe-tomahawk and gun-shaped war club of the Mandan Indians. One mark of the significance of guns to Audubon's identity is that all major portraits of him show him with rifle in hand (instead of presenting him in a double role, with gun and portfolio). One of Audubon's watercolours for his *Birds of America* depicts the artist as trapper, with a gun and dead bird slung over his back and a tomahawk in his right hand (even though the golden eagle in the picture was one he had bought rather than caught).[39]

While the killing of individual animals may be explained away as necessary for Audubon's art, his appetite for hunting was of much larger dimensions. Although he railed against the 'brutal propensity' of the Labrador 'eggers', whose object was 'to plunder every nest' and 'kill every bird' that came their way, Audubon's own narratives reveal that he delighted in 'rare sport', often went out in the field simply for the enjoyment of the chase and the kill, and exhibited little restraint when doing so. Even when he recognised that certain types of hunting were 'probably too well understood and too successfully practised in the United States', Audubon hoped to 'induce' his readers to take to the woods with their guns.[40]

This passion for hunting is clearest in Audubon's account of his expedition to the Florida Keys – an area rich in ibises, godwits, flamingos, frigate pelicans and fish-crows. When Audubon first approached Indian Key, his 'heart swelled with uncontrollable delight' at so many new birds and he 'longed to make a more intimate acquaintance with them'. His method of doing so was crude. As he explained it, 'students of nature' spent 'little time in introduction'. 'In a trice', he and his companions had a boat at their service and just 'a short pull' had them on a large Key. A few minutes later, 'shot after shot might be heard, and down came whirling through the air the objects of our desire'.[41]

A few days later, Audubon and his friends turned their hand to 'egging' when their pilot took them to an area rich in ibis nests, 'each containing three large and beautiful eggs'. When 'all hands fell to gathering', the birds 'gave way' and before long they had 'a heap of eggs that promised delicious eating'. Their breakfast over, their pilot told them to prepare 'for fun'. As Audubon described it,

> Each of us provided with a gun, posted himself behind a bush, and no sooner had the water forced the winged creatures to approach the shore, than the work of destruction commenced. When at length it ceased, the collected mass of birds of different kinds looked not unlike a small haycock.[42]

Photography played no part in the decline of this kind of slaughter which went far beyond the demands of art. To begin with, photography was also too slow and cumbersome to be of much use in recording animals in the field. But with the invention of dry plates in the 1870s, photography offered a means not just of recording animals while alive but also of catching movements too fast to be followed by the eye. Before long, the camera – literally as well as metaphorically – became a substitute for the breech-loader. One of the French pioneers of photography of birds in flight called his new camera a 'photographic gun'. Soon there were endless word-plays about the different methods of 'shooting' – one which destroyed the target; the other which left it intact. The idea of 'sport' was also re-cast so that the challenge became that of pitting one's skill against the natural shyness of the animal. In similar vein, the new breed of field naturalist-photographer delighted 'in obtaining a big "bag" without harm to a single creature'.[43]

Photography, therefore, worked both for and against preservation of the environment. So far as the landscape was concerned, the new technology was destructive where the old had been relatively benign. But when it came to natural history illustration, photography facilitated nature preservation, allowing animals to be recorded without even trapping them. So great was interest in photography among Australian ornithologists that their journal, the *Emu*, began carrying a regular column on 'Camera Craft'. As the *Emu* described it in 1915, the number of ornithologists abandoning the rifle for the camera was 'steadily on the increase'. It was 'becoming recognized' that the work of the naturalist who could 'bring living animals before the eyes of others' was 'of higher value than the work of the collector of specimens'. By 1919 there was a Nature Photographer's Club of Australia; by 1920 a book of their work edited by the nature writer, Charles Barrett, who made much of how 'hunting with a camera' satisfied the 'instinct for the chase' that lurked 'in every man' without causing that destruction of animal life which was 'hateful to all lovers of Nature'.[44]

Why does all this matter? After all, axes and guns were more or less ubiquitious in the nineteenth century. If all travellers including artists used them to get firewood and hunt up dinner, why should we care if painters and photographers also used them more directly for their art?

One reason is that we need to qualify if not abandon the assumption, widespread in writing about photography, that nature is immovable – that photographers have been limited to seeking out subjects which happened to conform to compositional conventions established by landscape painters. While photographers cannot move mountains, they can fell, uproot and transplant trees and have not always hestitated to do so. One example is probably the Anson Brothers' view of Lake St Clair in Tasmania chosen by Ann-Marie Willis to demonstrate how photographers selected subjects which happened to comply with the picturesque, 'seeking out elements such as framing trees, foreground logs, winding paths and rivers'.[45] Taken most likely by John Watt Beattie who became a partner in Anson Brothers in 1882, it looks to me as if Beattie did not simply find this subject. He constructed it, characteristically, by felling the tree in the centre both to clear the view down the lake and also to give interest to the foreground.

The enthusiasm of artists for the axe and the gun has, however, greater significance for our understanding of artists' attitude to the land – particularly in the United States where so much has been made of artists as key figures in the emergence of a new respect for nature. This connection between art and environmental concern has been a commonplace in the writing of both art history and environmental history since the late 1940s, when Hans Huth of the Art Institute of Chicago began publishing the articles which resulted in 1957 in his *Nature and the American*.[46] But its main public embodiment is much older: in 1886 George Bird Grinnell formed the Audubon Society for the Protection of Birds.[47]

This identification and celebration of artists as conservationists has recently been attacked in the United States as part of the larger movement in art history which looks on nineteenth century artists as agents of imperialism, colonialism, capital (or, in the case of England, still the aristocracy). This revisionism is exemplified by the catalogue for the National Museum of American Art's 1992 exhibition, *America as the West*, in which Nancy Anderson equated artists such as Sanford Gifford, Albert Bierstadt and Thomas Moran with 'the miners, loggers, farmers, and ranchers who traveled cross-country to capitalise on the material resources of the American West'.[48]

Anderson's identification of artists as one of many brands of carpet-bagger who flocked to the frontier rests on what these painters both included and omitted from their work. When they celebrated the sublime, Anderson argues that these artists were exploiting the land in the same way as resource-getters – 'mining' the landscape 'for the raw materials from which they fashioned studio paintings'. By failing to depict the despoilation of the environment, she suggests that they misled their public back east by implying that all was well on the frontier, that there was little or no conflict 'between the spectacular natural beauty of the land ... and the inevitable changes that accompanied the conversion of minerals, forests, and water ... that the West could endure both as symobl and resource'.[49]

If the celebration of the artist as conservationist went too far – elevating an avid gun-man into the namesake of one of the most significant environmental organisations in the United States – so this revisionism is also too extreme. Just as to depict something may be to legitimise it, so to ignore something else may help to promote the belief that it does not exist. But it is nonsense to suggest that to omit something is as bad as to destroy it. Whatever the failings of artists on the American frontier, there is still a large gap between the devestation wrought by miners and loggers on the one hand and the artists' celebrations of nature on the other. Where miners and loggers laid waste, artists on the whole left the environment intact.

Much of the recent criticism of nineteenth century painters also begs the question what one can expect of artists – particularly those working on the frontier. Is it fair, for example, in the manner of Paul Fox and Jennifer Phipps in a recent Victorian exhibition, *Sweet Damper and Gossip*, to indict colonial artists for their adoption of the picturesque even if this compositional device can fairly be characterised as an agent of dispossession 'born of the eighteenth century enclosure movement and the subsequent construction of the gentleman's park from communally used land'?[50] Is it reasonable to imply that artists should have quickly invented a new visual language for a new place (or, just as difficult, adopted one not identified with the rich and powerful)?

It is also worth asking what would have happened had painters – not just in the United States or Australia but in any of the white settler countries – tried to 'expose' the destruction which was occuring on the frontier. Almost certainly, they would have found no market for paintings of this type, at least in the mid-nineteenth century, and probably not even in the 1880s or 1890s. Then, as now, most artists were just small businessmen, at most minor entrepeneurs, who could not afford to paint works which they knew would not sell.

Not least, the type of revisionism exemplified by Anderson is remarkable for its failure to take account of the way in which artists most closely resembled miners and loggers, when they took up axes and guns in the pursuit of their art. If one wants clear examples of the painter or photographer treating the natural environment as a resource ripe for exploitation, it is the trigger-happy, axe-ready artist. If there is to be a villain, it should be the artist concerned only for what he took away, recorded in his sketchbooks or on his wet-plates, and not what he left behind on the ground.

This destructiveness does not matter if we are happy to separate a work of art from the circumstances of its production – to delight, like James Smith in 1857, in the 'sylvan solitude' of *Ferntree Gully in the Dandenong Ranges*, 'the magnificent group of fern-trees with their curving feathery frondage' and the 'swelling amphitheatre beyond'[51] – and to ignore what von Guerard may have done to secure this view. Nor perhaps is it all that troubling if, in considering the circumstances of production of these works, we recognise that what is precious now was so much more abundant in the nineteenth century; that what looks to us like destruction, then often seemed like improvement; and that the role of art itself was different when the artist was expected to better Nature.

This destructiveness matters a great deal, however, if we start from the premise that celebration of nature rests on appreciation and hence respect. The artists's use of the axe and the gun ruptures this nexus. This rupture is disturbing enough when the work of art includes some sign of what has gone on. While we may not know who felled the trees in a work such as Joseph Bischoff's panorama of the Grose Valley, at least there is tangible evidence of something awry. We have a chance of recognising the basis of the celebration offered. The breakdown between celebration and conservation is even more disturbing where the work itself gives no hint of what has gone on and only the written record may reveal how it was produced.

This problem is most acute in relation to a work such as von Guerard's *Ferntree Gully* which seems to treat Nature as Cathedral – the fern gully as a sacred place. Because this view of Nature is so close to that of contemporary environmentalism, it is easy to presume a complete identity of values. We should beware. The painting may not be what it seems. We need to accept the possibility that the colonial artist who, perhaps more than any other in Australia, seems to have valued Nature in all its detail, may have been happy to destroy it just to be able to present this view.

NOTES

[1] *Australian News for Home Readers*, 25 September 1865, p. 16; *Illustrated Australian News for Home Readers*, 12 June 1869, p. 133; 4 October 1869, p. 187; 31 December 1873, pp. 212-14, republished in *Illustrated Tasmanian News*, March 1874, pp. 12-13; *Victorian Naturalist*, vol. 24, 1907, p. 110. See, more generally, Peter Quartermaine, '"Speaking to the Eye": Painting, Photography and the Popular Illustrated Press in Australia, 1850-1900', in Anthony Bradley & Terry Smith (eds), *Australian Art and Architecture: Essays Presented to Bernard Smith*, Oxford University Press, Melbourne, 1980, esp. pp. 64-68; Linden Gillbanks, 'Charles Walter: Collector of Images and Plants in East Gippsland', *Gippsland Heritage Journal*, no. 13, December 1992, pp. 3-10.

[2] *Illustrated Australian News for Home Readers*, 23 March 1868, p. 8; 31 December 1873, pp. 212-14.

[3] *Illustrated Australian News*, 27 October 1866, p. 8; *Illustrated Australian News for Home Readers*, 23 March 1868, p. 8; 12 June 1869, p. 133.

[4] *Sydney Morning Herald*, 14 April 1900, p. 12; 22 September 1902, p. 5.

[5] Karen Current, *Photography and the Old West*, Abrams, New York, 1978, p. 30; Peter E. Palmquist, *Carleton E. Watkins: Photographer of the American West*, University of New Mexico Press, Albuquerque, 1983, pp. 19-21; Theodora Litsios, 'More than a Pretty Picture: Photography as a Tool in Wilderness Conservation', in Vance Martin & May

Inglis (eds), *Wilderness: the Way Ahead*, Findhorn Press, Forres, 1984, p. 208.
[6] 'Album of 20 albumen silver photographs of California by Carleton Watkins, 1861-1868', LTWEF 15, La Trobe Library; *Freeman's Journal*, 28 September 1872, p. 7; *Illustrated Australian News*, 7 August 1871, p. 128; 15 July 1873, pp. 122, 125; *Illustrated Sydney News*, 2 August 1873, p. 8; John Smith, *Wayfaring Notes (Second Series): A Holiday Tour Round the World*, Brown, Aberdeen, 1872, chaps 19, 20; Gael Newton, *Shades of Light: Photography and Australia 1839-1988*, Australian National Gallery, Canberra, 1988, pp. 184-5.
[7] *Sydney Morning Herald*, 11 November 1875, p. 5.
[8] *Australian Town and Country Journal*, 9 October 1875, p. 580; *Sydney Morning Herald*, 11 November 1875, p. 5; *Australasian Sketcher*, 15 April 1876, p. 10; *Railway Guide to New South Wales*, Richards, Sydney, p. 57. See, generally, Quartermaine, pp. 68-70; Tim Bonyhady, *Images in Opposition: Australian Landscape Painting 1801-1890*, Oxford University Press, Melbourne, 1985, p. 100; Catherine Snowdon, 'The Take-Away Image: Photographing the Blue Mountains in the Nineteenth Century', in Peter Stanbury (ed.), *The Blue Mountains: Grand Adventure for All*, Macleay Museum/Second Back Row Press, Sydney, 1988, ch. 9.
[9] Eccleston du Faur, Notebook, A1629, Mitchell Library, Sydney; *Sydney Morning Herald*, 4 October 1875, p. 2; 7 October 1875, p. 3.
[10] *Sydney Morning Herald*, 11 November 1875, p. 5; *British Journal of Photography*, 1876, pp. 310, 317.
[11] Joseph Bischoff, Album of Photographs of the Grose Valley, LTAF 340, esp. ff. 32-33, La Trobe Library, Melbourne.
[12] *British Journal of Photography*, 1876, p. 310.
[13] Nicholas Caire, 'Scene from the Black Spur', in *Views of Victoria*, Anglo-Australasian Photographic Co., 1877, no. 27. See also Caire, 'Scene at the Foot of Mt Strzeletzki', *Gippsland Scenery*, no. 7.
[14] *Sydney Morning Herald*, 7 October 1875, p. 3; 11 November 1875, p. 5; *The Railway Guide of New South Wales*, p. 59.
[15] David Robertson, *West of Eden: a History of the Art and Literature of Yosemite*. Yosemite Natural History Association/Wilderness Press, c. 1984, p. xviii.
[16] *Alta California*, 7 April 1872, quoted in *Edward Muybridge: the Stanford Years 1872-1882*, Stanford University, Palo Alto, 1972, p. 45.
[17] J.H. Harvey, 'A Photographic Trip to the Jenolan Caves and Kanangara Walls, N.S.W.', *Australian Photographic Journal*, June 1894, p. 14; January 1895, p. 147.
[18] Harvey, p. 148.
[19] Nanette Sexton, 'Watkins' Style and Technique in the Early Photographs', *California History*, vol. 57, fall 1978, pp. 246-7, 270.
[20] J.W. Beattie, 'The Picturesque West Coast of Tasmania', *Australian Photographic Journal*, 20 August 1897, p. 191; Margaret Tassell & David Wood, *Tasmanian Photographer: from the John Watt Beattie Collection*, Macmillan, Melbourne, 1981, pp. 79, 86.
[21] *Proceedings of the Royal Society of Tasmania for 1889*, p. ix; *The Giant Trees of Victoria*, Melbourne, 1890, plates 2, 4, 7, 8.
[22] James Mullens, 'Landscape Photography', *Philadelphia Photographer*, vol. 10, no. 117, September 1873, p. 466; quoted by Palmquist, p. 59; A.H. Wall, *Artistic Landscape Photography*, Percy Lund, Bradford, 1896, p. 166.
[23] *Illustrated News for Home Readers*, 17 June 1871, p. 125.
[24] *Walch's Literary Intelligencer*, March 1863, p. 136.

[25] Ann-Marie Willis, *Picturing Australia: a History of Photography*, Angus & Robertson, Sydney, 1988, p. 34.
[26] See Clarence S. Jackson, *William H. Jackson: Picture Maker of the Old West*, Charles Scribner's Sons, New York, 1947, p. 57; James Alinder (ed.), *Carleton E. Watkins: Photographs of the Columbia River and Oregon*, Friends of Photography, 1979, plates 18, 20, 21. See also, Palmquist, p. 59.
[27] See Barbara Novak, *Nature and Culture: American Landscape and Painting 1825-1875*, Oxford University Press, New York, 1980, p. 160.
[28] Letter, Alfred Howitt to Anna Mary Howitt, 7 October 1858, quoted by Mary Howitt Walker, *Come Wind, Come Weather: a Biography of Alfred Howitt*, Melbourne University Press, Melbourne, 1971, p. 95.
[29] *Dandenong Advertiser*, 4 July 1889, p. 1; Tim Bonyhady, *Australian Colonial Paintings in the Australian National Gallery*, Australian National Gallery/ Oxford University Press, Melbourne, 1987, pp. 170-9.
[30] *Age*, 16 October 1857, p. 5; *Transactions and Proceedings of the Royal Society of Victoria*, vol. 8, 1866-7, p. 319; G.W. Robinson, 'In the Dandenong Ranges Sixty Years Ago', *Victorian Naturalist*, vol. 28, 1911-12, p. 30.
[31] *Melbourne Punch*, 15 July 1858, p. 204.
[32] *Argus*, 4 December 1857, p. 5; *Dandenong Advertiser*, 4 July 1889, p. 1; Helen Coulson, *Story of the Dandenongs*, Cheshire, Melbourne, 1959, p. 148.
[33] Marjorie Tipping (ed.), *An Artist on the Goldfields: the Diary of Eugene von Geurard*, Curry, O'Neil, Melbourne, 1982, pp. 40, 56, 58, 60, 63.
[34] *Sydney Morning Herald*, 4 October 1875, p. 2 (emphasis added).
[35] *Argus*, 15 December 1888, p. 13; Sandra Bardwell, 'National Parks in Victoria 1866-1954', Ph.D., Monash University, 1974, p. 337 (note 111).
[36] *Argus*, 16 June 1888, p. 5.
[37] *Argus*, 16 June 1888, p. 5; 'National Park: Report of the Trustees for the year ended 31 December 1887', *Votes and Proceedings of the Legislative Assembly during the Session of 1888-9*, vol. 3; 'National Park: Report of the Trustees for the year ended 31 December 1888', *Votes and Proceedings of the Legislative Assembly during the Session of 1888-9*, vol. 2.
[38] Alfred J. North, 'On Two Early Australian Ornithologists', *Records of the Australian Museum*, vol. 6, 1906, p. 126; Rex & Thea Rienits, *Early Artists of Australia*, Angus & Robertson, Sydney, 1963, p. 125.
[39] *The Original Water-Color Paintings by John James Audubon for the Birds of America*, American Heritage Publishing Co., 1966, vol. 1, notes to plate 54; John Chancellor, *Audubon*, Weidenfeld & Nicholson, London, 1978, p. 87; Ann Shelby Blum, *Picturing Nature: American Nineteenth-Century Zoological Illustration*, Princeton University Press, Princeton, 1993, ch. 3.
[40] John James Audubon, *Delineations of American Character and Scenery*, Baker, New York, 1926, esp. pp. 68, 74, 253-8, 282, 286.
[41] Audubon, p. 181.
[42] Audubon, p. 189.
[43] W.P. Adams, 'Deer Stalking with a Camera', *British Journal of Photography*, 1889, p. 647; L.G. Chandler, 'Nature Photography', *Australasian Photo-Review*, vol. 27, 1920, p. 62; David Elliston Allen, *The Naturalist in Britain: a Social History*, Allen Lane, London, 1976, pp. 232-4; David Knight, *Zoological Illustration: an Essay towards the History of Printed Zoological Pictures*, Dawson, Folkestone, Kent, 1977, p. 67.

[44] *Emu*, vol. 15, 1915-16, pp. 47, 160; Charles Barrett (ed.), *Australian Nature Pictures*, Alexander McCubbin, Melbourne, 1920.
[45] Willis, p. 60.
[46] Hans Huth, 'Yosemite: the Story of an Idea', *Sierra Club Bulletin*, vol. 33, no. 3, 1948, pp. 47-78; Hans Huth, 'The American and Nature', *Journal of the Warburg and Courtauld Institutes*, vol. 13, 1950, pp. 101-49; Hans Huth,' The Poetry of Travelling', *Art Quarterly*, vol. 20, 1957, pp. 17-33; Hans Huth, *Nature and the American: Three Centuries of Changing Attitudes*, University of California, Berkely, 1957.
[47] See Frank Graham Jr, with Carl W. Buchheister, *The Audubon Ark: a History of the National Audubon Society*, Knopf, New York, 1990.
[48] Nancy K. Anderson, '"The Kiss of Enterprise": the Western Landscape as Symbol and Resource', in William Truettner (ed.), *The West as America: Reinterpreting Images of the Frontier, 1820-1920*, Smithsonian Institution Press, Washington, 1991, p. 242.
[49] Anderson, esp. pp. 241-3.
[50] Paul Fox with Jennifer Phipps, *Sweet Damper and Gossip: Colonial Sightings from the Goulburn and North-East*, Benalla Art Gallery, Benalla, 1994, pp. 7, 11. See also, Simon Ryan, 'Exploring Aesthetics: the Picturesque Appropriation of Land in Journals of Australian Exploration', *Australian Literary Studies*, vol. 15, no. 4, October 1992, pp. 282-93.
[51] *Argus*, 4 December 1857, p. 5.

Thomas Pringle's Plantation

Damian Shaw

A group of four thousand British settlers, their passage funded by the home government, arrived at the Cape in 1820. As Noël Mostert states: 'the operation was probably the most callous act of mass settlement in the history of empire'. The settlers were 'wholly ignorant in most cases even of how to plant a potato, largely innocent of any real knowledge of the historic background of the region they occupied, and certainly ignorant of how to cope with the natural dangers of their surroundings'.[1] Even though Thomas Pringle was an atypical 1820 settler, in that he was the leader of the only Scottish party and that he expected to gain a government post (whereas most settlers were English farmers and artisans), he shared the difficulties suffered by all prospective settlers in gaining adequate information about the Cape before departure. Before the arrival of the 1820 settlers in the Cape, Southern Africa had occupied very little space in the imagination of either the British public or in the works of British Romantic writers. Poets who regularly directed their poetic gaze eastwards, or, to a lesser extent, westwards, like Byron, Shelley, Keats, Rogers and Southey, rarely glanced towards the tip of the African continent.[2] Possible explanations for this lacuna include the limited British involvement in the Cape after its re-occupation in 1806. Indeed, Pringle had not shown any indication of interest in South Africa in his poetry or journalism before his decision to emigrate. Of the travel literature written about the Cape between 1719 and 1819, eight of the ten accounts known to Pringle by 1834 were written by non-British writers, and, where they were translated into English, had a relatively restricted circulation in Britain.[3] Of the two Britons, William Paterson, who is described as 'the first to write and publish in English a book entirely devoted to a description of experience at first hand of travel in South Africa' was a Scottish Linnaean 'naturalist'.[4] His book, *Narrative of four voyages in the land of the Hottentots and Kaffirs* (1789), despite the peoples mentioned in its title, was largely a document of South African 'geography, fauna and flora.'[5] The book was of more use to naturalists than prospective settlers. Similarly, the career diplomat John Barrow's *Travels into the Interior of Southern Africa in the Years 1797 and 1798* (1809) was 'a strange, highly attenuated kind of narrative that seems to do everything possible to minimize the human presence.'[6] They were of some use to settlers who were anxious to learn about the land they were to settle, but they gave very little information about its peoples. Even missionary involvement there, which could have made Britain more aware of conditions in the sub-continent, had been minimal before 1820. The first missionary in South Africa was the Moravian George Schmidt (1737), and the first member of the London Missionary Society sent out was Dr. Vanderkemp (1798).

Environment and History **5** (1999): 309–323

When the scheme to settle the Cape was announced in parliament in 1819, therefore, prospective settlers were extremely ill-informed about the territory they were about to claim for themselves.[7] It is true that Pringle began to read literature on the Cape voraciously before his departure, but he may be regarded as an exception.[8] The bulk of the settlers set off 'with profound ignorance as to what prospects there were of successfully establishing themselves as agriculturalists in the new home awaiting them'.[9] Notwithstanding these problems, the settlers were generally optimistic, a view supported by the British press and a rush of positive pamphlets and accounts of the Cape printed in 1818 and 1819,[10] even though 'one or two newspapers sounded notes of warning and a sixteen-page booklet was issued which violently opposed the whole scheme, and although two cartoons ridiculing emigration to the Cape of "Forlorn" Hope were published by George Cruikshank'.[11]

The general optimism of the settlers, however, does not imply that they were a culturally coherent group of people, originating as they did from Scotland, Ireland, Wales and England, and having widely divergent backgrounds.[12] Neither was there a coherent ideological approach to the colonies themselves in Britain in 1819, let alone towards Southern Africa. Christian Humanism and the 'civilising mission' were not to become the predominant ideologies of the British Empire until the Victorian period. In 1819, a time which saw the strengthening of social revolution and political reform in Britain, attitudes to colonial government in general had hardly been fixed, as is evidenced by rapidly changing colonial policies towards India ranging from those of minimal influence and interference within colonial society (Orientalism) to policies of complete assimilation (Anglicisation). But while British poets, philosophers and politicians continued through the first two decades of the nineteenth century to argue the often conflicting policies of Utilitarianism, Evangelism, Anglicisation and 'orientalism'[13] with regards to the empire in India, the roughly four thousand British emigrants who had landed at the Cape in 1820 were faced directly with the immediate problem of living in the 'contact zone' on the Cape frontier.[14]

As with the Pringle party, most groups of settlers, which were comprised largely of fairly uneducated parties in straitened though not desperate circumstances, knew that they had to work hard themselves in order to ensure their own survival.[15] They were led to believe that they were being offered a chance by the English government to re-establish themselves in a new colony solely in order to contribute to the prosperity of the settlement and to make their fortunes. Their contract with the British Government was one of land in return for labour. These men and women, unlike company or government officials who might return with ease to Britain, and who often had no direct interest in land for their own survival, had invested all their capital in the enterprise[16] and were, as Pringle puts it, about 'to draw an irrevocable lot for [them]selves and [their] childrens' children'.[17] In terms of reciprocity, settlers were led to believe that they were being given free land in return for their labour and industry, though this contract was practically 'irrevocable', as the vast majority of settlers did not have sufficient funds to return to Britain in the event of unexpected disaster. The circular issued to prospective settlers from Downing Street in 1819 emphasised the need for work, as well as the agricultural 'reason' for the settlement scheme. It stipulated that the head of each family be 'not infirm or incapable of work', and ended with a cursory 'P.S. In order to ensure the arrival of Settlers at the Cape at the beginning of the planting season, the Transports will not leave this country until the month of November.'[18] The British Parliament presented the settlement scheme to the public at large in exactly the same practical and economic light, government circulars not advancing any reason for settlement besides the promised prosperity of the colonists and the benefit they would be to the colony in terms of agricultural production. What the settlers did not know when they arrived was that the British Parliament's support for the scheme 'was influenced solely by strategic and not by philanthropic or economic considerations.'[19] They were to be allocated land on the Cape frontier just behind the border of the so-called 'Neutral Territory', a strip of land roughly thirty miles long between the Great Fish and Keiskamma rivers which had been cleared of all inhabitants after the fifth Frontier war of 1819, when the local groups were pushed back further out of the colony than ever before. After the 'Neutral Territory', which was closed to all except the military, the settlers were to form the next line of defence. The Cape Government could no longer afford to secure the border of the colony (the Great Fish River), most troops being required in India, and the existing white population of the colony was not large enough to settle the region. The warning of the Cape Governor, Lord Charles Somerset, to the Secretary for the Colonies, Earl Bathurst, that 'the settlers' property will in some measure be exposed in the first instance to be plundered by their neighbours unless their own vigilance and courage shall considerably aid in protecting it' was not communicated to applicants for the settlement scheme.[20]

Misled and uninformed, most settlers arrived in the colony prepared to labour for their success, unaware that they were to be settled on the border, or that they faced a potential threat of stock theft and military action from across it. Most desired, and believed that they would be able, to establish themselves and their families as prosperous land owners in a new country. It is not surprising that their primary interest was in the soil itself, in its fertility rather than the beauty of the environment.

However, in October of 1823, a series of devastating floods nearly annihilated all of the English settlers' land, housing and property in Albany. The Pringle party was unaffected owing to their geographical isolation from Albany, but the crisis provoked Pringle, as temporary secretary of the society for the 'Relief of Distressed Settlers' in Cape Town, to publish his first major piece of journalism on South Africa. By 31 October 1822, Pringle had already prepared a narrative description of Albany for publication – Walter Scott had suggested the idea before Pringle had departed – but had not attempted to publish it because of his desire 'to avoid publishing any thing that might clash with the views of the Government'.[21] The book, which consists of an introduction of fifty pages followed by a selection of letters by settlers who had suffered personally, was specifically designed to raise funds in England and India for the relief fund. Pringle, therefore, converted his account of Albany into a work of propaganda. The final manuscript was written in haste, then posted to Thomas Underwood on 5 January 1824. It was published shortly after it arrived in England as *Some Account of the Present State of the English Settlers in Albany, South Africa*,[22] and succeeded in raising an enormous sum of ten thousand pounds for the society.[23] Recognising the gravity of the settlers' predicament, Pringle appears to have written the document on his own initiative, for he mentions in the introduction that it is not an '*official* statement' in his capacity as secretary of the society, but that he is 'willing, however, to incur this responsibility, rather than lose time while [his] distressed countrymen are *ready to perish*'.[24] Political 'responsibility' could hardly be incurred by the publication of the settlers' letters themselves, for they are straightforward accounts of the actual losses suffered by individuals and blame nothing and nobody, besides the weather, for their misfortunes. Pringle's introduction, however, attempts to give a brief sketch of the general condition of the settlers in Albany. The chief purpose of the sketch is to reassure the British and Indian readership[25] that the settlers were not themselves to blame for four years of disaster, indebtedness and crop failure; indeed, that the predominantly English Albany settlers were an industrious group of people who were deserving of charitable treatment.

Pringle's first concern was to point out that the ignorance of the settlers with regard to their location was not their own fault. He provides the reader with a topographical description of Albany, because it will ensure a more correct notion of it than:

> can be derived from the too fanciful delineations of some late tourists. These gentlemen, whether scientific, sentimental, or religious in their other views, have almost universally concurred in representing the Zuureveld, as a fair and fertile region of unrivalled beauty and fecundity; – extending in luxuriant plains to invite the ploughshare, or swelling into verdant hills, which only wanted flocks and shepherds to be quite Arcadian; – adorned, moreover, with evergreen groves and forests, and with the superb and glowing allurements of euphorbias, strelitzas [sic], chandelier aloes, and scented acacias; – its lawny solitudes enlivened by sportive herds of elegant antelopes; and the whole landscape embellished (as they usually express it) "with all the picturesque scenery of a nobleman's park in England;" but rather, as transmitted through this "pictured medium," like a landscape in fairyland (pp. 4–5).[26]

These writers, says Pringle, have written in the style of Harvey's *Meditations on a Flower Garden*.[27] Pringle uses the language of these 'late tourists' with its 'glowing' adjectives in order to make the point that their descriptions are false to the extent of describing a place which does not exist ('fairyland'), as well as being of no practical use to the settlers. Fanciful descriptions can, thus, have dire practical consequences. Also of interest is that Pringle is criticising the use of an English model to describe the South African landscape. The English picturesque is of no utility, and can even be dangerous. It would have been better, Pringle continues, 'if practical information collected from the experience of even boors and Hottentots had been more carefully provided by the Government'.[28] Thus Pringle upbraids not only the writers for their rhetoric, but also the home Government for its lack of adequate and careful preparation. His criticism above makes it plain that more practical advantage is to be gained from the information provided by indigenous inhabitants than by the home government.[29] The colonists, says Pringle, 'were mistaken, many of them, doubtless, in giving credit to too flattering accounts of the character and capability of the country; but not more culpably mistaken than the Government, that partly countenanced these accounts, and sent them to colonize it upon an injudicious and ill-concerted plan' (p. 35). Here, Pringle lays the blame for the initial failure of the settlement scheme squarely at the feet of the British Parliament.

Having accused the British parliament of incompetence, and the Cape Government of not being liberal (in both senses), Pringle gives examples of the settlers' thriftiness and endeavour, in order to ensure that counter-accusations of laziness might not be directed against them, even though a few examples of 'the sloven, the sluggard, the drunken, and the improvident' do exist (p. 17).[30] A hardworking body of settlers is constructed in opposition to incompetent or mean spirited governments. Pringle does not proceed to blame the Others in South African society at the time for any disadvantages the settlers had suffered through pilfering and cattle raids. The Hottentots are 'trustworthy', even though they are 'long-oppressed' (p. 45). The slaves 'are *(and must be)* unhappy, debased, and dangerous in all countries' (p. 47 – Pringle's italics), but this is the fault of the system of slavery itself and its concomitant 'clouds of prejudice' (p. 46). As for the 'Caffers, even under the least favourable points of view, [they] are certainly an honest, humane, and civilized race, compared with the red or white [Canadian] savages' (p. 45).[31] Pringle, therefore, stresses the positive qualities of the Others in South Africa, and omits issues of violence relating to these groups. Pringle's purpose is to present the settlers as a coherent, hardworking group. As the prospectus of the *South African Journal*, appended to *Albany,* claims:

> No longer a disunited, wavering, and temporary assemblage of adventurers, with our ultimate views rooted beyond the ATLANTIC, we are fast acquiring, as a community, self-respect, and home importance, in which the prosperity of every country has its foundation.[32]

Pringle's focus in *Albany* is ultimately on the plight of the colonists themselves, but he also pays some attention to their identity as a group, which makes *Albany* more than just a factual report. The settlers themselves are beginning to take root in the soil of the Cape, a soil which should not be described as England.

The South African Commercial Advertiser (*SACA*), established by the printer George Greig, was first published on 7 January 1824. From Greig's 'Prospectus' of 20 December 1823, it is clear that the principal aim of the paper was to be a medium for business transactions and advertising, 'and any information that may tend to the advancement of *Trade* and *Commerce*, the Improvement of *Agriculture*, or the elucidation of *Science*'.[33]

After the second number, however, Greig invited Pringle and his fellow Scot John Fairbairn to take over the editorial side of the paper.[34] They duly accepted and assumed control of all editorial writing.[35] As editors they frequently expressed their sentiments about the new settlement in agricultural terms:

> To establish a flourishing Colony, therefore, in the midst of savage tribes, it is not merely a requisite to transplant thither a few hundred or thousand families of civilized people, and as soon as they have taken root to abandon them to nature and themselves; but the "*Plantation*" (to adopt the obsolete but expressive phraseology of our ancestors) must be fenced and sheltered, and unremittingly watered, and weeded, and pruned, and new-grafted, – and we must "dig about it and dung it," and watch over it with unsleeping diligence, if we wish to reap any return deserving our regard or worthy of the stock it was derived from. – If we act otherwise, and neglect the duty of good husbandmen, what can we expect but that our "Plantation" will either pine away in sickly and dwarfish degeneracy, or, on a soil of greater fertility, shoot up in wild and wasteful luxuriance, undistinguished for any profitable quality from the native thickets around it.[36]

In this passage, the editors directly conflate people with plant life. Success of the settlement relies on good husbandry and good gardening. Underpinning this are the (predominantly Scottish) moral precepts of profit and utility. Already we can see the logic of John Croumbie Brown's environmentalism starting to take root. Similar forces are at work in Pringle's sonnet 'Enon' (dated 1821, and presumably written just after Pringle's visit there):

ENON

By Heaven directed – by the World reviled –
        Amidst the Wilderness they sought a home,
        Where beasts of prey, and men of murder roam,
And untam'd Nature holds her revels wild:
There, on their pious toils their MASTER smil'd,
        And prosper'd them, unknown or scorned of men,
        'Till in the satyr's haunt and dragon's den
A garden bloom'd, and savage hordes grew mild.

So, in the guilty heart when heavenly Grace
        Enters – it ceaseth not till it uproot
                All evil passions from each hidden cell –

Planting again an Eden in their place –
Which yields to men and angels pleasant fruit,
And God himself delighteth there to dwell.[37]

The missionaries are portrayed as being threatened by an unspecified 'World' as well as savage [untamed] nature which includes the 'men of murder' and 'savage hordes' who live in it. In this way the missionaries' condition is parallel to that of Pringle and other settlers on the frontier who were hoping to make their 'gardens' bloom (achieve financial success) and see the 'savage hordes grow mild' (ensure their personal safety). The missionaries are being held up as ideal examples of how this might be possible. Life in Enon, however, was not as tranquil as it appears in the poem. The mission station had been 'destroyed by the Caffers in the war of 1819' before being re-occupied, as Pringle admits in the notes to *African Sketches* (1834).[38] In the same war, the land to be occupied by the settlers had been 'invaded' by the Caffers before being 'retaken' by the government. Pringle, here, is silent about land-rights. 'Enon' suppresses any narrative either of the violence used by the Caffers to destroy the mission station, or of the worse violence of the army used to drive them, in turn, off the land. The Caffers, however, are not blamed in the poem for destroying the mission station, nor is the army blamed for destroying them. Instead the solution of 'pious toil' acceptable to God, which is not always efficacious in the world of politics, is proposed. Indeed, it is already seen to have accomplished the aim of taming Nature in an Eden away from the 'World', just as the settlers desired to do for themselves. In this portrayal, the missionaries have been allowed their autonomy despite the government (or the secular World), and have succeeded in assimilating the colonial Other (the savage hordes/nature). It would seem that the simple, though arduous, task of planting a garden (which involves a human plantation) is sufficient to civilise 'nature' as well as the people living in it.

Pringle must have been impressed by the seeming tranquillity of Enon when he visited it in 1821, but the suggestion in the poem that 'pious toil' and the grace of God alone would be sufficient to secure the missionaries' respectability in the eyes of the world, and their security against 'savages'/'nature' is clearly idealistic. The mission had been destroyed in 1819 because of its lack of defences, a chance which Pringle was not prepared to take when it came to his own settlement.[39] Pringle, however, attempts to efface these unpleasant possibilities in this early work.

In 'Caffer Song' (1824), a poem free of any suggestion of violence besides that of hunting for a living, the persona of the 'hunter' is cast as an idealised, pastoral swain, encircled by peace and rural tranquillity.[40] The poem is a rendering of a Xhosa song (the original does not survive) but fits neatly into the standard contemporary trope of the 'noble savage' where 'the Negro reveres his parents, loves his wife, and is respected by his children. In the evening he dances.'[41]

CAFFER SONG
'Wena umfuhla linyaniza.'

Deep in the wild-wood lies hid a green dell,
Where fresh from the Grey Rock the bright waters swell,
And fast by that fountain a far-spreading tree,
Which shelters the home that is dearest to me.

Down by the streamlet my heifers are grazing;
Prone o'er the clear pool the herd-boy is gazing;
Under the shade my Ileza is singing –
The shade of the tree where her cradle is swinging.

When I come from the hill as the day-light is fading,
Though spent with the chase, and the game for my lading,
My nerves are new-strung and my light heart is swelling
As I gaze on that Grey Rock which towers o'er my dwelling.[42]

The language is that of containment and shelter, where gentle nature – as opposed to the savage nature of 'Enon' – encloses the mild and peaceful 'Caffer', certainly far from the settlers' or missionaries' experience of them by 1824. The motivation for the poem, then, is not immediately obvious. A reading which suggests that the poem was written in order to demonstrate to fellow colonists that the 'Caffer' was, in fact, harmless if left on his own in nature would seem unlikely. More likely is that the poem is an example of hymn-like, pastoral wishful-thinking which effaces the violence and injustices of colonial conflict by placing the 'Caffer' in a natural utopia with no obvious history.[43] It also effaces the threat of attack which was uppermost in the minds of most colonists, even though in most cases, as in Pringle's, colonists had not been in direct contact with the Caffers, seeing that the government did not allow them to keep slaves and forbade all trade between colonists and the native tribes settled across the frontier. Certainly, Pringle had had no direct contact with the Caffers by the time he left for Cape Town in 1822. Probably because his party had not been attacked, Pringle could afford to idealise the 'Caffer' unproblematically within the pastoral tradition, to view him as being contained by gentle nature, rather than by the colonists themselves and the military, which was actually the case. It is possible that Pringle had an ulterior motive in portraying 'The Caffer' as mild, isolated, peaceful – essentially concerned with the well-being of his own kin – in order to allay a fear of attack from 'savage hordes'.

Notwithstanding the above, by 1834, Pringle had obviously recognised the extremely idealised nature of the sketch when he changed its title to 'The Brown Hunter's Song'. With this new title, which refers instead to the 'Bushmen', who had already been virtually exterminated by 1824, the poem suddenly performs another function, that of idealising a lost state of innocence. The poem becomes an attack on those who had destroyed the idealised, defenceless, peace-loving 'Brown Hunter', who in the poem, poses no threat to colonial society.

In 'Enon' and 'Caffer Song', then, though the 'savage hordes' are portrayed negatively in the first, and the 'Caffer' positively in the latter, either 'pious' or pastoral toil is responsible for their redemption. There is no mention of military violence, land-rights, injustice, or oppression, themes which came to dominate his later poetry. According to Pringle, the best choice for a settler would be to become prosperous through pious toil, while remaining at peace with the government and with the natives alike.

'Afar in the Desert', Pringle's most widely published poem, was probably written in 1823, during or after his trip overland from the frontier to Cape Town. It was published in the *South African Journal*, 2, pp. 105-107. The narrator at first seeks refuge from the world in nostalgia for childhood and in recollections of his 'Native Land' (line 13), though this vision is swiftly shattered when he recognises that all is forsaken: 'All – all – now forsaken, forgotten, or gone – / And I, a lone Exile – remembered of none – / My high aims abandoned – and good acts – undone! / Aweary of all that is under the sun.'[44] The narrator who flees to the desert in the first verse is a person who has actually given up hope of being a patriot, who has capitulated to despair. The phrases 'my high aims abandoned – my good acts – undone!' may express Pringle's frustration with the colonial government, but the poem is too general to be certain that this was his intention. Rather, in the first stanza, the narrator flies into the desert to escape personal failure. In the second stanza, he again flies into the desert, but this time to escape the 'oppression, corruption, and strife' of the world. As the poem proceeds, the landscape is generally evacuated of its fauna and flora until the desert itself is described:

Where grass, nor herb, nor shrub takes root
Save poisonous thorns that pierce the foot;
And the bitter melon, for food and drink,
Is the Pilgrim's fare, by the Salt Lake's brink:
A region of drought where no river glides,
Nor rippling brook with ozier'd sides:
Nor reedy pool, nor mossy fountain,
Nor rock, nor tree, nor misty mountain,

Are found – to refresh the wearied eye:
But the barren earth, and the burning sky,
And the blank horizon round and round
Without a living sight or sound,
Tell to the heart in its pensive mood,
That this at length – is SOLITUDE![45]

This is very dissimilar to the effect the desert has on Mungo Park: 'In other parts the disconsolate wanderer, wherever he turns, sees nothing around him but a vast interminable expanse of sand and sky – a gloomy and barren void, where the eye finds no particular object to rest upon, and the mind is filled with painful apprehensions of perishing with thirst. Surrounded by this dreary solitude, the traveller [...] listens with horror to the voice of the driving blast, the only sound that interrupts the awful repose of the Desert.'[46] Pringle uses much the same language, suggesting that he was influenced by this passage, but to very different effect. The narrator finds refuge in a high-romantic solitude, which is redeemed by God, and the flight of the exile becomes a pilgrimage:

> As I sit apart by the desert stone,
> Like Elijah at Sinai's cave alone,
> And feel like a moth in the Mighty Hand
> That spread the heavens and heaved the land -
> 'A still small voice' comes through the wild
> (Like a Father consoling his fretful Child),
> Which banishes bitterness, wrath, and fear, -
> Saying – "MAN IS DISTANT, BUT GOD IS NEAR!"

In the light of Pringle's ambivalent position and fear of the colonial government when this poem was written, it is not surprising that he does not explicitly investigate the possibility of a political solution to the colony's troubles, whether it be revolutionary or not. The voice is God's, not his own. But the potential for dissent is made plain when Pringle identifies himself with Elijah, a prophet in the wilderness to an exiled nation: Elijah, after confronting Jezebel and slaying the priests of Baal (the forces of false religion) flees into the desert for his life, but wishing to die.[47] God, however, urges him to return to politics[48] and anoint Jehu as the new king of Israel.[49] Furthermore, Elijah proceeds to denounce King Ahab for stealing the vineyard of Naboth after Jezebel had had Naboth killed on false grounds, an action specifically involved with rights to land.[50] Elijah at Sinai's cave is a threatening figure, about to resume an active political career, to reinstate the 'high aims' which have been abandoned. The figure of Elijah represents an alternative path of political action, a figure about to pick up the gauntlet. Pringle eventually did just that. This had a profound impact on his later writings and approach to the South African environment, as I have demonstrated in my dissertation 'The Writings of Thomas Pringle'.[51]

But it can be seen here, however, that if – in Pringle's early writings on South Africa – people could be plants (a 'plantation'), and if properly nurtured plants could be moral weapons against degenerate native growths (and 'savage hordes'), and if the desert could be a place which both contains and is redeemed by God, then we can see the roots of the logic of Brown's environmental solution – simply plant trees (and God would see to their irrigation):

> Through the desert God is going
> Through the desert waste and wild:

Where no goodly plant is growing,
Where no verdure ever smiled;
But the desert shall be glad;
And with verdure soon be clad.

Where the thorn and briar flourished
Trees shall be seen to grow
Planted by the Lord and nourished
Stately, fair and fruitful too:
See! they rise on every side:
See! they spread their branches wide.

From the hills and lofty mountains
Rivers shall be seen to flow,
There the Lord will open fountains;
Thence supply the plains below.
As he passes, every land
Shall confess his powerful hand.[52]

NOTES

[1] Noël Mostert, *Frontiers, The Epic of South Africa's Creation and the Tragedy of the Xhosa People* (London: Pimlico, 1993), p. 533.

[2] Exceptionally, the figure of the 'Hottentot' occurs frequently in eighteenth and early nineteenth century discourse, most notoriously in terms of the 'Hottentot Venus'.

[3] They are Karl Peter Thunberg's *Travels in Europe, Africa and Asia*, 4 vols (London: 1796), Peter Kolb's, *The Present State of the Cape of Good Hope*, trans. Mr. Medley (London: Innys, 1731), François Le Vaillant's *New Travels in the Interior Parts of Africa*, 3 vols (London: 1796), Rev. Christian Ignatius Latrobe's *Journal of a visit to South Africa* (London: Seeley and Ackermann, 1818), Olfert Dapper's *Kaffrarie, of Lant der Kaffers, anders Hottentots genaemt* (Amsterdam, 1688), Martin Heinrich Lichtenstein's *Travels in Southern Africa, in the years 1803-1806*, trans. by Anne Plumptre, 2 vols (London, 1812), and Anders Sparrman's *A Voyage to the Cape of Good Hope* (London: G. and J. Robinson: 1785).

[4] Mary Louise Pratt, *Imperial Eyes: Travel Writing and Transculturation* (London: Routledge, 1992), p. 50.

[5] Pratt, p. 51: 'Where, [Pratt asks], is everybody? The landscape is written as uninhabited, unpossessed, unhistoricized, unoccupied even by the travellers themselves.'

[6] Pratt, p. 59. Pringle does not mention John Campbell's *Travels in South Africa Undertaken at the Request of the Missionary Society* (1815), Robert Semple's *Walks and Sketches* (1815), Capt. Robert Perceval's *An Account of the Cape of Good Hope* (1804), and *Gleanings in Africa*, Anon. (1805).

[7] The circular issued by the Colonial Office 'made no reference to the part of the country to which the settlers would be sent, nor the particular object which the Government

had in mind in aiding them to get there. To all enquiries for information on these points the Government gave evasive answers, going no further than to inform applicants that "the particular part of the Colony selected was the South-East coast of Africa".' Harold Edward Hockly, *The Story of the British Settlers of 1820 in South Africa*, 2nd edn (Cape Town: Juta, repr. 1973), p. 29.

[8] Even extensive reading could be misleading, though. Pringle states as much in 1824: 'Four years ago the advantages of the Cape Colony were held forth by ignorant and interested pamphleteers to the admiration of the world, in terms equally overstrained and delusive; and 100,000 Emigrants were eager to follow where 5000 have since lamentably failed' *South African Commercial Advertiser*, 4 February, 1824, p. 34.

[9] Hockly, p. 25. See also Mostert, pp. 520-521.

[10] Some examples are given by Hockly in his bibliography of Settler Africana, Hockly, pp. 254-263.

[11] Hockly, p. 25. For an examination of the Cruikshank cartoon 'The proposed Emigration to the Cape of Good Hope' see David Bunn, '"Our Wattled Cot": Mercantile and Domestic Space in Thomas Pringle's African Landscapes,' in *Landscape and Power*, ed. by W. J. T. Mitchell (Chicago: University Press of Chicago, 1994), pp. 127-173, (pp. 136-137).

[12] Of the 1455 adult male settlers among the group of 4000, Hockly (p. 31) analyses their professions as such:

Farming and country pursuits	42%
Skilled artisans and mechanics	32%
Commerce and Trade	12%
Army, Navy and Sea	5%
Professions	4%
Unspecified and miscellaneous	5%

[13] Nigel Leask, *British Romantic Writers and the East: Anxieties of Empire* (Cambridge: CUP, 1992), p. 91.

[14] I use the term 'contact zone' in the sense developed by Pratt: 'The space of colonial encounters, the space in which people geographically and historically separated come into contact with each other and establish ongoing relations, usually involving conditions of coercion, radical inequality, and intractable conflict,' Pratt, p. 6.

[15] 'Specific instructions were [...] issued that no settler should be allowed to own slaves or even hire Native labour, and that all work on the lands allotted was to be performed by free white labour, any contravention of these stipulations rendering the lands liable to instant forfeiture.' Hockly, p. 28.

[16] Hockly, p. 28.

[17] Thomas Pringle, *Narrative of a Residence in South Africa* (1834), *with an Introduction, Biographical and Historical Notes by A.M. Lewin Robinson*, ed. by A. M. Lewin Robinson (Cape Town: Struik, 1966), p. 9.

[18] In Hockly, p. 27.

[19] Hockly, p. 24.

[20] Hockly, p. 29.

[21] Pringle to Scott, National Library of Scotland, 3895.f.201. Pringle was already aware that he had to treat Lord Charles Somerset, the Governor, with caution. In the same letter he writes: 'Some person has informed him (or perhaps he has imagined from seeing my name mentioned much to my own upset in newspapers & magazines) that I am a violent Whig & formerly a supporter of the *democrat press* (as it is called) in Scotland.' He goes on to admit that he is a Whig, but denies any connection with party politics. Scott, of

course, was a well known, though at times ambivalent, Tory.
[22] *Some Account of the Present State of the English Settlers in Albany, South Africa* (London: Underwood, Edinburgh: Oliver and Boyd, 1824).
[23] Seven thousand pounds from England and India, and three thousand from the colony itself.
[24] *Albany*, p. 2.
[25] A relief fund had been set up in India.
[26] Pringle is, thus, already aware of three distinct modes of travel writing, i. e., 'scientific, sentimental, or religious'.
[27] Pringle excludes Barrow from having written in this style, but says, nevertheless, that he disagrees with many of his sentiments, especially regarding his condemnation of the Boers. *Albany*, p. 5. Pringle is referring to James Hervey's *Reflections on a Flower Garden*, in which the landscape is used as a springboard for sententious religious moralising.
[28] *Albany*, p. 5.
[29] 'A sort of Utopian delirium was somehow excited at that time in the public mind about South Africa, and the flowery descriptions of superficial observers seem to have intoxicated with their Circean blandishments not merely the gullible herd of uninformed emigrants, but many sober men both in and out of parliament' *Albany*, pp. 6-7.
[30] The thriftiest, of course, being the Scotch, who 'keeping profit and utility steadily in view, [...] allow embellishments and even accommodation to wait their leisure' *Albany*, p. 18.
[31] Pringle judges the groups according to their moral behaviour, not their skin colour, which makes possible his comparison of white, Canadian settlers with 'Caffers'.
[32] *Albany*, p. 117. The *South African Journal* had both commenced publication and already ceased operation, owing to Somerset's opposition, by the time this prospectus was published in *Albany*.
[33] 'Prospectus', *South African Commercial Advertiser* (South African Library: Cape Town, repr. 1978).
[34] Pringle says that Greig 'found himself in want of editorial aid, and solicited us to undertake the literary management of the paper' *Narrative*, p. 181.
[35] As Pringle and Fairbairn were joint editors and collaborated in writing the editorials, I assume that the opinions expressed in them reflect the attitudes of both editors, or at least were not accepted by one and wholly obnoxious to the other. A few copies of the *SACA* exist in which Pringle has noted the authors by hand. These show that he wrote the second editorials for the numbers of 28 January and 4 February, a note on the painter De Meillon (21 January), and a poem titled 'Speech of His Majesty King Mateebe' (21 January). See H. C. Botha, *John Fairbairn in South Africa* (Cape Town: Historical Publication Society, 1984), p. 18.
[36] *SACA*, 4 February 1824, p. 34. It is interesting to note that Pringle's use of the archaic term 'plantation' links it in a new sense to the West Indian plantations which he was to condemn so vociferously in later years as secretary of the Anti-Slavery Society.
[37] *SAJ*, p. 25.
[38] In *African Poems of Thomas Pringle*, ed. by Ernest Pereira and Michael Chapman, Killie Campbell Africana Library (Pietermaritzburg: University of Natal Press, 1989), p. 114.
[39] Pringle's plans to fortify his settlement, as detailed in the letter to Scott above, included building a small fort. He also arranged for a group of armed soldiers to guard his settlement. Certainly, by 1823, his letter to Mackenzie and his statements in *Albany* make it clear that, as a settler at least, military involvement might be necessary to ensure the settlers' survival, however dangerous that involvement might prove. Even though Pringle calls the Caffers 'humane' and 'civilized' in *Albany*, this does not imply that he did

not recognise the military threat they posed to the colony in general, and the settlers in particular. He says: 'the Caffers may be effectually checked, and their predatory inroads completely repressed or prevented, by establishing a line of small posts or fortified villages along a well-chosen frontier, and communicating with each other by constant patrols.' The system would be policed by 'a native militia of *free Hottentots* with an interest in the soil', *Albany*, p. 41.

[40] In later poems, like 'Makanna's Gathering', Pringle characterises the 'Caffer' as a warrior, rather than a hunter.

[41] Hoxie N Fairchild, *The Noble Savage* (New York: Russel and Russel, 1961), pp. 292-293. Pringle rapidly moved away from this sort of portrayal, the only other example being his 'ethnographic' poem 'The Coranna', where all the features in the quotation are evident.

[42] 'Ileza', according to Pringle's note, is a 'roebuck'. It is interesting to note that this poem contains the kind of celebration of the home which is found in many of Pringle's early works, except that the narrative persona is a 'Caffer'. The only features which identify it as 'African', however, are the title, inscription, and the word 'ileza'. *South African Journal,* 1, 1824, p. 25.

[43] Compare Leask (1992): 'Sir Walter Scott in his historical novel *Waverley* – significantly subtitled *Sixty Years Since* – evacuated and resolved the ideological divisions of early nineteenth-century Scotland into a romantic past, thereby constructing an image of the present as serene and untroubled' (p. 88).

[44] *SAJ*, 2, 1824, lines 19-22.

[45] Pringle deleted the final two lines above in the *African Sketches* version of 1834.

[46] Mungo Park, *Travels in the Interior of Africa*, ed. by John Keay (1799; London, Folio Society, 1984), p. 84.

[47] I Kings 19. 4.

[48] 'Go, return on thy way to the wilderness of Damascus,' that is, the city. I Kings 19. 15.

[49] I Kings 19. 16.

[50] I Kings 21. 18-22.

[51] Damian Shaw, *The Writings of Thomas Pringle* (unpublished doctoral dissertation, Cambridge University: 1996).

[52] John Croumbie Brown, *Pastoral Discourses* (1847), p. 108.

Ngugi Wa Thiong'o and the Search for a Populist Landscape Aesthetic

Renee Binder and G.W. Burnett

How does a given society perceive its environment? White (1967) attributed the West's environmental degradation to aspects of its Judaeo-Christian tradition and thereby made pursuit of comparative environmental ethics essential. Nonetheless, progress in comparative environmental ethics is, for want of insight, not easily achieved. One source of insight is the thought of the intellectual élite, among them serious novelists. This essay examines how Ngugi wa Thiong'o, East Africa's most prominent writer (Gaiownik, 1989), treats the landscape as a fundamental social phenomenon in two of his most important novels, *A Grain of Wheat* (1967, hereafter AGW) and *Petals of Blood* (1977, hereafter POB).

Ngugi uses the land as a projective symbol reflecting the emotional condition of his protagonists. The technique, recognized by his literary critics (see for example Jabbi, 1985; Ngara, 1985; Cook and Okemnimkpe, 1983; Killam, 1980; Muhoi, 1973; Sharma, 1988), arises from Ngugi's certainty that for the Gikuyu, his subjects, the land is the people, the central theme of society (Kenyatta, 1965, 22). Fixation with the land entails painstaking consideration of the landscape and this Ngugi provides through an apparently intuitively recognized landscape theory clearly resembling one recently developed in America. For Ngugi, a socialist, this theory is immoderately nostalgic. Ngugi's resolution of the dilemma between nostalgia for a lost landscape and the landscape's progressive potential suggests that many of Africa's environmental problems may arise from widespread alienation from the land. Incidentally, his approach questions the Western presumption that it is possible to manage a landscape separately from the society that depends on and shapes that landscape.

THE ARTIST

Ngugi wa Thiong'o's literary works include numerous plays and short stories, several in his native Gikuyu, but he is best known in the West for a series of five novels, *The River Between* (1965), *Weep Not, Child* (1964), *A Grain of Wheat* (1967), *Petals of Blood* (1977), and *Devil on the Cross* (1983). These novels explore the situation of the Gikuyu from the late pre-colonial period through the early years of Kenyan nationhood. They are most obviously political novels reflecting Ngugi's growing realization of his mission, political agitation of his own society. Because he portrays the independent government of Kenya as, if anything, worse than the colonial government, he has suffered both detention and self-imposed exile; nonetheless, he remains immensely popular with the *wananchi* (the Kenyan masses). Since his theme, the search for personal and collective freedom and dignity, is universal, his works have been popular both in Africa and among Western intellectuals.

The two novels *A Grain of Wheat* and *Petals of Blood*, being narrative, realistic 'whodunits', are stylistically and thematically the most available to Western readers. They are pivotal in understanding Ngugi's journey from humanism to socialism, and as his longest statements, they deal thoroughly with land alienation "from the historical point of view and as a process which continues in the present" (Gaiownik, 1989, 357). *A Grain of Wheat*, set in the days immediately prior to *uhuru* (independence), investigates the betrayal of Kihika, a fictional Mau Mau hero. *Petals of Blood* probes arson and political murders at a house of prostitution in postcolonial New Ilmorog. Both novels are complex, intricate stories laced with allusions to western philosophy and literature and African folklore, rich in symbolism, and full of characters acting their roles in a pageant of flashbacks that makes time into a labyrinth. Both works are major artistic achievements, and *Petals of Blood* attains, besides, a remarkable ideological synthesis and thereby considerable prominence in socialist literature (Ngara, 1985, 84).

AN ECOLOGICAL THEORY OF LANDSCAPE AESTHETICS

A Grain of Wheat and *Petals of Blood* embrace an ecological theory of landscape aesthetics that comprises both natural and cultural components while avoiding qualities of beauty and loveliness, or 'taste', as defining criteria. Ngugi's predicament, however, differs from that of Western theorists. Ngugi faces the problem of reconciling his society to landscapes transformed by imperialism and neoimperialism. Landscape theorists, particularly Americans, have sought to justify management, or active intervention in landscape deterioration, through an aesthetic free of individual and culturally sensitive standards of beauty. Without such an aesthetic perspective, landscape conservation is too easily dismissed as an individual response to offended personal taste, a taste which commands little public support. A broad aesthetic conceptualization can muster the consensus necessary to successful public action (Hiss, 1990, 126-223).

Appleton (1990, 21-2) defines the landscape as "the environment visually perceived", and the aesthetic as the pleasure in this perception. Pleasure is derived from appreciation of the two types of symbols contained in the landscape. One is natural, possibly genetic, "an intrinsic part of the survival behaviour of the species" (Appleton, 1990, 8). The other is cultural, one whose meaning must be learned for it to be understood and appreciated. The 'natural' symbol is "prospect and refuge" (Appleton, 1975, 69-75), in which satisfaction derives from the landscape's ability to meet the need to see without being seen. Response is intrinsic: prospect/refuge is not required in fact; rather, its mere symbol, for example light and dark, provokes an aesthetic response.

Subsequent theroreticians have accepted Appleton's biophysical bases for aesthetics but have emphasized the cultural symbols of identity, stability and control. Culturally, "...we do not so much discover aesthetically compelling properties in the environment ... as ascribe them to it on the basis of our individual and cultural beliefs, values and needs" (Costonis, 1982, 401). Groups protect their identity and stability by exercising control over landscapes, and landscapes symbolical of identity, stability and control are aesthetic (Bourassa, 1988, 250). Again, all that is required is the symbol, rather than the fact, of identity, stability and control. Locational patterns develop through the reciprocity of human impulses and natural agents, while aesthetics arise from these locational patterns consequent on the viewer's particular position and the landscape's relative size, scale, and physical diversity. The resulting landscape "promotes a sense of place and a sense of purpose within us not only as individuals but as societal groups" (Rodiek, 1988, 36). Landscape is, consequently, heritage to be shared with future generations as a cultural resource. It contains the material symbols of culture. People, as a result, inherit a responsibility to maintain control over their landscapes, thus making the future a serious part of their lives and thinking.

The ecological theory of landscape aesthetics recognizes several contrasts: cultural symbols and natural symbols; prospect and refuge; cultural identity and stability versus control and the ability to manipulate. How a society blends these contrasts results in a landscape unique in time, space and culture. The freedom to control and manipulate, recognized by Bourassa (1988), but fully articulated by Rodiek (1988), is critical; it is this that creates responsibility and requires that the future be taken seriously. Ultimately, landscapes deserve serious attention. They are conserved not because they are beautiful or pretty and quaint but because they contain the symbols that define civilization. To destroy a landscape is to destroy society and to control the landscape is to control society.

THE LANDSCAPE LOST

Ngugi embraces and adroitly uses an ecological theory of landscape aesthetics in his narratives. He avoids sublime description, and when he does use it, as in describing a moonlit Rift Valley, it is to tell the reader what a character did not see (AGW, 67). His characters perform in a magnificent setting, blind to the grandeur of the props. Rejecting romanticism, Ngugi's concern is the ordinary landscape of the *wananchi* which he introduces in the opening pages of *A Grain of Wheat* with the anti-hero and protagonist, Mugo.

The landscape's prominence at the novel's opening suggests its conspicuous role in the drama and its first appearance anticipates the changes Ngugi will diagram in words, the evolution of both landscape and ideology. Traditionally, the Gikuyu dispersed themselves in clans along their numerous ridges. Facing violent rebellion, the British gathered these dispersed rural people into centralized villages, the more easily to protect them from the rebels in the forest – and to prevent their support of the rebels. Colonial "new" Thabai, the focus of *A Grain of Wheat*, is such a village:

> When built, it had combined a number of ridges ... And even in 1963, it had not changed much from the date in 1955 when the grass thatched roofs, and mudwalls hastily collected together, while the whiteman's sword hung dangerously above people's necks ... Some huts had crumbled; a few had been pulled down. The village maintained an unbroken orderliness; from a distance it appeared a huge mass of grass from which smoke rose to the sky as from a burnt sacrifice. (AGW, 3)

Traditional houses have been thrown together non-traditionally as a result of foreign, imperial imposition. In a village of "unbroken orderliness from a distance", some huts have already tumbled and a few have been torn down. The landscape is already a contradiction portending destruction and rebuilding of society. This mass of huts commences Ngugi's ideological journey from an individualistic humanism to a collective Marxism, and the smoke rising up to the sky "as from a burnt sacrifice" warns of the human sacrifices necessary to the transformation.

Ngugi's initial humanism engulfs individuals in a love of land, grants them self-identity and calls them forth to action. When she speaks of the land, Mumbi's voice "trembles with passion", she feels the unity of her fiancé's workshop, Thabai, earth, and heaven (AGW, 78). She rides on strange waves, fights hunger and thirst, and struggles with demons to bring glad tidings to her people. Her excitement leads to the simple, fateful question, "Do you think it will always be like this, I mean the land?" (AGW, 79). Stories of "how the land was taken from the black people", harden Kihika, the warrior-hero, against "these people, long before he had even encountered a white face", and leads him to rebellion, the forest, and the betrayal and death on which Ngugi's story turns (AGW, 83).

The passion for landscape and the sorrow felt for its loss gives Ngugi a powerful opportunity to contrast, sometimes comically, Gikuyu and British landscape ideals. Mumbi's father's home, in all its chaotic glory, is remembered fondly:

> His home consisted of three huts and two granaries where crops were stored after harvests. A bush – a dense mass of creepers, brambles, thorn trees, nettles and other stinging plants – formed a natural hedge around the home. Old Thabai, in fact, was a village of such grass-thatched huts thinly scattered along the ridge. The hedges were hardly ever trimmed; wild animals used to make their lairs there. (AGW, 75)

The British willed to impose their "order" on the Gikuyu jumble and the epitome of contrast is the garden of District Officer John Thompson:

> A neatly trimmed hedge of cider shrub surrounded the Thompson's bungalow. At the entrance, green creepers coiled on a wood stand, massed into an arch at the top

> and then fell to the hedge at the sides. The hedge enclosed gardens of flowers: flame lilies, morning glory, sunflowers, bougainvillea. However, it was the gardens of roses that stood out in colour above the others. (AGW, 36)

Elsewhere an African contemplates another such garden: "A well finished application of sweat, art and craftsmanship over a number of years, so much energy and brains wasted on beautifying trees" (POB, 146). The "primordial trees", according to Thompson, awe the "primitive minds", and their "darkness and mystery" have led Africans "inside to magic and ritual" (AGW, 55). The primitive unkept landscape created primitive people so that by taming the wildness, the British tame the primitive man. Altering the landscape, in other words, asserts social control and advances imperialism. Thompson's garden is more than a focus for his private contemplation: it is a refuge from Africa and an inspiration for his imperialism. In *Weep Not, Child*, the owner of another such garden sums it up well:

> Mr. Howlands always felt a certain amount of victory whenever he walked through it all. He alone was responsible for taming this unoccupied wildness. (31)

From and through these sanctuaries, the British imposed "civilization" on Gikuyuland, creating a land of "paths in the neatly hedged fields – a result of land consolidation" and new villages of "huts, grass, lives crammed together" (AGW, 118). The approach of *uhuru* raises expectations that the landscape of the conqueror, as symbolized by Thompson's garden, will again be replaced with the landscape of the ancestors as symbolized by Mumbi's father's farm.

Nearing the conclusion of *A Grain of Wheat*, as the *uhuru* celebration approaches, rain, supposedly a symbol of hope, rebirth, and renewal, dominates the story and reinforces the expectations of the *wananchi*. Often brooding, oppressive, and sometimes torrential, Ngugi's water metaphors in *A Grain of Wheat* provoke uncertain critical interpretation (Jabbi, 1985), possibly because few of Ngugi's critics recognize that rain in the wrong amounts and at the wrong time in East Africa can be as destructive as no rain at all. This characteristic Ngugi finds it necessary to explain later:

> When a good crop was expected it was known through a rhythmic balanced alternation of rain and sunshine. A bad crop was preceded by sporadic rains or by a continuous heavy downpour which suddenly gave way to sunshine for the rest of the season. (POB, 33)

Nonetheless, the majority of the characters share the renewal interpretation of the rains, accepting its rejuvenating powers and the promise it provides. They rejoice:

> Murangu on high never slept: he always let his tears fall to this, our land, from Agu and Agu. As we the children used to sing:
>
> Ngai has given Gikuyu a beautiful country,
> Never without food or water or grazing fields.

> It is good so Gikuyu should praise Ngai all the time,
> For he has been ever so generous to them. (AGW, 178)

The rain and *uhuru* come together to culminate in a sort of rebirth of the landscape. But, is it rain that revives the landscape, or the new unity of the people, however fleeting and momentary?

> In the afternoon, the sun appeared and brightened the sky. The mist which in the morning lingered in the air went. The earth smoked grey like freshly dropped cow-dung. The warming smoke spread and thinned upwards into the clear sky. (AGW, 215)

This brightening, new freshness of the earth brings with it hope, a rebirth, and an opportunity to right the order of things. But as *uhuru* is achieved and as the land flowers, Mugo, the alienated, helpless antihero and false hero of Mau Mau, confesses his sin in a singular act of true heroism, which is also, ironically, his ultimate act of despair: it is an act that strangely reunites but also reveals the false mythology of the struggle of *uhuru*.

The landscape in this false mythology of freedom is a contradiction that Ngugi leaves unresolved. The ideal, Mumbi's father's farm, rests in nostalgia for a world that is no longer. The hope of the *wananchi* is that, with the British departure, the old ways and the old world will effortlessly return. They face *uhuru* with a foreboding, exhausted by its expectation and with a sense of disappointment in its arrival. Wambui possibly feels the lethargy as much as any character:

> Wambui sat on and watched the drizzle and grey mist for a few minutes. Darkness was creeping into the hut. Wambui was lost in a solid consciousness of a terrible anti-climax to her activities in the fight for freedom... Then she shook herself, trying to bring her thoughts to the present. I must light the fire. First I must sweep the room. How dirt can so quickly collect in a clean hut. But she did not rise to do anything. (AGW, 243)

Wambui is symbolic of the potential for action and at the same time the failure to act – action will bring about change for the collective good, failure to act will result in an endless cycle of despair. The cycle of rebirth and destruction has exhausted the participants but must continue in order to reach the ultimate landscape, the ultimate societal ideal.

The problem Ngugi presents but fails to resolve in *A Grain of Wheat* centres on nostalgia. The *wananchi* have lost their land to a foreign power and with it their ability to control and manipulate the landscape. Their identity has been shattered and with it their stability. The hope is that, with the departure of the foreign power, the landscape, like some ancestor of long-ago, will return and all will be right with the world. The hope and expectation romanticizes the past, and romanticism, of course, is anathema to socialism. Wambui recognizes that *uhuru* is a call to action, that the fire must be lighted and the room swept, but she fails to rise. The contradiction of nostalgia and a progressive social order is one that Ngugi must face squarely in *Petals of Blood*.

THE LANDSCAPE CORRUPTED

Petals of Blood, a good murder mystery, is also an examination of human alienation in a Kenya swept by neoimperialism. In this novel, two themes are intertwined and co-mingled: the landscape as the savaged product of human alienation, and as the product of capitalist exploitation. Ngugi's attempt to explain the former and contend with the latter, however, resolves the problem of nostalgia.

The savaged landscape of human despair is not a new theme, however, since it was introduced in *A Grain of Wheat*. Gikonyo, married to Mumbi, returns home from six years in detention only to discover that his wife has borne a collaborator's child. Intensely bitter, he drifts aimlessly through new Thabai and reflects, and his thoughts echo his alienation and disillusionment:

> ...one street led into another and dust trailed behind his heels. The very air choked him: Thabai was just another detention camp; could he ever get out of it? But go where? He followed the tarmac road which led him into Rung'ei. The Indian shops had been moved into a new center; the tall buildings were made of stones; electric lights and tarmac streets made the place appear as a slice of the big city. The sewage smelt, it had not been cleaned for a year. He went on and came to the African shops in Rung'ei; they were closed; tall grass and wild bush clambered around the walls of the rusty buildings and covered the ground that was once the market place... The African shops, as he learnt later, had been forced to shut as a collective punishment to the ridges. Blue smoke from a few huts was lost in the bright midday sun... Nothing in the new village now attracted him... Was there anywhere else to go? (AGW, 117–18)

Gikonyo has a clear vision of the future. This, the 'new Kenya', the land of the alienated, is the landscape of disorder, chaos, disgust, and the futility of smoke lost in the bright midday sun. The bush which has overtaken the African shops represents the suppression and decay of the whole of African society. Gikonyo feels trapped in this landscape, another detention camp.

The landscape of despair is concealed beneath the hopes and expectations of the *wananchi*. But, it is recognizable; a kind of rough, red lacerated, "bumpy, battered land ... sickly crops just recovering from recent drought, one more scourge which had afflicted the country...", filled with "...anxious faces of mothers dry and cracked ... scattered on the strips of shamba" (AGW, 9). It does not beckon nostalgia and it is to come into full flower in *Petals of Blood*.

In *Petals of Blood* an alienated *wananchi* have totally lost control of their land. The landscape itself is now corrupted and unproductive as if man, alienated from his labour, his fellow man, and himself, is now alienated from nature too. The landscape is eroded, raw, vicious and most often seen as vindictive or at best capricious and unpredictable. It yields little:

> Did you have a good gathano harvest in your place? Here it was poor and we don't know if the grains of maize and beans can last us to the end of the njahi rains. That is, if the rains come... (POB, 8)

And this failure to earn from the land destroys the fibre of society:

> The land seemed not to yield much and there was no virgin soil to escape to as in those days before colonialism. His sons had gone away to European farms and the big towns... So Njuguna, like the other peasants in all the huts scattered about Ilmorog Country, had to be contented with small acreage, poor implements and with his own small family labor. (POB, 9)

If rain sets the mood of expectancy in *A Grain of Wheat*, then the road provides that mood in *Petals of Blood*. In *A Grain of Wheat,* the railroad provides the imagery of colonial power, an iron thing devouring forests and linking African villages to a larger world. The railway station becomes a focal point for leisure, "...a meeting place for the young..." where on Sunday "...people just went there to meet one another, to talk, to gossip, to laugh..." (71). Indeed, poverty-and-drought-stricken and depopulated, Ilmorog, the center of action in *Petals of Blood*, is linked by natural roads to global events in the course of human history:

> Ilmorog plains themselves are a part of the Great Rift that formed a natural highway joining Kenya ... to the legendary waters of the River Jordan in Palestine. For centuries, and even up to this day, the God of Africa and the Gods of other lands have wrestled for the mastery of man's soul and for the control of the results of man's holy sweat... (POB, 68)

However, the road of greater concern to the characters is something more mundane and inglorious:

> The road had once been a railway line joining Ilmorog to Ruwa-ini. The line had carried wood and charcoal and wattle barks from Ilmorog forests to feed the machines and men of Ruwa-ini. It had eaten the forests, and after accomplishing the task, the two rails were removed and the ground became a road – a kind of a road – that now gave no evidence of its former exploiting glory. (POB, 11)

Poverty and drought finally stir the people of Ilmorog down this road and to action. Aroused by Abdulla, a maimed Mau Mau hero, the villagers are reminded that the ground on which they trod had been hallowed by those who had fought and died for Kenya and that they owe it to these ancestors to seek a better life, if not for themselves, at least for their children. En masse, the villagers take to the road, journeying to Nairobi to beseech their political representatives to take some action to assist Ilmorog. Their effort gains them little besides humiliation and insult, but upon returning from the journey, the rain finally comes to renew the endless cycle of life. Below the surface, however, is a new expectancy of a threatened future, one created by the journey itself:

> ...brooding not too far below their tranquil existence was their consciousness of the journey and the experiences which spoke of another less sure, more troubled world which could, any time, descend upon them, breaking asunder their rain filled sun-warmed calm... (POB, 197)

And so it comes to pass:

> ...we did not then know that within a year the journey, like a God who cannot let his generosity be forgotten, would send its emissaries from the past, to transform Ilmorog and change our lives utterly, Ilmorog and us utterly changed. (POB, 242)

The emissaries that come to Ilmorog are the forces of international capitalism and their local thugs and rascals. They bring the full fury of development creating a totally false, commoditized and commercialized landscape. Capitalism transforms the landscape to one of decay and decadence where alienated people feed on each other.

> This was the society they were building...in which a black few, allied to other forces from Europe, would continue the colonial game of robbing others of their sweat, denying them the right to grow to full flowers in air and sunlight.... (POB, 294)

Plots are carved from various farms to make a shopping centre and as shops are planned, people are required to apply for building permits. A mobile van from the African Economic Bank arrives to explain to the peasants and herdsmen how they can acquire loans. The loans sour and eventually town ownership is concentrated in the hands of the wealthy while the *wananchi* become debtors and servants in their own home. The new Ilmorog degenerates into a dehumanized landscape of:

> ...neon-lights; of bars, lodgings, groceries, permanent sales and bottled Theng'eta; of robberies, strikes; lockouts, murders and attempted murders; of prowling prostitution in cheap night clubs; of police stations, police raids, police cells... (POB, 190)

The landscape is chaos where all sense of identity, stability and control, the fundamentals of aesthetics, are hopelessly lost.

RESOLUTION

The socialist, Karega, is the one character to achieve something of a personal enlightenment. He asks the fateful questions, and accepting the implied answer, drives the logic to its full conclusion: "Must we have this world? Is there only one world? Then we must create another world, a new earth..." (POB, 294).

Karega's awakening is both existential and social. It is a private, personal realization demanding commitment and action: "...since the only thing he had now was his two hands, he would somehow sell its creative power to whoever would buy it..." (POB, 302). But at the same time it calls forth the *wananchi* to "...then join with all the other hands in ensuring that at least they had a fair share of what their thousand sets of fingers produced..." (POB, 302). And the awakening is compelling; the future depends on it:

> ... only then would the kingdom of man and woman really begin, they joying and loving creative labor... For a minute he was so carried on the waves of this vision and

> of the possibilities it opened up for all the Kenyan working and peasant masses that he forgot the woman beside him ... and he knew he was no longer alone. (POB, 344)

Karega's new awareness also resolves the problem of nostalgia, the hankering for a long gone world. Karega roughly equates the land with the ancestor, and thereby rests his call for collective action thoroughly in Gikuyu traditions of collective ownership:

> Why anyway, should soil, which after all was what was Kenya, be owned by an individual? Kenya, the soil, was the people's common shamba, and there was no way it could be right for a few, a section, or a single nationality, to inherit for their sole use what was communal any more than it would be right for a few sons and daughters to own and monopolize their father or mother... (POB, 302)

The call, however, is also Marxist. Karega's vision coincides with his new ideology and this futuristic view rejects a romanticized, idealized past:

> ...we must not preserve our past as a museum: rather, we must study it critically, without illusions, and see what lessons we can draw from it in today's battlefield of the future and the present. But to worship it – no. Maybe I used to do it: but I don't want to continue worshipping in the temples of the past without tarmac roads, without electric cookers, a world dominated by slavery to nature. (POB, 323)

DISCUSSION

In the West, sweeping structural changes following mass availability of the automobile have resulted in a considerable anxiety over the fate of landscapes that define ourselves, regionally and nationally. Preservation of structures, views and scenes on the basis of their beauty is a poor rationale. Beauty, it is commonly believed, is in the eye of the beholder, so that in egalitarian societies there is little to distinguish one scene from another, a situation compounded where land use decisions are based on maximum efficiency (Postman, 1993, 50). Over the past two decades, theorists, particularly in America, have attempted to confront the problem of the relativity of aesthetics by developing a concept for landscape evaluation that is ecological and therefore indifferent to beauty *per se* as an object of preservation. The result makes aesthetic virtues of the cultural identity, stability and control that a landscape can imply. The concept grants society much freedom and responsibility to determine the nature of the stage upon which it performs its drama, and it has considerably legitimized the idea, if not the specific targets, of landscape management.

In East Africa, imperialism and neoimperialism have also provoked a landscape crisis, which Ngugi wa Thiong'o analyses. Foreign political and economic power altered the symbols contained in the landscape, effectively disorienting the society they sought to control. Eventually commercializing the landscape, capitalism has taken from the *wananchi* the ability to control it and therefore their future. Society's freedom and sense of responsibility are reduced and the *wananchi* are denied the sense of identity and stability landscape control suggests. This alienation from the land, rather than the economics of subsistence agriculture and excessive population growth alone, may explain much of the decline in Africa's environmental condition. The *wananchi* can hardly be expected to feel responsibility for things, including the land, over which they have little control.

Ngugi's analysis, however, illustrates two issues about which conservationists should feel considerable discomfort. Through Karega, Ngugi makes it clear that progressive societies cannot afford the luxury of nostalgia. Conservation based on a bittersweet longing for the things of the past is objectionable, incompatible with the interest of the masses. Conservation requires, instead, a critical assessment of the past and preservation of those things that satisfy human biological needs or contribute to cultural identity and stability.

Furthermore, Ngugi rejects, out-right, professionalism and the bureaucracy as a valid force in making conservation decisions, preferring instead the image of thousands of fingers working together to shape the course of human history, including its conservation ethic. Sick societies produce sick landscapes; the cure is to change society. It is futile to think that a landscape can be 'managed' apart from the society that created it. Ngugi's assessment is based on his realization that colonial and nationalist Kenya are not democratic; however, this is also a realization that pluralistic societies are forced to base conservation on professionalism, a form of élitism, and that they fail to develop a landscape aesthetic that is fundamentally populist.

REFERENCES

Appleton, J. 1975. *The Experience of Landscape*. London: Wiley.

Appleton, J. 1990. *The Symbolism of Habitat*. Seattle: University of Washington Press.

Bourassa, Steven C. 1988. "Toward a Theory of Landscape Aesthetics", *Landscape and Urban Planning* **15**: 241-52.

Cook, David and Michael Okemnimkpe 1983. *Ngugi wa Thiong'o: An Exploration of His Writings*. London: Heinemann.

Costonis, J. J. 1982. "Law and Aesthetics: A Critique and a Reformation of the Dilemma", *Michigan Law Review* **80**: 335-461.

Gaiownik, Melissa 1989. "Ngugi wa Thiong'o". In *Contemporary Authors*, New Revision Series 27, pp. 355-8.

Hiss, Tony 1990. *The Experience of Place*. New York: Vintage Books.

Jabbi, Ba-Buakei 1985. "The Structure of Symbolism in *A Grain of Wheat*", *Research in African Literature* **16**: 210-42.

Kenyatta, Jomo 1965. *Facing Mt. Kenya*. New York: Vintage Books.

Killam, G. D. 1980. *An Introduction to the Writings of Ngugi wa Thiong'*o. London: Heinemann.

Muhoi wa Kikinyaga 1973. "Kenya: Trying to Silence the Truth", *The African Communist* **73**: 96-118.

Ngara, Emmanuel 1985. *Art and Ideology in the African Novel: A Study of the Influence of Marxism on African Writing*. London: Heinemann.

Ngugi wa Thiong'o 1964. *Weep Not. Child*. London: Heinemann.

Ngugi wa Thiong'o 1965. *The River Between*. London: Heinemann.

Ngugi wa Thiong'o 1967. *A Grain of Wheat*. London: Heinemann.

Ngugi wa Thiong'o 1977. *Petals of Blood*. London: Heinemann.

Ngugi wa Thiong'o 1983. *Devil on the Cross*. London: Heinemann.

Postman, Neil 1993. *Technopoly: The Surrender of Culture to Technology*. New York: Vintage Books.

Rodiek, J. 1988. "The Evolving Landscape", *Landscape and Urban Planning* **16**: 35-44.

Sharma, G. N. 1988. "Socialism and Civilization: The Revolutionary Traditionalism of Ngugi wa Thiong'o", *Ariel* **19**:21-30.

White, Lynn 1967. "The Historic Roots of Our Ecological Crisis", *Science* **155**: 1203-7.

'Penetrating' Foreign Lands: Contestations Over African Landscapes. A Case Study from Eastern Zimbabwe.

Heike Schmidt

INTRODUCTION

For the last few years Africanists have shown increasing interest in landscape. Themes like frontier, pioneers, explorers, and more recently, religious landscape, conservation, environment, national parks, and representations of landscape in literature and exhibitions, have been researched. A variety of disciplines is concerned with these topics, for example, history, and in particular spatial history, political geography, anthropology and literary criticism.[1]

Dealing with images and identities historically usually poses methodological problems. The high period of European expansion in southern Africa was the nineteenth century, for which written sources tend to be scarce, while oral sources seem to lack differentiation for the purpose of reconstructing locality. However, as the events discussed in this paper are located in the more recent past, a variety of sources were available: government files in the National Archives of Zimbabwe and the National Record Centre, as well as in the Provincial and District Administrator's respective Offices, mission records in the American Methodist Episcopal Church Archives, and papers in private possession. Further, interviews were conducted with the actual participants. Those interviewed include chiefs and traditional healers, 'commoners' living in the area, as well as employees of the tea estates.

This paper is based on a case study from the Honde Valley in eastern Zimbabwe on the border with Mozambique.[2] In 1952 the resident population was estimated to be 400 families.[3] Unusually late for the region, European influence only began to become significant in the 1950s. Although the northern part of the Valley had been owned by a succession of companies and multi-national concerns since the occupation in 1890, it was not surveyed until 1951 and 1952. In the following years two tea estates were established and in 1960 a road was completed which ran through the entire Valley.[4] Thus the 1950s were an important turning point in the history of land and landscape in the area.

This paper tells the story of the beginnings of two tea plantations between 1951 and 1958. These are situated on the western slopes of the Honde Valley, chiefly on rainforest land.[5] First, European and African readings of this landscape will be mapped out. Secondly, it will be demonstrated how competing imaginations followed from these readings which translated into contestations over land. Thirdly, a recent battle over spiritual landscape will be related. This is followed by a brief conclusion.

I. LOOKING FOR A SITE: DIFFERENT READINGS OF LANDSCAPE

In 1952 W.A.K. Igoe bought approximately 48,000 acres of land for £30,000 on behalf of Aberfoyle Plantations Limited, at that time a London-based company with rubber and sugar plantations in Malaysia and Mozambique.[6] The land was part of Inyanga Block, a farm which had previously belonged to a succession of companies. The first title deed to the Block, which initially consisted of roughly 154,400 acres (60,000 hectares), had been granted to the Anglo-French Matabeleland Company in 1895 and issued in 1897. This was part of the British South Africa Company's attempts to draw capital into the developing colonial economy.[7] In 1930 the Block was split. The southern part, called Holdenby Block, was bought by the London Rhodesia Company (Lonrho), and the northern portion, approximately 90,000 acres, was bought by the Hanmer brothers.[8] In 1948 Lonrho sold their part to the Rhodesian Government[9] which in turn sold it to a group of Rhodesian businessmen. These finally entered the agreement with Igoe in 1952[10].

Even such a brief sketch history of the ownership of Inyanga Block suggests a variety of interested parties over the years. It is important to differentiate a range of 'European' and 'African' interests in and attitudes to the land and landscape concerned, because these informed colonial land appropriation policies. Therefore the years from 1951 to 1952, when Igoe was looking for a potential site for a plantation in Rhodesia, will be analysed in depth in order to map out the different agendas of the main parties involved: multinational companies, explorers and experts, pioneers and settlers, colonial administrators, and Valley inhabitants.

EUROPEAN READINGS

Multinational Companies

In 1894 the Anglo-French Matabeleland Company applied to the Administrator of Rhodesia, Jameson, for land in Matabeleland. Instead, they were granted Inyanga Block in Manicaland on condition that they would spend '...£60,000 in mining or farming operations' during the following years.[11] By 1928, when Inyanga Block had been owned by the Company for more than thirty years, the land was still unexplored by Europeans. When the Anglo-French Matabeleland Company went into liquidation, they could not provide any detailed information to potential buyers. They had merely employed a European resident of the

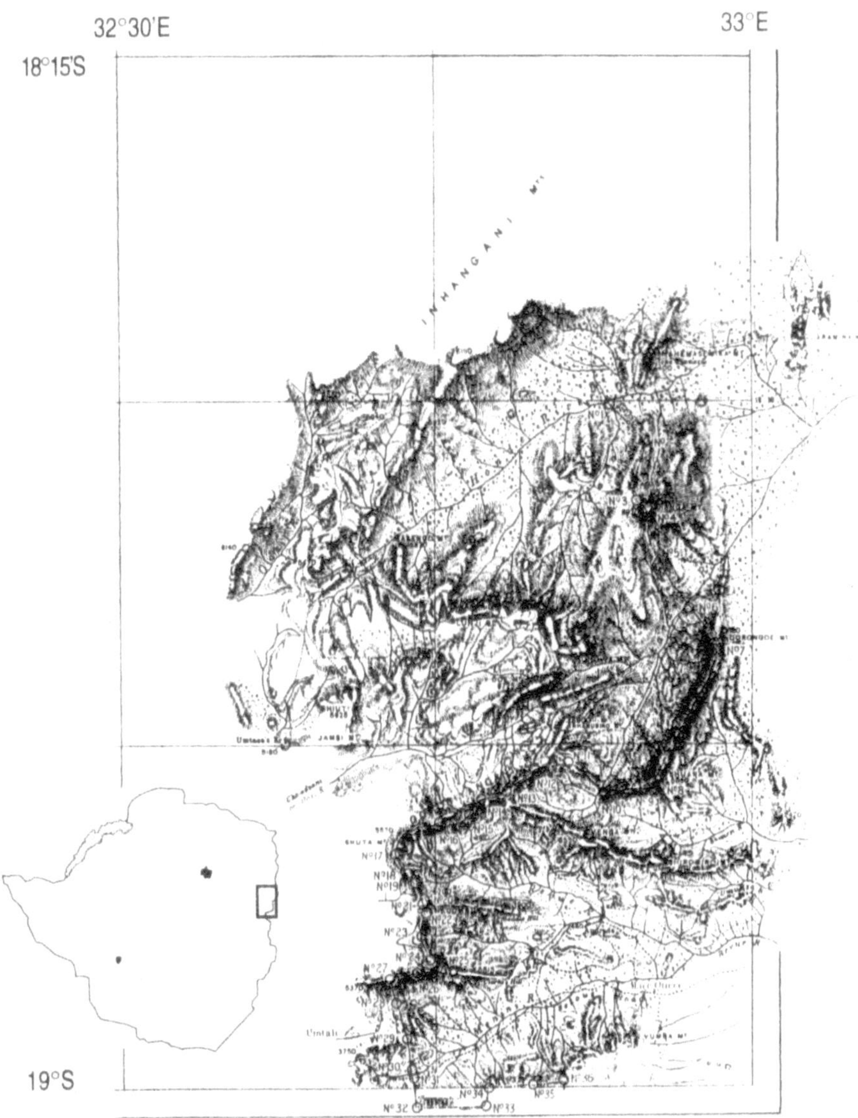

FIGURE 1. The Honde valley area in 1899. The northernmost marked boundary point (No.1) lies on the Honde river.

From Map of the Anglo-Portuguese Boundary in East Africa – Manica Section. Transferred at the Intelligence Division, War Office from I.D., W.O., No. 953(B). Reproduced by permission of the Syndics of Cambridge University Library.

District, Major van Niekerk, as a ranger.[12] This was a practice often exercised by absentee landlords, and van Niekerk held the same position at other properties in the area. His main task was to collect rent from Africans tenants and mission outstations and to represent the owner's interests towards local government representatives.[13] But it appears that he hardly knew the Block.

Therefore, interested buyers were forced to approach the Native Commissioner Inyanga in order to gain some information about the area. They inquired in 1928:

> Would you be so good as to favour us confidentially with a report on this property, referring to the class of land, any work being carried out there on, its approximate value and if it has any development possibilities.[14]

The Native Commissioner wrote in response that he had only recently arrived in the District and therefore did not know the area under question. Instead, he suggested, the District Cattle Inspector might be of help as he had recently visited the Block.[15] As late as the early 1940s Lonrho relied on a ranger, by now Miss I E van Niekerk, for information on their property.[16]

The 'explorer'[17] employed by Igoe in 1951 in order to find land for him in Rhodesia laconically summarised his view of the earlier owners of the Block:

> It was previously held by Europeans purely as a speculation and was sold to the Native Department a few years ago.[18]

He further explained in a report to Igoe:

> You must understand that in the early days large grants of land were made principally to mining companies. For instance the Inyanga block originally belonged to the Anglo French Corporation who of course took it off the map and never saw it until they sold it.[19]

Igoe expressed his surprise that the Block had hitherto been unexplored:

> ...it is still incomprehensible to me that the top plateau has never been completely explored and, except for a reconnaissance made 25 years ago by an old inhabitant, no Europeans have penetrated into the interior of this extremely large block.[20]

Previous owners' interest had been restricted to an acreage which could be located on a map, or – in other words – to colonial land speculation. Igoe was fascinated by the opportunity this left for him and understood his own role differently. He was a company director, but first and foremost he saw himself as a pioneer and settler. The *Farming Gazette Supplement* characterised him in 1985 as 'a London Irish businessman, fighter pilot and international rugby trialist', certainly not as a man usually to be found at the boardroom table.[21]

The attempt by Igoe and 'his explorer' to set their own interests aside from those of previous owners can only partly be convincing. Despite Igoe's preparedness to explore and invest, he did not look for plantation land for any specific use. Rather, he applied what could be called a negative definition of land: he was interested in those properties left over from the 'scramble for Africa'. This is exemplified in a report by 'the explorer', in which he tried to convince Igoe to buy Inyanga Block:

> I think that this bit of country is quite unique and I doubt whether the opportunity to acquire land suitable for the planting of crops requiring a heavy rainfall is likely to occur anywhere else in Rhodesia. This is in fact the last large block of undeveloped land in the heavy rainfall area in the Colony.[22]

Explorers and Experts

In the 1950s Igoe and Aberfoyle Plantations Ltd. were prepared to invest in this – as one of his sons later called it – '...comparatively isolated and little publicised land on the east side of the Nyanga escarpment'.[23] Once the Block was located, it was necessary to send explorers and experts in order to establish the value and potential of the property, and thus to permit useful future investment.

Again the explorer set himself and his task apart from earlier speculators:

> These large grants of land tended to prevent development in this area. Now they were gradually being cut up.

And he continued to explain,

> You must appreciate that Rhodesia is really not much more than fifty years old, and that until roads penetrated into these districts that [sic] the large holdings did not become broken up.[24]

What emerges from this report are images of potential and need for development. Once these were established, experts were employed in order to assess the viability of specific projects. This was the case with a tea expert who was hired to establish the tea growing potential on an inspection tour when the second plantation was being established. He recommended in a report written in 1955:

> We should go ahead in this good, rich and developing country. There may be better land in Africa but Inyanga is at least as good as the Anamallais, and we should lose no time in assessing the position in detail so as to ascertain the ultimate possibilities with the minimum of delay.[25]

Arguably, the images created by experts and explorers of the land and their own involvement with it differed in one regard. Whereas the expert stressed possibility, the explorer appears to have seen his specific role as overcoming the impossible by venturing into the 'unknown'. Both, however, emphasised that their project was different from that of settlers and early speculators, and both were interested in the development potential of land. Also, both stressed the inaccessibility of the area. One of the tea experts contended in 1952 that exploration had been limited to the fringes of the Block and that there was need for better means of communication:

> The whole area is very inaccessible and it is only within the last few months that a start has been made towards driving an inlet into the property; very slow progress is, however, being made, mainly owing to the nature of the country to be traversed coupled with the fact that very little labour is at the moment available, and a road-head has not yet penetrated sufficiently far to be of any practical use; the only means of access at the moment is therefore a very rough and mountainous jeep-track as far as the head of the Sumba River Valley, some three miles into the property from the northern boundary. From there on any investigation must be carried out on foot, and a thorough traverse of the block would entail several weeks in camp and much heavy walking.[26]

Pioneers and Settlers

Readings of landscape by pioneers and settlers produced probably the most dramatic counter-images. Peter Anderson in his work on the Fish River Bush in South Africa argues that the trekboers' '... wagons were the vehicles of frontier, the agents of encounter'.[27] Pioneers and settlers were the ones who created the frontier, who defined the boundary between the known and the unknown, between settlement and 'no-man's land'. Anderson shows how these people were successful in overcoming the apparent chaos of the undefined by inhabiting the foreign lands.[28]

The explorer, however, saw himself in this role of crossing and thus defining the frontier, and for this reason needed to point out the limitations of settler involvement in the imagination of landscape compared to his own capacity. Thus, he argued in the context of the absence of road construction on the Block, due to difficult terrain:

> ... this is, of course, one of the reasons why the country has not been developed as most places where an ox-wagon could be taken have been developed.

And he continued:

> In the early days you only developed places where you could get an ox-wagon in, and places where you could grow maize successfully.[29]

But a counter-image to the above exists, which gives a sense of unlimited power in the imagination and making of landscape. Because settlers and pioneers dared to 'penetrate the impenetrable', they had the great opportunity to transform 'wilderness' into 'known space'. This is, for example, apparent in Father Lewis's autobiography. He had been the resident Anglican priest in the Honde Valley in the 1960s and personally knew most of the 'European' population in the District. Writing about the northern part of Inyanga Block and adjacent land, both on the plateau, just beyond the Valley, he states:

> The Downs themselves, with their settled European population and their holiday cottages, were largely the work of a handful of pioneers who arrived in the nineteen-thirties. Major McIlwaine and the Hanmer brothers found bare wind-swept hills, planted trees (especially pines which spread like wildfire) and ended up with another Scotland, complete with man-made lakes and waterfalls and trout-streams. The steep and winding lanes were often shrouded in a Scotch mist.[30]

Native Commissioners

Finally, colonial administrators were also involved in the reading of African landscape. Their images mainly relate to the vastness, and to some degree to the improbability of their task: the administration of unknown and inaccessible lands. In 1951, the same year when 'Igoe's' explorer began 'penetrating' Holdenby Block, the Native Commissioner was commissioned to explore Holdenby Special Native Area. This area consisted of two territories on the Valley bottom, one directly adjacent to, and both east of Holdenby Block. The Native Commissioner described the area as follows:

> For the greater portion it is mountainous and has rivers flowing across it which pass through huge and grotesque gorges. It has been entered to a distance of six miles by road and it now remains to penetrate to the central parts and along the long narrow strip of the recently added Crown land adjacent to the Portuguese border.[31]

Thus features of the landscape were perceived to be 'grotesque' and the Valley '...a geographical oddity, its natural entrance being from Port territory.'[32] Six years later this area was still unexplored and another Native Commissioner reported:

> Holdenby, north of the Pungwe, is roadless, hilly, covered with tropical vegetation, and practically unknown.[33]

And in 1958 he stressed the need for a road:

> Lack of a road of any sort in the North East section of Holdenby is a handicap to the development of that area. This part of Holdenby is a wilderness of hills, streams and swamps, and a road will be difficult to construct there, but if funds are available next year an exploratory track will be cut into the area for a start to enable us to get in there.[34]

Now it was argued that exploration depended on the construction of roads – a curious image emerges: a Native Commissioner ordering a road gang of local people who know the area perfectly well to build a road which he can follow in order to find out where it leads to.

To sum up some of the interests and images evoked: The representative of a multinational insists that he does not speculate, but that he is prepared to gather information about the land in order to invest and develop. The explorer and the expert have a sense of potential of the land and their task is to investigate this potentiality. The explorer sets himself apart as the main perpetrator in moving beyond the frontier and sees the role of pioneers and settlers in the imagination of landscape as limited. A missionary on the other hand emphasises their great capacity to 'make' landscape. The Native Commissioner accentuates the vastness of his task and the inaccessibility of the land.

These European, and (as remains to be shown) African, constructions of the rainforest land served different interests. On the one hand, this surfaced in counter images. These are competing notions which need to be cross-referenced in the analysis in order to reconstruct a more complete picture. It appears that for all those involved it was important to set themselves apart from others in order to define and thus legitimate their specific role in the enterprise of European expansion. On the other hand, these images also informed each other. The most obvious examples are those of African agency, Africans as carriers, interpreters, and providers of food, and those of explorers and experts who were employed by the companies.

It is important to note that all the European images had one aspect in common, sexualisation of landscape: again and again there are images of penetration, opening up, getting in there, cutting into an area. It would be useful to deconstruct this sexualisation of foreign lands further and to show how far this related directly to European discourses on sexuality at the time.[35] In a different context Albert Wirz has argued that the construction of the primeval forest in nineteenth century Africa mirrors the construction of the male bourgeois self at the time.[36]

Another argument was put forward by the Comaroffs in their work on the first encounter between Tswana people and European missionaries. They emphasised the significance of the reading and transformation of African landscape by missionaries employed in order to establish power relations. To early nineteenth century missionaries, the vanguards of British colonialism, the African interior presented itself as virgin ground to be broken, landscape to be invested with history.[37] Here they follow T O Ranger and his argument that the colonial project, that is 'the transforming energies of capitalism, of literacy, of Christianity would at long last historicise the African landscape.[38] Therefore sexualisation in European narrative enabled the construction of landscape as wilderness, as uninhabited even if occupied,[39] and thus legitimated penetration. For this reason 'penetration' is an expression of more than mere imagery: real control over land was at issue.

AFRICAN READINGS

The rainforest is highly sexualised and gendered in mythology and prohibitions. Thus, local African men and women tell stories of trees with breasts and pools inhabited by female water spirits (*njuzu*).[40] There is not the space to attempt a complete reconstruction of African discourses. Rather, some dimensions will be highlighted in order to show the link between the imagination of landscape and the claim over land.

According to local belief, the rainforest on the slopes of the Valley is inhabited by spirits. If people dare to walk into the forest, the spirits will be tempted to tease them. They will appear in the shape of young girls, and trees themselves can look like women. Should the 'intruder' pay attention to the woman, or in particular, in the case of a man, show sexual interest, he or she is likely to disappear. An old man, 'traditional' healer (*n'anga*) and local 'kraalhead' (*sabhuku*) explains about the rainforest on the tea estates:

> All this area; if you walk through there, and you see, say, a tree – if you say something nasty about that tree, you get lost... There are strange trees there, which you might mistake for a person, and if you then say 'look at that girl' when actually it is a tree, you get lost.[41]

The reason given for this prohibition is that trees demand respect. The same belief concerns specific mountains which should not be talked about badly in their vicinity and fingers should not be pointed at them.[42] To give a current example: in 1992, a meeting was held at which government officials and male elders discussed the possibility of a pipeline from a pond on mount Nyangani to the city of Mutare. Chief Zindi, who understands himself as the keeper of the mountain, objected. Chief Zindi questioned the feasibility of the abstraction point and said it was a clear provocation of Nyangani, ancestral spirit.[43]

Another example is that of female water spirits (*njuzu*). They live in ponds up in the forest and appear as beautiful young women.[44] Again, the prohibition has a similar effect. If you see them in the distance and you pass by without paying attention, you are safe. But if you approach them, there are two alternatives. In the case of a man, if he attempts to have sex with a *njuzu*, he – or vital parts of his body – are likely to disappear. There are numerous stories of *njuzu* offering the 'intruder' to live with them at the bottom of the pond. In turn they are prepared to teach him or her to be a *n'anga*. If this offer is refused, the person disappears. Many *n'anga* claim to have started their career after having lived for days, or sometimes years with *njuzu*.[45]

An old man presented an interesting inversion of this narrative. He related that there is a pool on mount Nyangani, the slopes of which are covered with rainforest. In that pool there are *njuzu* who attract people by making the water look like gold. Hence white men tried to reach the pool. In this case not the people, but the pond itself disappeared:

> The white men tried to penetrate that place by dropping from planes using parachutes, but all was in vain: the place would disappear.[46]

All these stories have in common that they sexualise the rainforest. Or more specifically, they construct male human sexuality as being endangered by feminised landscape. This translates into gendered prohibitions: men are allowed to enter the forest for hunting, women for gathering of firewood, food and herbs, men post-sexual activity and post-menopausal women for annual rain rituals. Female discourses also depict the forest as a place of empowerment: in the forest young men are endangered through their sexuality, old men are teased for the absence of it.[47]

Arguably, the 'tabooisation' of the rainforest serves to protect environmental resources. Africans protected their agricultural production systems ecologically, by constructing the forests as spiritual landscapes.[48] As all the rivers and most streams in the area originate in the forest, it is of vital importance that the waterway should be protected from human waste. Also, prohibitions regarding approaching, not even to mention, of cutting down trees, protect the ecological balance between the high rainfall slopes and drier Valley bottom.

African readings of the rainforest state that the forest should only be entered on specific occasions, and not for daily land use. The landscape should be left untouched as far as possible. 'Not knowing the rules' and 'penetration' pose danger, which can be fatal. This exemplifies Ranger's argument that (pre-colonial) African claims to authority and to ownership of land were asserted through political and spiritual readings.[49]

To sum up, ideologically, contestations over land by Europeans and Africans become apparent in the sexualisation of landscape. Europeans legitimised their expansion into African territories by propagating the image of 'penetrating virgin forests'. For local Africans, on the other hand, penetration meant danger, a threat which arguably prevented forests from being turned into agricultural production areas.

II. ESTABLISHING A PLANTATION: HOW COMPETING IMAGINATIONS TRANSLATED INTO CONTESTATIONS OVER LAND

Recent literature on landscape in Southern Africa has emphasised the importance of cultural appropriation. The Comaroffs argue that European colonialism as a cultural project,

> .... depended, especially at first, on the construction of novel horizons and frontiers; on the export of signs and practices that would displace indigenous forms, recreating them in Europe's image.[50]

And Said, in the introduction to his book *Culture and Imperialism*, stresses the significance of narrative to imperialist land policies:

> The main battle in imperialism is over land, of course; but when it came to who owned the land, who had the right to settle and work on it, who kept it going, who won it back, and who now plans its future – these issues were reflected, contested, and even for a time decided in narrative.[51]

Nonetheless, it is important not to rest analysis with these imaginations and interpretations, as they translated into very real struggles over land and other environmental resources. Thus, the process of legitimising European expansion is related to African responses and perceptions.[52] Arguably, four changes occurred in European attitudes to land in the years 1952 to 1958, when Aberfoyle and Eastern Highlands tea plantations were established.

EUROPEAN TRANSFORMATIONS

First, recording turned into renaming. During the search for a site and in the process of establishing potentiality, the explorer's main task had been to record names, to draw maps, to learn about the locality. Now that the land had been bought, the emphasis shifted to making the unknown known and part of this was the introduction of new names which sounded more familiar. Anderson in his work on the Eastern Cape emphasises the significance of naming in the making of landscape:

> Naming, like travelling, is a primary activity in space. In this simple activity is prefigured settlement, survey, cartography, a whole history of spatial activity. A name is a tool for the further cognition of space, each one is a germinal noun in a sentence of spatial history.... Names are roots. They tell stories, they remember, they describe, they celebrate.[53]

Thus Igoe wrote in 1958 when he reconnoitred the land for the second tea estate:

> In order to prevent confusion arising with so many rivers in the area prefixed 'Nyam' we have renamed the principal ones as follows: the first river on the way in from the north entrance is the Honey, the next the Butterfly, and the third, the Buffalo.[54]

Secondly, 'wilderness' turned into acreage and rainforest into production area. Whereas by 1952 it was still considered to be extremely difficult to 'penetrate' the Block and establish acreage of the different areas, by 1954 exact acreage had been measured. Some production areas were beginning to be planted with tea, while others were set aside for future use. The tea fields appear to have tamed the wilderness of the forest.

Thirdly, the apparent remoteness was countered with a great effort to create communication networks. Both estates could only be approached from the plateau, down the escarpment on steep jeep tracks in the forest. As a result the European staff was forced to live in tents and to depend on local food supplies. They hardly ever had the opportunity to leave the Valley, the journey to the closest city for a weekend trip being too long and too cumbersome. This impaired the wellbeing of staff, and one of the early managers was forced to resign, as he failed to cope with the situation.[55] In order to improve the living condition of the European staff, but mainly for the transport of labour and produce to markets, the management began constructing roads in 1954.

This leads to the fourth, and probably most important, change. During the exploration of the Block African labour and expertise appears to have been obtained predominantly from areas adjacent to the Valley, and not from the Block itself. Once the plantation was being established, new need for an increased labour force arose. By 1952 Igoe still assumed that local labour would be cheap, as African tenants on the Block could be forced to enter into a labour agreement. Similar agreements were employed at the time throughout the Colony in order to create a stable workforce. Families were allowed to stay on the estate and cultivate limited areas of land, if, in return, the male adult members of the household worked at least 150 days per year for the Company.[56] Initially, therefore, Igoe reasoned that, 'being squatters, the natives are forced to work for us under pain of eviction'.[57]

However, soon the management had to realise that the task was more difficult. High hopes were set on the new road which would facilitate enforcement of tenant labour. This is reflected in a letter by Igoe from 1954:

> Male labour is still a little shy and difficult to coerce because of the scattered and remote positions of their rondavels. Better results will be obtained when the road is completed and it is made possible for us to use native policemen to round up absentees. The fact that the Native Commissioners can come into the Block by car (some are well beyond middle age) will make a great difference. As far as I know, no Native Commissioner has been right through our Block, although they are assumed to have intimate knowledge of the areas they control.[58]

But this attempt was not successful either, as their 'tenants' preferred to move off the land. Men refused to work on the plantations, only women, juveniles and children could be gained for seasonal work.[59]

In order to cope with their labour demands, attempts were then made to recruit men from neighbouring Portuguese East Africa, and indeed later from Malawi.[60] The management thought that the proximity to the border, which could easily be crossed, would be a major incentive. However, Igoe assumed that the apparent remoteness would pose problems:

> Labour which comes out at the present time is cut off from every type of commodity, food utensils, clothing and equipment, which civilisation, such as it exists there, has brought into the native's life as a necessity... to purchase even a needle is now two days' walk for a native. Therefore, it is important that one of the first buildings to be erected, even if it is of a temporary nature, is the native store. Wages will mean nothing without a purchasing point.[61]

CONTESTING IMAGINATIONS

It has been argued that European readings of the landscape changed when the plantations were being established. At the same time it began to become apparent that local African readings clashed with the dominant European image of remoteness. There are three dimensions to this disagreement which translated into acute shortage of local labour on the plantations.

First, the initial assumption by the plantation management had been that the Valley was so remote and inaccessible that there was little competition from other employers. This impression of isolation is easily gained, even today, when approaching the Valley from the western direction, i.e., the Zimbabwean plateau and the Nyanga mountains. A sudden, at times vertical drop, of up to 1000 meters and dramatic climatic change when entering the Valley, as well as its location along the border with Mozambique, underline this notion.

Yet Valley inhabitants have always crossed the border, since it was first drawn in 1898, and by the 1930s the Valley had become one of the routes migrant labourers took on their way into Rhodesia.[62] Old men relate how they began working at Penhalonga, a neighbouring mining area, in the 1930s.[63] Thus, by the late 1940s local African men were linked to information networks about local and regional labour markets, and many young men already had first hand

FIGURE 2. A tea plantation in the Honde Valley

experience of wage employment. In 1949 the Labour Officer for the Eastern Districts complained that new settlers in Inyanga District had great difficulty in recruiting labour. Africans preferred domestic work in nearby holiday resorts to the heavier and usually less-well paid farm work:

> There is a fairly acute shortage of labour among the new settlers on the Crown Land in the Inyanga area, where it seems possible that the proper development of farms may be held up on that account.

He further advised that the only solution would be for farmers to settle tenant labour on their farms. The labour officer reasoned:

> In this particular area, the labour position appears to be complicated by the better conditions and higher wages paid to hotel employees, and by holders of holiday plots, of which there are a considerable number in the locality.[64]

Secondly, the plantation management, as well as government agricultural extension workers, assumed that cash crops would be welcomed by Valley people. In the process of establishing the estates, a test plot was planted with sugar cane, exotic fruit and spices from Asia and other parts of Africa in order to establish suitability of the soil.[65] So far people in the northern part of the Valley had been largely excluded from the Government's attempts to introduce new crops to Africans. They grew millet (*rapoko*) as the staple food crop, dry-land rice, and vegetables, like yam (*madhumbe*). Fruit was also part of the daily diet.[66]

But local people were sceptical, not only towards growing cash crops themselves, but also towards the newly established tea estates. Again, contrary to the European notion of remoteness, people appear to have been very much aware of colonial land appropriation policies in adjacent areas. Just outside the Valley, in an area under the same paramount chief, a chieftainess had lost her land to the Lonrho-owned Wattle Company and other people were evicted when the Forestry Commission began planting on their estates.[67] Even though details are blurred in old people's memory, many do remember that the Wattle Company had first introduced exotic trees to Africans. When the soil proved to be suitable and the trees did well, the plantation took over and the local inhabitants were evicted, if they refused to enter a labour agreement.[68] By the 1960s, and particularly 70s, tea had become a political issue. An old man remembers that those in his community who resisted the introduction of tea did so, because they related this effort to earlier evictions from the forestry estates.[69]

Finally, there was a direct clash in perceptions of the rainforest. Whereas, as argued above, Europeans justified 'penetrating' the forest with its remoteness, African men refused to work in the forest. Arguably, local ideas of preservation, which clashed with those of penetration, prevented men from cutting down trees in the rainforest. Given the choice between a labour agreement and eviction, the local chief, Zindi, and most of his people decided to abandon the land. The resulting conflict again reflects different readings of landscape.

CONTESTATION OVER LAND

In 1954, when planting commenced in Aberfoyle,[70] Chief Zindi and his people moved into Holdenby Reserve. His new home was a mere 250 yards from the boundary with the plantation.[71] This move infuriated the manager of Aberfoyle who complained to the Native Commissioner Inyanga about it:

> We know you had already told all the Headmen and most of the natives in the area, that they could not move into the reserve, and that they are flagrantly disregarding your orders in doing so now.
>
> We have also been advised that Zindi has told all the boys not to carry their situpas [identity cards] when moving in our area, and that he is responsible for advising his followers to disobey your instructions.
>
> He is an extremely undesirable character to hold the position he has, and, if the above allegations against him are proved, I would suggest that you remove him from the district and demote him to shovelling coal at Wankie.[72]

Chief Zindi thus acquired a reputation of being rebellious. Later, during the war of liberation, he was sent into detention, because he supported guerrillas operating in his area.[73]

It seemed unlikely that the 'veteran rebel' had given up part of his land so easily. When talking to Chief Zindi in 1992, still in office since 1951[74] and now a very old man, assisted by an old male councillor and *sabhuku*, he remembered the beginnings of the plantation:

> When they [Aberfoyle] came here, we assumed they wanted to plough only a small portion of land.... And we let them be... I was not moved from there, no. They had told me that I was free to settle there, but then they would give me work to do. But I felt this was not beneficial – I could not stay on a farm – when I was ruler of the land. That is why I did not take long to leave that place. When they marked their boundary – I found myself living within their tea plantation. I was within the tea plantation. So I decided to move. I then shifted and came to stay here.[75]

But why did Zindi and his people move without putting up any resistance, particularly as only twenty years later, land and cash crops had become a major issue in the nationalist struggle in the area? Arguably, the reason was a boundary not visible to Europeans at the time.

In 1925 the Native Commissioner Inyanga reported that Zindi and his people lived on the fringes of the farm:

> The kraals on Inyanga Block are practically all on the borders of that farm, the centre being empty country.[76]

And again in 1947, the Provincial Native Commissioner wrote that the population on Holdenby Block lived in the foothills, neither up in the forest, nor on the Valley bottom.[77] Most of the Block was covered with rainforest, but it also extended to the Valley bottom just west of the Mapokana hills. It was on the very boundary between the two ecological zones that most settlements were located. Arguably, local people made a distinction between rain forest and forest which covered lower-lying areas, which consisted mainly of Msasa trees and bamboo. It was only the latter which was considered to be a potential agricultural production area. Therefore Zindi moved not only across the boundary between the plantation and the reserve, but also between landscape which was to be preserved, and landscape which could be utilised.[78]

The management of Aberfoyle, which could do nothing to prevent this move, appealed to the Native Commissioner for help. They defined the boundary at stake in yet another respect by drawing on the legal definition of land in Southern Rhodesia. The 1950 amendment of the Land Apportionment Act of 1930 stipulated that Africans should be evicted from European land, Crown land, and Native Purchase areas and that they were to be resettled into Reserves within five years.[79] In the following year the Native Land Husbandry Act was passed, which specified that the reserves were to be surveyed and the land to be newly allocated according to the Government's directives of land use. No African was allowed to move into a reserve during this process of evaluation. Neither could an African man apply for land rights who was not resident in a reserve at the time of the 'kraal appreciation'.[80] Thus the manager of Aberfoyle presented his interpretation of the new legislation to the Native Commissioner and demanded the enforcement of the Native Land Husbandry Act:

> We would be extremely grateful for your assistance in squaring the move before it really gets out of hand. We rely on these natives and their wives to assist us in the development of the Estate, and as we are potential food growers and therefore an asset to the country, we feel that we should have the support of all concerned in stopping the present movement of our labour force which is detrimental to our producing the crops we intend producing, and therefore detrimental to the country.[81]

But for a few years, the new legislation left the Government in a limbo: on the one hand, Africans were supposed to be evicted from European land unless they entered a labour agreement, but on the other hand, an uncontrolled move into one of the reserves was not allowed.[82] Thus, according to law Chief Zindi and his people could neither be forced to return to Aberfoyle, nor should they be allowed to stay in Holdenby Reserve. The matter was referred to the Provincial Native Commissioner who saw the Government unable to help Aberfoyle, as according to the Land Apportionment Act Africans could not be moved onto privately-owned land. He gave his opinion on the case to the Native Commissioner:

> I very much doubt if you can force them to return to Aberfoyle Plantations, because by doing so you would be forcing them to commit a statutory offence i.e. illegally entering a European area.... However, I realise that the natives should be encouraged to enter into a labour agreement and I suggest you do what you can to bring this about.[83]

Zindi and his people refused to return to Aberfoyle and local labour supply remained a problem.

III. EPILOGUE: A RECENT BATTLE OVER SPIRITUAL LANDSCAPE

This paper deals with the 1950s, and here is not the space to discuss in any detail the contestations over land in the nationalist period of the 1960s, nor during the liberation war in the 1970s, nor the so-called squatter problem of the 1980s. But one battle which Chief Zindi and his elders fought over the forest after independence should be briefly mentioned: his claim to spiritual landscape has remained an issue to the present day.

In 1954 Aberfoyle plantation was sold and renamed Eastern Highlands Plantation Ltd.[84] When the production area was expanded and the forest increasingly cut down, the management came to an agreement with Chief Zindi that the ancestral graves were to be spared.[85] These graves are situated on a hill top on the estate. Today it is striking to see the intensity and skill of landscape gardening, with tea fields covering entire hills. One of the few areas indeed spared is the ancestral grave yard where the annual rain ritual is performed.[86]

In 1991 the plantation management planned once more a major transformation of landscape: they decided to cut down the trees on the grave yard in order to construct a helicopter landing place. The argument put forward was that top level management of the parent company needed easy access to the estate. The trees were cut, notwithstanding the fact that during the liberation war a landing strip was built nearby which can comfortably be reached from the estate offices in less than thirty minutes by car on a tarred road.[87]

In 1991-92 Zimbabwe experienced a severe drought and in the Valley this was the worst drought in living memory. By September, when the elders started preparing for the rain ritual, they were told that they had no longer a right of access to the graves. The rains failed to break. This caused heated debate in the homesteads of villagers, as well as in the labour compounds on the estates.[88] The drought was attributed to the cutting down of the trees, the desecration of the grave yard. When Chief Zindi was interviewed in early October the issue was brought up repeatedly. He emphasised his ritual duties:

> My duties include performing rituals for the area... Yes, and also to maintain order in the area, by performing rain-rituals. The people come to assemble here.... If the dry season persists, the people assemble here and try to work out a solution.

And his councillor added that even the estate manager used to consult the chief in matters of rainfall:

> The white man who was there used to visit here and tell us that the tea was getting dry due to lack of rain, so we had to do something.

He continued to explain the current conflict:

> The changamire [Zindi] went to them and told them not to desecrate the graveyard, if they did not want to disturb rainfall. They refused to listen to him, saying that they had bought the land.... And that whoever had died would not resurrect, so they refused to compensate for the graves.... 'He died, he is dead – finish. We don't bury any more', so we had to keep quiet.... We were no longer allowed to visit the 'dense foliage' and perform our rituals.[89]

The drought persisted. Aberfoyle was forced to close down completely for one month in November, and Eastern Highlands was forced to reduce their capacity and lay off labour. Finally, the management was prepared to make a concession: compensation of a small amount of money and some bags of millet for the brewing of beer for the ritual were paid to Chief Zindi. The following day, on the 10th of November, torrential rains broke – exactly within the boundaries of Chief Zindi's territory (*dunhu*)![90]

CONCLUSION

An attempt has been made to demonstrate the link between images of landscape as ideological metaphor of space[91] and the legitimation of European expansion in a case study from Africa. It has been argued that Europeans sexualised African rainforest through images of 'penetration' and imagined it as 'wilderness'. However, this 'no-man's land' was inhabited by Africans with their own sexualised and gendered reading of the forest. These European and African imaginations of landscape translated into real contestations over resources and informed the strategies employed by the parties involved. Arguably, similar processes can be located elsewhere.

Methodological drawbacks in some of the literature on landscape arise from the limitation of sources. This is particularly apparent where attempts are made to portray African identities through European narrative.[92] The deconstruction of text in order to depict counter-discourses, as propagated by 'post-modernist literary criticism' should be part of any historian's skills. But arguably, this is not sufficient: Moore and Vaughan, in their recent book *Cutting Down Trees*, aspire to 'develop new methodological practices for the writing of African historiography and anthropology'.[93] They claim that in order usefully to reconstruct identities historically, it is important to draw on different discourses, as well as on local practices.[94] This paper is an attempt to show that a variety of oral and written sources needs to be 'blended in' and to be read in different ways in order to come to an understanding of some of the complexities of the process of European expansion.

NOTES

Earlier versions of this paper were presented to the Third European Science Foundation Course on the History of European Expansion, Sant Feliu de Guixols, Spain, 18-24 July 1994 and to the African Studies Association of the UK Biennial Conference, University of Lancaster, 5-7 September 1994. I would like to thank the participants, as well as Christian Wagner and Georg Deutsch for useful comments. I am grateful to Albert Wirz for drawing my attention to European images of the rainforest. Thanks also to the Centre for Modern Oriental Studies, Berlin, for financing the final writing up period of my D.Phil. thesis.

[1] For the bulk of literature on landscape in Africa, see, for example, Kopytoff, I. (ed) 1987; Ranger, T.O. 1987; Comaroff, J. and J. 1991; Croll, E. and Parkin, D. (eds) 1992; Anderson, P.R. 1993; Moore, D. 1993; Wirz, A. 1994; and Felix Driver's current work on imperial exhibitions.
[2] The evidence for this paper was collected as part of fieldwork in Zimbabwe, conducted for my doctoral dissertation, 'The Social and Economic Impact of Political Violence in Zimbabwe, 1890-1990; A Case Study of the Honde Valley', (Forthcoming D.Phil. thesis, Oxford, 1995). A number of the issues only touched upon here, are discussed in more detail in my thesis.
[3] National Archives of Zimbabwe, (NAZ), S2827/2/2/2, Annual District Reports, vol.V, Inyanga District 1952, p. 1.
[4] Construction had begun in the early 1950s, but was only completed in 1959. National Archives of Zimbabwe (NAZ) S2827/2/2/7, vol.II, Annual District Reports, Inyanga District 1959, p. 6. In 1960 the estate road was linked to the main Manga road. NRC, boxnumber 62328, PNC Umtali, File: Annual Reports 1959 and 62, Inyanga District 1960, p. 5.
[5] Inyanga Block, Eastern District, Southern Rhodesia, Report, George Williamson and Co Nairobi, 1952. Some of the written sources cited here are private papers and will henceforth be referred to as [Holdenby Papers].
[6] Copy of Agreement of Sale, 1952. [Holdenby papers].
[7] (NAZ), L2/1/6/1, Land Settlement Department, Letter from the Surveyor General's Office to the General Manager, Anglo-French Matabeleland Co. Ltd., Belingwe, 04.08.1905. In 1926 Inyanga Block changed hands several times in quick succession. S604, NC Inyanga, Letter from Native Commissioner (NC) Inyanga to Superintendent of Natives Umtali, 'Holdenby Private Location', 12.02.1926 and NC Inyanga to Chief Native Commissioner (CNC), 'Private Locations License', 20.07.1926.
[8] (NAZ), S603, NC Inyanga, Letter from the local secretary of Lonrho Salisbury to NC Inyanga, 'Holdenby Native Location', 13.01.1930 and letter from NC Inyanga to the CNC, 'Private Location: Northern Portion of Inyanga Block: Hanmer Brothers (Inyanga) Ltd', 29.12.1930. For a detailed history of this land, see Donald Moore's Ph.D. thesis, (Stanford forthcoming).
[9] The Government had been interested in Holdenby Block for 'native settlement' from as early as 1943 and bought the land, roughly 77,000 acres, at 6 shillings per acre in 1948. An area around the Mtarazi Falls, some 2,400 acres, was excluded from this transaction. National Record Centre of Zimbabwe (NRC), boxnumber 150768, NC Inyanga, File: LAN 4, 'CNC to NC Inyanga, 'Acquisition of Further Land for Native Settlement: Inyanga District', 06.09.1943 and boxnumber 62328, Provincial Native Commissioner (PNC) Umtali, Minute from CNC to Under Secretary, Department of Lands, 'Holdenby

Estate: Inyanga District', 27.02.1948.
[10] Wightwick, Umtali, to Igoe, Incomati Sugar Estates, Lourenco Marques, Portuguese East Africa, 21.11.1951. [Holdenby papers]
[11] (NAZ), L2/1/6/1, Land Settlement Department, Copy of letter from Little, Managing Director, Anglo-French Matabeleland Company, to the Manager of the British South Africa Company, 19.10.1900.
[12] Van Niekerk had come to Rhodesia with his wife in 1892 and settled in Inyanga district in 1897. (NAZ) Hist.Mss. WO 5/9/1, Pioneer Reminiscences, Letter from M. van Niekerk to Mrs de Groot, 29.11.1950.
[13] Colonel van Niekerk, for example, collected the rent for a Methodist mission site on the Block between 1913 and 1923. Old Mutare Mission Archives, File: Correspondence Concerning Leases 1916-20 (Umtassa Reserve), north-wall, shelf A, boxfile 31.
[14] (NAZ) S603 NC Inyanga, Letter from the Manager of the Standard Bank Umtali (for client) to NC Inyanga, 13.07.1928.
[15] *Ibid.*, Letter from NC Inyanga to the Manager,Standard Bank Umtali, 18.07.1928 and Letter from the Manager, Standard Bank Umtali, to NC Inyanga, 26.07.1928.
[16] (NRC) boxnumber 150768, File: LAN 4, 'CNC Record No. 119: Land Apportionment Act, 1941, Part VI'. Major van Niekerk was employed at least as late as 1927. CNC to NC Inyanga, 'Private Location: Holdenby: Inyanga District', 04.10.1927.
[17] The term 'explorer' appears appropriate in this context, even though D Wightwick is not referred to as such in the sources. His main task in the context of the case study was to explore land in order to provide information to Igoe. This he did on contract basis. Unfortunately, it has not been possible to establish Wightwick's professional or personal background other than that he was living in Mutare at the time.
[18] D. Wightwick to W.A.K. Igoe, London, 19.03.1952. [Holdenby papers]
[19] *Ibid.*
[20] Report by W.A.K. Igoe, Inyangani (Inyanga) Estates Ltd, 09.07.1952. [Holdenby papers]
[21] 'Aberfoyle: The Story of a Tea Estate', *The Farming Gazette Supplement*, 03.05.1985.
[22] H.D. Wightwick, Umtali, to Igoe, Incomati Sugar Estates, Lourenco Marques, Portuguese East Africa, 21.11.1951. [Holdenby papers]
[23] This notion of remoteness of the land was given as a reason for the much later development of tea in the Valley, compared to Chipinge District, the only other tea growing area in Zimbabwe. There tea plantations were started in the 1920s. *The Farming Gazette Supplement*. Aberfoyle: The Story of a Tea Estate. 03.05.1985.
[24] D. Wightwick to W.A.K. Igoe, London, 19.03.1952. [Holdenby papers]
[25] Copy: 'Report on Inyanga Land', by Angus Cameron, 21.04.1955. [Holdenby papers]
[26] 'Report on the Tea-Growing Possibilities of the Inyanga Block, the property of Inyangombi Estates (Inyanga) Limited: Mr. W.A.K. Igoe', by H.O. Thomas, 23.10.1952. [Holdenby papers]
[27] Anderson, 'The Human Clay', p. 23.
[28] *Ibid.*, p. 47.
[29] D. Wightwick to W.A.K. Igoe, London, 19.03.1952. [Holdenby papers]
[30] Lewis, A.R. 1992. *Too Bright the Vision? African Adventures of an Anglican Rebel.* London: Convenant Books, p. 184. In 1952 Igoe had reported that the general appearance of the Block was reminiscent of Scotland. Inyangani (Inyanga) Estates Ltd, report by W.A.K. Igoe, 09.07.1952. [Holdenby Papers]
[31] (NAZ) S2827/2/2/1, Annual District Reports, vol.V, Inyanga District 1951, p. 11.

[32] Inyangani (Inyanga) Estates Ltd, report by W.A.K. Igoe, 09.07.1952. [Holdenby Papers]
[33] (NAZ) S2827/2/2/5, Annual District Reports, vol.II, Inyanga District 1957, p. 8.
[34] (NAZ) S2827/2/2/6, Annual District Reports, vol.III, Inyanga District 1958, p. 6.
[35] For the growing literature on empire and sexuality, see, for example, Hyam, R. 1990. For the discussion of 'penetration' and expansion, see, Callaway, H. 1993, pp. 37-8 and Groot, J. de 1989, pp. 110-11.
[36] Wirz, 'Die Erfindung des Urwalds'. For the Rhodesian self-image as 'civilisers of wilderness', see Chennels, A. 1991.
[37] Comaroff, J. and J., 1988, p. 6.
[38] Ranger, 1987, p. 159.
[39] For the distinction between occupied and inhabited space, and land and landscape, see, Anderson, 1993, pp. 3 and 50.
[40] For simplification nouns in chi-Manyika, the local dialect of Shona, mentioned in the text are used in their singular form.
[41] Interview with informant A, 05.10.1992.
[42] Interview with Chief Zindi and 'Kraalhead' (*sabhuku*) Gogodi, 07.10.1992.
[43] (DAO) File: Chiefs and Headmen: Meetings and Assemblies Including Elections of Chiefs, Report on a Meeting Held by Traditional Leaders of Mutasa District on Friday 10.04.1992. See also, *Horizon* October 1994. Battle for the Pungwe, Pipeline Plan Raises Fears of Bleeding Honde Valley Dry, and Troubled Waters, Angry Gods, pp. 14-18.
[44] Interview with informant B, an old male *n'anga*, 06.10.1992 and with informant C, a young woman, 18.10.1992. From another area in Zimbabwe, the Midlands Province, stories are related which describe *njuzu* as beautiful white women with blond hair. See Hansson, G. 1994.
[45] Interview with informant D, an old woman, 01.02.1992 and with informant E, the young daughter of a *n'anga*, 05.10.1992. See for a recent example, Hansson, 1994.
[46] Interview with informant A, 05.10.1992.
[47] Interview with informants C and F, two young women, 10.11.1992. Even soldiers of the Zimbabwean army were mocked in such stories. Interview with informant G, a young woman, 26.10.1992.
[48] For the '...idea of social causation of environmental ills', see, for example, Werbner, R. 1993 and Schoffeleers, 1979, p. 8.
[49] Ranger, 'Holy Places', pp. 165-166.
[50] Comaroff, J. and J., 1988, pp. 7-8.
[51] Said, E. 1993, p. xiii.
[52] Donald Moore follows a similar objective in a paper on the northern part of Inyanga Block, where he seeks '....to show how struggles over land and environmental resources are simultaneously struggles over cultural meanings.' Moore, D 1992.
[53] Anderson, 1993, p. 22.
[54] Report to the Board of Directors of Aberfoyle Plantations Ltd on My Visit to the Company's Rhodesian Property – September/November 1958, by W.A.K. Igoe, November 1958. [Holdenby papers] Today the 'Nyam'-prefixed names of rivers are in use.
[55] Kirkwood and Peter Ring, for example, lived with their wives in tents for more than 15 months. Aberfoyle, Tea Report – 1954, by W.A.K. Igoe, 08.04.1954. [Holdenby papers] Ring worked for and lived at Aberfoyle since the beginnings, in 1952, until early in 1994, when he died. He is much talked about by employees of the estate, but rarely mentioned in the documentation. Paddy O'Shea, Aberfoyle's manager from 1954, was not able to take any leave for four years. Report to the Board of Directors of Aberfoyle Plantations

Ltd on My Visit to the Company's Rhodesian Property – September/November 1958, by W.A.K. Igoe, November 1958. [Holdenby papers]

[56] In an adjacent area the Forestry Commission imposed a labour agreement which forced male tenants living in Nyamukwarara Valley, on Stapleford Forestry Estate, to work a minimum of 180 days a year for the estate. 'Report on the Tenant Area; Stapleford Forest Reserve', by K.W. Groves, October 1956, p. 15. [Stapleford Papers]

[57] Director Aberfoyle Plantations Ltd to W.W. Halliday, Directors of Aberfoyle Plantations Ltd, 'Inyanga', u.d. [1952]. [Holdenby papers]

[58] 'Aberfoyle, Tea Report – 1954', by W.A.K. Igoe, 08.04.1954. [Holdenby papers]

[59] *Ibid.*

[60] In 1954 Kirkwood visited the administrator of Vila Goveia in Portuguese East Africa in order to come to a rather unusual private agreement involving baby food and whisky for the father of four, in return for access to the supply of 'native labour'. Letter from Kirkwood to W.A.K. Igoe, 18.03.1954. [Holdenby papers]

[61] Aberfoyle, Tea Report – 1954', by W.A.K. Igoe, 08.04.1954. [Holdenby papers]

[62] For the boundary commission, see, (NAZ) L2/2/6/6-8, T2/30/8 and A3/4/1.

[63] Interview with informant H, an old man, 15.08.1992. Chief Zindi himself remembers that he worked in Rezende mine in Penhalonga with men from his area. Interview with Chief Zindi, 07.10.1992.

[64] (NAZ) S1012/27, NC Umtali, 'Report of Labour Officer, Eastern Districts, October 1949', p. 3.

[65] (NAZ) S2827/2/2/1, Annual District Reports, vol.V, Inyanga District 1951-52 and S2827/2/2/4, Annual District Reports, vol.II, Inyanga District 1956.

[66] Interview with informant I, an old man, 15.08.1992 and informant J, a middle-aged woman, 23.08.1992. (NRC) boxnumber 62328, File: Reports on Lands and Reserves, Land Inspector Umtali to the PNC, 'Preliminary Report on the Remaining Portion of Holdenby', 09.11.1948.

[67] For chieftainess Muredzwa's struggle over her land, see, Schmidt, H. 1993.

[68] Interview with informant K, an old man, relative of Muredzwa, and resident in the Valley from 1951 to 1977. A *sabhuku* in the Holdenby area emphasised the grievance when relating that the only people ever forced to live in the Honde Valley were those who had been evicted by the Wattle Company and the Forestry Commission. Interview with informant L, 08.06.1992.

[69] Interview with informant M, 16.08.1992.

[70] The first 36 acres of tea were planted in the 1954/55 season. 'Report on Mr. A.R.A.G. Cameron's Visit to Luleche, October 1957', by Angus Cameron, 27.10.1957. [Holdenby papers]

[71] Before this move, Chief Zindi had been living about 250 yards from the boundary on the Block. (NRC) boxnumber 93786, NC Inyanga, File: CP6 to CP12, NC Inyanga to PNC Manicaland, 'Headman Zindi: Application for Removal by Aberfoyle Plantations Ltd', 21.09.1954. Today, after forced resettlement and the upheavals experienced during the war of liberation, Chief Zindi lives again in proximity to the boundary with the tea estate.

[72] (NRC) boxnumber 93786, File: CP6 TO CP12, Letter from Kirkwood, Manager Aberfoyle Plantations Ltd., to NC Inyanga, 14.06.1954.

[73] Interview with Chief Zindi, 07.10.1992. District Administrator's (DA's) Office, File: PER 5 Headmen, Letter from H.C.A. Gomes for DC Mutasa to the Secr. for Internal Affairs, 'Headman Zindi: Allowance Payment Vouchers Book No. 0395', 23.06.1977 and Provincial Administrator's (PA's) Office, File: PER 5 Headman Zindi, A.J. Bundock,

DC Mutasa District, to PC Manicaland, 'Fezayi 1A 1018: Headman Zindi', 17.07.1978.
[74] DA's Office, File: PER 5 Headmen, Letter from M.C. Hagelthorn to PNC Manicaland, 'Appointment of H/M Zindi', 11.06.1951.
[75] Interview with Chief Zindi and *sabhuku* Gogodi, 07.10.1992.
[76] (NAZ) S604, NC Inyanga, NC Inyanga to the District Veterinary Umtali, 'Cattle Cleansing Ordinance', 13.11.1925.
[77] (NRC) boxnumber 62328, File: Reports on Lands and Reserves, PNC to CNC, 'Holdenby Farm', 26.02.1947.
[78] An exception to this taboo is being made during times of crisis. To give but two examples, in the late 19th century people living in the northern part of the Valley moved up into the rainforest in order to seek protection from invading Shangaan warriors. Also, in 1992, during the severe drought a senior spirit medium (*mhondoro*) gave permission to cut trees and to expand fields into a sacred forest.
[79] (NAZ), S2807/4 and S2807/7, Land Apportionment Act: 1941-1951 and S1194/190/27/6/1, Natives Occupying Crown Land. See also, Moyana, H.V. 1984. *The Political Economy of Land in Zimbabwe*. Gweru: Mambo Press, p. 129.
[80] See various correspondence in, (NRC), boxnumber 93785, File: Tribal Trust Lands.
[81] (NRC) boxnumber 93786, File: CP6 TO CP12, Letter from Kirkwood, Manager Aberfoyle Plantations Ltd. to NC Inyanga, 14.06.1954.
[82] By 1961 demarcation in Zindi's area had still not been conducted. (NAZ) S2827/2/2/8, Annual District Reports, vol.II, Inyanga District 1961, p. 8.
[83] (NRC) boxnumber 93786, File: CP6 to CP12, PNC Manicaland to NC Inyanga, 'Headman Zindi: Application for Removal by Aberfoyle Plantations Ltd', 30.09.1954.
[84] Igoe carried on to develop Inyangombi forestry estate on the northern part of Holdenby Block. From 1958 he begun planting tea on the eastern portion. This new tea estate was again, rather confusingly, called Aberfoyle Plantation.
[85] Aberfoyle, Report on visit to the Estate by Mr. B.I. Barry 21st Feb. to 18th March 1960. [Holdenby Papers]
[86] The ancestral graves of the neighbouring chieftainship, Chikomba, are situated on what now is Aberfoyle estate. Chief Chikomba and his elders have been allowed access to the graveyard and in recent years even been transported by an estate lorry to the annual rain ritual. Letter from H/M Chikomba to the Manager Katiyo, 'Request for Transport for the Annual Rain Ceremony to and from Aberfoyle 27th-10-1990', 22.10.90 [Chikomba Papers]. The higher-lying portion of Chief Zindi's land (*dunhu*), mainly mount Nyangani and forest areas, was appropriated to Nyanga National Park.
[87] The landing place attracted much interest in the local press, for example, in the *Manica Post*.
[88] Great interest in the contestation was also expressed to the author by young men from Zindi who are working in urban areas, as was the case with a bank teller and an airport customs officer in Harare.
[89] Interview with Chief Zindi and *sabhuku* Gogodi, 07.10.1992.
[90] The author was 'trapped' in the factory of Eastern Highlands tea estate, as for a few hours it was impossible to move outside.
[91] Anderson, 1993, p. 60.
[92] See, for example, Anderson, 1993, and Comaroff, J. and J., 1991.
[93] Moore, H.L. and Vaughan, M. 1994, p. xv.
[94] *Ibid.*, pp. xviii to xxv.

REFERENCES

Anderson, P.R. 1993. The Human Clay: An Essay in the Spatial History of the Cape Eastern Frontier, 1811-1835. Oxford: M.Litt. thesis.

Callaway, H. 1993. Purity and Exotica in Legitimating the Empire. Cultural Constructions of Gender, Sexuality and Race. In: Ranger, T.O., and Vaughan, O. (eds) 1993. *Legitimacy and the State in Twentieth-Century Africa*, pp.31-61. London: MacMillan.

Chennels, A. 1991. Cultural Violence During the Pax Rhodesiana: The Evidence from Rhodesian Fiction. Paper presented to the Conference on Political Violence in Southern Africa, Oxford 25-27 June 1991.

Comaroff, J. and J. 1988. Through the Looking-glass: Colonial Encounters of the First Kind. *Journal of Historical Sociology* **I**(1): 6-32.

Comaroff, J. and J. 1991. *Of Revelation and Revolution. Christianity, Colonialism, and Consciousness in South Africa*. Chicago: University of Chicago Press.

Croll, E. and Parkin, D. (eds) 1992. *Bush Base: Forest Farm. Culture, Environment and Development*. London: Routledge.

Groot, J. de 1989. 'Sex' and 'Race': The Construction of Language and Image in the Nineteenth Century. In: Mendes, S. and Rendall, J. (eds) 1989. *Sexuality and Subordination*. London: Routledge.

Hansson, G. 1994. Religious Innovation in Zimbabwe. Mbuya Juliana Movement. Paper presented at the Zimbabwe Research Day on Religion, St Antony's College Oxford, 23.04.1994.

Horizon October 1994. Battle for the Pungwe, Pipeline Plan Raises Fears of Bleeding Honde Valley Dry, and Troubled Waters, Angry Gods, pp. 14-18.

Hyam, R. 1990. *Empire and Sexuality: The British Experience*. Manchester and New York: Manchester University Press.

Kopytoff, I. (ed.) 1987. *The African Frontier: The Reproduction of Traditional African Societies*. Bloomington and Indianapolis: Indiana University Press.

Lewis, A.R. 1992. *Too Bright the Vision? African Adventures of an Anglican Rebel*. London: Convenant Books.

Moore, D 1992. Competing Claims to Land and Legacy: Resource Conflicts in Nyanga, Zimbabwe. Paper presented at the Symposium entitled 'Parks, People, Crops and Wildlife: Contesting Terrain in Southern Africa' at the American Anthropological Association Meeting, San Francisco, December 1992.

Moore, D. 1993. Contesting Terrain in Zimbabwe's Eastern Highlands: Political Ecology, Ethnography, and Peasant Resource Struggles. *Economic Geography* **LXIX**(4): 380-401.

Moore, H.L. and Vaughan, M. 1994. *Cutting Down Trees. Gender, Nutrition, and Agricultural Change in the Northern Province of Zambia, 1890-1990*. Portsmouth: Heineman; London: James Currey; Lusaka: University of Zambia Press.

Moyana, H.V. 1984. *The Political Economy of Land in Zimbabwe*. Gweru: Mambo Press.

Ranger, T.O. 1987. Taking Hold of the Land: Holy Places and Pilgrimages in Twentieth-Century Zimbabwe, *Past and Present*, **117**: 158-194.

Said, E. 1993. *Culture and Imperialism*. London: Chatto and Windus.

Schmidt, H. 1993. Muredzwa Superwoman: Mapping Areas of Female Power in Eastern Zimbabwe. The Mutasa Mamboship. Oxford: Ms.

Schmidt, H. 1995 (forthcoming). The Social and Economic Impact of Political Violence in Zimbabwe, 1890-1990; A Case Study of the Honde Valley. Oxford: D.Phil. thesis.

Schoffeleers, J.M. 1979. Introduction. In: *id.* (ed.) *Guardians of the Land. Essays on Central African Territorial Cults* pp. 1-46. Gweru: Mambo Press.
The Farming Gazette Supplement. Aberfoyle: The Story of a Tea Estate. 03.05.1985.
Werbner, R. 1993. The Making of Moral Knowledge: Local-Global Displacements. Paper presented at the Association of Social Anthropologlists IV Decennial Conference, 26-30.07.1993.
Wirz, A., 1994. Die Erfindung des Urwalds oder ein weiterer Versuch im Fährtenlesen. *Periplus*: 15-36.

Engineering Miracles:
Water Control, Conversion and the Creation of a Religious Landscape in the Medieval Ardennes

Ellen F. Arnold

Medieval monks often represented themselves and others as converting the landscape itself as part of their religious mission. One of the best-known expressions of this is tree-chopping missionaries piously destroying sacred trees or pagan groves. This became a standard image and represented both the transformation of nature and the conversion of pagans to Christianity through monastic and saintly intervention. Yet this is not the only way that nature was tied to monastic mission. The stories from religious communities in the Ardennes provide a good example of this because despite monastic forest clearance and the ubiquity of trees in the landscape, they did not emphasise the felling of pagan groves. Instead, their stories described the conversion of water sources.

The legends about the foundation of Stavelot-Malmedy, for example, describe how Remacle, a seventh-century bishop, missionary and monk, built his monastery on a former pagan cult site. He tore down not the trees, but the pagan idols and he drove out evil spirits from a local spring that was 'fit for human purposes but polluted by pagan error' and subject to 'demonic infestation'. He then tamed it by channelling the spring through a lead pipe, controlling the resource and marking the new Christian control of the landscape.[1]

This is one of a series of medieval religious stories from the Ardennes that emphasise the importance of monastic control over water resources, water technology and religious practice. Such religious accounts, when used alongside administrative sources, allow us to explore the way that interactions with nature shaped and supported medieval cultural identities. The monks of the Ardennes created this and other stories in part to explain and heighten the importance of monastic engineering efforts which gave them temporal power and allowed them to tame and control both nature and religious practice.

INTRODUCTION

During the Middle Ages water was central to agricultural pursuits, commercial ventures and daily concerns, and control of water resources brought social as well as economic power. This article discusses the importance of water resources for the Benedictine monasteries of Stavelot-Malmedy and Andages/Saint-Hubert during the early and high Middle Ages (ca. 600–ca. 1150).[2] These monasteries were founded in the Ardennes during the seventh and eighth centuries. As they

Environment and History **13** (2007): 477–502.

grew in religious and economic power, they exerted wide administrative control over much of the Ardennes. Centuries before the Cistercian monks would become famous for such activities, these Benedictine monasteries began the process of domesticating and managing the region's waters. They canalised and managed streams, built mills and aqueducts, and drained swamps, creating new ponds. Through these activities, the monks displayed their economic wealth, their power as landlords and their social control over the secular landscape.

Because water also had spiritual meanings, this active engineering of water resources was also tied to the monasteries' religious culture. Medieval Christianity associated water with spiritual fertility, healing and religious conversion. Stavelot-Malmedy and Saint-Hubert were associated with famous evangelising saints and linked the conversion of people with water and with God's control of nature. The monks told stories about their founders destroying pagan shrines, erecting crosses and religious buildings, taming the rivers and streams and marking their presence in the landscape. Monastic communities combined and blended their secular and religious authority, and their responses to nature were both practical and abstract. Their control of water resources and the stories they told about water demonstrate the dynamics of this process.

As the monasteries grew in authority and prominence, the monks told and retold stories about their foundations. They also developed new stories that reflected both the continued power of the saints and the monasteries' long-established presence. They engineered water resources and maintained these structures over the centuries, and then constructed and designed miracle stories that highlighted these efforts. This linked their economic and agricultural power directly to their control of religious writing and of access to the saints, and fused their own seemingly separate identities as landlords and shepherds of souls.

The religious glorification of controlling and taming nature for economic power is at odds with some of the widely acknowledged religious goals of monastic groups. Many early medieval monasteries are associated with seeking out deserted, wild locations. According to the king who helped found Stavelot and Malmedy, these houses were built 'in our forest of the Ardennes, in an empty place of solitude'.[3] Located along rivers that snaked their way through densely forested peaks, the monasteries were established only miles away from one another, and were, for the most part, run as a single entity. Their founder, St Remacle, decided, in the words of his ninth-century biographer, to 'go to this deserted space (*eremus locus*), and there, remote from men, [live] without anything but God'.[4]

Such early descriptions of the area's solitude are part of an idealised interpretation of the local landscape which in reality included other secular and religious settlements. Though not all monastic communities sought out such isolation, Remacle and the generations of monks who came after him needed to be able to see their forest as a desert. Monastic tradition idealised the 'desert' and many monks sought out less-settled landscapes or places that seemed geographically isolated by natural barriers such as swamps, cliffs or forests. Because of the importance of the desert ideal, in many analyses of medieval attitudes towards nature, forests such as the Ardennes have become synonymous with medieval wilderness. Yet though many monks claimed to seek out wilderness, they rarely found it, and when they did, they did not long leave it as such.[5]

The desire for finding an isolated landscape was accompanied by a sense of the importance of converting that wilderness so that it became 'fit for human purposes' (*hominum quidem usibus apti*). In part, this transformation of landscapes was a part of the daily reality of living in the world and supporting communities of monks with clean water and food, and creating a physical place to worship God. But the large-scale monastic clearance of forest land, farming of arable land, and harnessing of rivers and streams were also tied to their goals of converting local pagan groups. Wild nature could be associated with paganism and demons and the monks saw themselves as bringing order, control and right religion to these untamed landscapes.[6]

The monks of the Ardennes manipulated the water resources of the region, turning them to human profit, thereby increasing their own prominence in the economic landscape. They also increased the prominence of the monasteries and their saints by telling miracle stories that reinforced the image of monastic resource control and the role of the monks in water miracles. By controlling both the water resources and the stories told about water, the monks ensured their continuing control over the natural and religious landscapes they oversaw.

CREATING A RELIGIOUS LANDSCAPE IN THE ARDENNES: REMACLE'S FOUNTAIN

Although there was some Christian presence in the Ardennes during the Roman and perhaps the Frankish periods, widespread Christianisation did not begin until the seventh century.[7] This process was led by evangelising monks such as St Remacle, who founded Stavelot-Malmedy around 648 and remained abbot until his death in 670. He was then buried at Stavelot, where his body (or relics) later became a focal point of the region's religious devotion.[8]

Over the course of the next century, Stavelot and Malmedy continued to develop their relationship with secular and religious patrons, to increase their economic power base, and also to establish their identity as a religious centre. Remacle's successor, Babolenus, began the process of connecting the houses to saintly power; Pope Vitalian gave him the relics of St Semetrius, which became the first focus of the houses' religious cults. By the start of the next century, as the royal dynasty changed and Remacle and the Merovingian foundation faded from living memory, the monasteries actively promoted their founder and their own history.[9]

In order to increase Remacle's prestige and to retain and promote the history of their monastery, the monks of Stavelot produced and commissioned several narrative accounts of the events of his life and the miracles that he performed after his death. The earliest of these, the *Vita Remacli Prima*, or the first biography of St Remacle, was written by an anonymous author (probably a monk at Stavelot) in the early ninth century. The second biography, generally referred to as the *vita Remacli*, was commissioned by an abbot of Stavelot and a bishop of Liège in the late tenth century. In addition to these biographies (or *vitae*), the monks also produced a collection of miracle stories (the *Miracula Remacli*) that was begun in the ninth century.[10]

The monastery of Andages or Andagium was first established in the Ardennes in the early eighth century. Around the time that Stavelot was beginning to promote Remacle, Andages acquired its own patron saint. The monastery was re-founded in 817, when the Bishop of Liège and Emperor Louis the Pious sent a group of Benedictine monks to renew the small monastery. As part of this process, the body of St Hubert was moved in 825 from Liège to provide the core of Andages' new religious identity. These events led to a flurry of religious writing intended to link the revitalised monastery with their new patron saint.[11]

The monks produced several biographies of St Hubert and books of miracle stories. The first biography of Hubert (the *vita prima sancti Huberti*) had been written (possibly at Liége) during the mid-eighth century, before the saint was moved to Andages. It set the stage for the later cult that would develop in the Ardennes. A second biography was written after 825 and includes the story of the saint's relocation, emphasising the new importance of the Ardennes in the saint's identity. After Hubert was moved to Andages/Saint-Hubert, a cult began to develop, and the monks began to record and broadcast stories of his miracles. The first book of miracles was written shortly after the second *vita* (ca. 840–845) by an unknown author. The second book of miracles was written during the eleventh century, again by an unknown author (since they were used to establish the saint's cult, both were most likely written by monks from Saint-Hubert or on behalf of the monastery).[12]

The narrative sources associated with the foundations and early histories of these monasteries establish the monks' religious goals and show the degree to which they associated their saints with the control of nature and the landscape. The *vita Remacli prima*'s account of the foundation of Stavelot and Malmedy links isolation and solitude with the physical landscape occupied by the monasteries. The site was described as an empty place where Remacle could live a religious life far removed from the secular world. There is no mention of a pre-existing population in the first account. The author of the later *vita Remacli* perpetuated the idea of isolation by describing the environment more closely. Stavelot and Malmedy, in the 'forest of the Ardennes' were dominated by their harsh and inhospitable environments. Stavelot was 'confined by mountains', and the construction of buildings at Malmedy was 'impeded by the swamps'.[13]

Despite these problems, Remacle chose this site because, unlike a nearby place 'full of springs' it had enough space for future building programs. The biography thus acknowledges and praises the monks' physical presence in the landscape. As Stavelot and Malmedy grew, they attracted visitors and attention. The monks had to reconcile this popularity with their desire for solitude. The author of the *vita Remacli* attempted to do this by choosing natural metaphors to describe the process, noting that a 'stream' (*agmen*) of monks and Christians flowed into the region.[14] This connected the secular and spiritual growth of the monasteries back to the isolating properties of the natural location and to the ability of the monks to control and direct this powerful force.

Though there are many nature metaphors found in Stavelot's religious writings, one story stands out both for its strong image of the control of nature and for its longevity within Stavelot-Malmedy's historical memory. Through the story of Remacle's fountain, the *vita Remacli* uses one of the streams near the new monasteries to show the ability of the monks to domesticate the wild landscape. By describing the religious conversion of the stream alongside its domestication, the monks tied their practical control of nature to their identity as evangelisers.

According the *vita Remacli*, when Remacle first visited the area around Malmedy he went to the Warche River. He found a place with 'waters full of fish' and abundant meadows. But he also found signs of former pagan cult practices. The local population had been 'bound up by idolatry' and signs of their pagan practices were still present in the landscape. These signs included effigies and mysterious 'stones of Diana', (*lapides Dianae*), possibly a religious site or altar linked to Diana of the Ardennes, an amalgamation of a local nature goddess and the Roman huntress. Remacle exorcised the spring, freeing the place of evil pagan influences by invoking Christ's name and making the sign of the cross over the water, which was 'polluted by pagan error'. The demonic infestation appears to have been represented by the drying up of the spring, because the biographer notes that once the saint had made the sign of the cross over it, water once again flowed from it, drop by drop. Remacle did not stop there; after exorcising the spring, he took care to make the resource more useful and stable. He made a leaded pipe for the spring, causing water to gush forth, converting the wild spring into a managed resource. Wishing to establish monastic practical and spiritual authority permanently over the site, he erected a stone cross and built an oratory and dwellings for the monks. These actions physically marked the presence of the Christian group and connected religious conversion with the engineering of water resources and the conversion of the landscape.[15]

By including this episode in their foundation story, the monks reinforced their permanent presence in the landscape and established their identity as the representatives of the true religion. According to monastic memory, the freeing of this water source from evil spirits was even at the root of Malmedy's name (*Malmundarium*), because it had been freed from evil spirits ('*malorum spirituum infestatione mundaverat*'). Remarkably, in spite of the importance of this conversion, there are no examples in the *vita Remacli* of the conversion of people. The author chose to use the natural landscape (stones and streams) to stand in for the larger populations, perhaps in order to retain the false impression of a landscape of isolation, idealised elsewhere in the foundation accounts.[16]

Another story from the *vita Remacli* links this idea of isolation directly to water sources. In a vision, Remacle allegedly revealed to a later monk a fountain 'fit for human purposes' and 'a place that was always quiet'.[17] Though it is not possible to determine if this is the same fountain as the *fons Remacli*, the author's statement that this spring was 'fit for human purposes' ties it to the other fountain and the foundation story. The author of the *vita* shaped the early legend of the origin of 'Remacle's fountain' and introduced the idea of miracles associated with it, but it was the later collection of Remacle's miracles that ensured that the fountain remained a clear point on the religious landscape. Some of these stories connect Remacle's fountain and other water associated with the saint to miracles of healing. For example, the monks told the story of a blind woman whose sight was restored after washing her eyes in and drinking from the fountain.[18] This miracle is similar to a healing miracle (discussed below) associated with St Hubert and linked to monastically controlled waters.

The similarity of miracle stories to one another is a reminder that Remacle's fountain is by no means unusual. As noted above, water was a powerful symbolic force in the Christian Middle Ages, and stories of saints and holy men controlling water and other forces of nature abound. That does not, however, lessen the significance of this story. On the contrary, this story, which is set in their own landscape, remained an active part of the monasteries' self-identity and the monks continued to highlight Remacle's taming of the landscape.

As Amy Remensynder shows, stories emphasising the founding of monasteries and Christian sites on earlier pagan sites were common in the early Middle Ages. However, she argues that by the twelfth century this aspect vanished from many of the retold narratives, since by then 'the landscape, at least as remembered, was safely Christian'.[19] Interestingly, this temporal shift is not seen in the foundation legends from Stavelot-Malmedy; the conversion of the landscape is most prominent in the tenth-century *vita Remacli* but continued to be found centuries later.

In the twelfth century, a famous abbot of Stavelot-Malmedy named Wibald commissioned a golden altarpiece. This work prominently featured the Christianisation of the landscape. It depicted several scenes from Remacle's life, including the foundation of both houses. One panel depicted the foundation of Malmedy and the establishment of Christian features on the pagan landscape. The Malmedy panel was dominated by the clearing of the forest and the construction of the monastery. One monk knelt on the roof of the monastery, and near the almost completed building two others were in the process of felling tall, leafy trees. Another monk held a hammer, with which he drove a cross into the ground above a naked, two-headed female figure, two cart wheels and a small animal. This was a graphic representation of the pagan symbols described in the *vita Remacli*, and the altarpiece labeled them as associated with Diana. The pagan statue of Diana lay upside down on the ground underneath a cross. Remacle was shown blessing the cross, with a stream or fountain flowing by his feet.[20]

This recreation of the legend of Remacle's fountain shows the afterlife of that story. In the twelfth century, images that tied the foundation of the monasteries and the establishment of Christianity in the region closely to control of the natural world were still a vivid part of monastic memory and imagination. The golden depiction of the conversion of the pagan fountain reminded its viewers, standing in the large and rich church built in the former wilderness, that the saint's religious power was linked to the conversion of the landscape. This also continued to validate the monks' physical presence in and control over that same landscape.

Another religious narrative from Malmedy, the *Translatio Quirini* further links the monks with a wonder-working water source, and with control of the saints. The narrative recounts the relocation of portions of the bodies of saints Nicasius, Quirin and Scubicule to Malmedy. In 1042, some of the local inhabitants doubted the authenticity of the relics, and the abbot opened the casket which reportedly contained the body of St Quirin and relics of his companions, relics of St Just and St Ouen, and two of St Peter's teeth. This crisis of belief in the relics, combined with competition with Stavelot, might have been the background for Malmedy's production of the *Translatio Quirini*.[21]

According to the *Translatio*, while the monks were bringing the relics to Malmedy, they arrived at a fountain near the monastery. Because of the heat, they decided to rest by the fountain. While they were there, a crippled woman was miraculously healed, and the fountain became an established place on the religious landscape. It was thereafter called the *fons sancti Quirini* or the 'fountain of St Quirin'. The name and memory of the fountain endured 'and not without merit; it is not only sweet for drinking, but indeed it brings health to the faithful who seek it'. Remacle's fountain had also been characterised by its simultaneous usefulness and sanctity, and the story of Quirin's fountain may have deliberately reflected the older stories. In this and other ways, the *Translatio Quirini* appears to have been intended, at least in part, to compete directly with the miracles and cult locations associated with St Remacle. The stories about St Quirin were written during a period in which cults at both monasteries were growing, as were tensions between Stavelot and Malmedy.[22]

Some of the further miracles associated with the relics of St Quirin show how saints were believed to be able to leave their mark on the landscape much more directly. At another place, the monks came to a river where it was customary for the women to come from all over 'to put their flax in the running waters, so that, taking the power from [the stream], it would be malleable'. One woman, inspired by the presence of the martyr's relics, confessed in front of a crowd of onlookers gathered to see the saint that she was in the habit of secretly taking the flax left by different people, 'so that I might look after my own poverty from out of the abundance of others'. In recognition of her confession, at the place where the relics had rested 'the grass kept its greenness eternally; it was neither burned by summer's heat nor taken away by winter's freeze'.[23]

This miracle reflects the peaceful and 'eternally quiet' site revealed by Remacle and also closely resembles another miracle found in the *Passio Agilolfi*. This hagiographical source was likely written by the same author as the *Translatio Quirini*, and describes the location of the martyrdom of St Agilolf. On that site, 'the seed of the place was preserved in perpetual greenness'. Borrowing from his own earlier work, he then reported that the greenness of the spot 'was neither burned by summer's heat nor taken away by winter's freeze'.[24]

According to this anonymous monk from Malmedy, both of these places were set apart from the rest of the agricultural world because of their sanctity. The site of Agilolf's death 'remains to this day unable to be cultivated and, as the inhabitants can testify, frequently glows with light during the night'.[25] The site where Quirin's body rested was similarly (though less explicitly) distinguished by its transformation from practically to spiritually useful. The eternally verdant grass near the river was part of a Christian landscape. But before it became a religious site it had been a part of the local economic landscape, and the story both marks holiness and suggests how the monks could connect religious authority to their economic identities. By reporting the 'customary' uses of the river and the woman's guilty confession, this story reflects the monastic role in regulating local land-use customs. This is not unique; many of the miracle stories from Stavelot-Malmedy have such double roles. The *Miracula Remacli*, for example, shows the saint punishing violators of pasturing customs and of bans on holy-day labour.[26] Such stories were rooted in and validated the monasteries' actions as landlords and social authorities.

MONASTIC HYDRAULIC ENGINEERING: EXERTING ECONOMIC POWER AND SOCIAL CONTROL

How should such religious stories be incorporated alongside archival records and archaeological evidence to understand medieval relationships to the environment? Studies of medieval water technology such as mills tend to focus almost exclusively on normative and administrative sources such as charters, legal formulae, polyptychs or property lists.[27] These sources share the advantage of providing potentially plotable and countable mill sites, and help historians make arguments about settlement history, expansion of the technology, the economic management of estates, and the degree to which a particularly landscape had been transformed. Medieval mill studies emphasise such questions, and many could be classified as histories of technology or as agricultural or landscape histories.[28] Such concerns encourage the use of sources that seem to be more objective than hagiographic works and to reflect reality.

When religious sources are used, they are, for the most part, incorporated to provide further examples of possible locations for mills, descriptions of mill technology, or economic and industrial uses for water mills. Rare is the attempt to discuss the meaning of the inclusion of mills in religious literature, or to explore the cultural and religious significance of the fact that the monastic authors inhabited a world that they had so successfully transformed.[29] Hagiographical sources are mistrusted, in part because they reflect one another, as in the case of St Quirin's fountain, which builds on the earlier stories of Remacle's fountain. Often overlooked is the fact that these hagiographical sources did not interact only with other religious narratives. Like the altarpiece that contained both religious stories and a property list, religious narratives were closely associated with the houses' charters, letters and other documents.

The sources related to Stavelot-Malmedy's foundation are a good example of this. There are several important royal charters that officially sanctioned the houses' foundations in the seventh century. These Merovingian royal charters and several early papal charters remained a living part of the houses' later identity. The manuscript tradition highlights this; an eleventh-century codex from Malmedy contains hagiographical writings about Remacle and then a series of copies of the early charters. In this context, these legal documents had become part of the religious history of the monasteries.[30]

The charters were not only preserved alongside religious narrative; they were also incorporated into it. The commissioner of the *vita Remacli* noted the rich trove of charters housed at the monastery, and the *vita* was quite indebted to the language and the narrative presented in the earliest charters. For example, when describing the foundation of the monasteries, the *vita* author engages directly with charter vocabulary, attempting to define and clarify a measurement term (*leuga*) from a Carolingian confirmation of one of the early charters.[31]

Miracle collections borrowed the format of charters to add a sense of authority and temporal context. A miracle from the second collection of St Hubert's miracles describes a storm. The story begins like a charter, noting that the storm took place 'in the 837th year from the incarnation of the word, when Louis the Pious was in the twenty-fifth year of his reign, and Walcaud, the bishop of Liège, had served for 28 years'.[32] Charters in turn reflected the language of religious sources in order to add a sense of sanctity. For example, many of Stavelot's charters take care to note that Remacle's relics 'were resting quietly there'. This blending of legal record and religious narrative further challenges us to acknowledge that hagiographical sources were both in dialogue with broad Christian themes and at the same time intimately bound up with local events, people and landscapes.

The stories about Remacle's fountain connect miracle to history and also tie the monasteries of the Ardennes into the broader context of early medieval monastic engineering. In the late seventh century, the monastery of Saint-Denis in Paris had an underground aqueduct supplied by a fountain that was named 'St Remigius' fountain' after the monastery's founding saint. At Malmedy, Remacle reportedly poured lead into the source of the spring, likely following the practice of channelling small streams through the use of lead conduits. This practice is evident in several other German monasteries, though at a later date. Regensburg had two managed water supplies by the twelfth century, and at St Emmeran an abbot was memorialised on his tombstone for having 'built the lead water conduit'.[33]

Monastic hydraulic engineering extended well beyond channelling streams or springs and included complex systems of canals and water drainage systems that ensured both the supply of fresh water and the removal of waste water. The Maulbronn monastery, for example, had an elaborate canal system that flowed through many buildings, including the forge. It carried non-drinking water throughout the monastery and provided for sewage disposal. The canal at places ran underground, and in other places ran in an open stream bed that was channelled and lined; this system included at least one mill race.[34]

As the many studies of mill technology have shown, monastic communities throughout medieval Europe participated in hydraulic engineering projects. The monks of the Ardennes did not need to irrigate land because of a lack of water; instead, their water engineering would likely have been designed to harness the power of the mountain streams and rivers and to try to control runoff. The region is mountainous, with steep and highly variable terrain, and major mountain ridges surround both Stavelot-Malmedy and Saint-Hubert. Several rivers course through the mountains and hills, and there is a complex network of springs, brooks and smaller tributaries. The water table is generally high, and the soils of the Ardennes do not respond well to heavy rains, which can lead to erosion, swampy conditions and floods. The soils' unsuitable reactions to water, either excessive drainage or the creation of swamp land, are exacerbated by the region's cool and wet conditions.[35]

To control and redirect the waters, the monks of Stavelot built and maintained an aqueduct or waterworks, to which they made significant repairs at least once. In a letter he sent to an absent abbot, the deacon detailed the changes to the infrastructure that had taken place. Among other things, the aqueduct had been rebuilt and a wall had been built around a new apple orchard. Although not specifically linked, the rebuilding of the water system corresponded to a new plantation, which suggests that the system may have been used to divert water to or away from the orchard. It might also have been used to drain or empty the area that had been turned into a new cemetery. One of the more complex examples of monastic waterworks in the Ardennes may have been the one described in a religious source from Saint-Hubert. It appears to have conducted fresh spring water throughout the monastic complex, channelling it through many of the buildings.[36]

Monasteries were able to be leaders in hydraulic engineering throughout the Middle Ages because they were some of the most powerful landholders. They had the ability, knowledge and resources to create and maintain larger-scale waterworks. Their interest in doing so was in part because of the religious importance of water. Some Roman aqueducts, for example, were used to feed Late Antique baptisteries. They also engaged in this process because of the social and economic status imparted to those who controlled water technology.[37]

Water-powered mills were among the most common forms of medieval water control, and show the pervasiveness of monastic control of water resources. As expensive, successful and necessary parts of the agricultural infrastructure, mills were a visible sign of the wealth and status of their owners, and of human control of the landscape. Though the large-scale use of mills and hydraulic power tends to be associated with the twelfth century, mills dotted the early medieval landscape. There is evidence for water mills in Gaul by the beginning of the first century A.D.. One milling complex has been excavated near Arles that was built in the second century, and the Mosel had a mill by the 350s. In England, Richard Holt suggests that watermills were used from Late Roman times into the early Middle Ages, 'probably without interruption'. On the continent, monastic records show that throughout the Carolingian Empire, most peasants had access to mills within five kilometres of their villages. A survey of the Loire valley has shown that before the year 750 there were already at least 138 mills in operation. The 820 polyptych from St Germain-du-Pres shows that the monastery owned at least eighty-four mills.[38]

Unfortunately, no comprehensive property list exists for either Stavelot-Malmedy or Saint-Hubert, and there is very little archaeological evidence for these communities. One short survey of irrigation canals and field drainage in the medieval Ardennes includes discussion of the scant traces of irrigation networks. This survey discusses two charters from Stavelot-Malmedy and briefly investigates the history of one of the properties that the houses controlled, the fisc of Wellin. However, the authors are able to draw few firm conclusions, in part because of the almost total lack of archaeological traces of mills in the Ardennes.[39]

Nonetheless, the scattered evidence suggests that the rivers of the Ardennes flowed through numerous monastic mills. Through the twelfth century, surviving documents from Stavelot-Malmedy name at least eighteen mills on fourteen properties. Saint-Hubert controlled at least sixteen properties with mills.[40] One of Stavelot's tenth-century charters names two properties with mills: the manors at Nohas and Baldav. The manor at Baldav was described in a property or holdings list as 'a good *curtis*, but badly devastated by its enemies; having good fields, a bakery/brewery, a mill and a large woodland'.[41]

Sources from Saint-Hubert are not very detailed, but a few comments can be made about the monasteries' mills. Like the manor of Baldav, several of Saint-Hubert's mills were on properties that had ovens or bakeries. Several of the properties had more than one mill, such as the property where Saint-Hubert received permission to build a third mill on the same site. Because of the brevity of the chronicle notice, no details of construction are noted, but most of the mills are associated with fishing. Mills, fisheries and 'still and running waters' are commonly linked in the chronicle and other sources. One charter describes a property with 'two fisheries in the water above the mill', and another records an apparently independent mill 'named Cheterners'. Because of the brevity of the Saint-Hubert sources, however, most recorded mills appear only in short property descriptions, such as that for the property of Summoulum (Somal) in the pagus of the Ardennes that included 'a mill, a fishery, a woodland, cultivated and uncultivated lands, and all of the servants who belong to the estate'.[42]

Most of Stavelot-Malmedy's mills are also recorded in such property lists, and for some properties little is known other than names. One of the exceptions to this is Stavelot-Malmedy's mill at the villa of Germigny, which provides an example of continuity of mill use and location. The villa included a multiple mill ('two mills under one roof'). This milling complex would have included two millstones in order to produce a higher output for the villa, which was one of the more substantial and important of the monasteries' holdings.[43] In addition to the actual mills, the monastery also possessed explicit rights to the villa's water resources, including not only the river and any man-made diversions, but also ponds and other still water.

The two mills in Germigny are first recorded in a charter from the year 650 but were of an even earlier origin, since at the time the charter was issued, the mills were already established. They then appear in two more seventh-century royal charters, both of which confirm monastic control of the property. With these initial privileges Remacle attempted to establish the monasteries' core estates early and clearly. His efforts seem to have paid off, because the mills appear again in a papal confirmation from 1049, which includes notice of Stavelot-Malmedy's continued ownership of the multiple mill, with no major changes noted.[44]

The mills at Germigny show up again in four papal confirmations from 1143 to 1154.[45] Though these papal confirmations are further removed from the mill's physical location, the monks of Stavelot were quite actively involved in procuring papal concessions and even in shaping their contents.[46] Though the details are masked by the repetitive nature of confirmation charters (though it should be noted that Stavelot-Malmedy's charters rarely repeat older ones verbatim), the existence of these mills through five hundred years of documents suggests continuity of mills on the site.

Another set of mills, at the estate of Calchus (or Chooz), are also recorded in some level of detail. Unlike the documents of Germigny that recur over centuries and rightly or artificially give a sense of continuity and stability to monastic properties, Calchus appears to have been a long-standing problem that the monks found various ways of dealing with. The property appears in a miracle story included in the *Miracula Remacli*. This portion of the collection was probably written between 980 and 1007, and it suggests that Calchus was a significant property already posing administrative problems.

The story opens by explaining that the estate had important fisheries and that 'it was the custom to set over them a monk from the monastery about whose faithfulness there could be no doubt'.[47] This suggests that there were administrative reasons that the monks would take an exceptionally active role in the day-to-day running of this estate. The concern for the productivity and reliability of Calchus' water resources would surface again. At the time described by the miracle, an elderly monk named Leutfrid had been the supervisor for a year, and he had made sure that there were always sufficient fish caught for the monastery. At this point, fishing seems to have been based on the river. The local fishing practice included using nets (*retus*) thrown from boats and setting out seins (*sagenae mittuntur*).[48]

The story is a further example of how the miracle collections reflect the local landscape and economy even though they contain generic Christian themes. After describing the monk and his fishing skills, the miracle quickly takes on a traditional Biblical theme: the miraculous catch. It so happened that it was the feast day of St Remacle, which increased the demand for fish for the monastic table. Yet no matter what he tried, he was unable to catch any fish. Worried a personal shortcoming on his own part had led to this dearth of fish, he prayed to Remacle. Suddenly, a wave swamped over the boat, leaving a fish and a puddle of water. Inspired, the monk began to put his seines back in and quickly caught enough fish both for the feast day and for distribution to the poor.[49]

By describing so explicitly the religious reasons the monks needed the fish (rather than the economic ones), the author of this miracle justifies the direct monastic management of the estate, and their participation in what could be a very lucrative use of the local waters. The monks directly managed a potentially valuable and problematic fisc, and then by telling a miracle story, attempted to sacralise these economic activities. The saint recognised that the waters needed to serve monastic purposes, and the blessing of an abundant catch validated these efforts.

Despite the monks' attempt to assert both practical and spiritual authority, it appears that Calchus and its waters fell out of direct monastic control. In 1126, more than a century after the compilation of the miracle stories, a charter tells another story of administrative problems, monastic intervention and control of water resources. Monastic investigation found that the estate had fallen into disrepair. The granary and the cow barn were ruined and the mill above the Meuse River was at that point completely useless, yielding no profits. The monks drastically altered the property's economic and administrative status, and assigned the management and rebuilding of the estate to a hunter named Hugo, who was charged with restoring the mill.[50]

The monks made plans to improve the pre-existing fisheries. This was another benefit of mill technology: millponds could serve as artificial fishponds and the canals and lined watercourses associated with mills could also be connected to weirs. Calchus' mill had active fisheries connected with it, and its manager was given the authority over the professional fishermen (*piscatores*) that the monks appear to have previously exercised in person. Evidence for the importance of fishing at the estate comes both from the miracle story and from the charter, which reports the payments and economic return of the estate. During the Middle Ages incomes from mills could be rendered either in currency or in grain tithes. Calchus was to supply the monks with grain and fish cakes, composed of brined fish, grain and pepper. This composite product of the fishery and the mill suggests the degree to which mills and river fishing were bound together in the Middle Ages, and is a reminder of the value of these water resources to monastic owners.

Though the restoration of the Calchus mills is not detailed, the surviving record of monastic mills at the property of Leignon provides more information on the technology and engineering process. The monks controlled the estate which had two mills 'from more ancient times'. By the early twelfth century both were dwindling in profits. There is no hint of the type of neglect the monks found at Calchus. Instead, the water supply for the two mills had largely dried up, and the work to restore their productivity had not yet been carried out. In the early twelfth century, the monks restored the old mills and built a third, new mill.[51]

This example shows the extent to which the monks were capable of transforming landscapes. In the process of restoring the mills at Leignon, the monks used their ability to direct the labour of their dependants and gathered a large work force with which they diverted the course of the stream. In addition to restoring water to the older mills, they blocked the stream ('*fontium obstruens meatum*'), drained nearby swamp land, and constructed a mill pond, where they built the new mill. The profits of the restored old mills belonged to the monastery, and to protect their investment, the monks pledged support monies to be used to prevent the mills from again becoming neglected and run-down. They specified that the money was to be used for materials for roofing, millstones, blades or wheels and everything else necessary for the repair of the mill.[52]

The ability of monks to endow and support mills in part explains the general success of monastic control of water resources. Evidence of preventative measures also shows that the monks were concerned with the tendency of mills to become run-down or obsolete. Around the same time as the restoration of the mill at Leignon, the monks also built a mill on the Amblève River, near the monasteries. (The two projects are recorded in the same charter.) They included provisions that reveal the monks' long-term interest in the mills. For the first generation of its operation, the mill's four builders (*constructores*) were given operational control and ownership of the mill and its incomes, but only for their lifetimes. This grant can be seen as a shrewd attempt by the abbot to ensure that the mill would be built to last; these men would have a personal interest in their work. The abbot also ceded to the mill the tithes from four nearby properties.

The tithe moneys would be used for the renewal and maintenance of the mill. This extra income was specifically intended to prevent the neglect or disrepair of the mills. Both of the clauses show concern for the long-term stability of the mill, highlighting what Richard Holt has described as the 'clear contrast between the short-term mentality of secular lords and the long-term, corporate, mentality of monastic lords'.[53]

Long-term planning was not the only thing that distinguished monastic control over water resources from that of secular landlords. Monks were, first and foremost, religious leaders. They viewed the natural landscape as a part of the world that could be controlled and even converted as a part of their religious mission. The monks therefore used their control over water resources, their engineering efforts and the resultant economic and social power in order to back up and reinforce their religious power. They also told stories that clearly linked the power of the saints to the natural landscape that they themselves had shaped and controlled.

ENGINEERING MIRACLES: EMPOWERING THE CANALS OF SAINT-HUBERT

As noted above, St Hubert was, like Remacle, one of the great missionaries of the Ardennes. The earliest of St Hubert's biographies highlights his early actions, noting that he freed the local population 'from error' and 'washed away [their paganism] by the waters of baptism'. Like Remacle, he was associated with the destruction of pagan sites and the Christianisation of the landscape. The first biographer writes that Hubert 'destroyed the many idols and sculptures that were gathered together in the Ardennes, which deserved to be burned by fire'. When the 'fanatical' locals persisted in venerating and honouring the ashes of their idols, Hubert ordered them to observe harsh penance, incorporating them into the Christian social structure. Finally, Hubert transformed the landscape by building churches dedicated to the holy martyrs 'in many different places'. The author of the biography signals this creation of a religious landscape with nature metaphors, noting that once Hubert had done this, the kingdom of the Franks was lit up 'by a most splendid illumination, as if by the rays of the sun'.[54]

Such descriptions of the sun breaking through darkness or storms as a symbol of miracle and divine favour is common in hagiographical sources. However, it should be noted that many of the sources from the Ardennes chose to use this image, especially in the context of frightening or uncontrollable rainstorms. For example, the author of the first collection of St Hubert's miracles, written in the eleventh century, described the ending of a terrible storm: 'and the darkness of the dense clouds, broken through by the radiant beams of the sun, was soon brightened'. Both of Hubert's *vitae* and the first two miracle collections contain many detailed descriptions of rivers swollen with flood waters or too shallow for boat travel; there are storms, floods and devastating rains, and water metaphors abound.[55]

Hagiographical stories written and crafted in and about the Ardennes evoke not only larger Christian messages, but also the local landscapes. Rain, storms and violent weather were common occurrences, and the authors of religious sources responded to the local landscape by creatively adapting older *topoi* and literary passages. They called upon their readers (and those being told the stories) to relate broader messages to their own experiences, and to associate their immediate surroundings to miracle. In this context, the ability of saints to tame and control natural forces becomes a mark of spiritual power. The monks also described themselves as tamers of their environment, and incorporated the landscape they lived in and shaped into the religious and cultural world that they constructed around themselves.

The second biography of St Hubert, written after the saint's body had been transferred to Andages, follows the same basic structure of the first biography, adding the story of the relocation of the saint. The first two miracle collections are similarly linked. The later hagiographical materials parallel and reiterate but do not exactly duplicate the earlier versions. This repetitive structure reinforces the problem of what to do with monastic tropes—but the presence of novelties and notable differences between the versions suggests that they should not be offhandedly dismissed, and that the repetition of stories and metaphors may increase their cultural significance rather than dull it.

The author of the second biography of Hubert picked up the nature metaphors found in the first account: 'Throwing the seeds of the good work on to good earth', the 'holy cultivators began to flow towards that place from all sides'.[56] By linking the monks' religious success to cultivation metaphors, the author tied religious purpose directly to the monastery's success as an agricultural landlord. Most relevant for the current discussion, the image of the monks flowing towards the monastery from all directions to aid in the cultivation of souls is reminiscent of the flowing of water through irrigation networks. This image, which mirrors the language of the *vita Remacli*, was used many times in the writings associated with St Hubert, most notably in a miracle story about the healing of a blind woman.

This miracle is a direct example of monastic attempts to reconcile their economic and agricultural control of the landscape with their religious purpose. It is recorded in both early miracle collections; the first book describes it in greater detail. An unnamed woman who had been blind from birth went with her parents to give alms at the monastery. When they entered the monastery, there was a teeming crowd of people. The mass of unseen people overwhelmed her, and she asked her parents to take her outside. Once outdoors, she asked them to take her to the place 'where the irrigation stream that had been diverted ... from the spring called "Andaina fontana" flows through canals for various monastic purposes'.[57]

The miracle is filled with watery language, drawing attention to the monastically controlled waters. When the woman enters the church, the people are described as a mingled mass of people and as a flowing wave (*'fluentibus undequaque plebis commixtæ catervis'*), whose chaotic motion she tries to flee. When she asks to be brought away, the author uses a Latin word that could also be used to describe water diversion (*'citatim me deviate'*). Her movement from chaos to monastically imposed order is further highlighted by the description of the water. It is specifically described as a diverted stream (*limpha ... derivatur*), flowing through canals into the monastery, where it was redirected to suit monastic needs.

When the woman's companions brought her to the water, their description of the site further highlighted the structure of the monastic hydraulic works. 'Look', they said, 'water is flowing through the canals.' The attempt to link monastic engineering to religious message is here reinforced by a tone of religious command: '*Ecce aqua per canales defluens*'.[58] The woman then washed her face three times in the water, and 'light filled her eyes'. Although derived from a natural spring, the water that cured the woman was monastically engineered. The woman sought out the diverted, managed waters controlled by the monastery. These waters became the vehicle for the saint's power. By telling the story in a way that emphasised the role of the monks themselves in constructing the healing canals, the author of this story was asserting monastic dominance over not only the water, but also the miraculous landscape.

Medieval miracle stories, though probably based in part on local lore and oral tradition, survive because monks decided to commit them to writing. These collections, though often compiled over several generations, were deliberately selected and arranged in a way that would glorify the saints who performed the miracles. A secondary and often more immediate goal of these collections was to draw attention to the monastery or church that held the body or relics of the saint, in order to encourage pilgrim traffic and trade and to garner the support and patronage of elite donors.

The narrative structure that the monks of Saint-Hubert designed in order to tell the story of the blind woman's healing expresses these multiple functions. The story showcased their technological achievement—the complex water system that they had constructed to channel and redirect the natural spring. This redirection of the spring not only reinforced their control of nature, but reminded those who saw it or read about it of the monastery's economic power and social status. But there were many ways the monks could have highlighted this secular power, and the impact of this story is broader. By using religious miracle, the monks linked their own manipulation of nature with that of their saint. The saint (and God) transcended nature by restoring the woman's sight. The vehicle through which he did so was not the natural spring, but instead the water the monks had engineered for their own purposes. The monks of Saint-Hubert thus balanced their secular and religious powers, ultimately reinforcing both.

The importance of these images of water control is reinforced by the second book of St Hubert's miracles, written almost two centuries later. The anonymous author of this second miracle collection also relates the story of the healing of the blind woman. However, this second account is drastically abridged, and most of the details of the story are left out. For example, all reported speech is removed, even a direct invocation of the saint. Interestingly, a statement of the woman's desire to travel on pilgrimage to the monastery is also omitted. In spite of the abridgement, the author chose to retain the watery images of the flood of people in the church (*eam confluentibus turbis*). Most importantly, the author retained the woman's request to be led 'to the waters, which flow through the canals for the use of the monastery (*in usus monasterii*)'. Once there, the author reports, she washed her face three times, 'and in between washings' (*inter abluendum*) prayed to the saint. Her sight was restored. The canals are the only substantial detail retained, and they again deliberately represent monastic power over nature and miracle.[59]

The monks of Saint-Hubert were able to tell and re-tell a story that associated the healing power of their saint with a specific economic resource, a canalised stream that had been engineered by the monastery. The significance of the creation of such a story is underscored by its repetition. This is similar to the telling and re-telling of the story surrounding the foundation of Malmedy. By creating a story in which St Remacle controlled and harnessed a spring, the monks of Stavelot-Malmedy tied their saint to the natural landscape and connected monastic hydraulic engineering directly to the religious conversion of the Ardennes. By retelling this story, and by enshrining it on an altarpiece, the monks reinforced their claims over that landscape and justified their economic control of the region. By claiming saintly approval of waterworks, irrigation canals and similar parts of the agricultural infrastructure, the monks of the Ardennes used their religious identity to justify and reinforce their social and economic power.

The canal system at Saint-Hubert was described as being intended to serve monastic purposes or uses ('*ad diversos monasterii usus influit*' and '*in usus monasterii*'). This language is similar to that found in the sources from Stavelot and Malmedy, which several times describe monastic fountains as 'fit for human purposes' ('*hominum quidem usibus apti*; *humanis usibus opportunem*'). Though this can reflect the repetitive nature of hagiography, it may also highlight a regional theme, and suggests that the hagiographical sources of the Ardennes were in dialogue with one another. Local context was important, and these sources engaged local experience, local cult practices, and even the local engineering efforts of the monks.

Despite the value of such stories, monastic narrative sources such as the *Translatio Quirini* and the *Vita Remacli* have been under-utilised in attempts to understand medieval attitudes towards nature. Unlike charters, which despite their repetitive and formulaic nature are generally treated as unique sources reflecting specific events and moments in time, hagiographic sources exhibiting a similar type of patterned language are often treated as generic rather than specific. However, though they contain echoes of earlier works, many were composed and compiled locally with clear agendas, including that of tying saintly power closely to a specific local landscape.

The Ardennes were full of monastically engineered water sources, and unsurprisingly, such efforts appear in their religious literature. The stories about Saint-Hubert's canals and Remacle's fountain are both centred on a natural spring that was harnessed and tamed by monks. Both of these springs became associated with the healing and transformative power of evangelising saints. The conversion of the waters stood for the conversion of the wider Ardennes, and the monastically engineered water systems represented the power of the monks who were the successors of the saints. Miracle stories linked the mundane and the miraculous, the natural and the super-natural. Medieval authors created continuity between practice and interpretation, and environmental historians interested in the Middle Ages need to actively address this by paying more attention to the ways that cultural sources intersect legal ones and to the importance of investigating medieval ideas alongside medieval practice.

NOTES

I have benefitted from the help and advice of many people, most particularly Ruth Karras and Richard Hoffmann. I would like to thank the ESEH for a travel grant that allowed me to present an earlier version of this article, and the editor and the anonymous readers for *Environment and History*, whose advice made this a stronger work.

[1] 'hominum quidem usibus apti sed gentilismi erroribus polluti'; 'daemonum infestationi obnoxii'. *Vita Sancti Remacli Trajectensis Episcopi* auctore Notgero, Migne *Patrologia Latina* 139, col. 1147–1168 (hereafter *Vita Remacli*), 12.

[2] Stavelot and Malmedy were twin institutions, and thus are often referred to as Stavelot-Malmedy. Because of their history of conflict with each other, at times I refer to the monasteries as separate institutions. Throughout this article, I refer to the monastery of Andages as Saint-Hubert in order to distinguish the monastic institution from the person, St Hubert.

[3] The medieval monastic idealisation of solitude had its roots in legends from the deserts of third- and fourth-century Egypt and emphasised the monastic goal of separation from the world. For an introduction to this topic, see Jean Heuclin, *Aux Origines Monastiques de la Gaule du Nord; ermites et reclus du Ve au XIe siècle* (Lille: Presses Universitaires de Lille, 1988) and C. H. Lawrence, *Medieval Monasticism: Forms of Religious Life in Western Europe in the Middle Ages*, ed. David Bates. 3rd ed. (New York: Longman, 2001). For a discussion of the monastic desert as wilderness, see Jacques Le Goff, 'The Wilderness in the Medieval West', in *The Medieval Imagination* (Chicago: University of Chicago Press, 1988), 47–59.

'in foreste nostra nuncupante Arduinna in locis vaste solitudinis'. This is the first surviving use of the word *forestis*. Halkin, Joseph, and C. G. Roland, eds. *Recueil des chartes de Abbaye de Stavelot-Malmedy. Publications de la Commission royale d'histoire*, 37 vol. 1, (Brussels: Kiessling et Cie, P. Imbreghts, successeur, 1909), [hereafter abbreviated HR] 2 (ca. 648). For further discussion of this charter and of the nature of forest vocabulary, see the third chapter of my dissertation, where I argue that the term (along with others such as *silva*) was used flexibly during the early Middle Ages. This flexibility was useful to the monks who did not want to construct either a single view of forested landscapes or an artificial divide between their own spiritual and secular uses of the natural world. Ellen Arnold, "Environment and the Shaping of Monastic Identity: Stavelot-Malmedy and the Medieval Ardennes" (Ph.D. diss., University of Minnesota, Twin Cities, 2006), 211–21.

[4] *Vita Remacli Prima* auctore Monacho Stabulensi anonymo, *Acta Sanctorum* [AASS] 3 September, 692–6. 'Post non multum vero temporis impetravit tandem a rege, quatinus relinquens successorem post se in sede pontificali, ut diu desiderabat, hunc eremi locum adiret, et ibi ab hominibus remotus, soli Deo vacaret.'

[5] Although the Cistercians are best known for promulgating the idea that their houses were founded in such solitude and wilderness, the Benedictines were also frequently concerned with promoting this image of their foundations and social relations. The literature on wilderness in civilisation is broad. For a survey, see Max Oelschlaeger, *The Idea of Wilderness from Prehistory to the Age of Ecology* (New Haven, CT: Yale University Press, 1991). However, Oelshleger's account of the Middle Ages takes up only four of his 353 pages. Discussions of medieval wilderness and sense of nature include Vito Fumagalli, *Landscapes of Fear; Perceptions of Nature and the City in the Middle Ages* trans. Shayne Mitchell (Cambridge: Polity Press, 1994) and Jacques Le Goff, 'The Wilderness in the Medieval West', in *The Medieval Imagination* (Chicago: University of Chicago Press, 1988), 47–59.

[6] *Vita Remacli* 5. Although the Latin sources use only the term *fons*, this word can imply both natural springs and artificial or enhanced fountains. Since in this case, it is clear that the spring was engineered, I have chosen to make a distinction in translation that might not have been readily apparent in the Latin. Indeed, since the Latin terms are indistinguishable, perhaps the phrase 'fit for human purposes' is intended as a marker of human manipulation of a natural spring.

[7] Because of the dearth of pre-monastic sources, very little is known about the pre-Christian religion of the Ardennes. The only clear evidence comes from the predictable merging of the native and Roman pagan gods. Édouard DeMoreau, S. J., *Les Abbayes de Belgique (VIIe–XIIe siècles)* (Brussels: La Renaissance du livre, 1952), 14. Alain Dierkins, 'De la christianisation de l'Ardenne à l'époque mérovingienne', in *Saint Remacle l'apôtre de l'Ardenne*, ed. Albert LeMeunier (Spa: ASBL fête de Saint-Remacle, 1995), 42–3. Édouard DeMoreau, *Les Abbayes de Belgique (VIIe–XIIe siècles)* (Brussels: La Renaissance du livre, 1952), 15. Helga Müller-Kehlen, *Die Ardennen im Frühmittelalter: Untersuchungen zum Königsgut in einem karolingischen Kernland* (Göttingen: Vandenhoeck & Ruprecht, 1973), 39.

[8] Medieval Christianity recognised the intercession of saints, and both formal and informal religious practices developed around places associated with the lives of saints. The most important sites of such saint cults were the places where the saints were buried. These cult practices included, but were not limited to, formal liturgies, informal devotional practices,

pilgrimages, and (importantly for the monasteries) donations of goods and property to the saints. For an introduction to early medieval saints' cults, see Peter Brown, *The Cult of the Saints: Its Rise and Function in Latin Christianity* (Chicago: University of Chicago Press, 1982) and Thomas Head, *Hagiography and the Cult of Saints: the Diocese of Orleans, 800–1200* (Cambridge: Cambridge University Press, 1990).

[9] HR 5. For a more detailed discussion of the early history of the houses and their relations to the Merovingian and Carolingian monarchs, see the first chapter of my dissertation, 'Environment and the Shaping of Monastic Identity'.

[10] For more information on the religious writings from Stavelot and Malmedy, see François Baix, 'L'Hagiographie à Stavelot-Malmédy' *Revue Benedictine* 60 (1950): 120–62.

[11] See Georges Despy, 'Questions sur les origines de l'abbaye de Saint-Hubert' *Saint-Hubert d'Ardenne, Cahiers d'histoire* 8, (1991), 242–56 and Satoshi Tada, 'The Creation of a Religious Centre: Christianisation in the Diocese of Liège in the Carolingian Period' *Journal of Ecclesiastical History* 54, no. 2 (April 2003).

[12] *Vita Prima Sancti Huberti*, auctore anonymo, AASS 1 November, 798–805. John of Orleans, *Vita Secunda Sancti Huberti*, AASS 1 November, 806–18; *Miraculorum S. Huberti post mortem, liber primus*, auctore coaevo, AASS 1 November, 819–23 [hereafter *Miracula Huberti prima*] and *liber secundus*, auctore anonymo, AASS 1 November, 823–9 [hereafter *Miracula Huberti secunda*]. The issues associated with using a series of biographies and miracles is discussed below.

[13] *Vita Remacli Prima* 2; *Vita Remacli*, 12: 'Arduennam silvam paludibus et montibus impeditam', 13: 'ad Amblavam fluvium in cujusdam montis confinio substitit'.

[14] Vita Remacli 4. 'Etsi autem locus ille multos haberet fontes, tamen quod angustus esset … videt locum spatiosiorem futuroque operi accommodatiorem.' The *agmen* of monks is interesting, because it has many possible meanings, including that of an 'army' of men. Thus, it simultaneously reflects both the connection to nature metaphors (the monks of Stavelot are elsewhere referred to as bees swarming around a hive) and to the image of monks, saints and martyrs as soldiers of Christ. There are many nature words that could be similarly flexibly applied, such as *fons* or *forestis*. Often the ambiguity may be deliberate, in order to allow the monks the greatest possible range of expression and meaning.

[15] *Vita Remacli* 12. 'Videns autem vir sanctus locum illum tum piscosis aquis tum pascuis uberrimiis …'; 'Igitur adhibita adjuratione per Christi nomen, et S. Crucis signo expresso, locumillum a daemonum incursatione vindicavit et expiavit, moxque aqua ab ipso suo meatu guttatim dilapsa evanuit'; 'plumbum in foramina infundens'. This description of Remacle's actions is a reminder that Christian sacred landscapes, though rooted in the natural world, often involved human (or divine) manipulation of nature. John Howe describes the 'firm' medieval belief that 'even a *locus amoenus* could be improved'. In idem. 'Creating Symbolic Landscapes: Medieval Development of Sacred Space', in John Howe and Michael Wolfe, eds., *Inventing Medieval Landscapes: Senses of Place in Western Europe* (Gainesville: University Press of Florida, 2002), 211.

[16] *Vita Remacli* 12.

[17] *Vita Remacli* 5. '*perpetuae quietis locum*' and '*humanis usibus opportunem*'.

[18] *Miracula S. Remacli episc. et conf.* ed. Io. Veldius. AASS 3 September, vol. 1 [hereafter *Miracula Remacli*] 1.3.

[19] Amy Remensnyder, *Remembering Kings Past: Monastic Foundation Legends in Medieval Southern France* (Ithaca: Cornell University Press, 1995), 45.

[20] Unfortunately, the work was destroyed, but a detailed drawing of the altarpiece was made, and then copied. A thorough discussion of this artwork and its problematic transmission is found in Susanne Wittekind, *Altar - Reliquiar - Retabel: Kunst und Liturgie bei Wibald von Stablo* (Cologne: Böhlau, 2004). This panel has been discussed in the context of the conversion of the pagan natural cult sites by Pierre Koumoth, who presents a useful survey of early Christian reactions against nature cults. Pierre P. Koumoth, 'Des arbres sacrés païns à l'Arbre-de-Vie chrètien dans le retable de saint Remacle à Stavelot', *Folklore; Stavelot-Malmédy* 54 (1993), 42–67.

[21] These saints were originally buried at Vadiniacus (Gansy l'Ile), but during the Viking invasions they were transported to Rouen along with the body of St Ouen. Later they were moved to Condatum (Conde), and then finally to Malmedy, where the cathedral still claims to house them. Balau, *Étude Critique*, 227. Benoît van den Bossche, 'Saint Remacle, moine: eléments de biographie'. In *Saint Remacle l'apôtre de l'Ardenne*, 47–54.

[22] *Translatio Malmundarium et miracula ss. Quirini, Nigasii, et. al.*, AASS 11 October [Hereafter *Translatio Quirini*], 2.22. In discussing the *Translatio Quirini*, Baix notes: 'Telle est la dernière production hagiographique de combat, sortie du 'scriptorium' de Malmédy.' Baix, 'L'Hagiographie à Stavelot-Malmédy', 162. The same monk also appears to have composed the *Passio Agilolfi*, a fictionalised account of a local saint. This is edited and published as the *Vita Agilolifi*. AASS 2 July, col. 714–23 [hereafter *Passio Agilolfi*].

[23] *Translatio Quirini* 2.24, 'ut ex aliena abundantia consulerem paupertati meae'; 'viriditatem sui perpetuo conservat gramine, ut nec aestivo exuratur fervorenec hiemali adimatur frigore'.

[24] *Passio Agilolfi* 2. 'Locus ... viriditatem sui perpetuo conservat germine, ut nec aestivo exuratur fervore, nec hiemali adimatur frigore.'

[25] Ibid. 'sed et inarabilis mantet usque hodie, et, ut testantur incolae, crebro per noctem micat lumine'.

[26] *Miracula Remacli* 1.1 and 2.15.

[27] For an example, see Dietrich Lohrmann's exhaustive study of the early medieval mills in the Loire and Escaut river valleys. This article relies heavily on the polyptychs of Saint-Germain-du-Prés and Saint-Bertin, and incorporates monastic charters, Merovingian formulae, toponymy, later maps and other polyptychs in order to assess and quantify the status of mill-building and mill-usage during the seventh–ninth centuries. He does cite annals and a few religious sources, including Gregory of Tours, but does not attempt to connect the motives and purposes of these sources, nor to use them in any way other than to find examples of early mills. Dietrich Lohrmann, 'Le moulin à eau dans le cadre de l'économie rurale de la Neustrie (VIIe–Ixe siècles)' in H. Atma, ed., *La Neustrie: Les pays au nord de la Loire de 650 à 850*, vol. 1, 367–404

[28] There is a long historiography on the questions of mills and milling technology. For a recent critique of the historiography see Miquel Barceló, 'The Missing Water-Mill: A Question of Technological Diffusion in the High Middle Ages' in Miquel Barceló and François Sigaut, eds., *The Making of Feudal Agriculture*, (Leiden: Brill, 2004) 255–314. For overviews of the technological diffusion of mills, see Richard Holt, *The Mills of Medieval England* (Oxford: Basil Blackwell, 1988) and the more recent work by John

Langdon, *Mills in the Medieval Economy: England 1300–1540* (Oxford: Oxford University Press, 2004). Both of these works focus on issues of technological development in England (where much of the work to date has been done).

For the Continent see Paolo Squatriti, *Water and Society in Early Medieval Italy: AD 400–1000* (Cambridge: Cambridge University Press, 1998) and Paul Benoit and Joséphine Rouillard, 'Medieval Hydraulics in France', in Paolo Squatriti, ed., *Working with Water in Medieval Europe* (Leiden: Brill, 2000), 161–215. Benoit and Rouillard point out that until recently, French studies of water technology were primarily done by archaeologists, local historians and legal historians, whose goals and questions further reinforce the emphasis on location, technology and legal control of mills and their profits. Squatriti's work is broad in scope and incorporates social history alongside the history of technology, exploring both uses of water and the social attitudes towards water use.

[29] Studies of Cistercian agriculture are an exception to this. For overviews, see Constance H. Berman, *Medieval Agriculture, the Southern French Countryside, and the Early Cistercians. A Study of Forty-three Monasteries*. Philadelphia: The American Philosophical Society, 1986; Constance Brittain Bouchard, *Holy Entrepeneurs: Cistercians, Knights, and Economic Exchange in Twelfth-Century Burgundy* (Ithaca: Cornell University Press, 1991).

[30] Halkin and Roland, eds., *Recueil des chartes*, xlv–xlvi.

[31] *Vita Remacli*, preface, 20.

[32] *Miracula Huberti secunda*, 1. 6

[33] On Saint-Denis, Benoit and Rouillard, 'Medieval Hydraulics in France', 167. This original hydraulic system was abandoned by the end of eighth century, when it was replaced as the primary water source by a stream. On Regensburg and St. Emmeran, Klaus Grewe, 'Water Technology in Medieval Germany' in Paolo Squatriti, ed., *Working with Water in Medieval Europe*, 137.

[34] Ibid., 141. Susanne Arnold, 'Wasserwirtschaft im ehemaligen Zisterzienkloster von Maulbronn' in *Water Management in Medieval Rural Economomy: Les usages de l'eau milieu rural au Moyen Âge. Ruralia* 5, supplement 17, 183–7. Even this well-known monastery has yielded very little archaeological evidence of its mills and water system; though traces are visible in the landscape, the system that extended beyond the monasteries' walls is still little known.

[35] Giovanni Hoyois, *L'Ardenne et l'Ardennais. L'évolution économique et sociale d'un région*, vol. 1 (Brussels: J. Duculot Press, 1949), 21–3, 30–33. M. Terlinden, 'La Forêst du Hodinfosse et la station de sechage de bois de Haute-Ardenne (Vielsalm) (Excursion des 15 et 16 septembre 1987)', *Bulletin de la Société Royale Forestière de Belgique* no. 2, March–April (1987), 91. René Noël, 'Pour une archéologie de la nature dans le nord de la "Francia"', in *L'Ambiente Vegetale Nell'Alto Medioevo* (Spoleto: Settimane, 30 marzo–5 aprile, 1989), 779.

[36] For Stavelot, Philipp Jaffé, 'Wibaldi epistolae', in *Monumenta Corbeiensia*, (Darmstadt: Scientia Verlag Aalen, 1964), no. 256. For Saint-Hubert, *Miracula Huberti*, 1, 8.

[37] Grewe, 'Water Technology in Medieval Germany', 133. Squatriti, *Water and Society*, 139–42.

[38] Benoit and Rouillard, 'Medieval Hydraulics in France', 169. Richard Holt, 'Medieval England's Water-Related Technologies', in Paolo Squatriti, ed., *Working with Water*

in *Medieval Europe*, 57–8. Lohrmann, 'Le moulin à eau', 368. Benoit and Rouillard, 'Medieval Hydraulics in France', 171.

[39] Philippe Mignot and Johnny De Meulemeester, 'A propos de l'hydraulique en Ardenne belge' in Jan Klápšt, ed., *Water management in medieval rural economy. Les usages de l'eau en milieu rural au Moyen Âge*, 3–10. Památky archeologické, Supplementum 17, Ruralia V. Prague: Institute of Archaeology, Academy of Sciences of the Czech Republic, 2003.

[40] Most early charters from Saint-Hubert were lost in an 1130 fire, but Saint-Hubert's chronicle, written between 1098–1106, drew heavily on now lost records of property donors and donations. The chronicle was integrated into the surviving charter base by Godefroid Kurth, *Chartes de l'abbaye de St Hubert en Ardenne* (Brussels: Academie Royale de Belgique, 1903).

[41] HR 74. 'curtem bonam sed ab hostibus valde vastatam, agri culturas bonas, cambam, molendinum et silvam magnam'.

[42] Kurth, *Chartes de l'abbaye de St Hubert*, nos. 49, 63, 92, 90 and 30. The property list reads: 'cum molendino, piscatura, silva, terris cultis et incultis et cum tota familia ad ipsum pertinente'.

[43] The mills were also surrounded by a cleared area that probably, if better-documented English mills can provide analogy, contained outbuildings such as storage sheds or even a house for the miller. Holt, 'Medieval England's Water-Related Technologies', 67. Multiple mills were described as consisting of two mill engines, 'under one roof' or 'in one building'. Although most multiple mills were on the same banks, one multiple mill excavated at Abbotsbury in Dorset had two engines opposite each other on different sides of stream.

[44] HR 3, 8–9, 111.

[45] HR 178. Celestine II confirmed of ownership of the mills in a longer list of holdings. The mills were confirmed again by Lucius II (HR 179), Eugenius III (HR 182), and Adrian IV (HR 248).

[46] This point is especially relevant for the papal charters issued between 1143 and 1154 during the abbacy of Wibald. Wibald was an active correspondent with the popes, had a close relationship with one of the papal chancellors, and even drafted official imperial correspondence to the popes. It is unlikely that he would expend papal favour and support on a property that the monastery was no longer interested in developing.

[47] *Miracula Remacli* 1. 18. 'in ea igitur, eo quod sit piscaturae habilis, ante moris erat monachum a monasterio statuere, de cujus non dubitaretur fide'. Calchus also appears in the second book of the miracle collection, 2.2.

[48] Richard Hoffmann refers to this miracle story as evidence of weir fishing. See Richard Hoffmann, 'Economic Development and Aquatic Ecosystems in Medieval Europe', *American Historical Review* 101, no. 3 (June, 1996), 636 n. 18.

[49] Ibid. 'elevataque subito a flumine unda navim concite tamquam acta flamine petiit, ac magnum in ea piscem cum latice simul injecit'.

[50] HR 145. The report noted that the monks were unable to draw any produce or profits from the mill: 'que nulla omnino habebantur'.

[51] HR 141, 'ab antiquis temporibus'; 'que dum propter nimium aque defectum illis non valerent sufficere'.

[52] Ibid. 'in tecto, mola, rotis, sc[erptis]' Since the millpond was built explicitly for the new mill, Leignon may have had both of two common medieval water-mill types, the weir and leat mill and the millpond mill. There are some later English examples of both types existing in combination or at the same sites. Langdon, *Mills in the Medieval Economy*, 76–7.

[53] Holt, 'Medieval England', 88.

[54] *Vita Huberti prima*, 3. 'baptismi unda ablutos'; 'Idola plurima et sculptilia, quae colentes erant in Ardoinna, igne cremanda destruxit'; 'fanatici'; 'et velut radius solis splendiflua inluminatione ... inluxit'.

[55] *Miracula Huberti prima,* 1. 6. 'opacitasque nubium mox percussa solis radio suo enitesceret jubare'.

[56] *Vita Secunda Sancti Huberti* 31. 'sed super optimam terram jacto verbi semine'; 'in eumdem locum religiositatis cultores confluere'.

[57] *Miracula Huberti prima,* 8. 'ubi irriguosa foret limpha, quæ de fonte vocabulo Andaina fontana dirivatur ... et eam ubi per canales ad diversos monasterii usus influit, illuc postulando perduci impetravit'.

[58] Ibid.

[59] *Miracula Huberti secunda*, 9. 'petiit ut ad aquam, quæ per canales in usus monasterii influebat, deduceretur'.

Environmental History and the Construction of Nature and Landscape: The Case of the 'Landscaping' of the Jutland heath

Kenneth R. Olwig

THE 'NATURE' OF THE NATION STATE

It can be argued that environmental history was born, in its modern form, as a child of national romanticism. If the Enlightenment was a cosmopolitan age which idealised the universal, the romantic era was more concerned with the particular. The unit of government was not to be based upon a hierarchy of rational knowledge descending from a geometrically perfect heavenly order, but was rather to be the expression of the will of a specific people from a specific area. Thus, whereas the absolute monarchies saw themselves as the highest earthly link in a chain of being descending from the cosmos, the nation state was to be an expression of the place in which the language and culture of its folk developed. According to Arthur O. Lovejoy, the emphasis upon diversity and particularity is the one common factor in the otherwise diverse tendencies which have been termed 'romantic':

> the quest for local color; the endeavor to reconstruct in imagination the distinctive inner life of peoples remote in time or space or in cultural condition; the *étalage du moi*; the demand for particularized fidelity in landscape-description,... the cultivation of individual national, and racial peculiarities. (Lovejoy 1973: 292-93)

It was in this intellectual loam that the notion of national democracy could grow and develop. It also provided fertile soil for the idea that the condition of the nation and the condition of the environment were interrelated. This idea, however, represented something of a Pandora's box, containing both the seeds of the worst type of nationalism, and the blessings of a progressive environmental consciousness. A key to understanding the Jekyll and Hyde nature of this phenomenon lies in an understanding of the double character of the concept of nature which developed at this time.

THE BIRTH OF MODERN ENVIRONMENTAL HISTORY: THE DANISH CONTEXT

Because of its size, Denmark provides a useful social microcosm in which to study the interlinkages between various areas of endeavour which may be more

Environment and History **2** (1996): 15-38

difficult to perceive in larger and more complex societies. In Denmark, one person may be a prominent figure in various fields which, in larger societies, would involve several persons. Furthermore, the links between this person and other people generating changes in other fields are often easily established, not only because of the size of the society, but also because of the intensity of the Danes' penchant for recording and storing their national history. This means that we can work not only on the large scale of ideas and movements, but also on the micro-scale of the individuals who create such movements, and carry them out. It then becomes possible to re-examine developments in larger societies in the light of insights thus gained on a smaller scale. In some cases, furthermore, it might be that the small scale of Danish society has enabled certain individuals to see a 'larger', interconnected, picture which would be more difficult to grasp in bigger societies. This, in turn has enabled them to exert an influence on an international scale which would not otherwise be expected, given only the statistical odds of someone from such a small place being recognised. One such person was Joachim Frederik Schouw (1789-1852), who, I would argue, was one of the Protean fathers of modern environmental history.[4]

J.F. Schouw

Joachim Frederik Schouw combines, in a fascinating way, the emerging ideals of modern, objective, natural science and enormous political and environmental commitment. As a botanist he was a leading figure, helping to create, through his research and his theoretical work, the modern discipline of plant geography. He was also an important organisational figure, helping to create an international scientific community committed to comparative science. His geography of Europe was used, in translation, throughout the continent. At the same time, however, he was also politically active on a scale warranting comparison with Thomas Jefferson. He was a key figure in the peaceful Danish transition from absolutism to democracy which occurred in the 1830s and '40s, not only as a leader of the transitional proto-democratic assemblies, but also as an author of the new constitution. Part of his political work was his engagement in the movement for freedom of speech, and his use of this movement to enlighten the general public about scientific and environmental issues through publications, lectures and educational reform. It is for this reason that he co-initiated, in 1833, The Danish Natural History Society, becoming the editor of its journal. The essays he produced for this forum were published in book form in a number of languages, in the English translation, under the title *The Earth, Plants and Man*. In the preface the publisher, Bohn (who also published Alexander von Humboldt's *Cosmos*) wrote:

> The author of 'The Earth, Plants and Man' is so well known to all who made any acquaintance with Physical Geography, that no apology seems necessary in present-

> ing a work of his to English readers – the less when it is one so entertaining and instructive as the present. (Schouw 1852: preface)

Though Schouw is here identified as a physical geographer, the book is in many respects a cultural geography, with a strong historical dimension, on the general theme of man and nature. It influenced readers as varied as Karl Marx and George Perkins Marsh. Marsh, the author of *Man and Nature: or, Physical Geography as Modified by Human Action* (1864), was also, of course, a force in the foundation of modern environmental history, as well as of the environmental conservation movement. Like Schouw, he was deeply committed both to science and to the importance of democratic social engagement (Marsh 1967; Lowenthal 1958; K.R. Olwig 1980).

Denmark at this time was in the throes of an economic and political crisis which threatened the very existence of the country. For Schouw, the solution to this crisis was not only political, it was also environmental. The Danish environment, its forests and fields, had become seriously depleted because of excessive exploitation, which Schouw blamed ultimately on the social conditions fostered by the absolute monarchy. For Schouw, this meant that a national revival depended not only on political reform, but also on an environmental reform which would engage the entire populace. As a natural scientist, Schouw had the ability to analyse and engage in this process on the level of the practitioner as well as that of the publicist. For him, dissemination of scientific knowledge about the environment was critical to this endeavour. The following statement shows just how the ideas of science, democracy and environmental improvement were linked in Schouw's mind:

> It is one of the advantages of more recent times that the sciences are no longer the property of a certain class, but are increasingly distributed amongst the people. This is because the flow of the sciences is not only increased by the reception of new sources, it also must be led, in endlessly divided canals, over the country so as to make it fruitful. (Schouw 1832: 221)

Schouw's choice of metaphor is no doubt influenced by the observations of environmental degradation which he made in the Mediterranean area, and his conclusion that the cause was fundamentally social:

> Sicily, formerly the granary of Italy, certainly produces much less corn now; many tracts of land lie desert, but this is to be ascribed to the deficiencies of social circumstances, not to the climate .... If the social conditions of Algeria could be reduced to order, the fertility there would certainly not be inferior to what it was in antiquity. (Schouw 1852: 238)

NATURE AND NATION

It was the notion of the unity of identity between a people and their environment that made possible the environmental awareness of a person such as Schouw. However, as he himself recognised, this idea was somehow also the root of its greatest weakness. To understand this weakness we must look to the links between nature, landscape and the environment. The interaction of these concepts engenders the Achilles' heel of the kind of environmental understanding, and history, which Schouw and like minded thinkers elsewhere sought to promulgate – an Achilles' heel which, I believe, still hobbles us today.

Schouw regarded the nation as a product of the interaction between a people and its environment through time. However, he recognised the danger of this view being co-opted by a much more simple interaction in which the nation is seen to be the direct product of a given environment. His membership of a society with a dual national identity, both Danish and Scandinavian, was particularly helpful in providing an intellectual antidote to such forms of nationalism. The battle against the absolutist state had fostered an awareness of the common cultural roots of the Scandinavian people, leading to a growing pan-Scandinavian form of nationalism which ran against the grain of nationalisms more narrowly focused on the nation state. In a lecture to the Scandinavian Society on 'Scandinavia's nature and people' he was thus moved to criticise those who argued for the determination of national character by the physical environment. The importance of this critique was acknowledged by George Perkins Marsh who proposed to translate a version of it under the title 'Nature and nations', because it combated 'the common notion that national character is influenced by physical causes'. In this essay Schouw wrote:

> Denmark's nature is therefore not Scandinavian in the narrow sense, it is more similar to the German than to the Norwegian or Swedish. But then one should also conclude that the Danish people are more German than Scandinavian? This would be so if it were the case that it were true that a people's character is determined by or is significantly dependent upon the nature of that land which the people inhabit. But even though this view is very widespread and continually taken as given by philosophers, historians, natural scientists and poets, it is nevertheless a misconception which has only become so common because the relationship between nature and man is still in need of scientific treatment. With regard to this subject conclusions have been drawn with a superficiality which would not be tolerated in any other science. (Schouw 1845: 8)[5]

Schouw polemicised against the idea that social man was determined by nature, arguing that, quite to the contrary, different nationalities can share similar environments (as in Switzerland) and similar nationalities can share divergent environments (as in Scandinavia). For Schouw, the character of such societies:

> ...has its soil, its intellectual soil in *History,* out of which it springs, – has its intel-

lectual climate in *Language*, in which it lives and moves (Schouw 1845: 15).

It is not the laws of physical nature that determine their character, but the laws governing the 'soil' and 'climate' of a social environment. If the reverse were seen to be true, Schouw's entire project for social and environmental transformation would be threatened. The argument that nations were, and ought to be, 'natural' reflections of their environment, was fundamentally conservative, leaving no room for Schouw's coupling of social reform and environmental restoration.

The problem for Schouw, I suggest, is that various, ideologically potent, meanings had become attached to the word 'nature'. This had the effect of derailing discourse, so that apparently sensible individuals and disciplines expressed views which, though easily demolished by Schouw's form of argument, nevertheless defied the sort of scientific logic which he applied to them. Environmental determinism, in various guises, became a leading current of geographic thought in the course of the 19th century, and even though the excesses of German *'Blut und Boden'* ideology helped pave the way for its disgrace in the post WWII era, it nevertheless survives in various guises to this day (K.R. Olwig 1993).

NATURE, NATION AND LANDSCAPE

The primary reason why discussions of the relationship between society and nature became so volatile is that the somewhat parallel concepts of nature and landscape tended to merge at this time, thus reifying and camouflaging meanings of nature which had hitherto been the object of much more conscious discourse. This process of reification was, in many respects the end result of a long series of social, material, and ideological transformations beginning in the Renaissance, which lay the groundwork for the development of the modern national state.

The term *land* was originally applied in the Germanic languages to a unit of territory which often was identified with a people or quasi ethnic group – Östergötland, in Sweden, was thus the *land* of the Eastern 'Goths.' These areas were often of some legal importance in the Middle Ages as areas covered by a given body of a law which was generated by the operation of the so-called *ting*, a representative body which met periodically, and which was rooted in unwritten customary law. The location of the *land's ting* became a de facto capital – e.g. Viborg was the locus of the *ting* for the land of the Northern Jutlanders. Modern Danish law thus begins with the writing down of the laws of various *lands* at the close of the 12th century. The writing down of these laws, however, at the same time marked their end as a judicial unit which was dependent upon oral tradition – and hence some form of organic cultural continuity. The writing down of law made it possible for a central power to appropriate the law to itself. The nascent state initially consisted of a sort of conglomerate of *lands* to which the regent regularly paid a visit in order to manifest state power.

The salience of the *lands* in subsequent national discourse was that while they disappeared as a functional political unit at an early date, they retained importance as a locus of place as opposed to state identity. The name which was eventually applied to these areas of felt identity was 'landscape'. The term *landskap/landskab/landschaft*, which is found throughout the Germanic speaking nations, is virtually synonymous with the term *land*, except that it is usually applied to areas which are smaller than, or sub-units of, a nation state.[6] State authority in Scandinavia replaced the *land* as regional sub-unit of the state with the *Amt* in Danish and *Län* in Swedish, a territory directly under the control of the king, possibly with different boundaries from the *land*. This occurred in Sweden, for example, in 1634. The early date of the disappearance of the *land(skap)* as a viable political unit of the state reflecting antiquated, community based, notions of law and governance contributed to its perpetuation, particularly in Sweden, as a 'felt' region. The more ancient and obscure the origins of an institution, the more 'natural' and inviolable it appears to be. *Lands* thus became a locus of quasi-ethnic, regional identities, which counterpoised to state identity. When a Swede, for example, is asked where he is from, he will invariably tell you the name of the *landskap* – and *not* the *Län* – from which he originates. At the university of Uppsala the students belong to fraternity-like clubs, called 'nations', in which membership is based upon *landskap* of origin. This distinction between the *landskap* as a locus of felt, cultural, identity and the state as a political unit is particularly clear in the context of the last remaining *landskap* which still functions as a unit of governance, the Aaland Islands. Though they officially belong to the Finnish state, they are culturally Swedish, and because of their strong ethnic identity they have been allowed to exercise considerable rights to self-government under the official title of *Landskap* – the world's last functioning 'landscape' in the territorial sense!

The suffix 'scape' is cognate to the suffix 'ship' and it can be assumed that, like most such affixes, its particular meaning has normally been as neutral as the 'ship' in 'township' is for most people today. The suffix occurs in a variety of similar contexts, such as the Danish *Grevskab* – meaning an area which is the domain of a count (County). This does not, however, preclude the term being used with a certain poetic license to refer to the landscape as a felt locus of identity, the domain of a people. The suffix 'scape' thus means shape, which in the Germanic languages means create, as well as shape in the more ordinary English sense of the word. It is a word which has organic, biological – and thereby also reproductive – connotations, and it is often applied to the activity of the supreme creator, God. The connotations of the prefix 'land' – for example as a synonym for country or nation – are, of course, familiar to English readers. The term landscape thus bears with it connotations which can give it a meaning along the lines of 'area shaped or created by a people'.

The earliest 'landscape' paintings, *per se*, were those of the Dutch, who began to gain European prominence for their homely, detailed, depictions of their native provinces in the 17th century. They, quite naturally, applied the

Dutch equivalent of the word *landskap*, *landschap,* to paintings of particular areas of territory within their country. It has been argued by Simon Schama that these paintings reflected the peculiar character of the emerging bourgeois Dutch sense of national identity, which defied the feudal states which sought to bring Holland under their control (Schama 1987). These paintings were characteristically of rather humble places, often reflecting the special way the Dutch had managed literally to shape 'lands' from the sea bottom. If Schama is right, that these paintings reflect a nascent form of nationalism, then it is not improbable that the notion of landscape, even then, carried important connotations as a place shaped by a people.

The Dutch landscape paintings subsequently became popular in 17th century England where they were, characteristically, imported at a time when Dutch hydrologists and engineers were engaged in a somewhat more material 'land shaping' in the Fens and other wetlands. Along with the paintings, the English also imported, or rather re-imported, the term landscape – which had long since become obsolete in English. Since the English no longer attached the original territorial meaning to the term it was natural that they would interpret it to mean: 'a picture representing a view of natural inland scenery'. A landscape was something you hung on the wall. In this context the suffix 'scape' simply came to mean 'a view or picture of a (specific) type of scene'. When re-defined in this way it became equally natural to apply the term landscape to paintings of scenes that were the product of other artistic traditions than that of the Dutch (Webster 1963: 'landscape').

OF BATS, MICE AND BIRDS

In Renaissance Florence a tradition for painting rural scenes emerged, parallel to the Dutch tradition, which was much more fundamentally symbolic and ideal in its thrust. In this tradition both subject and form are marshalled in the expression of an ideal vision of the natural. The subject could be a scene inspired by Virgil's vision of the natural life in Arcadia, while the form could be that of a framed perspective drawing in which the form itself – the 'perspective' of the world as being fundamentally a scene – was seen to be an expression of natural principles. Such principles are embodied in expressions such as 'all the world is a stage' or 'theatre of war'. Even though paintings in this tradition – e.g. paintings by Claude Lorraine (1600-1682) – might appear to be reasonably realistic representations of a particular place, they were normally essentially figments of the painter's imagination (K.R. Olwig 1993). Since the status of art tended to be gauged by the status of its subject matter this tradition tended to be given a higher status by English art critics than the Dutch, which because of its plain, humble, subjects, tended to be derided as being unimaginative and overly slavish to detail. This Mediterranean tradition, furthermore, laid the groundwork for the profession of landscape architecture. Put bluntly, what a landscape architect did was to take an actual place, which might look like the plain subject matter of a Dutch painting, and turn the place into something which might look like one of Claude's ideal visions – particularly when seen (and framed) from a particular location. Through the act of landscaping, the architect literally created 'landscape' out of topography by exploiting its 'capabilities' as artistic material, as the architect Lancelot 'Capability' Brown was wont to say. In this way, the landscape architect helped facilitate the transition in meaning, which occurred in the English language, from the sense of landscape as 'a picture representing a view of natural inland scenery', to the meaning 'a portion of land that the eye can comprehend in a single view' and, eventually, 'vista, prospect' (Webster 1963: *landscape*). The meaning of landscape was transferred from the signifying medium, the painting, to the material subject to which the painting referred through depiction in order to signify some form of meaning. Landscape thereby became a segment of the world seen as if it were in a painting. In this way the meaning of the word landscape was restored to something approaching its original sense, but now it is no longer an area or territory, bounded and shaped by a collectivity, but a scene perceived, as in a theatre, from a particular point by an individual: 'a portion of land that the eye can comprehend in a single view' (Webster 1963: *landscape*).

The popularity of things English, not the least English landscape gardening and landscape art on the continent, at the time of Joachim Frederik Schouw, no doubt facilitated the transferral of the English concept back to the continent from which it had come. By this time it had superseded, and, in fact, all but

FIGURE 1. The landscape gardens at Stourhead, England

obliterated, the original meaning of the term in both the German and the Dutch language. When, under the influence of German nationalism, German scholars revived the term in the course of the 19th century as a concept applied to a unit of territory, it continued to retain the English idea of landscape as a *natural* scene, with all the normative connotations born by this word (Hard 1970). It thus became a 'bat-like' term, at once a mouse (an actual territory) and a bird (a scene, perceived from a particular perspective, like a theatre scene). In this way, it also tended to conflate the character of actual places with esthetic ideas of the ideal and natural, tied to particular modes of viewing (i.e. from particular vantage points) and ideal notions of the natural which western society had learned to identify with certain kinds of scenery (e.g. the Arcadian).

The same fate that befell the term landscape also, quite logically, befell the term nature. Paintings in the ideal tradition represented a vision of the natural gestalted in the form of framed perspective representations of ideal scenes. When this tradition merged with more realistic artistic traditions of the sort identified with the Dutch, nature increasingly became identified with the scenes of actual places represented in art. The meaning of the word nature shifted from its primary meaning, as 'inherent character' or creative force, and became reified and concreticised as that which has been created. Nature as 'scenery' became virtually synonymous with landscape as 'vista/prospect'. This process by which the meanings of the words nature and landscape were conflated was facilitated by the fact that they have similar connotations. The word nature derived from the Latin *nascere* meaning birth. It referred to the same sort of creative birthing process as the Germanic *scape,* and, in fact, the two terms are closely identified in the examples given in dictionaries in these languages – eg. 'organic growth' 'determined by nature' (*Ordbog over det Danske Sprog* 1931: *'skab', 'skabe'*), or 'the creative power of nature' (Collins-Klett 1983: *'schaffen')* or 'to create, fashion, form ...(said of God or Nature)' (*Oxford English Dictionary* 1971: 'shape').

The problem with the conflation and reification of the meanings of landscape and nature within the bat-like figure of a something which is both territory and view, much as a bat is both mouse and bird, is that it tends to have a disjunctive effect on discourse. One person, in a given context – e.g. Schouw writing as a physical scientist – may thus discourse on nature in a way that represents it in much the same matter of fact way as a Dutch painter – e.g. as a bat. Here we are dealing with a nature which reflects the creative (or destructive) efforts of a given people *vis-à-vis* their material environment. In this discourse, there will necessarily be symbolic overtones, related, for example, to the nature of the society involved, but we will essentially be dealing with a nature which is amenable to scientific analysis. Another person, perhaps a poet, may look at the same place as nature, or landscape, and see a 'bird', an ideal Arcadian unity between man and environment, or the expression, sanctioned by God or Nature, of manifest destiny. It is this sort of language which, in turn, surfaces in the discourse of an historian such as Oswald Spengler in his reference to 'cultures that grow with original vigour out of the lap of a maternal natural landscape, to which each is bound in the whole course of its existence' (quoted in Sauer 1969: 325). This language amply illustrates the metaphorical, and ideological, potency of the term landscape when linked to that of nature and culture in this way. The culture which refuses to conform to its apparent determination by a given maternal landscape is *ipso facto* unnatural.

The problem, of course, is that it is one thing to read the discourse of a poet in the text of a poet, and it is another to read it when it is presented in the quasi-scientific text of an historian. It is now very difficult to know whether we are dealing with a mouse (an actual relationship between a people and their environment), or a bird (a more aesthetic representation, taken from the more narrow perspective of an ideal vision). It is this mouse/bird problem, I believe, which led to the situation which caused Schouw to exclaim that: 'with regard to this subject conclusions have been drawn with a superficiality which would not be tolerated in any other science'.

THE HEATH

The problematic character of the conflation of meaning which occurred with the concepts of nature and landscape can be exemplified in relation to the characteristic northern European environment termed heathland. Because the heathlands were thinly populated with a poor transport infrastructure, and only extensively grazed and cultivated, they were perceived as wild nature. To the rational mindset of the Age of Reason, the unproductive heaths were an eyesore, and the people who lived there were perceived to be as useless as the environment they inhabited, and responsible for its condition. The romantic mindset turned this idea on end. Suddenly the people of the heathlands came to be seen as natural Arcadian shepherds who expressed, in their culture, the nature of the unspoiled landscapes which they inhabited, and, hence the unspoiled ideal nature of the nation to which they belonged. The perception of this group's relation to its environment thereby moved from one extreme to the other, from the degenerate producers of a degenerate environment, to the natural expression of the natural people of a natural environment. The corollary of the latter view, however, is that it would be 'unnatural' for these people to defile themselves, and their environment, by changing this relationship.

One of the earliest Danish expressions of 'heath romanticism'[7] is to be found in the writing of the author Jens Baggesen (who identified with German culture and wrote extensively in German). In 1792-93, he wrote the following about the Lüneburger Heide, in present day Germany:

> The further I penetrated into my desert/wilderness,[8] the more delightful and interest-

FIGURE 2. An artist's rendition of the heaths as they appeared in 1855

> ing it became. It is true that my external eye discovered nothing but heather and, here and there, single stunted pine trees – everything about me lay spread out in one inexpressible gray-black naked flat surface. But despite this, all the more beautiful rare sights floated past my inner eye in a thousand undisturbed phantasies. Soon came a long bearded hermit, soon an honorable old Dervish with water in the palm of his hand, soon a Chinese prince who had gone astray, soon a fleeing princess of Tiflis, soon a pilgrim who, for every two steps forward, took one backwards, soon a wandering knight, soon three disheveled prophets, soon twenty-four fearsome rovers, soon a whole caravan with dromedaries.

The women here are described as 'courteous heather nymphs, whose cheeks' roses and neck's lilies more than sufficed to replace the lack of flowers in this district '...they were herders; and truly! they were the most Arcadian I have hitherto seen' (Baggesen 1973: 104-108).

Even though such expressions seem overwrought and a bit ridiculous – and there may have been an element of self-satire in this text – it has been shown that the perception of the heath as Arcadia permeated even the most respected natural scientific work at this time, such as that of the geographer Alexander von Humboldt (Hard 1965). It found, however, its most characteristic expression, as might be expected, in the work of poets and artists; and, as I will show, it also required a poet to capture its problematic character.

STEEN STEENSEN BLICHER AND FAUST

Unlike Jens Baggesen, the Danish poet Steen Steensen Blicher, his contemporary, was born and raised on heathlands (in Jutland) resembling those described in the passage described by Baggesen. He appears to have recognised that an essential element of Baggesen's perception of the heaths was its egocentricity. The heaths maintain their idyllic character only so long as it suits the phantasy of the romantic wanderer. Thus as soon as Baggesen begins to feel lonely the heath changes color, and becomes every bit as dreary as it was romantic earlier:

> Nothing except heather, and heather and more heather! All that was elevated had disappeared – and even though I attempted to call back the living phenomena of my phantasy – everything was empty, uniform, dry, cold, dead, unimportant, unendurable. (Baggesen 1973: 104-108)

It is a similar transformation in a passage in a short story by Steen Steensen Blicher (which appears to be a literary paraphrase of Baggesen's) that provides a key to understanding Blicher's ambivalence toward this kind of romantic idealisation of the landscape. It begins with the following description of the narrator's confrontation with the Jutland heath:

> Sometimes when I have wandered across the great heaths with nothing but brown heather about me and a blue sky above me; when I have strolled far from human beings and the marks of their puttering here below – mere molehills that time or some restless Tamburlaine will level to the ground; when I have flitted, light of heart, proud of my freedom like the Bedouin whom no house, no narrowly bounded field ties to one spot, who possesses all that he sees, who lives nowhere, but roams as he pleases; when in such a mood my roving eye has caught sight of a house on the horizon unpleasantly arresting its airy flight, then I have wished – God forgive men the passing thought, for it was nothing more – would that this human dwelling were not there!

The narrator's protest that he didn't really desire to wipe out the human population of the heaths is suspect, however, because he clearly 'doth protest too much', and the frightful wish is soon repeated:

> A forester has proposed that the entire colony of settlers on the heath should be wiped out, and that trees be planted in the fields and on the site of the razed hamlets. I have sometimes been seized by a far more inhuman idea. What if we still had the heather-grown heath, the same that existed thousands of years ago, undisturbed, its sod untouched by human hands! But, I repeat. I did not mean it seriously. For, when exhausted, weary, languishing with heat and thirst, I have longed intensely for the Arab's hut and his coffee-pot, then I have thanked God for a heather-thatched cottage – though miles distant – promising me shade and refreshment. (quoted in K.R. Olwig 1984: 29-31)

The point, it would seem, is that when an area is viewed aesthetically as landscape scenery the people of the area become reduced to just another expression of that landscape scene – just so much ornament to be blotted out with the flick of a brush, so much stage scenery, to be changed at the close of a scene. Blicher also includes the same sort of fanciful mirages as Baggesen described, but the problem, as he suggests, is that this type of commanding view is not just limited to aesthetes. As he notes, a forester has proposed to wipe out human habitation in the area in order to plant trees. The problem, furthermore, is double edged because, in the end, the romantic aesthete imaginatively destroys the very environment upon which he himself depends for mental and physical sustenance.

Blicher was not alone in perceiving that this viewing of an area as landscape had a hidden, dæmonic dimension. In a famous passage from Faust, Goethe depicts Faust, together with the dæmon of dæmons, Mephistopheles, taking in a view in which the elements of the landscape spread out below become so much stage scenery, to be manipulated at will; its dwellers destroyed, should they spoil the scene:

> This drives me near to desperate distress!
> Such elemental power unharnessed, purposeless!
> There dares my spirit soar past all it knew;
> Here I would fight, this I would subdue!
> ...'And it is possible! ...Fast in my mind, plan upon plan unfolds.'

Suddenly the landscape around him metamorphises into a site. He outlines great reclamation projects to harness the sea for human purposes: man-made harbors and canals that can move ships full of goods and men.

The only thing which stands between Faust and his dream is an old couple who live in pastoral harmony with their surroundings, and who are a model of community virtue. He desires to replace a self-generated natural idyll with a new designed idyllic scene of his own creation. Faust becomes obsessed with this old couple and their little piece of land:

> That aged couple should have yielded,
> I want their lindens in my grip,
> Since these few trees that are denied me
> Undo my world-wide ownership...

They must go, to make room for what Faust comes to see as the culmination of his work: an observation tower from which he and his public can 'gaze out into the infinite' at the new world they have made (quoted in Berman 1982: 60-7).

This passage plays a central role in Marshall Berman's classic study of the modern temperament, which takes its title *All that is Solid Melts into Air,* from a statement in Karl Marx's *Communist manifesto* about the exigencies of modern life.[9] It is rooted, I would argue, in the fundamental way of seeing which is represented here, in which nature flicks between being a material relationship, to a mode of seeing which dissolves as soon as the eye's focus is changed.

Blicher was engaged in a critique of the perception of the nature of the world as landscape scenery. His critique was rooted in fundamental transformations in western cosmology beginning in the Renaissance which, in effect, transformed it literally into a world *view*. He was concerned, I would argue, with the same fundamental bat-like problem as Schouw. At the one moment the heath is a 'mouse', the humble abode of a poor marginal peasantry, the next it is a 'bird', an Arcadian fairyland in which the people are a romantic expression of the scene. So long, however, as we are only dealing with the visions of a romantic wanderer these transformations are as reversible as a magician's spell, but when we are dealing with the physical transformations of the forester, or of the Faustian developer, then they become more permanent, and destructive.

ALL THAT IS HEATHER MELTS INTO AIR

In retrospect, Blicher's passage has taken on a prophetic quality.

Enrico Dalgas (1828-94), nephew of Joachim Frederik Schouw, sought to realise the visions of Blicher and his uncle not as romantic phantasy, but in terms of social and environmental transformations which restore both economic and cultural life. He was a road engineer who became the charismatic leader of a national movement to transform the heathlands into forest and farm as a means of compensating for the loss of Schleswig-Holstein in 1866. What is fascinating about his project, seen from the perspective of this discussion, is that environmental history was at the centre of his agenda. Thus his first priority, when launching the Heath Society in 1866, was to publish a pamphlet called *Geographical Pictures from the Heath*, which was essentially a popular environmental history of the heathlands. This work, which Dalgas, through the years, supplemented with lengthy geographical studies, was a pioneering attempt to use the topography of the heath as historical source material, the interpretation of which provided an understanding not only of the historical development of the heathland environment, but also of the steps which would be necessary to restore it to its original fertility. To tell this story Dalgas pioneered the development of methods which characterise environmental history writing to this day. We thus find him correlating, for example, place name evidence concerning the presence of prehistoric barrows and forest with choropleth maps in order to show the effect of human settlement.

We likewise find him, spade in hand, cutting segments from the soil in order to show the podzolisation which could result from changes in land use and soil cover. It is no accident that a number of the modern pioneers of pollen analysis were Danes, working in the heathlands. They were often basically working to answer questions raised by Dalgas. In Dalgas's version of history, the natives of the heath were neither the desultory destroyers of the environment – as they

FIGURE 3. Enrico Dalgas

were seen to be in the enlightenment – nor the 'natural' product of their environment, as the romantics saw them, but rather pawns in a complex social and political process which, under the given circumstances, made heathland agriculture the only viable choice.

Through his ability to comprehend the complex of infrastructural, environmental cultural, and social factors governing heathland agriculture, Dalgas succeeded in becoming the catalyst of a remarkable process of transformation which virtually eradicated the heath. The hitch, however, was already present in the title of his first publication, *Geographical Pictures*. When communicating with the heathland peasantry he didn't need pictures. As a road builder working in the area he had a well developed understanding of the mentality of the local populace. When he spoke of increasing soil fertility through irrigation systems, he spoke to an age old concept of nature which had direct non-visual appeal to a cultivator. In order to sell his project to the burghers of Copenhagen, however he needed pictures: he had to transform the heathlands into a landscape scene which needed changing. Initially, his strategy worked, too. He managed to get the burghers to provide the capital to plant the trees which provided the coulisse which enframed the efforts of the heathland farmers to restore the fertility of the soil. The trees, furthermore, served a useful purpose both in terms of wind shelter and in terms of the capital which the planting effort, indirectly, gave to the population of the region. The problem was that the landscape picture captured the public imagination to the extent that it came to supersede the original purpose of improving the conditions of the people who lived in the area. This proved especially to be the case after Dalgas' death in 1894.

Dalgas had emphasised that the heath movement was concerned with people in their environment, not with the environment for its own sake, as he exclaimed at a meeting of the Royal Agricultural Society: 'It is not only for the sake of the

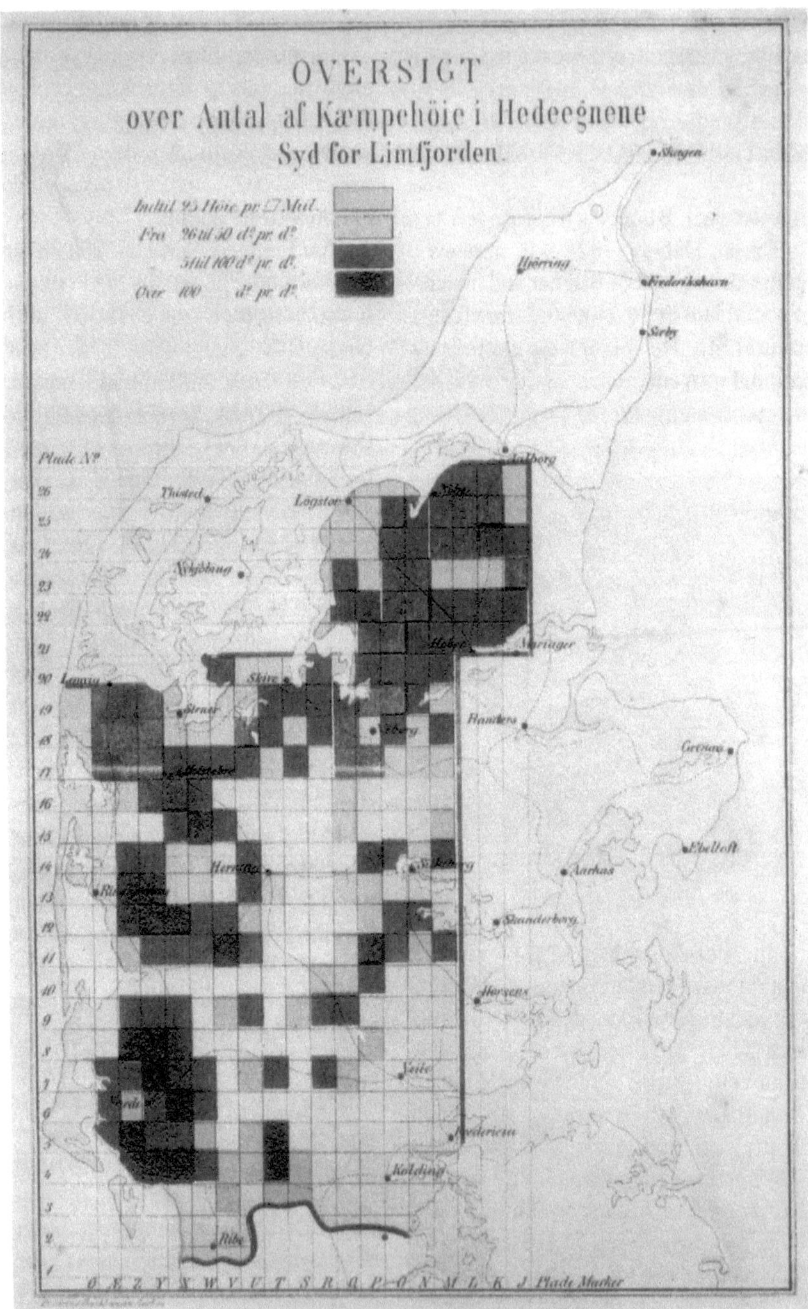

FIGURE 4. A chloropleth map by Enrico Dalgas showing the number of barrows per square mile. The barrows are an indication of early human settlement.

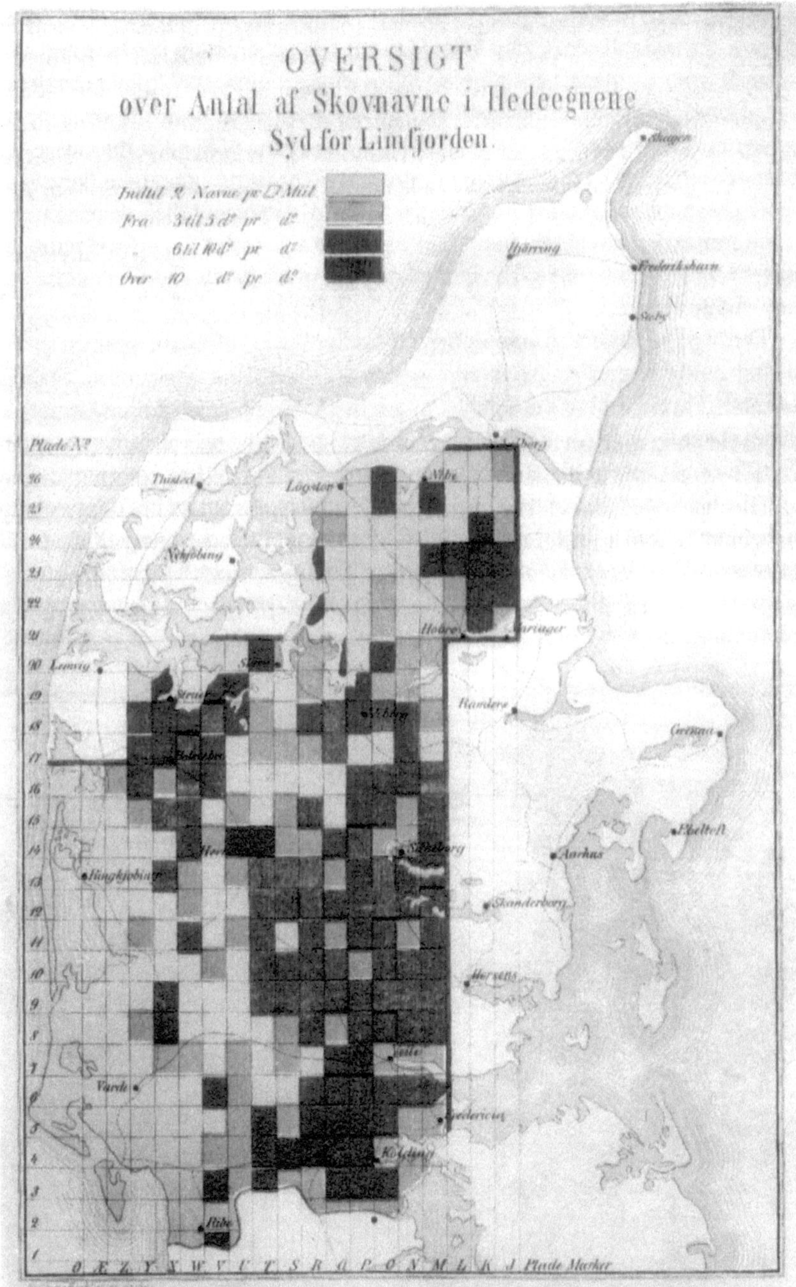

FIGURE 5. A chloropleth map by Enrico Dalgas showing the number of place names per square mile indicating the presence of forests at the time of settlement.[10]

dead earth that we have come here, but also for the living people, who also have a claim to make' (quoted in K.R. Olwig 1984:85). After his death, however, the scene became the focus of the national movement. This resulted in a concerted effort to cultivate and afforest areas which Dalgas himself saw as being un-cultivable. In 1916, out of disgust with the way poor cottars were enticed to break their lives and backs on fundamentally infertile soils, the poet Jeppe Aakjær, himself a native of the region, wrote of the Heath Society:

> Those who describe the Heath Society as a conqueror are correct. West Jutland is, in my eyes, a conquered country. Any Jutlander who thinks about what has occurred must regard the Heath Society and its so-called cultivation of our forefathers' land with the same eyes as a conquered people looks upon the monuments to victory which the enemy raises upon the land of the conquered (quoted in K.R. Olwig 1984: 86).

Aakjær became a pivotal figure in mobilising a heath preservation movement which eventually was to eclipse Dalgas' cultivation movement. This movement was, furthermore, vital to the generation of the then nascent nature preservation movement. The irony was that in order to combat the Heath Society Aakjær found it necessary to use the rhetorical weaponry of his enemy, with the result that the

FIGURE 6. The extent of the Jutland Heaths (a) c.1800, and (b) c. 1950. Maps prepared by the University of Copenhagen Geographical Unit.

living environment of the Jutland farmer, whose cause Aakjær otherwise championed, became subsumed to the cause of a nature reified as heathscape scene:

> ...no conquering horde could have gone more ruthlessly to work against a province's original aesthetic values. It is a Society which threatens all that we hold holy ...the landscape, the view, the mile vaulted horizons (quoted in K.R. Olwig 1984: 87).

The pendulum has swung so far today that we now find the Ministry of the Environment, in response to public demand, buying up farmland and, in the name of 'nature restoration', transforming that farmland into forest and heath – much to the consternation of a local population once feted as heroes of the nation because of their efforts to cultivate these same areas. Even this goal is a will-o'-the-wisp, because the heathland environment was the product of a historical process of human interaction. It therefore cannot be managed back, in the name of nature, to some hypothetical 'original' state as if it were so much stage scenery. All the king's horses, and all the king's men, cannot put this landscape back together again. While the public stands hypnotised, distracted by a vision of landscape as scene, the landscape, in its original sense as an expression of the creative activities of its natives, is destroyed. Nature, as a generative physical force, is transformed into a scenic illusion, reflecting the eco-architectural state of the art of today's environmental planners.

FIGURE 7. Dalgas and friend, spying out over a reclaimed heath

CONCLUSION

The case of the 'landscaping' of the Danish heathlands exemplifies the way the conflation of the concepts of landscape and nature result in the sort of 'bat-like' transformations which allow the perception of the environment to undergo a sudden and disjunctive shift in meaning. Both Baggesen and Blicher, in their own ways, exploited and elucidated the poetic effect of this shift. Schouw, on the other hand, taking his point of departure in the language and logic of science, could not comprehend how otherwise rational thinkers, against all evidence, could not understand the argument against environmental determinism. He did not understand that this determinism was not seen to be an act of nature, in the scientific sense, but an act of the *nature* of the nation conceived as an all encompassing landscape scene which, like the designs of the scenographer and playwright, determine the plot to be acted out by the players. The plot was that of a national drama, acted out by the people, and it was just such a plot that Dalgas was able to stage.

The Danish case is hardly unique. In the United States of America, for example, vast areas are set aside, in the name of nature, as virgin wilderness parks. There is nothing, in and of itself, that is questionable about setting aside land for parks. Quite the opposite, this is an activity which humans have engaged in to the benefit of flora, fauna, and themselves, for centuries. One should not overlook, however, that these parks too, are scenery in a national drama, preserving the memory of an era, as Everhart writes, when the 'exemplary virtues of rugged individualism and free enterprise were the foremost commandments of Manifest Destiny' (Everhart 1972: 6; see also K.F. Olwig 1980). I think it is to the U.S.

FIGURE 8. A carefully tended, preserved heath

Park Service's credit that it appears to be taking more and more consideration of the fact that the American landscape is not only the scene of the national drama of Manifest Destiny, but also the place of dwelling of, among others, indigenous people for whom the blessings of this destiny were not particularly apparent. The problem here is less a recognition of the symbolic importance of landscape, but rather, the unraveling of the strands which bind 'mouse' and 'bird' together in our conception of the natural environment. The fact that certain landscapes are of enormous visual beauty, and the fact that their preservation thereby takes on considerable symbolic and emotional importance – which can be vital to the conservation movement as a whole – does not mean that they are actually of particular significance to the health of the environment as biosphere. Flat, fetid, dank, and visually unaesthetic swamps can have considerably more ecological importance than, for example, the environment of the Grand Canyon.

The issue, as I see it, is that both causes are good on their own terrain of discourse. The one is related to vital cultural, and hence abstract, issues concerning ideals and norms for the relations within society and between society and its environment, whereas the other involves more concrete issues concerning the health of the biosphere. The problem is that the first tends to overshadow the second. This happens, for example, when apparently neutral scientific terms such as environment, milieu and ecology take on a dual identity, like the dual identity of 'nature'. We thus find that words like environment and ecology become virtually synonymous with 'nature' in many of the contexts – such as advertising – where the value laden connotations of words and concepts are important.

Perhaps our 'bat' has a tendency to turn into a vampire, but if so, unfortunately there is no wooden stake which can put it to permanent rest. The solution, rather, lies in developing an historical understanding of the way in which the fabric of our present day conception of nature, and the values which we attach to it, have been woven together. It is only then that we can begin to weave a new fabric better suited to a world in which the nation state is no longer the measure of all things. Though it is difficult to predetermine what will be the stuff of such a new conception of nature, my guess is that it will have to be less visual, and more keyed to the totality of our senses, and the organic needs to which they are tied. Ecologically speaking, the environmental ideal will probably be less the barren mountaintop, and more the fertile meadow. This, in some respects, would be a return to the original concept of landscape, conceived of as a locus of dwelling.

NOTES

[1] On the importance of social engagement in modern environmental history see Cronon 1990; Worster 1990.

[2] On the concept of deconstruction as applied to nature see Olwig 1989.

[3] This article represents a new theoretical approach to material treated in depth in Olwig 1984.

[4]For a more in depth presentation of Schouw see Olwig 1980.
[5]A version of this lecture is found in English translation in Schouw 1852: 240-46, under the title 'Nature and Nations.'
[6]The importance of the addition of the suffix 'scape' might derive from the necessity to distinguish between ancient territorial units identified with ancient peoples, called *lands*, and the larger states which encompassed several of these *lands*, and which, themselves, accrued the name *land*. Though these *lands* have lost their independent status, they still have the 'shape' of a *land*. On the Scandinavian use of the term *land* and *landskap*, see Rona 1965: *Landskap, Landskabslove, landskapsnämn.*
[7]The correct literary term for authors of this period, who characteristically swooned for wild sublime landscapes, is actually 'pre-romantic', but most lay people, I would venture, would apply the term 'romantic' to this sort of writing. Romanticism, *per se*, as a conscious literary movement, identified with people like William Wordsworth, comes later.
[8]The Danish word *ørken* meant both desert and wilderness at this time. The author plays with this double meaning, thereby also playing upon the fact that the heath bore some physical resemblance to the Arabian desert due to its sandy flatness, and the occurrence of mirages. It also bore a literary resemblance stemming from the tradition of viewing the Arabians as happy pastoralists.
[9]The phrase 'all that is solid melts into air', as I have argued elsewhere, appears to derive from Shakespeare's *The Tempest* (Olwig 1990). It is not impossible that both Baggesen and Blicher had this passage, which reflects on the relationship between theatre scenery and the real life world, in mind when they described their ephemeral visions on the heath.

...be cheerful, sir.
Our revels now are ended.These our actors,
As I foretold you, were all spirits, and
Are melted into air, into thin air;
And, like the baseless fabric of this vision,
The cloud-capp'd towers, the gorgeous palaces,
The solemn temples, the great globe itself,
Yea, all which it inherit, shall dissolve,
And, like this insubstantial pageant faded,
Leave not a rack behind. We are such stuff
As dreams are made on, and our little life
Is rounded with a sleep (Shakespeare 1954: 103-4).

[10] From an article of 1884-5, entitled 'The past and future forests of the Jutland Heaths'.

REFERENCES

Baggesen, Jens. 1971. *Labyrinten*. Copenhagen: Gyldendal.
Berman, Marshall. 1982. *All That is Solid Melts into Air: The Experience of Modernity*, pp.60-71. New York: Simon and Schuster.
Collins-Klett. 1983. *German-English Dictionary*. London: Collins
Cronon, William. 1990. 'Modes of Prophecy and Production: Placing Nature in History', *The Journal of American History,* **76**(4): 1122-1131.
Dalgas, Enrico 1869-9. *Geographiske Billeder fra Heder.* 2 vols. Copenhagen: C.A. Reitzel.
Everhart, William C. 1972. *The National Park Service*. New York: Praeger.
Hard. G. 1965. 'Arkadien in Deutschland, Bemerkungen zu einem landschaftlichem

Reiz', *Die Erde*, **96**(1).

Hard, G. 1970. *Die 'Landschaft' der Sprache und die 'Landschaft' der Geografien: Semantische und forschungslogische Studien*. Colloquium Geographicum, Bonn b.11. Bonn: Ferd. Dümmlers Verlag

Lovejoy, Arthur O. 1973. *The Great Chain of Being*. Cambridge, Mass.: Harvard University Press.

Lowenthal, David. 1958. *George Perkins Marsh: Versatile Vermonter.* New York: Columbia Univ. Press.

Marsh, George Perkins. 1967 (orig. 1864). *Man and Nature*, ed. David Lowenthal. Cambridge, Mass.: Belknap, Harvard University Press.

Ordbog over Det Danske Sprog. 1931. Copenhagen: Gyldendal.

Olwig, Karen Fog 1980. 'National parks, tourism, and local development: a West Indian case', *Human Organisation* **XXXIX**(1): 22-31.

Olwig, Kenneth R. 1980. 'Historical Geography and the Society Nature "Problematic": The Perspective of J.F. Schouw, G.P. Marsh and E. Reclus', *Journal of Historical Geography* **VI**(1): 29-45.

Olwig, Kenneth R. 1984. *Nature's Ideological Landscape*. London: Allen and Unwin (this book is also available in Danish translation under the title, *Hedens Natur: Om Natursyn og Naturanvendelse Gennem Tiderne*, (Copenhagen: Teknisk forlag, 1986).

Olwig, Kenneth R. 1989. 'The Childhood Deconstruction of Nature', *Children's Environments Quarterly*, **6**(1).

Olwig, Kenneth R. 1990. 'Nature, Structure, and Daily Life: Planning, Landscape, and the Idea of Nature'. In *Fysisk Planlegging i Forvandling: Natur-Struktur-Hverdagsliv*, ed. Sigrun Kaul. Stockholm: Nordiska institutet för samhällsplanering. Also published as: 'Literary Perspectives on Planning, Landscape and the Idea of Nature', *The National Geographical Journal of India*, **36**, March-June 1990.

Olwig, Kenneth R. 1993. 'Sexual Cosmology: Nation and Landscape at the Conceptual Interstices of nature and Culture, or: What does Landscape Really Mean?' In Barbara Bender (ed.) *Landscape: Politics and Perspectives*. Oxford: Berg.

Oxford English Dictionary 1971. Oxford: Oxford University Press

Rona, Georg (ed.) 1965. *Kulturhistorisk Leksikon for nordisk middelalder,* v. X. Copenhagen: Rosenkilde og Bagger.

Shakespeare, William 1954, *The Tempest*, Arden Edition, Frank Kermode, ed., 'Epilogue':1-20. London: Methuen.

Schama, Simon. 1987 'Dutch Landscapes: Culture as Foreground'. In Peter C. Sutton, *Masters of 17th-Century Dutch Landscape Painting*, pp.64-83. London: Herbert Press.

Sauer, C.O. 1969. 'The morphology of landscape'. In *Land and life*, J. Leighly (ed.), 315-50. Berkeley: University of California Press. First published 1925

Schouw, Joachim Frederik 1832. 'Om Naturvidenskabernes Fremstilling for Folket', *Dansk Ugeskrift*, **15**(I): 221-31.

Schouw, Joachim Frederik 1845. *Scandinaviens Natur og Folk: Et Foredrag holdt den 22nde November 1844 i det Skandinaviske Selskab*. Copenhagen: Reitzel.

Schouw, Joachim Frederik 1852. *The Earth Plants and Man: Popular Pictures of Nature*. London: A. Henfrey (trans.).

Webster's Seventh New Collegiate Dictionary 1963. Springfield, MA: Merriam

Worster, Donald. 1990. 'Transformations of the Earth: Toward an Agroecological Perspective in History', *The Journal of American History*, **76**(4): 1087-1106.

'Forsaken Spot' to 'Classic Ground': Geological Heritage in Australia and the Recuperative Power of the Deep Past

Kirsty Douglas[1]

The meaning of landscapes takes novel forms in Australia's topographically understated but climatically dramatic interior. The dearth of lush valleys, navigable rivers and forested alpine scenery west of the Great Divide encourages a landscape aesthetic shaped instead by the provision of a fourth dimension, a sense of the grand temporal scales represented by deep-time landscapes, objects and Indigenous cultures in Australia. Building on ideas about cultural and natural heritage in Australia, and taking literature on geological heritage buried in reports and in-house journals, this paper begins to construct a theory of geological heritage and of the recuperative power of the deep past. By this I mean the language of merit and significance attached to landscapes on the basis of their age, when they or their material productions are recognised as geologically or archaeologically significant. Here I have concentrated on three landscapes celebrated for their geological particularity but elsewhere categorised as waste or barren (Figure 1).

The Hallett Cove Conservation Park is about twenty kilometres south of Adelaide. It was preserved from encroaching suburbia in 1975, primarily because of its 280 million-year-old Permian glacial features and their contribution to geological debates spanning one hundred years, from the possibility of southern hemisphere glaciation, which was first postulated in the 1880s, to the plate tectonic revolution of the mid-twentieth century. The second case study involves the Lake Callabonna Fossil Reserve south-east of Lake Eyre in South Australia, or more particularly, the graveyard of giant extinct marsupials first delivered to western science in 1893. It was placed on the Register for the National Estate in 1980 for the quantity of pleistocene bones eroding from its surface sediments. But it entered the canon of significant geological landscapes in the 1890s and the South Australian Government declared it the new nation's first 'Fossil Reserve' in 1901. Further to the south and east, the dry lakes of semi-arid western New South Wales' Willandra Lakes Region were inscribed on the World Heritage List in 1981 for their cultural, archaeological and geological significances. This third episode hinges around a moment in February 1968 when the Victorian geomorphologist Jim Bowler found a collection of split and charred bones protruding from a blowout on a sand dune bordering Lake Mungo. This bundle of bones, identified as a Pleistocene human cremation, is known colloquially as Lake Mungo 1 or Mungo Lady.[2]

Environment and History **12** (2006): 269–96

Earth scientists and others involved in the classification of geological heritage have written extensively on how to identify, protect and define it, but as yet, the practice of geological heritage remains largely untheorised in Australia, in contrast to other sorts of cultural and natural heritage.[3] It is not my purpose to negotiate the complexities of modern heritage discourse and method. Nor have I attempted to plot a path between the often-conflicting requirements of State and Commonwealth heritage legislation. Instead this paper is a first step towards a theory of geological heritage in Australia through an examination of ways in which three landscapes can be described as having been, in a sense, 'saved', or recuperated via the discovery and articulation of a deep past. Value in a landscape is negotiated at the boundaries of the sometimes incompatible sacralisations of science versus heritage, education and training versus preservation, indigenous and other patrimonies and the requirements of tourism or industry.

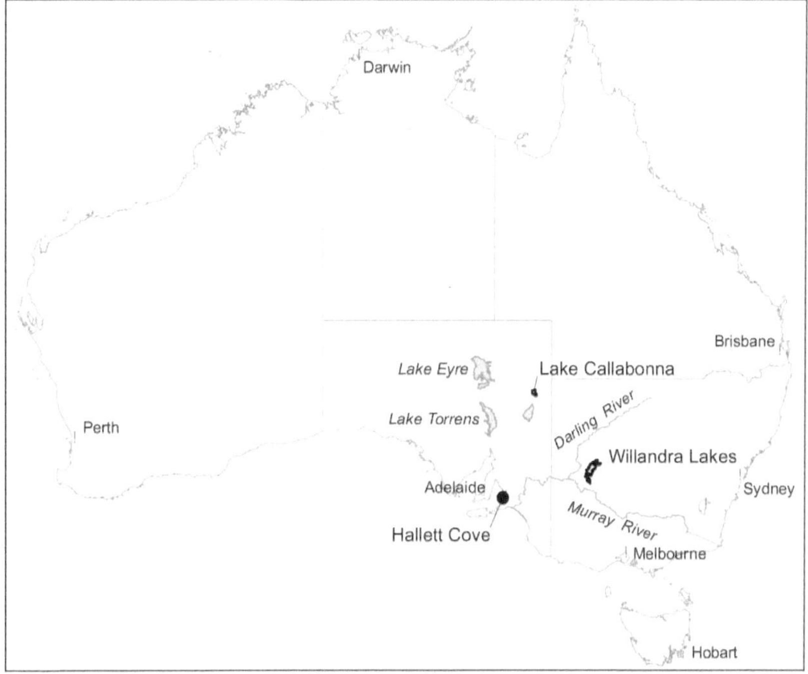

FIGURE 1. Locality map. Hallett Cove Conservation Park, Lake Callabonna Fossil Reserve (SA), Willandra Lakes World Heritage Area (NSW). (produced by Heritage Information Section, Heritage Division, Department of the Environment and Heritage, Canberra, Australia)

WHAT IS GEOLOGICAL HERITAGE?

Australian geologists, vertebrate palaeontologists and archaeologists regard each of these three areas as more or less canonical in the annals of their respective disciplines. They form part of the ill-defined, expanding catalogue of sites or features which make up the nation's geological heritage. The human geographer Graeme Aplin, reflecting on the nature of heritage management in the late twentieth and early twenty-first centuries, declined to prescribe a definitive answer to the question he posed, 'What is "heritage"?'. Graeme Davison refused a simple answer to a similar question in *The Use and Abuse of Australian History*. David Lowenthal described 'the cult of heritage' as 'a newly popular faith ... a self-conscious creed, whose shrines and icons daily multiply and whose prose suffuses public discourse'. As such, a broad, all-weather definition may be futile, because nothing about the word is definitive: according to Lowenthal, 'heritage relies on revealed faith rather than rational proof'. Even a discussion of its plurality of meanings and origins will not satisfy everyone. Still it is worthwhile briefly to consider some antecedents and counterparts to the practice of geological heritage in Australia.[4]

In 1985 the Australian archaeologist Isabel McBryde wrote in an introduction to a collection of essays about the control of cultural heritage that the site as 'national symbol' emerged in the nineteenth century 'as part of the historical self-consciousness of a number of European states'. Demands for guidelines for the protection of this national heritage were framed 'in terms of the site as both symbol and patrimony'. Sites and artefacts physically and metaphysically linked the past with the present. States thereby re-invented both past and present to serve national and political agendas in the pursuit of 'collective self-conscious identity'. Ten years later Denis Byrne, an archaeologist, connected 'the concept of heritage' inextricably to the practice of archaeology in Australia 'since at least the 1970s'. In keeping with McBryde's argument, Byrne wrote that 'archaeology and cultural nationalism march hand in hand in virtually every country in the world'. The historian Tim Bonyhady mused on the 'forgotten' pre-Federation antecedents of the 'preservationist usage' of heritage by the Whitlam Government a century later. He provided a contemporary legal definition of its bedmate, the National Estate, 'defined in the Australian Heritage Commission Act as those parts of the natural or cultural environment that "have aesthetic, historic, scientific, or social significance or other special value for future generations as well as for the present community"'. Section 2 of the new Australian Heritage Council Act (2003), which replaced the earlier Act, retains the same phrase.[5]

This list of prerequisites from a small sample of available literature foregrounds attributes considered important by people involved in the identification, interpretation and conservation of geological heritage, but it also highlights an important difference between the articulation of geological and mainstream heritage values. The custodians of geological heritage such as the Geological

Society of Australia (GSA) find particular resonance in references to scientific value, 'other special value' and the allusion to posterity in the phrase 'future generations'.[6] They regard aesthetic significance, given priority in the Australian Heritage Council (AHC) Act, as marginal, although recently the GSA has considered the ill-defined 'aesthetic values' as an 'avenue for further research', not to mention financial support.[7] Furthermore, there are several recent examples of close collaboration between tourism boards, local people and museum and geological workers. National Parks and Wildlife Services (NPWS) and scientists at the Naracoorte Caves World Heritage Fossil Site in south-eastern South Australia have worked fruitfully together to build ties with the South Australian Tourism Commission, better to integrate scientific and aesthetic values in marketing the site and to position the state as 'a unique and diverse tourist destination'. At 'Kronosaurus Korner', the Richmond Marine Fossil Museum in central Queensland, palaeontologists and curators work with people in the region to promote fossil conservation, research and commercial tourist potential, while encouraging local employment. The Queensland Museum also attempts to foster such links. However, for all their focus on community involvement and the marketing of geo-heritage, these collaborative exercises still emphasise function, in the sense of geological processes, training and preservation, over form.[8]

In contrast in the United Kingdom, building on thirty years of work through the Geological Conservation Review begun in the late 1970s, the 'Regionally Important Geological-geomorphological Sites', or 'RIGS' programs involve local organisations and people with site protection and management, including the assessment, maintenance and promotion of 'aesthetic character'. The former convenor of the GSA's standing committee on geological heritage, Bernie Joyce, noted that in Australia, 'Pioneering work on the assessment of aesthetic values was carried out during the Central Highlands study', which was the second Australian Heritage Commission joint assessment of National Estate values. There is space between the AHC criteria and the pragmatic, scientistic approach of the GSA to harness geological heritage and notions of deep time to landscape aesthetics, thereby fostering a broader, geologically informed appreciation of both geology and landscape in the general public.[9]

Geological heritage identification and management is an evolving methodology with a corpus of literature often buried in reports and submissions by the various bodies associated with its articulation and implementation. The movement has to some extent (reciprocally) adopted the rhetoric of the United Nations Organization for Education, Science and Culture's (UNESCO) World Heritage Convention with its ranking of 'significance' into local, regional, national and international categories and the apparent contradiction of 'uniqueness' or 'outstanding value' tempered by 'representativeness'. Joyce described the two approaches in the following terms, as located along a 'spectrum of importance' whereby 'at the rare end of the scale we may have a *unique* site. At the *common* end we may have a group of features, from which a *representative* example could be selected'. He justified representation as allowing 'a significance to be attached to one or several features which can best represent a group of similar features'. Such an example 'need not be outstanding or striking, but need only be typical of the group it is to represent'. Other assessment criteria include educational potential, historical significance and importance for ongoing research or reference.[10] Despite the shared language, only around 20 sites inscribed on the World Heritage List are there primarily because of their geological interest, from a total of 690 sites worldwide of which 138 are natural, 23 mixed and 529 cultural.[11]

Geological heritage may be embodied in a 'site' or a 'feature'. A site is an area of land of geological interest, like the Hallett Cove Conservation Park or the Lake Mungo National Park (Figure 2). A feature shows an aspect of geology or geomorphology which does not necessarily have a 'particular extent': it may be a process such as erosion or a discrete site, exposure or object like a type section or a fossil locality. For example, the park boundaries at Hallett Cove protect exposed objects such as Tate's Rock and processes such as the badlands erosion of the Amphitheatre (Figure 2). The Lake Callabonna and Lake Eyre basin fossil localities separately constitute 'features', although they can also be described as 'sites'. The terminology, like much about geological herit-

FIGURE 2. Hallett Cove Conservation Park. View of the Amphitheatre from the south. (Photograph K. Douglas)

age, reflecting the discipline from which it takes its name, is both specific and slippery. Earth scientists have used the term 'geological monument' to embody sites or features of geological heritage significance, or, to quote Bernie Joyce again, 'those features of a region which form the essential basis of geological education, research and reference'.[12] Control of meaning is as important to the community of earth scientists as to other heritage practitioners.

Partly an attempt to rectify the perceived low public profile of sites of geological heritage, the institution of a system of Global Geoparks is another initiative encouraged by those such as UNESCO involved in geological heritage and geoscience education world-wide. It is further regarded as a complement to eco-tourism, preserving global 'Geo-diversity' by making it economically sustainable. The official web-site of the China-based Office of the World Geopark Network explains the Geopark philosophy as

> educating the general public in environmental matters. They also serve as tools for demonstrating sustainable development and for illustrating methods of site conservation as well as remembering that rocks, minerals, fossils, soils, landforms and landscapes are both the products and record of the evolution of our planet Earth and, as such, form an integral part of the natural world.[13]

The first International Geopark Conference was held in Beijing in late June, 2004. Through its Earth Sciences Division (now subsumed within the Ecology and Earth Sciences Division), UNESCO set up an Advisory Board for Geoparks in 2001. There are now 33 UNESCO-accredited Global Geoparks. Of these, 12 are in China, from a total of 85 Chinese National Geoparks. The rest are in Europe. The proposal for acceptance into the Global Network of the first Iranian national Geopark, on Qeshm Island in the Persian Gulf, has just been assessed (June 2005).[14] UNESCO's support is underpinned by the Geopark Network's undertaking to promote geo-heritage for the purposes of preservation (of sites, objects and processes), education, tourism, sustainable development and the creation of jobs for local people. Since 2002, Dr Sue Turner, Australia's lone Geopark advocate and a vigorous proponent of Geo-tourism, has been building an Australian-Pacific Network, in the interests of obtaining UNESCO assistance and accreditation.[15] Despite its philosophical links to eco-tourism and World Heritage, the language of Geoparks, at least in Australia, is still notably utilitarian, again focussed on finance, education, training and sustainability rather than aesthetics. Turner has noted by way of contrast that in her talks in Beijing and Paris, she is encouraged to emphasise 'links to landscape for cultural reasons and human resonance'. Instead in Australia, the funding bodies she approaches require 'practical finance-based facts'.[16]

Notwithstanding a shared vocabulary, shared legislation and some shared sites, geological heritage is distinct from other types of natural and cultural heritage, with different emphases. Landscapes embody it as *earth history*, revealed like the cyclical climate change evident in the Lake Mungo badlands stratigraphy;

and as the *history of a discipline in Australia*, illustrated by certain landforms or material remains, for instance Tate's Rock or the site of the 1893 South Australian Museum campsite at Lake Callabonna. Earth scientists therefore value a geological monument for its physical qualities or for the stories it tells about the development of their discipline. The GSA terms the latter 'classic sites'.[17] The distinction converges with Graeme Aplin's umbrella notion of heritage, as, in an Australian context at least, 'Two sets of ideas – heritage as a set of ideals, and heritage as things – merged in the 1960s so that heritage now refers to things that represent ideals'. The recognition of geologically significant sites and their ongoing protection help to ensure the continuity and integrity of earth science research in Australia. The landforms, as receptacles in which scientists locate geological knowledge, keep the history and the future of the discipline.[18]

The performance of geological heritage also differs from broad ideas of cultural and natural heritage because of its emphasis on practical research over patrimony (with the possible exception of Geoparks, whose rhetoric implies a notion of global patrimony). Barry Cooper and Maud McBriar, both past-convenors of the Sub-committee on Geological Conservation of the South Australian branch of the GSA, and Bernie Joyce, have all stressed the importance and difficulty of finding a balance between the incompatible requirements of conservation and of industry. The GSA as a national body representing a membership drawn from among Australian earth scientists in industry and academia is uniquely and tenuously poised. It has been slow to adopt Geoparks discourse.[19] The needs of extractive sciences and earth heritage are often in conflict. Extraction is anathema to many National Parks representatives who share the custodianship of geological monuments within national park boundaries. Conversely, in the eyes of many geologists the point of geological conservation is to aid present and future geological research, which is sometimes necessarily destructive. Some members of the GSA perceive a potential and irreconcilable conflict of interest for the society between the requirements of the extractive industries and the requirements of conservation. They anticipate that the protection of sites and features on the grounds of geological significance will set a precedent with potentially awkward ramifications for the mining industry.[20]

On the other hand, sites of geological heritage form part of the national estate. With respect to cultural heritage, Isabel McBryde wrote that 'New visions of the past, or new versions of the past, may serve social and political ends'. This applies equally to natural and geological heritage. The site or feature becomes a symbol of national unity. The GSA regards geological heritage as patrimony of a different kind, ostensibly harnessed not in the interests of fortifying collective national identity but pragmatically, as a scientific or educational resource.[21] But in a nation like Australia which has not reconciled its precolonial and colonial pasts with its 'post'-colonial present, 'geological patrimony' is conveniently located in a prehuman past that can be made national and international. Non-Indigenous Australians, accused by cultural historians like Paul Carter of co-opting landscape history and Aboriginal heritage as a sort of prosthetic past to compensate for our shallow roots, can embrace the superlatives 'oldest', 'largest', 'outstanding', 'world-class', freed from the burden of someone else's history. Lake Callabonna, we are told, 'represents a unique accumulation': there is 'no other site like it in the world'. Hallett Cove achieves, as the South Australian Science Teachers' Association put it, 'world-wide significance' because of its links to other Gondwanan sites across the globe.[22]

In this context any notion of archaeological patrimony is immediately problematic. Some archaeologists argue (from a sound genetic basis, according to modern scientific orthodoxy) that Pleistocene human remains like those at Lake Mungo transcend race and ownership because of their great age (upward of 45,000 years B.P), the impossibility of tracing modern affiliations or of gauging the wishes of the long dead, and their impact on debates about the origin and geographic radiation of modern human beings. The eminent Australian historian and archaeologist John Mulvaney has convincingly made such arguments regarding the 'handback' of Kow Swamp burial remains in the 1990s.[23] Professor Mulvaney is an impassioned advocate for the protection of heritage as 'a national possession' vital for the construction of collective identity. Furthermore, as the British archaeologist Colin Renfrew expressed it, 'The world archaeology is something in which we can all share': this is justification by globalisation.[24] Some Indigenous Australians argue that the remains are the ancestors of the traditional custodians of the region and therefore constitute Indigenous cultural property and should be 'returned' to the Indigenous 'owners' for appropriate disposition.[25] On the one hand is the assumption of the 'universality of [archaeological] values' and the importance of cultural heritage to national collective self-perception, as Mulvaney has argued.[26] On the other are the unassailable moral claims of dispossessed people to what they perceive as their cultural property and the assumption of a homogeneous community of Aboriginal meaning and culture through time. These debates are of course not restricted to Australian archaeology. The predicament of many North American archaeologists is characterised by situations like the ongoing, often acrimonious debate surrounding the discovery, acquisition, investigation and disposition of the so-called 'Kennewick Man', found in 1996 in eastern Washington State, one of the most complete and oldest skeletons excavated in North America. Questions of its 'cultural and genetic affiliations' are balanced by questions about the nature of the truth claims of Western science versus those of indigenous traditions and the ownership of pre-Columbian material culture.[27]

Philosophical issues attached to the notion of geological heritage are at first glance less thorny than those linked to the material remains of the human past. The questions of 'who owns the past?' – its physical remains – and 'who controls the past?' – or perceptions of the past – are clearly less sensitive when dealing with 280 million-year-old glacial deposits at Hallett Cove or the fossil traces of Precambrian 'jellyfish' at Ediacara in the Flinders Ranges of South Australia, as opposed to the remains of somebody's meal or great aunt in the human past. Geological heritage operates very differently at the archaeological sites of the Willandra Lakes compared to Hallett Cove and Lake Callabonna. But the issues become hazier when dealing with material that might have informed Aboriginal understanding of their own pasts. Is there such a thing as non-cultural heritage in country as saturated with meaning as Australia?

I do not necessarily mean, with this question, to conflate geological heritage and indigenous cultural heritage, but they are clearly sometimes mutually referable, as in the examples which follow. Nineteenth-century naturalists and their informants reported many Aboriginal accounts which linked megafaunal bone accumulations such as Callabonna's with ancestral figures and the formation of the land and its features. In 1996, fossil poachers removed some 120 million-year-old dinosaur footprints from Crab Creek, near Broome, Western Australia. Among other stakeholders, the ensuing media and scientific attention focussed on the Rubibi people, to whom the trackways were a sacred link to ancestors.[28] Furthermore, it is naïve to assume that debates about 'ownership' are somehow answered by encouraging indigenous people to manage 'their own' sites (as Geoparks regulations require), as witnessed by ongoing challenges to A<u>n</u>angu management of the Ulu<u>r</u>u-Kata Tju<u>t</u>a National Park in central Australia. Governed by the precedent-setting Northern Territory Aboriginal Sacred Sites Act, 1989, the World Heritage Area is a model for Indigenous/government co-management. Nonetheless, many issues undermine efforts by A<u>n</u>angu to preserve and manage the site, and the cultural and spiritual heritage there embodied.[29] Such legislation does little to settle challenges by non-Aboriginal tour and resort operators who claim that 'Ayers Rock' is a national 'icon' and therefore belongs to all Australians, or by the many visitors who assert their right to climb 'the Rock', against the wishes of the A<u>n</u>angu owners.

HALLETT COVE AS 'CLASSIC GROUND': GEOLOGICAL HERITAGE AND THE BATTLE FOR MEANING

The South Australian division of the GSA has played a central role in the preservation of geological heritage in that state since 1966 when the glacial pavements of Hallett Cove became the movement's flagship.[30] To date its Geological Heritage Subcommittee has collated over 400 geological monuments in the state into the eight-volume *Geological Monuments in South Australia* (The 44,800 hectare Lake Callabonna Fossil Reserve also numbers among these). From 1958 to 1975 campaigners fought to prevent housing developers from building over coastal landforms and geological exposures with historical and educational significance at the cove. The society declared the glacial landforms a geological monument in the 1960s and the 50 hectare park, opened in 1976, was placed on the Register for the National Estate in 1981. The perceived danger to Hallett Cove's geological 'integrity' posed by the proposed suburban developments mobilised academic geologists, teachers and those concerned more generally with lack of public consultation and the state's natural heritage. The material remnants of its deep past elevated the site from a somewhat degraded coastal landscape to a geological feather in South Australia's heritage cap.[31]

Many of the Hallett Cove campaigners continue to represent their victory as the vindication of a geological awareness of landscape. By invoking the fourth dimension, they effected a local appreciation of places worth saving in the state in counterpoint to the monumentalism sometimes associated with the establishment of national parks in, for instance, North America and New Zealand or on the east coast of Australia. But their declarations were no less hyperbolic. The campaign literature of Hallett Cove insisted on the need to preserve the site, with its 'almost unbelievable glimpses of the past', for 'the future'. If South Australia's geographical 'circumstances' required a 'system that could overcome the paucity of snow-clad mountain-top scenery' then the grandeur of deep time in the intimate setting of Hallett Cove provided just that. For example, the GSA(SA)'s nomination of Hallett Cove to the Register for the National Estate in 1977 describes the glacial features as the 'best of the (late Palaeozoic) Australian glacial pavements... amongst the best in the world'. The park boundaries protect a 'world renowned area of geology' preserving the glacial pavements 'in relation to older and younger rocks' thus revealing aspects of 'the geological history over the last 600 million years'. Not only qualitatively the 'best in the world', the cove rocks tell a story of South Australia spanning the top eighth of earth history.[32]

Conservationists and developers faced each other across front page headlines in the Adelaide *Advertiser* in a battle to determine the shape of meaning and to control landscape aesthetics at the cove. The literature of the conservationists likened processes of urbanisation to the spread of a disease or an alien terror, employing such images as the 'tentacles of urban sprawl', 'menacing encroachment', 'developer's devouring teeth' and 'senselessly scraped off the map'. Pre-'development' Hallett Cove was, somewhat misleadingly, a botanical refuge, 'close to its natural condition', 'nature in its untamed state', 'magnificent and unspoiled', 'a beauty spot', 'a picturesque landscape', 'a source of beauty and pleasure', and 'St Vincent Gulf's most beautiful natural cove'.[33]

This is patently at odds with the reality of a landscape which had been grazed, mined and farmed for well over one hundred years, as pointed out by spokesmen for the development companies who declared that 'there has been some emotional thinking on the subject'.[34] It was disingenuously heedless of evidence for pre-European modification of the landscape in the form of Aboriginal 'tool factories' and fires which, as related in the conservationists' own literature, Matthew Flinders reported in 1802. But the campaigners' rhetoric is tempered by real grief at the perceived or imminent loss to the South Australian public of 'yet another unique landmark' and anger at the bureaucratic opacity, hypocrisy and lack of consultation that leads to such 'decay'. As an editorial in the *Advertiser* claimed in September 1971, 'the best of the environment cannot be left to the hands of local government'. In contrast, the vocabulary of would-be developers, while acknowledging the 'magnificence' of the 'outlook' and the 'panoramic views', stressed the 'deficiency' of the beach, the lack of scenic attraction of the 'steep and broken landform', the 'rapid degeneration' of the area which has been 'defaced', 'denuded' and 'degraded', not by subdivision but by agriculture and by 'uncontrolled public access' resulting from the site's 'isolation'. This could best be countered with judicious application of the town planner's salve.[35]

Hallett Cove is an equivocal success. Some geologists and members of the National Trust maintain that the scientific value of the park and reserve is compromised because potentially important sites whose geology has not been investigated were and continue to be lost to housing.[36] Nevertheless, some gains were made in the interests of education, research and the history of the discipline. The GSA successfully and opportunistically mobilised South Australia's deep past, its material remains and intellectual legacy, public opinion and landscape aesthetics in the interests of geological heritage and the establishment of a collective national treasure chest of places worth saving. The stories of Hallett Cove thus begin to demonstrate the capacity of deep time to salvage and recuperate a threatened, degraded, domesticated landscape.

LAKE CALLABONNA: A 'MOST UNEXPECTED LOCATION'

The sediments of Lake Callabonna preserve the largest assemblage of diprotodon remains yet discovered (Figure 3). These rhinoceros-sized marsupials were mired in the drying lake and died of thirst up to 100,000 years ago. While the fight for Hallett Cove was a test case for the geological heritage movement in South Australia and has become in a sense emblematic of a perceived paradigmatic shift in environmental policy in the state during the 1960s and 1970s, public contest has not marred the frosted gypsum surface of Callabonna for a hundred years. Its desiccated landscape illustrates a redemptive aspect to deep time objects and palaeoenvironmental reconstruction in a different way from Hallett Cove. In its evocation of dying diprotodons in a dying lake, the standard palaeontological *Just So* story refreshes the trope of the watered inland in a Cainozoic land of plenty, reiterated later in the Willandra Lakes-Lake Mungo story.[37] The material remains of Callabonna's Pleistocene past and their interpretation gives the modern landscape layers of meaning otherwise unintelligible and unimaginable.

Before the revelation of its palaeontological wealth in 1892, Lake Mulligan as it was then known was chiefly renowned as the easternmost shore of Edward John Eyre's great 'horseshoe lake' of impassable salt flats and mud, which supposedly curved northward around the Flinders Ranges, stretching from Lake

FIGURE 3. South Australian Museum expedition to Lake Callabonna in 1893, looking south-west. (Photograph from E.C. Stirling and A.H.C Zietz 1899. 'Fossil remains of Lake Callabonna, Part I…'. *Memoirs of the Royal Society of South Australia* 1[1]).

Torrens in the west, Lakes Eyre and Gregory in the north to the south-eastern Lake Frome. Successive expeditions by B.H. Babbage, P.E. Warburton, John McDouall Stuart and A.C. Gregory during the 1850s shattered the horseshoe as pastoralism 'opened up' the interior of South Australia. Gregory, the leader of the first European expedition to pass between Lakes Blanche and Callabonna in search of the lost Ludwig Leichhardt, dismissed this country to the north of the Flinders Ranges with devastating brevity as 'sterile and of little practical value'.[38]

Creek beds and clay pans tell of other hydrological regimes when rivers flow and the dust turns to mire. An eyewitness, Harold Fletcher of the Australian Museum, described an enigmatic, provocative landscape stretching 'away to the north', 'completely devoid of vegetation', producing feelings 'of gloom and loneliness' in the viewer:

> Even bird life was practically non-existent, and this introduced a hushed stillness adding an aura of mystery to the desolate countryside... Away in the distance, towards the centre of the lake, a cluster of vegetation was miraged up, seemingly to float in the air.[39]

The lake is overwritten by another emerging from Fletcher's understanding, as a natural historian, of an 'empty' landscape and a deeper palaeontological past. But before it was a graveyard there were other lakes there: inland sea, horseshoe lake, saltbush plain, swamp, desert, too boggy, too dry, wasteland, midden, refuge, larder. These stories intersect with the lake's geological heritage. Meaning is as unstable as the lake surface.

The *South Australian Register* earlier adopted a similarly cabbalistic voice after John Meldrum, a well digger from Callabonna Station, brought the first collection of bones to Adelaide from Lake Mulligan. In August 1893 the newspaper linked the 'sterile' landscape to the wonder of the deep past: 'the gigantic creatures of a bygone age whose relics are embedded in the hardened mud and débris of what were once the huge swamps of the Far North-East'.[40] Another anonymous source in the *Register* described the Callabonna site in 1894 as located in 'a series of "claypans" in the vast desert north-east of Farina. It is a "lake" only in flood times – an arid waterless region of sand and salt pools'. Ornamenting this scene are 'the bones of these monsters' which lie as they died, by the hundreds. But far from contributing to the Hadean character of the site, the bones raised questions which began to recuperate the environment of Callabonna:

> On what did they feed? Why were they made so enormously strong?... What astonishing changes in the climate and rainfall must have occurred since these beasts roamed in the jungle as the rhinoceros, or in swamps as the hippopotamus?... These things are among the buried secrets of the great past, which secrets science is unlocking.[41]

Again in the *Register,* in May 1893, the bleakness of Callabonna as 'a more apparently uninteresting and forsaken spot' than which 'could not be found in the whole of Australia' is juxtaposed with a fulsome account of its glorious deep past, as revealed once again by heavily reified Science :

> What a different picture of the past history of this country is brought to light by the new discoveries! [Nearby] Mount Searle... was probably at the period of which we speak fully twice [its present] elevation. On its sides grew huge trees, and all around was a dense tropical growth, exceeding in luxuriance the forests of the eastern slopes of the Andes in South America. Every form of life on the whole earth was at that time huge and uncouth... [These skeletons] are a magnificent treasure in the interests of science... Of very far-reaching significance is the story which is told by these mute relics of a remote age.[42]

The discovery 'in the most unexpected' location, 'of incalculable value to science', went some way to redeeming the lake as a functional colonial landscape.[43] At first glance, the story reads as degeneration from a Pleistocene Eden to a modern desert. Closer reading shows that value in the modern landscape is clearly attached to the wealth of meaning the bones provide. E.C. Stirling, as Director of the South Australian Museum, visited the museum's campsite in 1894 and worked on the fossil material from 1893-1913, with his assistant

Amandus Zietz. In an article in the journal *Nature* in 1894, Stirling dismissed the scenic merits of the lake in unflattering terms as 'Almost unsurpassable for barrenness and utter desolation'. Names 'such as Mount Hopeless, Dreary Point, Illusion Plains, Mount Deception, Mirage Creek' invoked the 'character of the surrounding country' in which 'Scarcely any vegetation relieves the prevailing desolation'. As for the lake itself, 'not a bush relieves the unbroken monotony of the level, white crystalline surface'. But he tempered his criticism of the region's sparse severity considerably with his statement that 'There is compensation for the uncompromising physical features' of the lake 'in the fact that its bed has lately been shown to be a veritable necropolis of gigantic extinct Marsupials and Birds, which have apparently died where they lie, literally in hundreds'.[44]

Sixty years later, the lake was a successful port of call for the Berkeley palaeontologist and Fulbright Scholar Ruben Stirton and his graduate student Dick Tedford on their first trip to Australia in 1953. Stirton, whose name is inextricably linked to Callabonna in the annals of South Australian science, is credited by many of his students with inspiring a renaissance in the study of mammalian palaeontology in Australia in the 1950s.[45] By the time he first set eyes on the lake in May 1953, rediscovering the museum's 1893 camp, the desolation of the landscape barely warranted comment. The laconic Texan explorer-geologist with an eye for detail was making science instead.

> I finally wandered back on the lake floor and came into the high dune ... I could see saline flats island-ward from the dune before I reached it ... Off to my left I saw an object that looked like a box-board. So I strolled over that way ... I then came upon a kangaroo skeleton that commanded my attention for a few minutes as I looked for the cranium and mandibles. We have been picking up the best ones ... Next I saw some forked posts about half buried that seemed to form the uprights for a shelter. All this and other objects about rather convinced me that I had found Zietz' camp site. Then I thought, '[Diprotodon] must be about'. In the water and at the edges of the water were objects that could be what we had been looking for, within 5 minutes I had located the weathered remains of 9 Diprotodon skeletons.[46]

The landscape only intruded into Stirton's account negatively when he headed 'the long distance back to the car'. Perhaps his equanimity derived partly from the expedition's mode of transport, by Land Rover and truck instead of camel, and partly from the difficulties of field work in his arid Texan home state, but the rigours of a one-month journey were still considerable. The landscape provided compensation as much as tribulation. He had rediscovered a site of great contemporary significance and palaeontological wealth, against the predictions of his colleagues at the museum.[47]

Although he was in Australia principally to search for older fossils than the Pleistocene Callabonna remains, Stirton's joy in discovery, even of these 'young' fossils, is palpable. On 1 June, after their first full day working on the Callabonna fossils, he wrote: 'we hit bone ... It is a pleasure to give a field number to a fossil'.[48] The landscape featured only in so far as it thwarted or facilitated science. It intruded as a mild inconvenience, a recalcitrant container unwilling to relinquish palaeontological knowledge: 'The mud is so sticky it is a fight to get it off the shovel ... we were standing in slush and water half way up our shoes ... It is difficult to get close to the water because of the soft mud'. The fossils and the traces of past scientific endeavour are both *features* of the landscape – for example, Stirton recorded that his 'favorite place is on the femur of a partly eroded Diprotodon exposed at the water's edge' – and *measures* of its stability – 'It was in a mound like this that I found one of the whiskey jars indicating [the] stability [of the mounds] for as long as 50 years'. So taken together fossils and the history of vertebrate palaeontology can form the connecting threads in an investigation of the power of deep time to replenish and recuperate country which, like Lake Callabonna, has been in other contexts deemed useless or barren.

Fossils are to some extent moveable heritage. The South Australian Museum and other collections in Queensland and New South Wales stand in for and replace the physical site at Callabonna. The pragmatics of climate, distance, collection and preparation ensure that it remains a lode to be mined or left in place, not a museum or teaching resource in its own right, as is Hallett Cove. The lake itself, in its distance from scientific institutions, and its bones, in their fragility and extraordinary preservation, have a mystique and morbid fascination lacking in the everyday utilitarianism of Hallett Cove's readily accessible 'outdoor laboratory'. This mystique, unrelated to conventional Western evaluations of landscape beauty, cannot be divorced from its scientific value and interpretation, showing that geological heritage can be harnessed in the development of a landscape aesthetic appropriate to the 'arid', 'flat', 'monotonous', 'barren' country of north-eastern South Australia.

LAKE MUNGO: 'FORSAKEN SPOT' TO 'LAND OF LAKES'

During the 1880s, surveyors' reports in western New South Wales noted the presence of collections of bivalve shells and fish bones around the rims and on the surfaces of broad dry ovoid saltbush plains. As early as 1838, Major Thomas Mitchell identified these plains with their leeward arcuate dunes as dry lakes, by analogy with extant salt lakes.[49] The scientific salvation of the Willandra Lakes Region lies in the more recent past. It was not until the 1940s that geologists described the formation of these crescent-shaped leeward dunes, or *lunettes*, as being driven by cycles of aridity and humidity and prevailing south-westerly winds during the last ice age (Figure 4).[50]

Still characterised as poor grazing country, semiarid, fringe, degraded, the lakes landscapes nonetheless began to be redeemed by the 'unparalleled record' of Quaternary climate change revealed in their sediments. But they remained

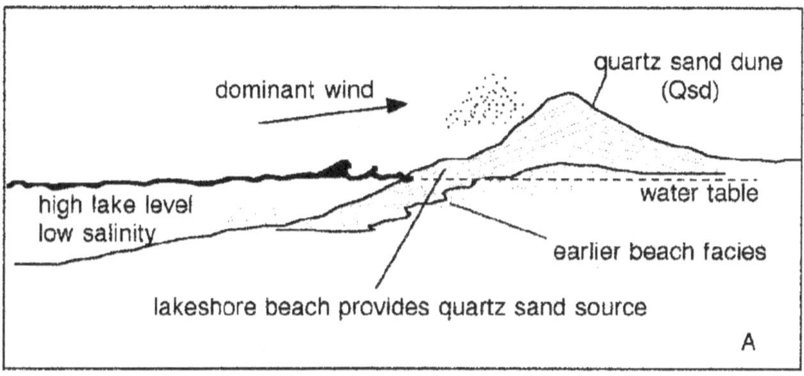

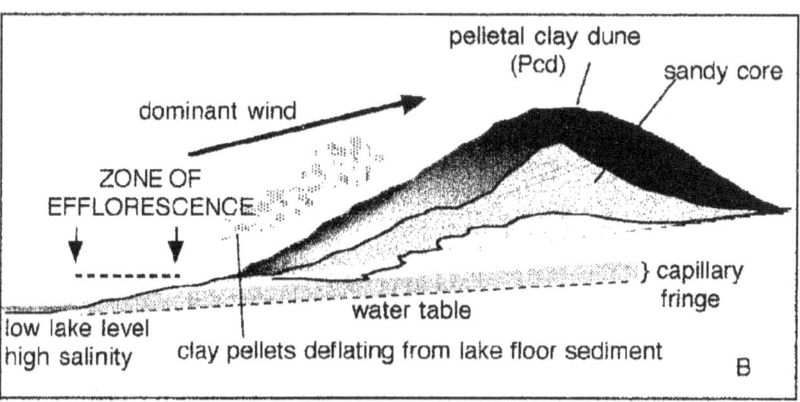

FIGURE 4. Lunette formation. A. Formation of a typical quartz sand lunette. B. Formation of a typical clay lunette. Modified after J.M. Bowler 1986. 'Quaternary landform evolution', in *The Natural Environment*, ed. D.N. Jeans. Sydney: Sydney University Press.

marginal landscapes. Then Jim Bowler's discovery of ancient human remains in 1968 coming as it did at a time when John Mulvaney and certain other Australian archaeologists had begun to insist on a Pleistocene antiquity for Aboriginal Australians, catapulted Lake Mungo and the rest of the lakes into the global archaeological canon. The cultural significance attached to the burials attracted World Heritage classification. Without the concomitant funding and publicity, the lakes region would still be a mere geomorphologic footnote, the abode of goats and emus. As a World Heritage Area, it offers instead global standing, national significance, shared heritage and an incomparable timescale.

In *The Custodians*, Nicholas Jose's epic meditation on Australian identity, 'Ralph Kincaid', a Welsh archaeologist (and thinly disguised proxy for the late

Rhys Jones) argued that archaeology's 'real treasure was not gold or silver, but time itself ... And the latest arrivals ... wove themselves into the story as excavators and articulators ... Australian prehistory was an essential nation-forming discipline'.[51] The mystery and the monumentalism of the deep past evoke reverence in the Willandra Lakes as at Callabonna, but with this human past comes wider recognition and celebration. Lake Mungo has become a tourist site of pious pilgrimage. Despite its World Heritage classification under both natural and cultural criteria, it is for illumination of the human past that the area is chiefly and popularly celebrated, even by geomorphologists, as this quote from Bowler, a geologist, demonstrates:

> The association here of complex burial ritual (Mungo III) involving anointing with ochre at this time presents one of the dramatic mysteries of ancient human cultural development. In death, the story of that person illuminates our understanding of those ancient occupants and the Ice Age environments that supported them.[52]

This is problematic. Western science requires that knowledge be shared and global (notwithstanding the demands of institutional brinkmanship, market forces and intellectual copyright). Consequently, antique human remains, even those that have already been studied, must be stored against the possibility of new insights into human descent, demographics, diversity and disease. On the other hand, Aboriginal people of Mutthi Mutthi, Paakintji and Nyiampa descent claim custodianship of the land and human remains, severely limiting the freedom of scientific research there. Such issues of the 'ownership' or 'custody' of material remains of the past have not yet clouded non-archaeological localities such as Callabonna and Hallett Cove, except where they overlap with cultural or archaeological sites. But geological and national heritage are perceived by some as being under siege by a 'non-scientific', 'anti-scientific' or 'creationist' indigenous activism.[53]

In a twist on the nineteenth-century vision of cultivation rejuvenating marginal country, palaeobotanist and science writer Mary E. White cited Lake Mungo as an example of a degraded landscape, ruined by pastoralism.[54] She attributed the mobility of the landscape to overstocking, which threatens its aesthetic and scientific value. But it is in this badlands erosion that geologists read cycles of climate change and discover archaeological material. In a landscape with as little natural exposure as western New South Wales, and indeed much of the Australian continent, geological researchers rely to some extent on human intervention. More recent scientific accounts of the Willandra Lakes landscapes suggest that even these erosional patterns – which facilitated geological understanding – are evidence of older climatic cycles at work. Sheep and goats have undermined the stability of the lunettes, but in a repeat of patterns found deeper in the stratigraphic record.[55] What level of pastoralism is acceptable in a World Heritage area? With particular regard to the establishment of Lake Mungo National Park, Jim Bowler recently acknowledged the Barnes families, pastoralists on the former Mungo and Joulni Stations who, as he explained, 'endured the climatic and economic vicissitudes of life in the Western Division of NSW, lives frequently compounded by the complexities that followed on the heels of scientific discoveries and subsequent heritage complications'. He insisted that 'the nation in general [owes] a profound debt' to Albert and Venda Barnes who 'forfeited their heritage, Mungo Station, to permit the investment of that region's scientific treasures in the national interest'.[56] The deep past and geological heritage thus redeem human failing in the recent past.

Elsewhere in *The Custodians,* Jose shifted the barely disguised 'Lake Moorna' to west of the New South Wales border. He evoked 'Lake Moorna' with an archaeologically informed sense of majesty, age and mystery, but one which was intrinsic to this landscape, independent of the works of humanity:

> without breaking into features of even the simplest narrative, the country went on for miles. The dry sunken bed of Lake Moorna, when at last she reached it, was the dominant feature only because it was even more minimal than the surrounding plain... the irony of a grandiose name from elsewhere, the Walls of China ... The negation of landscape as conceived in the pictorial tradition: no alps, no crags, no ruined towers, no nestling hamlets; in that lay its teasing eloquence.[57]

For Jose and his protagonists, geology provided meaning, a new way of 'seeing' a landscape in the fourth dimension. Jose's geomorphologist Fritz Vogel 'had seen through the surface of the land with his X-ray eyes to pictures of time beneath'.[58] The mystical experience was vindicated, not created by 'Moorna Woman's' discovery.

Meaning is established neither by physical geography nor palaeontology nor archaeology nor fiction nor heritage guidelines alone. Cultural and intellectual overburden distinguishes the Willandra Lakes World Heritage site, as it is viewed and imagined, from broad ovoid saltbush plains fringed by eroding dune deposits. Lake Mungo's deep-time overburden imbues it with a grandeur or spectacle at odds with its flat, dry landscape. The power of deep time to add contour and colour to 'dead' country is akin to the transformative effect of Technicolor on Dorothy's experience of the shift from Kansas to Oz, as we move from the eroding Mungo lunette, via the fourth dimension, to a fully treed and watered landscape: the Pleistocene land of lakes.[59]

CONCLUSION

Geological heritage resists simple definition. Indeed, part of its value to this study rests in its flexibility. It has not proved easy for earth scientists to divorce geological heritage from 'non-scientific' agenda like tourism, politics and nationalism. The celebration of landscapes on the basis of their geological significance alone is often not enough. The Hallett Cove campaigners found it necessary to harness archaeology, social history, botany, entomology, the history of science, notions of egalitarianism, government corruption and non-consultation to ensure the preservation of some of the cove's geologically important features. The success of the Willandra Lakes World Heritage nomination can be linked to patrimony, landscape aesthetics and cultural heritage as well as the significant archaeology and geology of the region. Lake Callabonna's geological significance has long been linked to South Australian parochialism and institutional rivalry, although the Stirton and Tedford expeditions appear to have been rather successful exercises in cross-institutional and international cooperation. The material landscape as a repository of 'knowledge about the past' is a national resource, inseparable from ideas about patrimony. It should be possible to embrace the aesthetics agenda of heritage rhetoric and the popular appeal of the deep past and deep-time objects to create the space in which new notions of geological heritage and landscape aesthetics begin to be articulated.[60]

NOTES

[1] I would like to thank the History Program, RSSS, ANU and my colleagues therein for financial, collegial and intellectual support during my PhD, from which some of this material is drawn. For comments on drafts and discussion of related issues, I am particularly grateful to Tom Griffiths, Libby Robin, Bronwen Douglas, Richard Baker, Chris Ballard, Jane Carruthers, Bernie Joyce, Maud McBriar, Joy McCann, Lawrence Niewojt, Emily O'Gorman, Stephen Pyne, Tim Rowse, Barry Smith, Sue Turner, Rod Wells, participants in the inaugural postgraduate Environmental History Workshop, 2002 (sponsored by the Centre for Resource and Environmental Studies (CRES), the History Program RSSS and the National Institute for the Environment [ANU]), the audience at a seminar which I delivered to the History Program Seminar Series in May 2003, and two anonymous referees.

[2] Howchin 1895, 61; McBriar 2000; Pledge 1994; Bowler et al 1970, Bowler 2002. See also Douglas 2004 for further development of the ideas in this paper.

[3] See for example Joyce and King 1980; Joyce 1995; and IUCN 2004, for evaluation of geological and geomorphological values within the World Heritage Convention. But it should be noted that the wonderfully versatile historian of science, environmental historian and geologist, George Seddon, has written extensively on the culture of geology in Australia, and on changing attitudes toward landscapes. For example see Seddon 1996; Seddon 1997, 7–14, 64–72, 109–12.

[4] Aplin 2002, 7–15; Davison 2001, 123–30; Lowenthal 1997, 1, 2.

[5] McBryde 1985, 2, 7; Byrne 1996, 82; *Australian Heritage Commission Act 1975* (Cth), s. 4(1), quoted in Bonyhady 1996, 147. For new Acts, see Environment Protection and Biodiversity Conservation Act 1999 (*EPBC* Act), Section 528, at http://scaleplus.law.gov.au/html/pasteact/3/3295/top.htm, and the Australian Heritage Council Act 2003 No. 85, an Act to establish the Australian Heritage Council, and for related purposes, at http://scaleplus.law.gov.au/html/comact/browse/TOCN.htm. The other document recognised Australia-wide as a guide to heritage principles is the *Australia ICOMOS Burra Charter,*

1999, for the conservation of cultural heritage. It uses similar language to the EPBC Act to define heritage values, and has been an important tool for the promotion of multiple values (Kerr 1983; see also http://www.icomos.org/docs/burra_charter.html).

[6] The history of science and its relationship to a site and to past workers (scientists or collectors) is also regarded as important for heritage value. The GSA has a History of Geological Science Group (ESHG) that works closely with the heritage committees and holds joint meetings at biannual conferences. Similarly the International Union of Geological Sciences (IUGS) has INHIGEO (the International Commission on the History of Geological Sciences) (Susan Turner, pers. comm. 2 July 2005).

[7] Joyce 1995, 15.

[8] Bourne 2005; Clark and Wells 2000; Hocknull 2005; Morrell 2005; Reed and Bourne 2000, 61–90; Reed et al 2005; Wells 1996.

[9] See Harley 1994, 313–17 for discussion of RIGS. See Joyce 1995, 19 for assessment on aesthetic values in the Central Highlands study.

[10] Joyce 1995, 4–5, 7.

[11] Office of the World Geopark Network, http://www.worldgeopark.org/chi-geointro/list.htm.

[12] Joyce and King 1980, 156.

[13] Office of the World Geopark Network, http://www.worldgeopark.org/chi-geointro/list.htm.

[14] Susan Turner, pers. comm. 2 July 2005.

[15] Office of the World Geopark Network, http://www.worldgeopark.org/chi-geointro/list.htm; Turner 2004a, 37–8; Turner 2004b, 173 (see 182–90 for an appendix of potential Australasian and Pacific Geoparks); Turner 2005.

[16] Susan Turner, pers. comm. 2 July 2005.

[17] Bernie Joyce, pers. comm. 23 Feb. 2000. Contrast this to Geoparks, which, especially in China, emphasise cultural associations (Susan Turner, pers. comm. 2 July 2005).

[18] For quote, see Aplin 2002, 15. Also see Aplin 2002, 1–2 and Thorsell 1995, 8–11, for the argument that it is often not appropriate to divide heritage into separate 'natural' and 'cultural' realms. To this end, Sarah M. Titchen (1996, 235–42) has indicated that a future challenge for the World Heritage Committee 'will be to ensure a seamless approach to heritage previously categorized and separated as being either natural or cultural, and to adopt an inclusive plurality in the identification and assessment' (240). It recently began this process with new legislation, reclassifying World Heritage sites such as Uluru, which formerly qualified under both natural and cultural criteria as 'cultural landscapes'.

[19] Turner 2004a, 37–38; Susan Turner, pers. comm. 2 July 2005.

[20] Bernie Joyce, pers. comm., 23 February 2000; Barry Cooper, pers. comm., 26 January 2000; Maud McBriar, pers. comm., 30 January 2000. See also Swart 1992.

[21] Sue Turner has emphasised differences here between GSA notions of geological heritage and those espoused by Geoparks UNESCO, which are more in line with conventional heritage discourse (Susan Turner, pers. comm. 2 July 2005).

[22] For quotes see McBryde 1985, 7; Wells and Tedford 1995, 3, Tedford 1973, 354; South Australian Science Teachers Association 1971, 3. For the accusation of appropriation of Aboriginal pasts, see for example Carter 1992, Introduction.

[23] Mulvaney 1990, 104–5; Mulvaney 1991, 12–21.

[24] Renfrew and Bahn 1991, 483. It is worth noting that over the past two decades, the views of Mulvaney and those of Renfrew have been and continue to be contested by many archaeologists.

[25] Jopson 1999.

[26] McBryde 1996, 66–7.

[27] See for example, Johnson 1996; Wilford 1999; Egan 2000.

[28] For some accounts of megafaunal bone accumulations like Callabonna, which were assimilated into Aboriginal understanding of landscape change, see Howitt and Siebert 1902, 525–32; Gregory 1906, 3–9. For reports of the Broome theft and the distress of local Aboriginal people, see Reynolds, 1999. A detailed account of the incident, and the hunt to recover the footprints, appears in Long 2002. The theft was reported on the front page of the *Australian* on 16 October 1996. Dr Sue Turner, Australian representative on the International Advisory Group for Geoparks, had this to say about Lake Callabonna's Geo-heritage credentials: 'This is perfect Geopark! ... The Broome stories of the dinosaur footprints also add to the scientific interest and in Carnarvon it is clear some past Aboriginal people could differentiate between dinosaur and emu footprints even if they were not aware that dinosaurs were extinct. We need to learn much more about Aboriginal "scientific" perceptions and their interpretations – others are using them to investigate volcanoes and tsunamis in the past in Australia – all potential Geopark material' (Susan Turner, pers. comm. 2 July 2005).

[29] For example, see Uluru-Kata Tjuta Board of Management and Parks Australia 2000, 28–9, 152–61.

[30] Hutton and Connors 1999, 109.

[31] Douglas 2004, 75–83.

[32] For quotes see Caldicott and Geering 1974, 20; Hall 1992, 128; GSA(SA) 1977.

[33] Quotes from miscellaneous correspondence (Hallett Cove Papers, private collection of E.M. McBriar) and Adelaide's *Advertiser* and *Sunday Mail* from 1965–71.

[34] Chapman 1971; see Martin and Associates 1971 for Kadima and Silesia Development Companies' comments on the degradation of the land due to clearing and farming.

[35] Martin and Associates 1971; Nancarrow 1971, 8.

[36] Barry Cooper, pers. comm. 26 Jan. 2000; Harris 1971.

[37] A number of authors has discussed the expectation of many early European settlers and explorers that the centre of Australia contained an inland sea or giant freshwater lake (see for instance Black 1962–3; Cumpston 1971; Douglas 2002). Explorers John Oxley, Thomas Mitchell, Charles Sturt and Edward Eyre, among others, all expected or hoped to find an inland sea, lake or trans-continental navigable river. Not until John McDouall Stuart finally reached the point he determined as the centre of Australia in 1860 was this particular misconception shaken. Dreams of inland seas live on in Lake Eyre's sporadic flooding, and in geologists' and palaeoclimatologists' reconstructions of former climates and geographies, when 'Australia' *avant la lettre* was more humid.

[38] Memorandum by A.C. Gregory on the provincial division of the northern portion of the Australian continent, from *Votes and Proceedings of the Queensland Parliament,* 1861. Quoted in Cumpston 1971, 117.

[39] Fletcher 1996, 150–2.

[40] Anon. 1893a, 4.

[41] Anon. 1894, 5.

[42] Anon. 1893b, 4–5.

[43] Anon. 1893b, 5.

[44] Stirling 1894, 185–6.

[45] Tedford 1985, 39–59.

[46] Stirton 1953, 31 May 1953.

[47] For example, see Stirton 1953, 1 June 1953.

[48] Stirton 1953, 1 June 1953.

[49] Mitchell 1839 [1838], 373. (See 268 for description of lakes).

[50] Hills 1940, 15–21; Stephens and Crocker 1946, 302–12.

[51] Jose 1997, 354.

[52] Bowler 1998, 120.

[53] For opposing views see Jopson 1999 and Johnson 1996.

[54] White 1997, 91.

[55] Douglas 1996, 30; Jim Bowler, pers. comm. 25 July 2002.

[56] Bowler 1998, 154.

[57] Jose 1997, 348.

[58] Jose 1997, 250–2.

[59] Bowler and Jones 1979.

[60] Turner has also noted that 'My colleague the former Director General of the Geological Survey of Iran in promoting the new Qeshm Geopark has emphasised that such landscapes are also "recuperative" in the medical sense and provide havens for relieving stress of the modern world. They take this literally too as the Geopark is linked to the Persian Gulf Biotechnology Research Centre which seeks medicines etc from natural products and also from the cultural history of the islanders who have used the geology and landscape intimately for thousands of years to harvest freshwater (rainfall).' (Susan Turner, pers. comm. 2 July 2005).

REFERENCES

Unpublished

Bourne, S.J. 2005. 'Managing beyond the World Heritage boundary'. Paper delivered at the *10th Conference on Australasian Vertebrate Evolution, Palaeontology and Systematics (CAVEPS 2005) and Quaternary Extinctions Symposium*, Naracoorte, 29 March 2005.

Chapman, R.C. 1971. Letter to G.R. Broomhill, Minister for Conservation and the Environment from the Hallett Cove Development Company. 23 July. Adelaide: Hallett Cove Papers, private collection of E.M. McBriar.

Clark, Brian and Rod Wells 2000. 'Site report from the Australian Fossil Mammal Site Naracoorte'. Report delivered at the World Heritage Fossil Site Conference, 22 September 2000.

Douglas, Kirsty 1996. 'Land systems and stratigraphy of Lake Mulurulu: Examination of Quaternary palaeoenvironments'. Unpublished Honours report. University of Melbourne.

Douglas, Kirsty 2004. '"Pictures of time beneath": Science, landscape, heritage and the uses of the deep past in Australia, 1830-2003'. Unpublished PhD thesis. Canberra: Australian National University.

Fletcher, Harold O. 1996. 'Delving into the past: Incidents in the career of a palaeontologist and a brief introduction to interesting fossils of Australia'. Unpublished TS. Sydney: Australian Museum. Archive ref. 96/14P.

Geological Society of Australia (SA Division) [GSA(SA)] 1977. 'Nomination of Hallett Cove to the Register for the National Estate'. Unpublished TS. Adelaide: private collection of Barry Cooper.

Hocknull, Scott 2005. 'Palaeotourism in Queensland'. Paper delivered at the *10th Conference on Australasian Vertebrate Evolution, Palaeontology and Systematics (CAVEPS 2005) and Quaternary Extinctions Symposium*, Naracoorte, 29 March 2005.

IUCN 2004. 'A global strategy for geological World Heritage: A contribution to the Global Theme Study of World Heritage Natural Sites'. Consultation document. http: //www.geoconservation.com/conference/Docs/WHGeol.pdf.

Joyce, E.B. 1995. 'Assessing the Significance of Geological Heritage: A Methodology Study for the Australian Heritage Commission'. Report prepared for the Australian Heritage Commission by the Standing Committee for Geological Heritage, GSA. Melbourne: Geological Society of Australia.

Martin, T.S. and Associates 1971. Hallett Cove development application. Unpublished report prepared for Kadima Pty Ltd and Silesia Pty Ltd. Adelaide: Hallett Cove Papers, private collection of E.M. McBriar.

Morrell, Adam J. 2005. 'Research at Kronosaurus Korner'. Paper delivered at the *10th Conference on Australasian Vertebrate Evolution, Palaeontology and Systematics (CAVEPS 2005) and Quaternary Extinctions Symposium*, Naracoorte, 29 March 2005.

Nancarrow, H.F. 1971. 'Conservation of geological features – Hallett Cove project'. Unpublished report. Adelaide: Hallett Cove Development Company Pty Ltd. Adelaide: Hallett Cove Papers, private collection of E.M. McBriar.

Reed, E.H., Roderick T. Wells, S.J. Bourne and Anne Sellar 2005. 'Discovering the history of life on Earth in South Australia'. Paper delivered at the *10th Conference on Australasian Vertebrate Evolution, Palaeontology and Systematics (CAVEPS 2005) and Quaternary Extinctions Symposium*, Naracoorte, 29 March 2005.

South Australian Science Teachers Association 1971. 'The need for the Government to acquire and preserve an extensive area of land at Hallett Cove as Major District Open Space'. Unpublished report. Adelaide: private collection of C.W. Bonython.

Stirton, R.A. 1953. Field journal, February 12 1953 to August 23 1953. Unpublished TS. Berkeley: University of California Museum of Vertebrate Palaeontology Collection.

Swart, Rosemary 1992. 'Environmental protection of Geological Monuments in South Australia'. Unpublished Masters thesis. Adelaide: University of Adelaide.Turner, Susan 2005. 'Australian-Pacific Network promoting UNSECO assistance to Geoparks for sustainable development'. Paper delivered at the *10th Conference on Australasian*

Vertebrate Evolution, Palaeontology and Systematics (CAVEPS 2005) and Quaternary Extinctions Symposium, Naracoorte, 29 March 2005.

Uluru-Kata Tjuta Board of Management and Parks Australia 2000. *Fourth Uluru-Kata Tjuta National Park Plan of Management*. Canberra:

Published

Anon. 1893a. 'The fossil remains at Lake Mulligan'. *South Australian Register*. 12 August.

Anon. 1893b. 'Extinct animals of Australia'. *South Australian Register*. 24 May.

Anon. 1894. 'The fossils from Lake Mulligan'. *South Australian Register*. 12 September.

Aplin, Graeme 2002. *Heritage: Identification, Conservation, and Management*. Melbourne: Oxford University Press.

Bennett, M.R., P. Doyle, J.G. Larwood and C.D. Prosser 1996. *Geology on your Doorstep: The Role of Urban Geology in Earth Heritage Conservation*. London: Geological Society.

Black, E.C. 1962–3. 'The Lake Torrens hoodoo'. *Proceedings of the Royal Geographical Society of Australasia* (South Australian Branch) 64 (December): 43-51.

Bonyhady, Tim 1996. 'The stuff of heritage'. In *Prehistory to Politics: John Mulvaney, the Humanities and the Public Intellectual*, ed. Tim Bonyhady and Tom Griffiths. Melbourne: Melbourne University Press: 144–62.

Bowler, J.M., R. Jones, H. Allen and A.G. Thorne 1970. 'Pleistocene human remains from Australia: A living site and human cremation from Lake Mungo, western New South Wales'. *World Archaeology* 2: 39–60.

Bowler, J.M. and R. Jones 1979. 'Australia was a land of lakes'. *The Geographical Magazine* July: 679–85.

Bowler, J.M. 1986. 'Quaternary landform evolution'. In *The Natural Environment*, ed. D.N. Jeans. Sydney: Sydney University Press: 117–47.

Bowler, J.M. 1998. 'Willandra Lakes revisited: Environmental framework for human occupation'. *Archaeology in Oceania* 33(3): 120–55.

Bowler, J.M. 2002. *Lake Mungo: Window to Australia's Past*. CD-rom. Melbourne: University of Melbourne and Murray-Darling Basin Commission.

Byrne, Denis 1996. 'Deep nation: Australia's acquisition of an indigenous past'. *Aboriginal History* 20: 82–107.

Caldicott, Ron and Adrian Geering 1974. 'Development and disaster – Hallett Cove'. *Habitat* June: 20–22.

Carter, Paul 1992. *Living in a New Country: History, Travelling and Language*. London: Faber.

Cockburn, Stuart 1971. 'Blood is up at the cove'. *Adelaide Advertiser*. 15 September.

Cooper, H.M., M. Kenny and J.M. Scrymgour 1972 [1970]. *Hallett Cove: A Field Guide*. 2nd edition. Adelaide: South Australian Museum.

Cumpston, J.H.L. 1971. *Augustus Gregory and the Inland Sea*. Canberra: Roebuck Society Publications.

Davison, Graeme 2000. *The Use and Abuse of Australian History*. Sydney: Allen & Unwin.

Douglas, Kirsty 2002. 'Scarcely any water on its surface'. In *Words for Country: Landscape and Language in Australia*, eds Tim Bonyhady and Tom Griffiths. Sydney: University of New South Wales Press: 68-83.

Editorial. 1971. 'Conservation and the cove'. *Adelaide Advertiser*. 15 September.

Egan, Timothy 2000. 'US takes tribes' side on bones'. *New York Times*. 26 September. http://www.nytimes.com/2000/09/26/science/26SKUL.html Accessed 30 January 2001.

Gregory, J.W. 1906. *The Dead Heart of Australia: A Journey around Lake Eyre in the Summer of 1901-1902, with some account of the Lake Eyre Basin and the Flowing Wells of Central Australia*. London: John Murray.

Hall, C. Michael 1992. *Wasteland to World Heritage: Preserving Australia's Wilderness*. Melbourne: Melbourne University Press.

Harley, M. 1994. 'The RIGS (Regionally Important Geological/geomorphological Sites) challenge: Involving local volunteers in conserving England's geological heritage'. In *Geological and Landscape Conservation,* ed. D. O'Halloran, C. Green, M. Harley, M. Stanley and J. Knill. London: Geological Society, pp. 313–17.

Harris, R.F. 1971. 'Cove not studied'. Letter to the Editor. *Adelaide Advertiser*. 22 September.

Hills, E.S. 1940. 'The lunette: A new landform of aeolian origin'. *Australian Geographer* 3(7): 15–21.

Horr, N. 1971. 'Preserving heritage'. Letter to the Editor. *Adelaide Advertiser*. 22 September.

Howchin, W. 1895. 'New facts bearing on the glacial features of Hallett's Cove'. *Transactions of the Royal Society of South Australia* 19: 61–70.

Howitt, A.W. and Otto Siebert 1902. 'Two legends of the Lake Eyre tribes'. *Report of the Australasian Association for the Advancement of Science* 9, Hobart: 525–32.

Hutton, Drew and Libby Connors 1999. *A History of the Australian Environmental Movement*. Cambridge: Cambridge University Press.

Johnson, George 1996. 'Indian tribes' creationists thwart Archaeologists'. *New York Times*. 22 October.

Jopson, Debra 1999. 'Lay ancient Mungos' bones to final rest, say custodians'. *Sydney Morning Herald*. 31 May.

Jose, Nicholas 1997. *The Custodians*. Sydney: Pan Macmillan.

Joyce E.B. and R.L King 1980. *Geological Features of the National Estate in Victoria: An Inventory Compiled for the Australian Heritage Commission*. Melbourne: GSA (Victoria).

Kerr, J.S. 1983. 'The Burra Charter of Australia ICOMOS'. In *Protecting the Past for the Future. Proceedings of the UNESCO Conference on Historic Places, Sydney 22-28 May 1983*, ed. M. Bourke, M. Lewis and B. Saini. Canberra: Australian Government Publishing Service.

Long, John 2002. *The Dinosaur Dealers*. Sydney: Allen & Unwin.

Lowenthal, David 1997. *The Heritage Crusade and the Spoils of History*. Cambridge:

Cambridge University Press.

McBriar, E.M. 2000. 'The protection of Hallett Cove as a geological monument'. In *Records and Reminiscences: Geosciences at the University of Adelaide, 1875-2000*. Adelaide: University of Adelaide: 79–80.

McBryde, Isabel (ed.) 1985. *Who Owns the Past?* Melbourne: Oxford University Press.

McBryde, Isabel 1996. 'Past and present indivisible? Archaeology and society, archaeology in society'. In *Prehistory to Politics*, ed. Bonyhady and Griffiths: 63–84.

Mitchell, T.L. 1839 [1838]. *Three Expeditions into the Interior of Eastern Australia with Descriptions of the Recently Explored Region of Australia Felix and of the Present Colony of New South Wales*. Volume II. 2nd edition. London: T. & W. Boone.

Mulvaney, John 1990. 'Bones of contention'. *Bulletin*. 9 October: 104–5.

Mulvaney, John 1991. 'Past regained, future lost: The Kow Swamp Pleistocene burials'. *Antiquity* 65(246): 12–21.

Pledge, N.S. 1994. 'Fossils of the lake: A history of the Lake Callabonna excavations'. *Records of the South Australian Museum* 27: 65–77

Reed, E.H. and S.J. Bourne 2000. 'Pleistocene fossil vertebrate sites of the South East region of South Australia'. *Transactions of the Royal Society of South Australia* 124: 61–90.

Renfrew, Colin and Paul Bahn 1991. *Archaeology: Theories, Methods, and Practice*. London: Thames and Hudson.

Reynolds, Steve 1999. 'Fossil thefts'. *MLSSA Newsletter* 261, November issue. Marine Life Society of South Australia. Online http://www.mlsaa.asn.au/nletters/november99.htm

Schwerdtfeger, P. 1974. 'Outrage at Hallett Cove'. Letter to Editor. *Adelaide Advertiser*. 17 July.

Seddon, G. 1996. 'Thinking like a geologist: The culture of geology'. Mawson Lecture. *Australian Journal of Earth Sciences* 43: 487–95.

Seddon, George 1997. *Landprints: Reflections on Place and Landscape*. Cambridge: Cambridge University Press.

Stephens C.G. and R.L. Crocker 1946. 'Composition and genesis of lunettes'. *Transactions of the Royal Society of South Australia* 70: 302–12

Stirling, E.C. 1894. 'The recent discovery of fossil remains at Lake Callabonna, South Australia'. *Nature* 50(1286): 184–8, 206–11.

Stirling, E.C. and A.H.C. Zietz 1899. 'Fossil remains of Lake Callabonna, Part I: Description of the manus and pes of *Diprotodon australis*, Owen'. *Memoirs of the Royal Society of South Australia* 1(1): 1–40.

Tedford, Richard H. 1973. 'The Diprotodons of Lake Callabonna'. *Australian Natural History*. September: 349–54.

Tedford, Richard H. 1985. 'The Stirton years 1953–66: A search for Tertiary mammals in Australia'. In *Kadimakara: Extinct Vertebrates of Australia*, ed. P.V. Rich and G.F. van Tets. Melbourne: Pioneer Design Studio: 39–59.

Thorsell, J. 1995. 'How natural are World Heritage natural sites?'. *World Heritage Newsletter* 9: 8–11.

Titchen, Sarah M. 1996. 'On the construction of "outstanding universal value": Some comments on the implementation of the 1972 UNESCO World Heritage Convention'. *Conservation and Management of Archaeological Sites* 1(4): 235–42.

Turner, Susan 2004a. 'Recommendation for national Geopark initiatives seeking UNESCO's assistance in Geological Heritage promotion'. *The Australian Geologist* 131, 30 June 2004: 37–8.

Turner, Susan 2004b. 'Australian-Pacific Network for UNESCO assistance to Geoparks'. In *Proceedings of the First International Conference on Geoparks*, ed. Zhao Xun, Jiang Jianjun, Doug Shuwen, Li Minglu and Zhao Ting. Beijing: Geological Publishing House: 173–90.

Wells, R.T. 1996. 'Earth's geological history – a contextual framework for assessment of World Heritage fossil site nominations. *Global Theme Study of World Heritage Natural Sites* No.1. IUCN: Gland, Swizerland.

Wells, Roderick T. and Richard H. Tedford 1995. '*Sthenurus* (Macropodidae: Marsupialia) from the Pleistocene of Lake Callabonna, South Australia'. *Bulletin of the American Museum of Natural History* 225: 1–111.

White, Mary E. 1997. *Listen ... Our Land is Crying: Australia's Environment: Problems and Solutions*. Sydney: Kangaroo Press.

Wilson, C. (ed.) 1994. *Earth Heritage Conservation*. London: Geological Society in association with the Open University.

Wilford, John Noble 1999. 'Archaeology and ancestry clash over skeleton'. *New York Times*. 9 November. http://nytimes.com/library/national/science/110999sci-kennewick-man.html Accessed 30 January 2001.

'Welcome to the Atomic Park': American Nuclear Landscapes and the 'Unnaturally Natural'

John Wills

In 1962, Alfred Hitchcock filmed *The Birds* at Bodega Bay, a quiet fishing community fifty miles north of San Francisco. Hitchcock used the peaceful coastal village as a backdrop for a harrowing story of nature out of control. His depiction of a flock of seagulls terrorising small-town America won substantial acclaim as a natural disaster masterpiece. At the same time that Hitchcock faked an avian menace on the shores of Bodega, town residents rallied against a formidable nuclear presence. A major California electrical utility, Pacific Gas and Electric (PG&E), hoped to construct an atomic power plant on the wild reaches of Bodega Head peninsula. PG&E officials insisted that their nuclear project posed no threat to the region. A billboard on the perimeter of the inchoate construction site announced 'Welcome to Bodega Bay Atomic Park'.[1] The 'atomic park' promised an outlandish blend of high technology and primordial nature, public energy provision and coastal recreation. Yet some northern Californians remained unimpressed. Anti-nuclear campaigner David Pesonen distributed a pamphlet entitled 'A Visit to the Atomic Park' highlighting the less welcome features of PG&E's nuclear enterprise. According to Pesonen, Pacific Gas had misled citizens of Bodega as to the true nature of its project, with 'the use of the word "park" to describe a massive atomic complex' just one example of corporate unreasonableness.[2] A state park, rather than an atomic park, appeared the safer option for Bodega.

Competing visions of Bodega Head as an atomic park and a state park reflected the immense cultural symbolism attached to the park label in the latter half of the twentieth century. In post-1945 America, the 'park' emerged as a mass-produced icon of pleasure. Seeking a higher quality of life, US citizens found solace in the open spaces of city and state parks. Increased leisure time fuelled a boom in recreation, with the park promising redemption from the ills of congested, urban society.[3] Business magnates, recognising the cachet attached to the word 'park', renamed their manufacturing complexes 'industrial parks' and 'research parks'.[4] Walt Disney called his carnival-like fairgrounds 'theme parks'.[5] However, it was the 'national park' that most captivated the imagination of America in the 1950s and 1960s. In laden station wagons, middle-class Americans travelled to national parks on the weekends. The great outdoors attracted droves of vacationers. In 1965, Yellowstone National Park received two million visitors for the first time in its history.[6] The national park, with its rustic signposts and inviting picnic benches, represented the ultimate park – the archetypal outdoor recreational experience.

The atomic park was something else entirely. Both the atomic bomb and the national park were born in the American West. Yet the US park ideal, often celebrated as 'the best idea we ever had', shared little in common with dreams of artificial energy sources and unassailable military might.[7] National parks and nuclear sites represented disparate landforms and mindscapes. One represented the apogee of American conservationist thinking, the other highlighted the destructive potential of high technology. Test sites were treated as verbatim wastelands. While US citizens celebrated the national park as a repository of wilderness values, landscape gardening at nuclear plants conjured images of scientifically managed and modified plant life, artificial lawns in white, futuristic cities. At Bodega, PG&E employed the park motif in the hope of naturalising the atom, but failed to elaborate on the abstruse links between nuclear energy production and nature protection, of how the construction of reactor sites could practically service the preservation of wilderness. While initially receptive to claims of a clean, environmentally friendly energy source, conservationists grew wary of atomic power, and became fearful of an accidental release of radiation into the biosphere. By the late 1970s, anti-nuclear activists had convinced the American public that there was nothing natural about atomic power.[8]

The axiomatic gulf between nuclear installations and nature preserves has traditionally barred any meaningful comparison between these two discrete forms of land use. However, exploring the history of the 'park' in its nuclear and preservationist incarnations suggests that apocalyptic and Edenic landscapes are not always polar opposites. The vigour with which nuclear lands have been derided, and nature parks exalted, owes more to entrenched social values than to any extensive consideration of the places involved. Nuclear landscapes have for too long been typecast as infertile no-mans-lands. Despite the irreverence of the comparison, the nature park offers a fresh perspective on atomic soil.

It is the intention of this article to explore the unexpected common ground between nature parks and nuclear landscapes. By considering how such lands were originally set aside, what practices (and attitudes) governed their early development, and what purpose they came to serve in the modern era, the 'atomic park' is intellectually set alongside more conventional park systems. Preservationist and military mandates are usefully compared. The term 'nature', employed in this essay to describe healthy biodiversity (usually due to a relative paucity of human impact), emerges as a complex, culturally laden, and idealistic reference point. In the light of what we know about radiation and its potential to cause genetic damage, it is hard not to think of atomic landscapes as 'unnatural'. In turn, the concept of the atomic park remains, at best, 'unnaturally natural'.

CHOOSING SUITABLE PARKLAND

In locating and appropriating land for atomic purposes, nuclear planners often followed rationales comparable to the motivations of early park stewards. This section considers how nuclear authorities searched for wild and remote regions for their projects, eventually coming into competition with the American conservation movement.

In 1864, Yosemite Park was set aside for 'public use, resort, and recreation'.[9] However, in contrast to city parks, Yosemite proved distant from white American communities and, at that time, inaccessible to all but the richest or hardiest travellers. Yosemite was located 'in nature'. The remoteness of the parkland, along with its unsuitability for settlement or farming, made public acquisition all the easier. Just as Yosemite was celebrated for its magnificent cliffs and waterfalls, preserved intact and 'inalienable for all time', it was also deemed 'worthless' by its marginal economic importance in terms of resource extraction.[10] Later parks, such as Yellowstone National Park (1872) and Death Valley National Monument (1933), were established according to a similar rationale. From the 1940s onwards, nuclear industrialists also laid claim to wild, remote, and marginalised places. The desire for secrecy, allied to concerns over radiation, encouraged nuclear developers to search for territories on the periphery of mainstream American society. Nuclear projects were best situated on uninhabited and undeveloped land, far from major cities.

Both nature park planners and nuclear industrialists imagined the landscapes about them. Gathered around a campfire at Madison Junction in 1870, members of the Washburn expedition articulated a desire for 'a great National Park' at Yellowstone.[11] Proponents envisioned a museum of natural curiosities preserved for public use, insulated from the worst excesses of private capitalism by arbitrary straight-line boundaries. Yellowstone duly became a national treasure, with the Madison campfire immortalised in popular memory as the birthplace of the American park idea.[12] The idea encouraged Americans to see land as virtuous due to its untouched and unpeopled status. Western regions were re-conceptualised. Park planners and nature preservationists mythologised spectacular mountain climes and plunging desert canyons as the pristine American 'wilderness'.[13] Meanwhile, Native American residents had no place in the virginal park scene. Like so many Euro-American concepts, the nature park ran roughshod over indigenous rights and customs. Remnant Indian nations were evicted from their ancestral territories.[14] Rather than primeval nature frozen in time, the park wilderness was an inherently modern construction, with its own destructive logic.

In *Savage Dreams*, environmental writer Rebecca Solnit described the assembly of 'physicists in the wilderness' at Los Alamos, New Mexico, in 1942.[15] Like park planners at the campfire, atomic physicists played out future scenarios in their heads, anticipating how atomic fires would transform both material and political landscapes. The Manhattan Project had brought nuclear science to the West. Seeking secret, remote and uninhabited terrain, military authorities had appropriated vast tracts of 'wilderness' for the manufacture of the world's first atomic bomb. Stretches of New Mexico and Washington were regarded as barren, unpopulated and readily available for atomic purposes. Like national park planners, atomic engineers superimposed their desires for vacant spaces onto the physical landscape. Native American nations and recalcitrant ranchers lost their lands during the expansion of military projects at Los Alamos and Hanford Engineering Works (Washington) in the early 1940s, and Nevada Test Site in the early 1950s. Lecturer in American Studies Valerie Kuletz labelled the process 'nuclear colonialism'.[16] In their capacity to annex Indian territories, atomic pioneers resembled Euro-American frontiersmen. Nineteenth-century homesteaders, miners, town developers and national park planners had all imagined the West to be theirs for the taking. The atomic imagination fed off prior misconceptions of landscape and lingering forms of racial prejudice.

In their search for land, park boosters and nuclear developers rarely competed for the same sites. However, in the 1960s, both conservationists and atomic industrialists fervently pursued the expansion of their respective territories. Recognising public support for outdoor recreation, conservationists campaigned for more state and national parks.[17] Meanwhile, the nuclear industry launched an ambitious reactor construction programme, tied to Eisenhower's promotion of 'Atoms for Peace'. Most conservationists at that time supported nuclear power as a preferred alternative to dam building. The American conservation lobby vilified hydroelectric projects as concrete behemoths threatening large-scale disruption of river ecosystems, while welcoming talk of ecologically benign, self-contained atomic energy facilities. However, support for the peaceful atom wavered when atomic developers chose sites of specific interest to the conservation lobby. A relatively small number of environmentalists, concerned at the loss of valuable coastal scenery and the chances of radioactive accident, had clashed with nuclear enthusiasts in the early 1960s at Bodega Head. In the mid 1960s, Pacific Gas and Electric announced plans for another nuclear plant on the California coast, on the Nipomo Dunes, 65 miles north of Santa Barbara.

As a potential site for a nuclear park, PG&E rated Nipomo as 'good' in terms of 'local topography', 'isolation', and 'physical features'.[18] Meanwhile, conservationists valued Nipomo for its rare sand formations and aesthetic beauty, and vowed to protect the region from industrial encroachment. Atomic aficionados and nature lovers converged on the same location. 'Another Bodega Head' loomed on the California coastline.[19] However, in an unexpected turn of events, PG&E representatives and directors of the Sierra Club, a national conservation organisation, agreed to a land deal in summer 1966. In order to free Nipomo for state park purchase, the Sierra Club endorsed an alternative site for PG&E's nuclear project. Leading members of the Club professed no antipathy towards atomic power, and merely pressed for the plant to be placed in a more

FIGURE 1. The American West (selected nuclear sites and nature parks)

convenient location. The nuclear park was relocated fifteen miles north along the coastline, to Diablo Canyon.

Separated from the nearest town by a line of steep hills, Diablo Canyon was a remote and secluded spot on an undeveloped promontory. PG&E engineers judged the canyon to be 'excellent' in terms of 'geology, seismology, and foundation'.[20] Diablo represented prime atomic material. Diablo also turned out to be a wild stretch of California coastline with potential as parkland. In the rush to save Nipomo, directors of the Sierra Club had mistakenly cast Diablo Canyon as a 'treeless slot' bereft of ecological significance.[21] However, on discovering that the 'real' Diablo featured unsullied tide pools and record-size coastal live oaks, a number of renegade Sierra Club members challenged the agreement with Pacific Gas. Director Fred Eissler drew attention to a favourable National Park Service survey of the headland in 1959.[22] Sympathetic Club stewards presented the Diablo lands as 'California's Last Unspoiled Pastoral Coastland'.[23] Fearing the collapse of the 1966 deal, defenders of Nipomo insisted that Diablo failed to meet state park standards. Local conservationist Kathy Jackson argued: 'Diablo Canyon has not been wilderness since 1832. It is an overgrazed oak woodland and chaparral canyon'.[24] Directors Ansel Adams and William Siri declared Diablo 'prophetically named', growing 'out of the moving sands and rare flora of Nipomo to sow doubt and dissension'.[25] The ensuing controversy almost split the Club.[26]

The same qualities that marked Diablo an ideal location for nuclear development also confirmed its potential as a nature reserve. Remoteness, wildness, and an absence of humanity appealed to conservationists and developers alike. 'Save-Diablo' Sierra Club members duly admonished PG&E for its inability to avoid wild and cherished landscapes in its quest to build a state-wide energy system. 'With its almost magnetic attraction for the untouched site, the clean sand and the blue water, [PG&E] selects a hitherto inviolated [sic] area, applies the blade of the bulldozer to it and then come tumbling down the ferns, the glens, the trees, the valley', commented one California Public Utility Commission staff member sympathetic to the 'Save-Diablo' cause.[27] PG&E rejected any claims that it was in competition with the state park system or conservationists. While corporate officials admitted that the Nipomo Dunes represented attractive parkland, Diablo Canyon was another matter entirely. As an 'undistinguished' headland of 'ordinary nature', Diablo was presented as worthless to all but hardy nuclear industrialists.[28] Once used as an argument *for* national parks in the late nineteenth century, worthlessness appeared on the side of the nuclear park system in the late 1960s. PG&E also reminded Californians of their increasing energy needs. The energy sufficiency of the whole state depended on a nuclear landscape at Diablo Canyon. By contrast, a nature park at Diablo promised an unwelcome return to the electrical dark ages.

IMPLEMENTING THE DESIGN

Even wilderness regions such as Yosemite and Yellowstone are now acknowledged as (at least partial) constructions of the human psyche, with wood cabins and paved roads practical attestations of federal presence. Meanwhile, nuclear landscapes carry the physical scars of prolonged military tests and reactor building programmes. This section explores the making of two kinds of landscape, and reveals how themes of mastery over nature, outbreaks of fear, and national pride can bind places together, as well as separate them.

In implementing their design plans, both national park stewards and atomic authorities at times demonstrated reprehensible attitudes towards resident flora and fauna. In 1953, following a series of atomic explosions at Nevada Test Site, over 4,500 sheep died from radiation burns on surrounding ranch land.[29] Military personnel hid behind a cloak of secrecy and scientific jargon, insisting that the herbivores died of eating toxic plants or malnutrition. Ranchers had trouble believing what they were told. The sheep appeared neither thin nor diseased, nor did rifles or ravenous predators kill them. The military-atomic complex was the true culprit. Authorities apparently realised the cause of animal deaths in the locality, but failed to disclose such information to beleaguered ranchers. Such malversation helped ferment a popular understanding of nuclear landscapes as places of nefarious scheming and malign portent in subsequent decades. That flora, fauna, along with 'guinea pig' soldiers, emerged as victims of the atomic age gave credence to the idea of nuclear terrain as inherently destructive. Nuclear protesters came to associate the secret designs implemented at nuclear landscapes with the failure of responsible government.

National parks, as paragons of democracy and public accessibility, avoided such intense scrutiny. The National Park Service remained a highly respected federal authority, with the public thankful for its transparent two-fold *raison d'être* of wilderness protection and recreational provision. While Americans expected the Nevada Test Site to have a woeful past owing to military exigencies, national parks were assumed to be in a pristine condition thanks to enlightened land stewardship goals practised by the Park Service. Yet, in a sense, national parks had their own secret past. Designs to protect 'nature' in early park systems (namely herds of local ungulates) entailed the premeditated killing of resident predators, with end results comparable to the radioactive sheep cull in Nevada in the 1950s. In national parks from the 1870s to the 1930s, hundreds of carnivores died from federal mismanagement. The United States Army assumed control of Yellowstone in 1886, and continued an anti-predator agenda inaugurated by early park stewards. Cavalry units also saw off any furtive enemies wandering Yosemite (1890), Sequoia (1890) and General Grant National Parks (1890). Sounds of gunshots and military patrols indicated that the first national parks began life as militarised zones. In 1916, the National Park Service, backed up by scientific dogma, institutionalised annual killing sprees. The grey wolf was one of the unfortunate species to be classified as a 'threat' to park ungulates and nature's balance. Just as likely to be killed inside as outside park borders, *Canis lupus* faced a torrent of prejudice. By the 1940s, the wolf had been extirpated from the continental United States.[30]

The burnt Nevada sheep and the castigated American wolves were the victims of large-scale human experiment. Military and park authorities relished exercising dominion over their respective territories. Federal officials sought absolute control of their surroundings. Destruction was tied to the creative process, with the laying of strychnine and the spread of plutonium part of the making of landscape.

Although at the time hidden from view, the scale of transformation that accompanied the nuclear age proved far-reaching. Manhattan Project engineers shaped vast expanses of the American West to match their World War and Cold War intentions. The Manhattan Project was huge in every way, from budgetary expenditure, to public deception, to the western lands appropriated for atomic testing. 'Secret' cities were constructed.[31] The wild western landscape was refashioned to meet an orderly military remit. Art historian Peter Hales located the Manhattan Engineering District as psychologically 'somewhere between an army base and a utopian social experiment'.[32] The Nevada Test Site, meanwhile, provided a 'massive outdoor laboratory' for the advancement of scientific knowledge.[33] Close to ground zero, army personnel packed beagles, mice, hogs and monkeys into wire cages to register the effects of atomic blasts, not realising that they too were 'experimental' animals. Nature incarnate represented the canary thrust into the mine as a meter of danger. In the 1950s, Project Plowshare took the nuclear experiment a stage further. Project proponent (and eminent nuclear physicist) Edward Teller insisted that atomic energy could be used to improve on nature's design. Grandiose plans included forging commercial ports, melting polar ice caps, and transforming deserts into lush green paradises with the aid of nuclear explosives.[34] Whole ecosystems seemed ripe for redevelopment. Atomic energy promised the transformation of place on an unlimited scale, with the nuclear physicist assuming the al fresco role of landscape gardener.

Albeit on a far smaller scale, national park wardens similarly operated by an ethos of management, control and scientific advancement. Plant and animal populations were stringently monitored to meet park guidelines. Most wildlife biologists regarded intervention as necessary to keep nature in 'perfect' balance. Yet scientific knowledge of ecological systems proved far from flawless. In the early twentieth century, park officials encouraged ungulate numbers in excess of ecological capacity, with disastrous results.[35] Natural fire was artificially prevented in national parks until the 1970s.[36] Authorities, meanwhile, shaped their dominions to meet public expectations. At Yosemite in the 1920s, bears and mountain lions were kept in cages so that tourists could view nature 'red in tooth and claw' without having to stray from the safety of the park village.[37] Roads, railroads, hotels and stores were all initially welcomed into the 'wilderness'. State and national parks signified constructed landscapes.

Branching roads and animal culls aside, park authorities remained committed to the protection of wild nature in principle, if not always in practice. National parks denoted the crown jewels of the American homeland, majestic sequoias and rock formations cast as nature's cathedrals to rival European stone spires. Park staff defended such places from ruination, protecting America's natural heritage from unscrupulous developers. National pride inspired the safeguarding of natural assets.

Systematically exploding more than a thousand bombs on western soil, nuclear pioneers lacked such noble land stewardship goals. Nevertheless, the work of the nuclear establishment was still tied to the defence of American territory. In 1953, the *Las Vegas Review-Journal* declared, 'We like the AEC [Atomic Energy Commission]. We welcome them to Nevada for their tests because we, as patriotic Americans, believe we are contributing something, in our small way, to the protection of the land we love.'[38] Crater sites, irradiated atomic veterans, and burnt beagles were a small price to pay for national security. The military-industrial complex protected the whole of the United States, including state and national parks, from the 'red enemy'. Park authorities meanwhile experienced their own territorial skirmishes with Native Americans and industrial capitalists. In Glacier National Park (1910), Montana, park staff engaged in a perennial battle with the Blackfeet regarding indigenous user rights on the Eastern slopes of the preserve, while neighbouring oil and gas operations threatened the ecological integrity of the park.[39] Both atomic and park landscapes concerned the protection of 'America the beautiful'.

American pride proved integral to both institutionalised landscapes. Park and nuclear boosters rallied to win over the American public to their respective projects. Rail tracks and luxurious hotels attracted the rich and influential to Yellowstone and Yosemite. The Atomic Energy Commission announced bomb blasts at Las Vegas hotels, inviting gamblers to temporarily leave behind the neon lights of their casinos for other bright sights across the desert. The *Nevada Highways and Parks* magazine for late 1953 used pictures of 'Doom Town' at Nevada Test Site to promote tourism, the beleaguered irradiated buildings offering a novel portrayal of state accommodation compared to the usual motel fare.[40]

Both the eruption of Old Faithful geyser at Yellowstone and the rise of giant mushroom clouds across Nevada drew outbursts of pride, wonder and horror from onlookers. Watching Yellowstone's Mud Volcano, Nathaniel Langford, member of the Washburn Party, wrote how 'The sensations inspired in me to-day, on again witnessing its convulsions, and the dense clouds of vapor expelled in rapid succession from its crater, amid the jarring of the earth, and the ominous intonations from belief, were those of mingled dread and wonder'. Yellowstone was deemed 'unnaturally natural'.[41] In *The Big Picture*, a 1950s military film, a chaplain described an atomic explosion: 'you look up and you see the fireball as it ascends into the heavens. It contains all of the rich colors of the rainbow, and then as it rises up into the atmosphere it assembles into the mushroom. It is a wonderful sight to behold'.[42] Observers claimed to have found god in the glow of ground zero and within the 'cathedrals' of Yosemite.[43] Nuclear tourism was never as explicit as nature tourism, but Americans were able to find divine beauty in both landscapes. The sublime inhabited both nuclear and natural domains.

What differentiated the nuclear park from the nature park was the level of fear assigned to it. Nature parks had successfully transformed the 'wilderness', once considered primeval by Euro-Americans, into a goodly and spiritual landscape. National parks were new Edens, providing honest pursuits for wholesome Christian families. By contrast, nuclear landscapes were insalubrious, malfeasant places, where invisible evils lurked. The nuclear priesthood readily sacrificed their lands in the pursuit of forbidden knowledge, the secrets of the atom. Meanwhile, atomic uses amplified, rather than wiped clean, lingering notions of the taboo and the unwelcome. Seeping radioactive barrels strengthened popular perceptions of arid lands in Nevada and California as desolate wastelands. The new nuclear wilderness had its roots in soil already deemed unfit for life.

For environmentalists, the barrenness of ground zero indicated the destructiveness of humanity and a fast approaching ecological doomsday. Nuclear landscapes signified tortuous practice grounds for a forthcoming holocaust. The spring 1971 edition of *The Living Wilderness* detailed 'The nuclear sword of Damocles', 'the greatest threat to the continuance of animal, vegetable and human existence', declaring 'not only the wilderness but the whole world is in peril'.[44] Released during the same year, saturnine science fiction movie *Silent Running* explored the possibility of life devoid of wilderness. With Planet Earth (and, more importantly, the United States) denatured to the point of supporting only the human species, American spaceships carried the 'last forests of our once beautiful nation' in giant bio-domes, with the distant hope of re-establishing the 'parks and forest system'. However, budget cutbacks led to the abandonment of the space project. All but one of the domes was destroyed using nuclear explosives. The last forest survived thanks to an extrovert nature enthusiast disobeying orders. He then taught two friendly robots to look after the wilderness. *Silent Running* reflected popular concern over environmental collapse and nuclear destruction, and made an emotional plea for better land stewardship.[45]

Fearing a rise in public opposition, the nuclear industry attempted to reconnect atomic sites with natural landforms in the 1960s and 1970s. Corporations located nuclear plants amidst newly created 'nature reserves', hoping that local wildlife would freely congregate alongside reactors and thus show their support of the atom. One industry advert proclaimed 'Go Play in the Atomic Park', alleging that children could safely play in nuclear landscapes without fear of fallout.[46] A number of movies suggested that radioactive decay was not altogether bad for the world. Bizarre post-apocalyptic utopias were expected to rise from the ashes of nuclear Armageddon. Film historian Joyce Evans explained the 'attraction' of 'nuclear war' as 'like a cloth that wipes away the accumulated ravages of history and allows a clean, fresh world to be reborn'.[47] Movies such as *Genesis 2* (1973) predicted a return to the virgin wilderness, with 'man' as survivor, an atomic Daniel Boone, with his ragged clothes testament to the abandonment of former cultural excesses.[48] Meanwhile, radiation mutants, savage and predatory, replaced the bears and serpents of the original wilderness.

FIGURE 2. Old Faithful geyser, Yellowstone (US National Park Service photograph)

FIGURE 3. 'Nancy' tower shot, Nevada, 1953 (US Department of Energy photograph)

THE MODERN PARADOX: THE POST-ATOMIC PARK?

This final section details recent debates surrounding the setting aside of former nuclear lands as protected park areas. While atomic aficionados put great store by the abundance of species to be found at testing grounds and reactor sites in the American West, environmentalists struggle to make sense of unfolding events. The true meaning of the 'post-atomic park' remains open to interpretation.

In the 1990s, many nuclear projects were downscaled or decommissioned. Nuclear energy had proven itself uncompetitive in the marketplace, while the end of the Cold War abruptly halted the nuclear arms race. Attention gradually turned to the ecological costs of the atomic era. While the scale of radioactive spoilage defied public expectations, equally shocking was the survival of nature in atomic 'wastelands'. At ground zero, native vegetation had reclaimed Trinity. Ravens nested in the plugs of former underground nuclear tests.[49] The 'nuclear wilderness' of the 1990s was far less 'alien' than depicted in the movies. If there were any radioactive mutants, they were kept secret and well hidden.

Those responsible for cleaning up atomic sites welcomed signs of natural recovery. The presence of endangered species testified to a healthy rather than terminally polluted landscape. Wild flora and fauna also bolstered nuclear tourism. Tour guides for Nevada Test Site stressed the natural legacy of the nuclear age. The Department of Energy proudly spoke of the 6000 acres surrounding Rocky Flats plutonium processing plant north-west of Denver, 'home to many species of animals and plants'.[50] The land had assumed a dual purpose, preventing nuclear contamination from reaching human settlements while protecting wild nature from increasing urbanisation and tourism. In May 1999, US Energy Secretary Bill Richardson announced the setting aside of 800 acres of Rocky Flats as Rock Creek Reserve, thus protecting 'a unique habitat that has been untouched by human development for 25 years'.[51]

Authorities stressed their commitment to preserving nuclear and post-nuclear wilderness. At Yucca Mountain, proposed site for high-level radioactive waste storage, and, as such, a nuclear landscape in the making, officials monitored the endangered desert tortoise and 'indicator species' such as the long-tailed pocket mouse for early warnings of environmental impact.[52] Just like national park rangers, nuclear authorities regretted their past record of land mismanagement, and vowed to make amends. Portland General Electric, as a gesture of 'responsible environmental stewardship' offered land occupied by Trojan nuclear plant to the state of Oregon for park use.[53] The atomic plant, dubbed 'Oregon's Trojan horse' due to its poor operating performance, was in the process of being decommissioned. Featuring 500 acres of woods and wetland, including 200 wildlife species and one concrete nuclear sarcophagus, the *Hanford News* commented, 'As far as parks go, it would indeed have a bit of everything'. The newspaper's headline read 'From nuclear to state park?'[54]

FIGURE 4. Nevada test site
(US Department of Energy photograph)

The gulf between the atomic park and the nature park appeared to be closing. Tennessee Valley Authority dams, along with other huge industrial adventures, had been accepted in the past for their accompanying picnic sites and boating lakes.[55] The atomic industry offered similar fringe benefits. The National Park Service assumed responsibility for a number of nuclear missile silos next to Badlands National Park as newly appointed national historic sites.[56] Park employees also restored the McDonald Ranch at Trinity Test Site, after rain (rather than atomic blasts) damaged its tin roof and mud brick construction. Environmentalists, ranchers, farmers, real-estate developers and Native Americans all competed for stretches of the Hanford Engineering Works. Only five percent of the reservation had suffered plutonium contamination, leaving 530 acres of 'prime habitat'. In June 2000, Hanford Reach National Monument, home to bald eagles and peregrine falcons, was set up as a shrub-steppe reservation. Battelle-Northwest biologist Larry Caldwell elaborated on the importance of Hanford, explaining that 'in a state that is losing thousands of acres of wildlife habitat each year... We're sort of an island, sort of a last bastion of sagebrush-dependent species'.[57] With many more acres to be freed for purchase, environmental hopes centred on expanding the post-nuclear National Monument.

While nuclear landscapes received unexpected plaudits, national parks came under fire from wilderness purists. The vulnerable ecology of nature parks had been meddled with and trampled on for too long. Park authorities were encouraged to manage humans, not nature. While the National Park Service appeared receptive to environmentalist pleas, they struggled with a sizeable tourist problem. At Yellowstone, recreational vehicles roared across park landscapes in the summer months. Snowmobiles invaded in the winter. Yosemite village was famous for its neon shopping experience. The 'wilderness' experience appeared in danger of devolving into a vacuous retail industry.

Nuclear landscapes had yet to be tarnished by consumer capital. Trinity Test Site, open to the public twice a year, featured only a few gift sellers. Neither was overcrowding a problem. Rebecca Solnit found the unpopulated zones of Nevada Test Site preferable to the claustrophobic Yosemite, shocked to discover

FIGURE 5. Traffic jam, Yellowstone (US National Park Service photograph)

'this country's national Eden so full of disturbing surprises and its Armageddon so comparatively pleasant'.[58] Solnit was not the only one to favourably compare nuclear lands with traditional park areas. One wildlife biologist claimed PG&E's Diablo property was in far better ecological condition than Montana de Oro State Park, its northerly neighbour.[59] Plans were put forward to protect Diablo Canyon following plant decommissioning.[60] While nature parks suffered from their own recreational success, nuclear lands, mostly off-limits to the nation, often resembled their pre-nuclear countenance. Buffer zones, as no-mans-land, had served as enigmatic wildlife refuges. Rather than national parks, nuclear parks boasted the human-less 'frozen' wilderness.

The nuclear wilderness nevertheless had its fair share of critics. Colorado environmentalists rejected claims of a 're-natured' Rocky Flats. The 'Rocky Flats Horror Picture Show', with over 170 contaminated hotspots, hardly qualified as wilderness.[61] Nor were its land stewards well-trusted nature lovers. One environmentalist described the Department of Energy as 'so focused on public image that they cast aside safety'.[62] The 'rebirth' of Denver's Rocky Mountain Arsenal (RMA), former chemical warfare site turned wildlife menagerie, was equally regarded with suspicion. According to the Army Corps of Engineers, the territory featured 'the most contaminated square mile on Earth'.[63] Reports of tumble mustard tree groves flourishing on Rocky Mountain soil seemed unlikely given the prodigious manufacture of mustard gas and other lethal concoctions.

FIGURE 6. Wild horses at Nevada test site (US Department of Energy photograph)

Attempting to bypass the issue of human access, unconscionable authorities had merely discovered 'a way to do less clean-up' by proposing wildlife reserves.[64] Even more suspect was a plan to make RMA part of a 'Central Park of the West'.[65] Both the Rocky Mountain Arsenal and Rocky Flats represented dubious additions to the US park system. Environmentalists fervently pushed their own 'toxic tours' of the sites surrounding Denver, showing a landscape connected by pollution, not protection.[66]

For several decades environmentalists had vilified atomic energy as an enemy of ecology. While clean-up authorities promoted stories of natural recovery and benign experimentation, anti-nuclear activists preferred to keep with their well-established narratives of environmental ruin. Along with cancer-suffering atomic veterans, nuclear and post-nuclear landscapes provided material proof of radiation damage. For vehement critics of the nuclear age, the landscape was itself a story of secret holocaust and the slow death of nature. 'Atomic photographers' in the late 1980s and early 1990s captured scenes of nuclear devastation in western territory. Carole Gallagher photographed brave but sickened residents of Utah and Nevada, and cloudy, contaminated landscapes.[67] Richard Misrach shot pictures of dead animal corpses and nuclear desolation in the desert.[68] The overwhelming image was one of needless human sacrifice and creeping ecocide.

Photographs situated the 'nuclear west' as a social creation, a landscape forged by atomic device. Unlike huge canvas paintings of national parks, or early portraits of the 'Great American desert', where humans were noticeably absent, the nuclear vista was an 'irrevocably social landscape' moulded by nefarious sapient endeavour.[69] To help magnify themes of poisoning, nature was often cast as a powerless victim of atomic 'progress' or a gloomy, deathly backdrop. Celluloid scenes of the nuclear landscape drew on deep-rooted fears of both atomic energy and harsh terrain. The tortured animal bones immortalised by Misrach resembled the buffalo skulls in classic paintings of the West by Charles Russell one hundred years earlier.[70] The myths of the American desert, 'wasteland' and 'wilderness', death and beauty, coincided. While tourists captured on film freakish geysers and the 'unnaturally natural' at Yellowstone, atomic photographers documented poisoned waterholes, misshapen military machinery, and the 'naturally unnatural' at Nevada Test Site. Nuclear industry pictures of healthy wildlife thriving in atomic spaces were fake and timid by comparison.

Environmentalists recognised that the 'nuclear park' ideal drew attention away from serious problems at atomic sites involving decontamination and waste storage issues. As well as supposed nature reservations, Rocky Flats and Hanford were also federal Superfund sites. Established by Congress in 1980, the Superfund program was designed to clean up the most polluted sites in the country, under the guidance of the Environmental Protection Agency. Peter Hales described 'the atomic spaces of the Manhattan Engineering District' as 'legendary deserts of toxic horror'.[71] Meanwhile, working uranium mines continued to spew toxins into the air and ruin neighbouring communities. The nuclear age was about pollution not preservation. Radioactive particles from more than a thousand nuclear tests had travelled the biosphere, tainting the Earth with poison. There was, in fact, no untouched wilderness thanks to atomic engineering. Even national parks fell victim to passing radiation clouds in the 1950s.[72] In the popular consciousness, nuclear landscapes remained the antithesis of the hallowed recreational paradises of Yosemite and Yellowstone. According to the *New Atlas of the West*, nuclear landscapes were the quintessential 'ugly west', despoiled lands marked by 'atomic leftovers'.[73] While park landscapes testified to wholesome recreation and fondness for wild nature, nuclear and post-nuclear landscapes manifested destruction and deception. The most revealing 'nuclear park' was to be found just a half-mile from Lawrence Livermore National Laboratory, a nuclear weapons research centre east of Berkeley, California. To the shock of Livermore personnel, plutonium particles had been found at Big Trees Park, popular destination for local parents and children, not to mention birds and wildlife. The *San Francisco Examiner* renamed it the 'Plutonium Park'.[74]

REINTERPRETING ATOMIC SPACES

At Bodega in the early 1960s, any useful discussion of the atomic park had been cut short by the discovery of the San Andreas Fault directly beneath PG&E's groundbreaking plant. A natural, seismic threat put paid to any chances of a nuclear park on the headland. Pacific Gas was forced to withdraw its plans. The land set aside for nuclear status passed into state park ownership, with the shaft dug for the atomic plant (known by locals as 'the hole in the head') claimed by birds as a duck pond. The nature reserve gradually covered up all traces of PG&E's atomic aspirations. Nature had been saved, and the full ravages of the nuclear landscape avoided. The choice had been between an atomic park and a state park, industry and despoliation or nature and recreation. A journalist, recounting events at Bodega Head, declared 'It's a park alright, but not an atomic one'. The difference appeared self-evident.[75]

Over a period of fifty years, nuclear landscapes served as popular icons of danger and destruction. Hanford Engineering Works and Nevada Test Site represented sacrifice zones, Armageddon wastelands where humans experimented with deadly materials. Unlike US national parks, set aside to preserve wild scenery, lands appropriated for the nuclear cause were subject to exploding bombs and the annihilation of nature. In the 1990s, nuclear lands taken over for clean up or decommissioning were expected to bear testament to their deadly purpose. Decomposing waste barrels were the anticipated legacy of the nuclear era. However, a bunch of coyotes hanging out at ground zero told a slightly different story. Battered and irradiated, nature had survived the holocaust. Just as national park managers had partly crafted the 'virgin wilds', natural forces had maintained an influence on the man-made nuclear landscape.

Nature's survival was treated as something of an enigma. While bears wandering in Yosemite symbolised a wild American landscape cherished by its keepers, the presence of wildlife at Nevada Test Site hardly matched with the destructive mandate of military authorities. Puzzling over how to interpret the atomic park paradox, commentators turned to effete narratives of the nuclear era. Pro-nuclear industrialists took credit for natural recovery, while environmentalists remained sceptical. Nuclear lands were inescapably tied to partisan interpretations of the nuclear age. In 1995, the Smithsonian revised a major exhibition on Enola Gay and the dropping of the atomic bomb to placate war veterans.[76] In 1994, New Mexico officials, fearing 'gatherings of peaceniks', rejected a request by thousands of US children for a peace park at Los Alamos, although a Missile Park at White Sands Missile Range Museum continued to attract its fair share of war technology enthusiasts.[77] The nuclear age, ended or not, had lost none of its controversy. American society and landscape still appeared gilded by their brush with atomic physics. Perhaps not the oxymoron that it first appears, the 'atomic park' is part of this contested territory. Just as US national parks remain fiercely controversial landscapes, subject to divergent interpretations, and imperfect monuments to America's past, nuclear parks are similarly contentious places.

Reaching a steadfast verdict on the ecological costs of the nuclear age is thus likely to remain out of reach until a scientific and intellectual common ground emerges. The advent of 'post-atomic parks' will need to be set alongside the trials encountered in burying mountains of nuclear waste. Despite a very different charter, Hanford Reach Monument shares its history with Yucca Mountain. Atomic landscapes need to be reinterpreted, and the nuclear story rewritten, to take into account themes of natural loss and recovery. This entails a greater role for environmental history in nuclear history, and perhaps a diminished role for studies based on Cold War mentalities.

Equally, nuclear issues have much to add to our understanding of environmental history, especially in regard to prominent terms such as 'nature' and 'park'. From this article, it is clear that much of the allure of the park rests on its wilderness imagery, of a landscape untouched by humanity, while nuclear landscapes are repugnant due to their overt military exigencies, and concomitant lack of naturalness. Situating nuclear landscapes and park territories as polar extremes reflects the influence of two important cultural paradigms, one asserting the nuclear age as intrinsically destructive, the other positing the conservation era as productive and praiseworthy. On a more profound level, nuclear landscapes are meant to symbolise the danger of human dominion and control, while parks embody idealistic notions of nature pure and unsullied by culture. However, the specific landscapes set aside as totems of cultural decay or biotic resurgence rarely conformed to their mantles. From abandoned, military vehicles to bustling concessionary stores, signs of human impact pepper both nuclear and national park landscapes. Meanwhile, nature (as a description of floral and fauna agents) fails to abide by the absolute definitions we foist on it. Endangered species rebound at nuclear wastelands, while grizzly bears struggle to maintain numbers in protected areas such as Yellowstone. Neat stereotypes disregard the complex interactions between nature and culture. Once a term used to describe the geologic curiosities of Yellowstone, today more appropriate to post-atomic wilderness, the 'unnaturally natural' remains not only a paradoxical phrase, but also leads to a sticky quagmire over how best to interpret the modern landscape.

NOTES

[1] A picture of the billboard can be found in Wellock 1992, 192.

[2] David Pesonen, 'A Visit to the Atomic Park'. The pamphlet reprinted articles published in the *Sebastopol Times* during autumn 1962. Held at the Bancroft Library, University of California, Berkeley.

[3] See Hays 1987, 23–4, 86–7.

[4] Eminent Western historian Richard White remarked how developers established 'park-like' industrial sites in Western states during the post-1945 era. Stanford Industrial Park, founded in 1951, was the first university-sponsored industrial park in the country. See White 1991, 547 and Findlay 1992, 117–59.

[5] For further insight into Disney landscapes, see Findlay 1992, 52–116.

[6] Yellowstone National Park received 2,062,476 visitors in 1965. Haines 1996 [1977], 480.

[7] Novelist Wallace Stegner is credited with having described the US national park system as 'the best idea we ever had' in 1983. Noted in Milstein 1996, 8.

[8] Throughout the 1970s, anti-nuclear protesters highlighted themes of radioactive contamination and even mutation, while offering solar power as a natural alternative energy source. Following the accident at Three Mile Island nuclear power plant, Pennsylvania, in 1979, mainstream American society adopted a critical stance towards atomic energy production, although nuclear weapons were still accepted as valuable 'peacekeepers' to counter the 'Soviet threat'.

[9] Yosemite Park Act, June 30 1864, U.S., *Statutes at Large*, 13 (1864), 325. Yosemite was expanded to become a National Park in 1890.
[10] Ibid.; See Alfred Runte's discussion of national parks as 'worthless lands' in Runte 1979, 48–64. California senator John Conness described the Yosemite bill as 'a grant of certain premises located in the Sierra Nevada mountains, in the State of California, that are for all public purposes worthless, but which constitute, perhaps, some of the greatest wonders of the world'. Runte, 48–9.
[11] Washburn expeditioner Cornelius Hedges is said to have first raised the idea of 'a great National Park'. See Milstein 1996, 39.
[12] Milstein 1996, 39. The origins of the park idea may alternatively be traced to events surrounding the establishment and operation of Yosemite Park (1864). See Runte 1990, 26–7, 33–5.
[13] For a study of the re-evaluation of wilderness in the late nineteenth century, see Nash 1982 [1967], 108–21.
[14] For park policy towards Indians, see Spence 1999 and Keller and Turek 1998.
[15] Solnit 1994, 136.
[16] Kuletz 1998, xiv. Solnit discusses Shoshone title to the Nevada Test Site in *Savage Dreams*, 28–30. For land issues at Hanford, see Ken Olsen, 'At Hanford, the real estate is hot', *High Country News*, 28/1, 22 Jan. 1996; for Los Alamos, Barbara Ferry, 'Homesteaders sue over ancestral land', *High Country News*, 32/6, 27 Mar. 2000.
[17] In 1956, the National Park Service also announced Mission 66, an extensive plan to expand the park system and attendant visitor services. Hays 1987, 117.
[18] PG&E, 'Summary Comparison of Sites for Nuclear Power Plant, South Coastal Area', Sierra Club Collection (henceforth SCC) 71/295c, box 189, file 30, Bancroft Library.
[19] In correspondence dated March 6, 1963, Sierra Club member Frederick Eissler suggested, 'There is every reason to believe that the Nipomo Dunes is another Bodega Head', SCC 71/103c, box 78, file 13. The Bodega analogy was later applied to controversies surrounding a nuclear plant at Diablo Canyon. In early 1967, the *San Francisco Chronicle* detailed events at Diablo, commenting 'once again, as at Bodega, a good power plant site was also a good park site'. *San Francisco Chronicle*, 12 Feb. 1967.
[20] PG&E, 'Summary Comparison of Sites'.
[21] Sierra Club Board of Directors, Minutes of the Annual Organisation (May 7–8, 1966), 8, SCC 71/103c, box 4, file 5.
[22] For example, memorandum 'To Board of Directors from Fred Eissler', (September 8, 1966), SCC 71/103c, box 110, file 1. Eissler first referred to the Pacific Coast Recreation Area Survey (1959), published by the National Park Service, at the May 1966 Club meeting.
[23] 'The Diablo Canyon Area: *California's Last Unspoiled Pastoral Coastland*', signed by David Brower, Polly Dyer, Jules Eichorn, Fred Eissler, Martin Litton, Daniel Luten, David Pesonen, Eliot Porter, and Georg Treichel, *Sierra Club Bulletin*, 52/2 (February 1967), 7, author's personal copy.
[24] Kathy Jackson, 'Correction: John Muir Would Vote No', (February 1969), SCC 71/103c, box 123, file 11. The letter was part of a cantankerous battle between members regarding how John Muir (1838–1914), co-founder and 'patron saint' of the Club, would have voted on Diablo if alive in the 1960s.
[25] William Siri and Ansel Adams, 'In Defense of a Victory: The Nipomo Dunes', *Sierra Club Bulletin* (February 1967), 4.
[26] See Schrepfer 1992, 212–37 and Wellock 1998, 68–94.
[27] William Bennett quoted in *Ramparts*, February 15, 1968, SCC 71/103c, box 117, file 33.

[28]PG&E, 'Special Report of Diablo Canyon', *PG&E Life* (June 1967), 15, SCC 71/103c, box 113, file 40. In the Aleutians off the coast of Alaska, Atomic Energy Commission officials similarly downplayed the natural worth of Amchitka Island to bolster support for nuclear testing in 1971. See Coates 1996, 22, 33.

[29]Keith Schneider's foreword in Gallagher 1993, xvii. The incident is discussed more fully in Hacker 1998, 157–75.

[30]Wolves survived in Alaska. For an overview of National Park policy towards *Canis lupus*, see McIntyre 1993.

[31]For more on the construction of nuclear cities, see Abbott 1998, 90–115.

[32]Hales 1997, 2.

[33]Here I use the Department of Energy's description of Nevada Test Site as a 'massive outdoor laboratory,' at http://www.nv.doe.gov/nts.

[34]However, Project Plowshare promised far more than it could ever possibly (let alone safely) deliver. The American public remained wary of radiation side-effects, while the test grounds of Nevada and White Sands, marked by dusty craters and military ditches, were hardly the best indicators of what nuclear engineering offered. For insights into a few of the controversies surrounding Project Plowshare, see Coates 1989, 1–31, O'Neill 1994, and Krygier 1998, 311–22.

[35]In the 1910s and 1920s, the National Park Service killed predators in order to encourage huge elk herds. However, the herds overgrazed suitable range, and vast numbers died during harsh winters. This led to more protection for elk, and the cycle repeated itself until policy revisions in the 1930s. For a highly critical look at Yellowstone National Park management and elk overpopulation problems, consult Chase 1987, 19–24.

[36]Yosemite and Yellowstone park employees endorsed natural-burn policies for the first time in 1972: Chase 1987, 70 and Runte 1990, 216. The seminal work on the use of fire through time remains Pyne 1982. On the 'creation' of national park landscapes, see McClelland 1998.

[37]Runte 1990, 133–4.

[38]*Las Vegas Review-Journal*, 21 May 1953. Cited in Fradkin 1989, 19.

[39]On the Blackfeet issue, see Warren 1997, 126–51 and Spence 1998, 29–49. On gas threats, see Buchholtz 1976, 78. On dangers to national parks in general, see Freemuth 1991.

[40]*Nevada Highways and Parks* magazine (June–December 1953). See Fradkin 1989, 103–4.

[41]Milstein 1996, 39.

[42]Gallagher 1993, xii.

[43]Upon witnessing the first atomic explosion at Trinity Test Site in July 1945, Los Alamos Laboratory director J. Robert Oppenheimer quoted a passage from the *Bhagavad Gita*, while the appropriately named 'Cathedral Rocks' and 'The Cathedral Spires' have been a source of inspiration for Yosemite visitors for decades.

[44]Lenore Marshall, 'The Nuclear Sword of Damocles', *The Living Wilderness* (Spring 1971), Papers of David Hartsough, American Friends Service Committee, San Francisco office.

[45]*Silent Running* (Universal Pictures, 1971).

[46]A copy of the advertisement can be found in Gofman and Tamplin 1973, 182–3.

[47]Evans 1998, 137.

[48]*Genesis 2* (TV movie, 1973) written and produced by Gene Roddenberry (of Star Trek fame), is brimming with atomic references. The post-nuclear war story (set in 2133) features a mutated race of humans (the Terranians) living underground, who depend on an arcane nuclear generator for their electricity. The surface has meanwhile become wild.

Dylan, suspended by cryogenic experimentation in the 1970s, awakes into this bizarre world. While initially upset at losing his local highway and airport to wilderness, he soon comes to admire the beauty of blue skies and clean water, exclaiming, 'it's like the earth has been given a second chance'. On behalf of a remnant (and enslaved) human population, he destroys 'Terrania' with a nuclear missile left over from the Third World War. Other nuclear movies posted an anti-survivalist message, such as *Massive Retaliation* (Massive Productions, 1984).

[49] Journalist James Abarr related on a visit to Trinity how 'Ground zero at Trinity offers strong testimony to the recuperative powers of nature. Radiation levels are virtually nil, and the once-blackened and scorched land has fully recovered from the nuclear devastation of a half-century ago. Plants, grass, soil and wildlife have all returned…'. James Abarr, 'The Legacy of Trinity', *ABQ Journal.com*, 28 Oct. 1999. According to one Nevada Test Site tour guide, a raven annually nests atop the plug of a crater caused by Bilby, a 1963 atomic test. Bilby has become a 'drive through' crater on tours of the test site, a modern-day version of the drive-through redwood at Yosemite National Park. Solnit 1994, 208.

[50] Department of Energy, 'Rocky Flats Closure Project: Rocky Flats Overview', http://www.rfets.gov. The DOE similarly declared that land use restrictions at Nevada Test Site assured that 'biotic communities are in a relatively natural balance', in 'Nevada Test Site: National Environmental Research Park', http://www.nv.doe.gov/nts/researchpark.htm.

[51] Department of Energy, 'Energy Department – U.S. Fish and Wildlife Partnership Creates "Rock Creek Reserve"', press release, 17 May 1999, copy available at http://www.rfets.gov. The agreement was reached between the US Fish and Wildlife Service and the DOE.

[52] Such details are noted in the 'Environmental Program' posted at the Department of Energy's Yucca Mountain website, http://www.ymp.gov.

[53] 'From nuclear plant to state park?', *Hanford News/Tri-City Herald*, 15 Aug. 1999. The article is posted at http://www.hanfordnews.com/1999/aug25.html.

[54] Ibid.

[55] The Tennessee Valley Authority, established by Congress in 1933, is responsible for the economic (and, in turn, social) development of the Tennessee River drainage basin. Alongside huge industrial projects (including over 30 dams), the TVA has also created campgrounds, beaches and parks. For further insight into TVA's industrial and natural legacy, see Wilson 1992, 259–66.

[56] 'Strangelove park', *High Country News*, 26/13, 25 July 1994.

[57] John Stang, 'Hanford habitat key to survival', part of a series on Hanford, entitled 'A matter of habitat', *Tri-City Herald*, 25–28 Feb. 1996.

[58] Solnit 1994, 367.

[59] Conversation with Sue Benech, biologist, Diablo Canyon, 21 Aug. 1997.

[60] David Sneed, 'Water board working to preserve PG&E land', *The Tribune*, 17 Aug. 1999, and Sneed, 'PG&E supports Diablo preserve', *The Tribune*, 3 Oct. 1999. *The Tribune* was formerly the San Luis Obispo County *Telegram-Tribune*.

[61] Michael Fumento used the phrase 'Rocky Flats Horror Picture Show' in the as titled 'Rocky Flats Horror Picture Show: Rocky flats Plutonium-Processing Plant', *National Review*, 5 Nov. 1990.

[62] Sierra Club member Susan LeFever, quoted in Camille Colatosti, 'A "Toxic Tour" of Denver: Working for environmental justice at the grassroots', *The Witness* (July–August 2000). A copy of this document is available at http://thewitness.org/archive/julyaug00/toxictour.html.

[63] Cited in Wilson 1992, 281.

[64] Colastosti, 'A "Toxic Tour" of Denver...'
[65] Governor Roy Romer put forward the idea of a 'Central Park of the West'. See Mark Obmascik, 'Arsenal Billions Away from Being Picnic Site', *Denver Post*, 14 Feb. 1987, reprinted in Cronon 1995, 65. Maria Streshinsky included the RMA in a list of 'Five fabulous makeovers for Mother Earth', in 'From Blighted to Beautiful' *Via Online* magazine (November 1999), available at http://www.viamagazine.com/top_stories/articles/environment99.htm.
[66] The Colorado People's Environmental and Economic Network (COPEEN) offer toxic tours. See Colatosti, 'A "Toxic Tour" of Denver...'
[67] Gallagher 1993.
[68] Davis 1999, 341–5 briefly discusses the work of Richard Misrach. A useful article on pro-nuclear photography is Kirsch 1997, 227–55. Kirsch argues that AEC photographs were 'designed, quite literally, to take the place out of the landscape', (229) so that the public felt no attachment to areas used for testing.
[69] Davis 1999, 347.
[70] For a brief discussion of Russell's work, see Dippie 1994, 692–4.
[71] Hales 1997, 5.
[72] Downwind of the Nevada Test Site, Zion National Park (Utah), Bryce Canyon National Park (Utah) and Grand Canyon National Park (Arizona) inevitably received fallout from aboveground nuclear tests during the 1950s.
[73] Riebsame 1997, 134. Details of 'A Nuked Landscape' are located in a chapter looking at the so-called 'Ugly West'.
[74] Jane Kay and Erin McCormick, 'Bay's nuclear leftovers', *San Francisco Examiner*, 25 Nov. 1997.
[75] Simone Wilson, 'How Bodega Bay Nixed the Atomic Park', *Albion Monitor*, 3 Dec. 1995. A copy of this document is available at http://www.monitor.net/monitor. See also 'Bodega's Bird-Dogs Saved Town', *San Francisco Chronicle*, 23 Dec. 1997.
[76] On the controversies surrounding the Smithsonian exhibition on the Enola Gay, see Kai Bird's article 'Silencing History', *The Nation*, 20 Feb. 1995.
[77] 'Peace Gets No Chance', *High Country News*, 26 Dec. 1994. The peace park was planned as a 'sister memorial' to the Hiroshima Memorial Peace Park.

REFERENCES

Abbott, Carl 1998. 'Building the Atomic Cities: Richland, Los Alamos, and the American Planning Language'. In *The Atomic West*, ed. Bruce Hevly and John Findlay. Seattle: University of Washington Press.

Buchholtz, C.W. 1976. *Man in Glacier*. West Glacier: Glacier Natural History Association.

Chase, Alston 1987. *Playing God in Yellowstone: The Destruction of America's First National Park*. San Diego: Harcourt Brace.

Coates, Peter 1989. 'Project Chariot: Alaskan Roots of Environmentalism'. *Alaska History* 4/2 (Fall 1989): 1–31.

Coates, Peter 1996. 'Amchitka, Alaska: Toward the Bio-Biography of an Island'. *Environmental History* 1/4 (October 1996): 20–45.

Cronon, William (ed) 1995. *Uncommon Ground: Toward Reinventing Nature*. New York: Norton.

Davis, Mike 1999. 'Dead West: Ecocide in Marlboro Country'. In *Over the Edge: Remapping the American West*, ed. Valerie Matsumoto and Blake Allmendinger. Berkeley: University of California Press.

Dippie, Brian 1994. 'The Visual West'. In *The Oxford History of the American West*, ed. Clyde Milner II, Carol O'Connor and Martha Sandweiss. New York: Oxford University Press.

Evans, Joyce A. 1998. *Celluloid Mushroom Clouds: Hollywood and the Atomic Bomb*. Boulder: Westview Press.

Findlay, John M. 1992. *Magic Lands: Western Cityscapes and American Culture After 1940*. Berkeley: University of California Press.

Fradkin, Philip 1989. *Fallout: An American Nuclear Tragedy*. Tucson: The University of Arizona Press.

Freemuth, John C. 1991. *Islands Under Siege: National Parks and the Politics of External Threats*. Lawrence: University Press of Kansas.

Gallagher, Carole 1993. *American Ground Zero: The Secret Nuclear War*. New York: Random House.

Gofman, John and Tamplin, Arthur 1973. *Poisoned Power: The Case Against Nuclear Power Plants*. London: Chatto and Windus.

Hacker, Barton C. 1998. '"Hotter Than a $2 Pistol": Fallout, Sheep, and the Atomic Energy Commission, 1953–1986'. In *The Atomic West*, ed. Bruce Hevly and John Findlay. Seattle: University of Washington Press.

Haines, Aubrey L. 1996 [1977]. *The Yellowstone Story: A History of Our First National Park, Volume Two, Revised Edition*. Niwot, Colorado: University Press of Colorado.

Hales, Peter Bacon 1997. *Atomic Spaces: Living on the Manhattan Project*. Urbana: University of Illinois Press.

Hays, Samuel P. 1987. *Beauty, Health, and Permanence: Environmental Politics in the United States, 1955–1985*. Cambridge: Cambridge University Press.

Keller, Robert and Turek, Michael 1998. *American Indians and National Parks*. Tucson: University of Arizona Press.

Kirsch, Scott 1997. 'Watching the Bombs Go Off: Photography, Nuclear Landscapes, and Spectacular Democracy'. *Antipode* 29/3: 227–55.

Krygier, J.B. 1998. 'Project Ketch: Project Plowshare in Pennsylvania'. *Ecumene* 5/3 (Fall 1998): 311–22.

Kuletz, Valerie 1998. *The Tainted Desert: Environmental and Social Ruin in the American West*. New York: Routledge.

McClelland, Linda Flint 1998. *Building the National Parks: Historic Landscape Design and Construction*. Baltimore: The John Hopkins University Press.

McIntyre, Rick 1993. *A Society of Wolves: National Parks and the Battle Over the Wolf*. Stillwater, Minn.: Voyageur Press.

Milstein, Michael 1996. *Yellowstone: 125 Years of America's Best Idea*. Billings: The Billings Gazette.

Nash, Roderick 1982 [1967]. *Wilderness and the American Mind, Third Edition*. New Haven: Yale University Press.

O'Neill, Dan 1994. *The Firecracker Boys*. New York: St Martin's Press.

Pyne, Stephen 1982. *Fire in America*. Princeton: Princeton University Press.

Riebsame, William (ed.) 1997. *Atlas of the New West: Portrait of a Changing Region*. New York: Norton.

Runte, Alfred 1979. *National Parks: The American Experience*. Lincoln: University of Nebraska Press.

Runte, Alfred 1990. *Yosemite: The Embattled Wilderness*. Lincoln: University of Nebraska Press.

Schrepfer, Susan 1992. 'The Nuclear Crucible: Diablo Canyon and the Transformation of the Sierra Club, 1965–1985'. *California History* 71/2 (Summer 1992): 212–37.

Solnit, Rebecca 1994. *Savage Dreams: A Journey into the Landscape Wars of the American West*. New York: Vintage Books.

Spence, Mark David 1998. 'Crown of the Continent, Backbone of the World: The American Wilderness Ideal and Blackfeet Exclusion from Glacier National Park'. *Environmental History* 1/3 (July 1998): 29–49.

Spence, Mark David 1999. *Dispossessing the Wilderness: Indian Removal and the Making of the National Parks*. New York: Oxford University Press.

Warren, Louis 1997. *The Hunter's Game: Poachers and Conservationists in Twentieth Century America*. New Haven: Yale University Press.

Wellock, Thomas 1992. 'The Battle for Bodega Bay: The Sierra Club and Nuclear Power, 1958–1964'. *California History* 71/2 (Summer 1992): 192–211.

Wellock, Thomas 1998. *Critical Masses: Opposition to Nuclear Power in California, 1958–1978*. Madison: The University of Wisconsin Press.

White, Richard 1991. *'It's Your Misfortune and None of My Own': A New History of the American West*. Norman: University of Oklahoma Press.

Wilson, Alexander 1992. *The Culture of Nature: North American Landscape from Disney to the Exxon Valdez*. Cambridge, Mass.: Blackwell.

Landscape and Ambience on the Urban Fringe: From Agricultural to Imagined Countryside

Joseph Goddard

INTRODUCTION

Over the last generation, historians have advocated the study of the interrelationship of the city and the environment, in part to stop the gaps in knowledge resultant from sub-disciplinary specialisation and to create a holistic understanding of the processes separately researched by environmental and urban historians. Joel A. Tarr (2000) noted that 'historians have paid limited attention to the effects of cities on the environments on their hinterlands'.[1] While Tarr conceived of influence flowing from the city to the hinterland, this paper suggests a more even interlacing of influences to create patterns of urban-rural hybridisations based on reciprocal flows of people, ideas and physical objects. In the process, pastoral urban hinterlands can also influence urban areas as ideal, idealised and aspirational states of mind and physicality are projected back.[2] Thus conceived, nature blends roles as a socio-cultural construction and an actor in its own right.[3]

Arguably the urban-rural borderlands stage the most significant negotiations of cultural ideas with physical environments in the U.S., as emplaced by diverse networks of actors – including farmers, urban émigrés, government administrators and corporations. In the process new landscapes emerge which are fashioned socially and culturally, yet are still reliant on physical surroundings. Swirling within this mix of countryside and urbanity is a form of stylised nature or 'socionature'; part constructed, part physical and partly dissembled.[4] Incomers to the urban fringe imagine such areas to be nature, or at least predominantly natural, whereas displaced farmers and others more clearly recognise resultant landscapes as being enacted upon both them and their locales by outside forces. Together a fragmented, uneasy and contested patchwork of amenity and agricultural landscapes may result, in which an incomers' landscape of leisure fizzles against, and fuses with, a landscape of production.[5]

Landscape transformation appears most visibly in the functional borderlands of urban areas.[6] Describing this phenomenon demanded new terms of the professionals and observers concerned. August Spectorsky (1956) coined 'Exurbia' as a description of elective farming and ranching on New York City's borderlands at mid century; William Whyte (1958) wrote of pervasive 'Urban Sprawl' at the city's edge in *Fortune* magazine; Jean Gottmann (1961) described America's eastern seaboard (Massachusetts to Virginia) conurbation as a continuous 'Megalopolis'; Richard Louv (1982) argued that Americans elected

Environment and History **15** (2009): 413–439.

to fuse tradition and nature with opportunity in a reworked and rejuvenated 'America II'; John Herbers (1986) showed how metropolitan edge migration left decentralised city-country mixes of settlement patterns which he depicted 'new American heartlands'; Joel Garreau (1991) recorded how urban life had spread to 'Edge Cities' on the metropolitan periphery; and Adam Rome (2000) highlighted the environmental effects of post-1945 spatial and demographic movements of 'the Bulldozer in the Country'; while Rob Lang and Jennifer LeFurgy (2007) described the texture of twenty-first century elusive and rapid urbanisation as 'Boomburbs'. At a crude level, these authors described the urban fringe in very different terms, from celebratory (Spectorsky and Garreau) to catastrophic (Rome), depending partly on whether they focused on physical or cultural phenomena.[7] More widely, concern over landscape and ambience change held the attention of people across the United States, the United Kingdom, and in other developed western nations, even as manifestations of change at the urban fringe varied.

Exurbia and sprawl emerged as the most durable terms for metropolitan edge growth by professionals and the popular mind respectively, with exurbia understood as extra-metropolitan urban and suburban growth rather than Spectorsky's electively rural lifestyle.[8] Exurban studies brought forth useful and innovative research, most of which was quantitatively based within the social sciences (economics, demographics and statistics) and presupposed that distance from urban area reduced the attractiveness of a location. Meanwhile, the softer culture of the urban fringe remained largely subsumed by the numbers, leading to oversimplifications and a lack of understanding of textual differences. For many, distance from urban areas – measured in commutes of up to two hours – continued to be a positive factor as it provided access to nature and protection from urban contamination. Fixations on the bricks and tarmac sprawl of monster homes on clustered subdivisions stifled discussion of cultural sprawl, of 'neo-ruralites', 'new-country' and 'neo-pastorals', who mobilised deep-set ideas and sought expansive, leisured lives in at the urban fringe. Moreover much recent research had the mournful loss of farmland and countryside to asphalt and bricks as its primary concern, rather than an assessment of landscape change and hybridisation. This paper scrutinises changing landscapes and ambience in three dissimilar metropolitan edge counties in the eastern U.S. – Loudoun County, Virginia; Howard County, Maryland; and Niagara County, New York – using census data, state reports, extension reports, news-media and interviews.

> Thirty-three percent of Loudoun's farms are really homesites .... This proportion appears to be rising and reflects the ... national trend among urbanites towards a return to rural living .... There are more takers for what Loudoun has to offer ... with Washingtonians crossing the Potomac in a ... discovery of her fertile possibilities in land and living.[9]
>
> (1949 Loudoun County promotional brochure)

People and ideas spilled between the cities and the countryside during the latter half of the twentieth century, as illustrated in the Loudoun booster brochure above – altering the character of the American landscape in the process. Some city dwellers forsook their urban homes for rural living, while others left the country for the city. Agricultural change contributed to this development, as did the actions of governments and others. Arable farming landscapes were lost in urban edge expansion, yet countryside vistas frequently and counter-intuitively became more complex, with greater diversity of flora and fauna. Grapes, horses, exotic animals, wildlife and new plant types thrived – replacing cereal and dairy farming – with fun or essentially non-commercial leisure farming taking over from hard nosed commercial farming. The minds and activity of new country dwellers – penurbanites – imagined, preserved and fashioned rich new pastoral landscapes in the unlikeliest of settings.

Loudoun County lies thirty miles from Washington D.C. in northern Virginia, Howard County lies about twenty miles from Baltimore, Maryland and Washington, D.C., and Niagara County lies some fifteen miles north and east of the Baltimore-Niagara urban complex (at their closest points). Rural backwaters in 1945, all three subsequently came under the sway of nearby metropolitan areas as transport links to them improved. Populations increased and diversified dramatically: in terms of religious, ethnic and racial composition. Secondly, settlement dispersed widely, with the development of suburbs and the infusion of urban concerns into local politics. Thirdly, metropolitan mindsets overlaid local societies, leaving them substantially changed. Fourthly, traditional agrarian livelihoods became marginal to local economies in value and employment terms. Lastly, physical urban frontiers – whether as tangible lines of development, linear tendrils, or as exclaves – advanced into these counties.

For observers, however, these counties remained predominantly rural and verdant, despite the roar of the bulldozer. In fact, portions of the counties seemed more rural to city eyes in 2007 than in 1947. Deliberate preservation schemes help to explain this, but just as often the pastoral feel stemmed from the collective result of individual actions as settlers moved in. Thus, county and regional governments in Loudoun, with a 2006 population (estimate) of 268,817 (up 98,000 since 2000), Howard with a 2006 population (est.) of 272,452 (up 24,000 since 2000), and Niagara residents with a 2006 estimate of 216,130 (down 2,000 since 2000) cultivated rural flavours in some areas – despite eight to tenfold post-war population increases for Loudoun and Howard.[10] This observation becomes doubly remarkable as the developed areas of these counties magnified beyond population increases.[11] Simultaneously, western Loudoun, central western Howard and eastern Niagara became greener, more forested, more diverse in plant, insect and animal life. In all three counties, larger populations jar against more verdant and less traditional farmland, challenging assumptions that the U.S. has become a 'suburban nation' and created a sprawling 'isomorphic geography of nowhere' in the process.[12]

To exemplify and analyse the construction of an urban borderland neo-pastoral landscape, five markers came under examination: the diversifying agricultural economy and landscape; the extent of the equine industry; agricultural fairs; the development of viticulture; and preservation and park development. The first four reflected ill-articulated cultural ideas operationalised by individuals, as they required a leisured use of extensive landholdings in order to create more of a 'dreamscape' than a productive landscape. As a prerequisite, such non-commercial use relied on incomes independent of agriculture or horticulture, relatively cheap real estate prices, and often well thought out business plans. To employ cultural capital in a transformative way economic capital probably helped. Preservation and park development resulted from collective action and relates how local societies collectively reacted to the growing influence of the city.

THE DIVERSIFYING AGRICULTURAL LANDSCAPE AND ECONOMY

Farming influences landscapes immensely, so changes in farming affect how people perceive places. Farming landscapes in the three counties transformed between 1945 and 2007. Incomers staked claims on the countryside, envisaged land differently, and prized aesthetics above utility. New country types saw land as a setting; the countryside conjured images of places to live in rather than work on. Not surprisingly, then, farmer and settlers clashed over attitudes, as one Maryland cattle farmer indicated:

> One reason for a lot of the conflict is what non-farmers think of farms .... Environmentalists call farms natural resources, planners call them open space, and most people relate to them as parks. We think of a farm as a factory.[13]

For penurbanites, land could never be a factory. The countryside altered as incomers employed their ideas, shown through changed crop and animal husbandry trends, the availability of alternative agricultural advice and research, and the growing influence of the leisure economy. Between 1964 and 2002, as farmland was built over or left fallow, nearly two thirds of farmland was withdrawn from commercial agriculture in Howard, and between one quarter and one third in Loudoun and Niagara.[14] The complexion of remaining fields changed, witnessing the influence of new farming practices and of the scale of farming. The most important agents of change in the three counties – apart from farmers and land consumers themselves – were the Cooperative Extension Services (CES) acting in concert with county governments' building and zoning policies.

Cooperative Extension Services reoriented themselves towards non-standard, 'alternative', or 'new' agricultural production from about 1980 as many commercial farms broke into mini-homesteads. Part-time 'farmettes' proliferated from the 1970s, starting a relative trend which extends to the present. Growing numbers of smallholdings grabbed media attention in a 1974 *Howard County Times* article which estimated that there were two hundred 25-acre and smaller farms in Howard alone.[15] Penurban farmers conducted small-scale hobby-farming (smallholder farming with limited commercial impact), dude-ranching (oriented towards leisure and tourists), horse farming, organic farming, subsistence farming, collective farming, themed farming, pumpkin patches, petting farms, advanced forms of animal husbandry including exotic herds of llamas, alpacas, angoras, water buffalo and ostriches, and horticulture, including viticulture. Some back-to-the-landers were inspired by Scott and Helen Nearing's mid-century 'good life'; others followed Spectorsky's wealthy weekend farmers of the 1950s; and still others sought ways of paying their property taxes.[16] Incomers worked both landscapes and perceptions of landscapes. New, elective farmers frequently relaxed commercial criteria, but still needed specialist advice. Smallholder Peggy Schultz captured the new farmers' motivations in a 1979 *Baltimore Sun* interview: 'Farming just makes you feel good'.[17]

Despite rural sympathies, many new farmers knew little about country life, so the CES offered support – such as Howard CES basic farming course which started in 2000.[18] The CES reacted to the ark-like diversity of alternative farming: the mindset of the 'farmette' organic wool producer grated with specialised agronomists. Few traditional farmers practised alternative agriculture, so alternative usually meant incomer farming – as CES personnel in all the counties confirmed during interviews.[19] The need for profits and the massive capital invested deterred alternative farming for traditional farmers; especially as globalising food markets left scant leeway for experimentation. As staff retired, the CES increasingly hired specialists with skills tailored to diverse contemporary farming, often in regional specialists groups such as for producers of wine and horses in Maryland, Virginia and New York.[20]

Small-scale producers complicated the marketing of food and fibre as niche and marginal farmers demanded more CES help in finding buyers for their goods, for instance by encouraging farmers' markets and subscription services to quicken the journey from field to table. Such marketing protected small producers from market price fluctuations by connecting them with local customers. Putting faces to produce, places for farms, and stories to consumers, were positive attributes that echoed with customers and allowed consumers to pitch their identities with the farming community. Nurturing niche products like lambs, goats, exotic vegetables, or items with value added on-site, such as cheese and wine also encouraged finely meshed penurban economies.

Recognising diversity, the CES support themed farming, including pumpkin patches targeting suburban families who could combine farm visits with pumpkin cutting, wine tours where the tippler could follow the grape from field to bottle, and the Bed and Breakfast weekend farming experience. Collectively, such initiatives 'humanised' farming for the outsider; which was especially important given mounting unease over the methods and the quality of agribusiness produce.[21] Overall, CES organisations reoriented themselves towards consumer-minded strategies. Loudoun County's 1998 rural development programme represented the clearest acceptance of the hybridisation of agriculture by reconnecting the agrarian dream with the metropolitan present.[22] The realisation that farming on the fringe held challenges and opportunities singled Loudoun out as a pioneer in deliberately weaving the seductive and productive landscapes which attracted incomers.

In recent years, agricultural crises associated with global markets, low commodity costs, and growth pressure hampered family farmers' ability to carry debt, improve productivity or add value to produce. Few traditional farmers could confidently pass their livelihoods on to their offspring, suggesting links between alternative and new farming and opening the door for incomers who could bear investment costs and low returns or think differently. 'Ethnic' farmers who cultivated intensive and high value products for émigré communities grew. After 1980, numbers of African, Asian and Latin American farmers rose seven-fold in the Washington-Baltimore region. Termed 'New American Farmers' by the *Washington Post*, they served between 500,000 and one million local customers through networks of supermarkets and speciality grocery stores. Ethnic farms looked little like traditional American monocultures and reinforced penurbia's exotic impression.[23]

Parts of the changing agrarian economy could only be inferred from qualitative sources, as census materials only registered them incompletely. Examples include organic farming and more exotic crops and animal husbandry, where figures were very shaky due to self-reporting and classification. Censuses did not distinguished between organic and non-organic farmers, and different states operated different classificatory regimes, making comparisons between counties and across time virtually impossible. Likewise, the variety of livestock types relied on self-reporting. Data for both sectors needed to be gleaned from elsewhere. Horses, wine and agricultural fairs provided good sources describing changing rural life that can be monitored over time. These are examined later.

TABLE 1. Farm Size and Distribution

	Total farmland acres	**Percentage area farmland**	**Under 50 acre farms**	**Under 10 acre farms**
Howard County				
1964	87,000	54%	137	17
2002	38,000	23%	222	72
Loudoun County				
1964	234,000	70%	251	73
2002	165,000	49%	977	99
Niagara County				
1964	181,000	54%	598	108
2002	148,000	44%	346	70

(Source: U.S. Census of Agriculture, see note 7.)

Farm sizes reflected the development of a hybridised pastoral landscape, characterised by the leisure farming and dude ranching where horses were present. Agriculture in all three counties transformed, as shown in Table 1 above. The distribution of farm sizes was squeezed as medium sized family farms fell to giant agribusiness on the one hand, and to the development of small lot and scarcely commercially viable leisure farming on the other. Micro lots gained much more significance. In Howard the total farm area fell from 87 thousand acres in 1964 (when suburbanisation took off), to 38 thousand acres in 2002 – from 54% of land area to 23%. Simultaneously, the number of under-50 acre farms nearly doubled, from 137 in 1964, to 222 in 2002. Eye-catchingly, the number of tiny farms (under 10 acres) shot up from 17 to 72 during the same period. Loudoun's 234 thousand acres of farmland in 1964 fell to 165 thousand in 2002 (with much of the fall after 1980 when development began to encroach) from 70% of land area to 49%. Here, sub-50 acre farm numbers rose nearly fourfold; from 251 in 1964 to 977 in 2002. Niagara also saw land in farms decrease; from 181 thousand acres in 1964 to 148 thousand acres in 2002 – from 54% to 44% of land area. Small farm numbers here, however, collapsed by half from 1964 to 1992 (598 to 273) as the county suffered rustbelt malaise. From 1992, however, the number recovered strongly (to 346).

The stunning growth of lifestyle farms is well established, with less farmland distributed among many more small plots – despite the effects of different data collection methods or tax code changes on statistics. The huge increase in plots of 10 acres in the most developed county – Howard – may predict the future for other metropolitan edge counties. Certainly, the visual impression of these smallholdings would be of greater diversity than for traditional arable dairy farm, or agribusiness. While too small to farm, a patchwork of 10 acre landholdings helps create pastoral landscapes and ambiences where monoculture once predominated. For urbanites, the horse and leisure country of western Loudoun, western Howard and eastern Niagara became more alluring as a potential homestead: a trend confirmed at the national level by successive Gallup polls since 1972. The motif value of hayfields and horse manes billowing in the wind captured the hearts of the country-minded urbanite.[24]

THE EQUINE INDUSTRY

Horses, the second marker of landscape construction, are a vital feature of the penurban fringe. Loudoun, Howard and Niagara counties saw rising numbers of horses within their areas between 1940 and 2002; despite mechanisation and despite declining arable farming acreages and employment. Increased horse populations relied on changes in farming: from for profit to for fulfilment. Local hay production rose even as dairying declined, suggesting that this hay was finding new markets.

The equine industry infused the feel of a community, as horses need space to feed and graze, for riding, and for hay and silage. Pasturage transformed cornfields into lush meadows. Simultaneously, the landscape was embellished with the feel of an elective, landed, leisurely and pastoral lifestyle: the 'country' ambience that drew city dwellers. State agricultural departments and local CES offices charted rising horse numbers through Equine Census Reports. Owning horses provided rich commercial returns, while servicing the equine market supported a growing equine economy, including blacksmithing and riding schools that can be tracked through city directories and telephone books. Descriptions for property for sale with equine references in publications such as the upper crust lifestyle monthly *Town and Country* suggest a spin off for real estate values. In recent years Maryland, Virginia and New York states reported spending for equine products of $476 million, $504 million and $704 million respectively. Capital employed reportedly exceeded yearly expenditure by a factor of ten.[25] Though county breakdowns of annual expenditure were not available, horse census numbers revealed rising horse ownership rates. Loudoun became Virginia's premier equine county, and increasing horse numbers refuted the idea that mechanisation and closeness to the metropolis meant fewer horses.

Equine surveys are innovations of the last two decades. State Equine Surveys recorded more horses and dollar values than Census figures, and showed that the equine market deserved serious attention. Bridging economics and lifestyle, equine industry numbers and values suffered under-reporting and uncertainty. Due to collection methods and the lack of incentives to report, this uncertainty remained even though owner interests including the American Horse Council and CES offices encouraged members to respond.[26]

Howard agricultural census figures listed 1,032 horses in 1997; less than the post-war high of 1,579 in 1987, but above the 935 reported in 1969.[27] In part, this rise in numbers from 1964 to 1987, and then fall thereafter reflected two distinct phases in the county's development; a first in which metropolitan attitudinal influence strengthened, and a second where penurban development within the county was superseded by physical development, leaving less land for leisure pursuits. Highlighting data uncertainty, the 2002 Maryland Equine Census counted 5,190 horses in Howard County – five times the census figures. Howard's horses were valued at $61 million dollars and located in 1,200 places totalling 11,200 acres, or nearly 5% of the county's total area. Howard stabled one horse per 25 inhabitants. The Maryland Equine Census noted that nearly half of the state's horses were located in five outer Baltimore-Washington region counties; intuitively where they would least be expected due to development pressures.[28]

Loudoun County reported a post-war high of 4,135 horses in the 1997 U.S. Agricultural Census, up from 2,405 in 1969. Strikingly, the 2001 Virginia Equine Report counted seven horses for every one tallied by the census: 15,800, or one for every fifteen Loudouners. Inventory value amounted to nearly $295 million, explaining why the Loudoun Department of Economic Development monitored the industry conscientiously. Rising numbers may result from greater distance from metropolitan cores than Howard. Loudoun dominated Virginia horse numbers and value rankings, along with adjacent Fauquier County, repeating the link between horse number and proximity to metropolitan areas seen in Maryland.[29] Niagara listed 871 horses in the 1997 U.S. Agricultural Census, down from 1,107 in 1964. In contrast, the 2000 New York Equine Survey estimated Niagara's equine population nearly four times higher, at 3,000 with a value of $12 million – unchanged from the 1988 report. Consistent with other states nationwide, the New York Survey found more horses in near-urban areas.[30]

Clear differences between 1997 U.S. Agricultural Census figures and 2000–2002 State equine reports underlined the growth and uncertainty of the equine market. The 2002 U.S. Agricultural Census returns greatly increased the reported number of horses in all three counties; from 1,032 in 1997 to 1,382 in 2002 in Howard (30%); from 4,135 in 1997 to 6,162 in 2002 in Loudoun (nearly 50%); and from 871 in 1997 to 1,698 in 2002 in Niagara (nearly 100%). More farms registered horses present in 2002 than in 1997; up from 111 to 158 in Howard; up from 401 to 731 in Loudoun; and up from 129 to 222 in Niagara. Three strong indicators emerge: the large size of the equine market, the growth of the market over the last generation, and the outer metropolitan fringe location of the industry. The precise size and value of the equine market probably surpassed even the higher equine report numbers.[31]

Farmers probably served the equine market for hay for cash from the barn door, especially given hay's weight, bulk and cost of transport. Substantiating barn-door sales would be impossible, although there is indicative data. Hay production in Loudoun increased markedly despite smaller yields per reporting farm; from around 50 thousand tons in the 1960s to around 70 thousand tons from 1987, and despite the collapsing dairy industry. Moreover, the average yield per reporting farm fell from the 1990s. Hay production in Niagara fluctuated wildly, while it dropped in Howard until the 1990s. Thereafter it stabilised, interesting because commercial dairying and ancillary industries had all but disappeared. Uncertainty reigns with regard to reporting criteria. Bountiful harvests and collapsing traditional markets beg the question of where the hay was going, with horses (and perhaps sheep, goats, llamas and other exotic species) providing a probable answer.[32]

Listings by equine-related businesses in City Directories and Yellow Pages recorded vital and growing activity in Howard and Loudoun measured over ten year intervals since the 1960s, revealing growth to be especially strong after 1980. Howard saw a lone entry for horses in the 1972 phone book rise to seventeen in 2003, including three horse centres, four breeders, four trainers and six saddle and equipment vendors: a staggering increase, especially as much farmland had been lost. For Loudoun, the increase was still more dramatic. Entries for a single harness maker and one blacksmith in 1962, multiplied to eleven breeders, eight dealers, three furnishers, 26 trainers, three transporters, six blacksmiths and 22 saddle and harness sellers in 2001. Seventy-nine entries, the 2001 sum of Loudoun area horse related businesses, described a dynamic, vibrant community. Even Lockport and the rural eastern half of Niagara County increased its listings of such businesses, from one lone blacksmith in 1949 to two racers, a breeder, a blacksmith and two riding academies in 2000.[33]

The huge increase in horse business entries could partially be explained by cross-county regional listings, multiple listings and a greater propensity for businesses to list. Yet together with census and survey numbers, increasing numbers of businesses testified to increasing horse numbers and the $368 million importance of the industry in the counties, and indicate an increasingly leisure-inspired landscape. What were people doing with all these horses? One answer is provided by county agricultural fair classifications: a huge expansion of showing categories took place, which is reflected in 2003 programmes. Howard's fair listed 24 categories, from pulling to horsemanship; Loudoun's included 30 riding categories; and Niagara included seven major categories.[34] Cooperative Extension Service (CES) were acutely aware of rural transformations through links with 4-H programmes and targeted programmes at the horse minded newly-rural incomers.

AGRICULTURAL FAIRS

Agricultural fairs – a third area attesting to landscape and attitudinal change – shaped, reflected and bound local identity by bringing people together, and shaping community and togetherness in an atmosphere of entertainment. Fairs showcased rural life and the changing face of rural society, the shifts in agricultural production, landscape consumption and attitudes through schedules of events, classifications and competitions. Two generations ago, fairs exhibited produce raised or grown for sale – such as food and fibre – and items made or transformed for home use, such as clothes, cooking and canning. Recent fairs demonstrated that rural life now included hosts of other activities. These new activities created feelings and transformed symbols (rather than objects), leavening traditional rural life with a penurban synthesis of country and heritage that celebrated ambience and consumed landscape. Examples included the Niagara Fair's native dancing, Celtic dancing, clog dancing and antique tractor and equipment parade, Howard Fair's hand spinning and hair goat exhibitions, and Loudoun Fair's quilting, crocheting and hunting categories.[35] These classifications imagined rural life in non-commercial terms through stylised impressions of tradition and emphasised the break between countryside as an arena of production, and its contemporary function as a field of dreams.

CES youth 4-H programmes (Heads, Hearts, Hands and Health) played active roles in Howard, Loudoun and Niagara county shows. Fairs grew in length from a day or two in the 1940s and 1950s, to a week by 2006/7. Show categories increased gradually in Niagara and more rapidly in Howard and Loudoun, especially after 1980. Howard categories in 1946 included meat, vegetables, beef, and farm crops, poultry, household and 4-H demonstrations; as did Niagara in 1957, which also included tractor-pulls and flower arranging; and Loudoun in 1954, which held classes for vegetable canning and freezing.[36] Post-war Loudoun fair programmes carried advertising for various staples of rural life: farm equipment, insurance, banking and feedstuffs. By 2007, CES programmes – which fed into show categories – served farm folk and other people interested in rural life, gardening, woodcraft and food production and treatment.

Many participants of recent CES programmes knew little of country life; consequently 4-H streamed programmes, with advanced instruction for farm children and basic skills for suburban kids. Fewer farm children, the massive suburban market, a wish to remain relevant, and incomer interest in rural life encouraged 4-H outreach to a broader public. County shows reflected change through the introduction of non-ownership categories for exhibitions so that everyone could join in, including the showing of borrowed sheep, and a prolific range of 'pet' categories including rabbits and goats, baked goods, fashion and ponies – all of which appealed to a non-traditional public.[37]

Fair categories demonstrated the un-commercial hybridisation of countryside connected to penurbia and the shortcomings of the Agricultural Census. Llamas debuted in the 1998 Loudoun show, despite no census listings recording llamas in the county. In Howard, hand spinning surfaced; since 1973 the county has hosted the annual Maryland Sheep and Wool Show, reinforcing its craft heavyweight-status.[38] While Howard registered sheep numbers halved between 1964 and 1997, the number of farms with sheep remained virtually unchanged, suggesting cottage rather than commercial production. Similarly, Loudoun saw more small producers emerging. The 2003 Howard fair included eight sheep divisions, fifteen wool categories and nineteen meat categories for sheep, and the Loudoun fair listed seven major ownership divisions with an array of sub-classifications. While goats, llamas and alpacas did not appear consistently in census statistics, fair entries insisted that the animals had to be there. The 2003 Howard show included five divisions and fifty categories for goats – incredible as the 1997 Census counted only 213 goats. The 2003 Loudoun fair offered two classes and eight classifications for a 1997 Census count of 412 goats, and the Niagara show offered four events for its 154 reported goats.

Almost certainly, agricultural censuses undercounted the diversity of marginal wool, milk and meat categories. Niagara offered a home winemaking competition, and all three counties included beekeeping.[39] The rearing of llamas, sheep, goats, horses, bees and ponies and the growth of winemaking painted a picture of agriculture and land use as arenas for a stylised, leisure economy. These agricultural leisure economy activities could be perceived to require part-time attention and self-management, although reality often turned out differently. Agricultural fairs showcased the rise of a leisured agricultural economy, increasing diversity and the hybridisation of countryside. Country-minded incomers moved to the fringe and tended intricate gardens of leisured, esoteric production that partly replaced traditional farming. Fair categories presented texture that census figures missed due to underreporting, especially on the most marginal micro farms.

VITICULTURE

Tending vineyards – a fourth indicator of landscape and ambience change – reflected the pastoral idyll in the ancient world, taken up by America's founding fathers who reflected upon ideas of natural purity and order. Winegrowing mixed idylls with the sophistication and urbanity informing America's revolutionary republican class. Penurbanites brought and bought the symbolic value of the vineyard to the present and fed the nationwide viticulture boom. Since 1970 winery numbers nationwide have probably more than quintupled.[40] A key 2005 report noted that 36 thousand New Yorkers owed their livelihood to grape products and the industry provided over $400 million in tax revenue. Three of the major producer areas (The Niagara Escarpment, The Seneca Lakes and Long Island) lay within commuter distance of the state's largest metropolitan areas: Buffalo; Rochester/Syracuse; and New York City.[41]) Virginia's biggest winegrowing counties also straddled the outer orbit of Washington, D.C. and Charlottesville.[42] A 2004 Maryland report reconfirmed the geographical link between winegrowing and penurban areas.[43]

New country people founded many wineries in the three counties after 1970. Loudoun boasted 54 winegrowers in the 2002 Agricultural census, up from 17 in 1978. Grape production in Loudoun rose one-hundredfold, to 836,000 pounds by 2006. The Loudoun Rural Economic Development Office responded vigorously by establishing the 'County Wine Trail'.[44] Niagara re-orientated its massive grapes-for-the-table industry towards added value wine production from 1964 to 2002.[45] In March 2004, Niagara County planned the distribution of 100,000 new Niagara Wine Trail Brochures to support the craft through agro-tourism. Even Howard managed an increasing number of producers from 1987. Howard's 15th annual 'Wine in the Woods' festival in May 2007 spotlighted local wines and drew over 20,000 visitors and 70 artisans.[46] The multi-year horizon for grape cropping meant that growers needed outside incomes before their first payday, confirmed by census data recording non-fruit bearing vines in the 2002 census which augurs for significant increases in the 2007 census.

Deep-set cultural dispositions and pragmatic responses to zoning rules together encouraged grape cultivation. Protective land policy in many counties stipulated minimum sizes for rural area housing lots, typically between two and fifty acres. Too big to mow, too small for traditional farming, these plots lent themselves to viticulture or horse keeping. The CES in Maryland, Virginia and New York honed their winegrowing expertise through regional viticulture coalitions. CES advice towards production, processing and marketing underscored the huge confidence in the wine business's potential – as an industry, to draw tourists, and to enhance rural qualities. Increasingly sophisticated winemakers fermented grapes from other producers, providing markets for micro-producers who could not make their own wine. Almost certainly wineries suffered undercount as some ventures simply amounted to loss-making hobbies, financed by salaries or home sale bonanzas. Winemaking's banner value overwhelmed its commercial value, as the rows of grape vines draped across plots of land endowed an area with genteel, rural sophistication. Rising wine production, wine country allure, and the greater prestige of local wines brought the producer, the consumer, and the imagination together in a collective appreciation, and confirmed that the cultural importance of wine trumped its economic value.

PRESERVATION AND PARK DEVELOPMENT

Cultural ideas drove landscape change at two levels. The four examples sketched above relied generally on individually chosen, functional factors, which then formed recognisable patterns for support services to deal with. Larger scale factors – as flagged earlier – were also important, in terms of zoning rules implemented by county governments and preservation and park creation policies advanced by municipality, county, state and federal policy.

Concern over sprawl affected near-metropolitan counties from the early twentieth century. Zoning became a common method of controlling development and directing land use. Women's organisations, such as the Garden Club of Virginia, led in campaigns to introduce rural zoning in Loudoun in 1941–2. Howard implemented zoning in 1948, whereas Niagara introduced zoning on a piecemeal township basis between the 1920s and the 1970s.[47] In all three zoning ultimately mandated minimum lot-sizes for homes in sensitive countryside areas or wilderness under 'Agricultural-Rural' or 'Agricultural Residential' classifications.[48] Rules covering lot-sizes also protected property values by ensuring exclusivity. Zoning regulations were tightened from 1970, revealing growing concern over encroaching development. Minimum agricultural plots in designated countryside areas grew: Howard quintupled lot-sizes to five acres, and Loudoun up-zoned from one to ten acres. Western New York used zoning to reduce linear 'ribbon' development by preventive zoning for road-front property.[49] Protective agricultural zoning bestowed rural feelings to countryside development by stopping intensive suburban-style development.

County services like water and sewer lines supported planning policy. Howard and Loudoun attempted to direct development through water and sewer provision by focusing services tightly on designated areas, and discouraging development in unserviced regions.[50] Both counties saw growth as given, while in Niagara water and sewer systems crisscrossed the county by the 1960s to facilitate development.[51] Large-lot owners beat servicing policy by relying on well-water and septic tanks, a factor influencing the lot size increases during the water pollution conscious 1950s and 1960s: Big plots were essential for well-water extraction and sewage disposal without the imminent worry of contamination.[52] More recently, small-scale private treatment plants coupled with high cluster-zone densities and favourable property prices increased the ability of developers to ignore county services. However, micro-treatment plants blighted the penurban landscape and fuelled resistance to further growth, as the *Loudoun Times Mirror* noted of one scheme: 'One major roadblock is the sewage and water treatment plant that will spray highly treated sewage on neighbouring undeveloped land.'[53] Many fringe settlers would have regarded human slurry as an intrusion upon the countryside vistas they imagined.

Large-lot rural development left penurban homeowners flummoxed over how to use their five to fifty acre mini-estates, while the difference between agricultural returns and development profits chased commercial farmers out of the market as some farmers could not afford to pay spiralling taxes. Using the land and earning a tax-offsetting return instead of hours of mowing strengthened the attraction of Cooperative Extension Service offerings for incomers.[54] The CES helped where it could – such as Virginia's 2004 courses in forest management which allowed small 'woodlot owners to see the forest beyond the trees', Niagara's environmental education programmes, and Howard/Maryland's 'Basics of Farming' short courses.[55] Capital costs of landholdings amounted to near zero for some, with land values being secondary to the house price. Contrastingly, traditional farmers had to invest heavily to produce profits. That incomers could discount their investment explains how the countryside diversified so rapidly since 1970. Paradoxically, large-lot housing, a product of zoning changes inspired by environmental concern, encouraged countryside transformation. Tax and investment factors helped explain the ageing of the farming profession: few younger farmers could finance a traditional farm as land values outstripped farmers' means to produce a return.

After 1980 zoning policies became more sophisticated in fighting the loss of open countryside through mini-estate privatisation. Cluster zoning (clustering), allowed more houses in one part of a plot in return for the preservation of the rest – with overall housing densities unchanged. Transferable Development Rights (TDR) programmes aimed to concentrate agricultural reserves and permit builders greater densities and profits on some sites if they purchased land elsewhere for preservation. For both, increased building densities on smaller plots saved infrastructure costs for builder and the county. Yet some observers felt cluster zoning and TDRs legitimised development. Suburbanites complained that building densities in their areas were already too high, while pretty rural areas enjoyed TDR protection paid for with their taxes. Sectional, suburban-country jealousy poisoned Loudoun politics from the late 1990s, as it had in Howard in the 1980s. Tellingly, zoning, clustering and TDR policies had limited success in staunching development. Howard and Loudoun – in line with other outer Washington-Baltimore region counties – grew despite policies targeted to maintain their rural character. A 2002 University of Maryland 'Landsat' satellite study recorded that development consumed 28,000 acres a year in the Washington region: build-outs actually accelerated as anti-development policies increased.[56]

Public concern over sprawl persisted, was recognised by political representatives, and manifested itself in ways two ways. Farmland protection enriched cultural landscapes, and parks framed natural landscapes. Both meetings saw dollar returns deluged by attitudinal returns and were generally implemented and administered by county governments. Voters supported park creation and land development rights because they saw enough intrinsic value in these programmes to bankroll them. This self-sacrifice – despite resistance – indicated that incomer-farmland and wilderness attitudes were actualised into constructed places. And even where other factors such as flood protection and water quality maintenance worked into decisions to preserve or establish parks, the parks quickly blended into the background natural vista.

Penurbia united worlds of consumption and preservation. Aesthetics and the economics of farming combined to create unique syntheses which maintained open, rural habitats, like Loudoun's horse and hunt country, Niagara's escarpment, and Howard's wool and crafts. Preservationism was important, yet penurbia's heritage-hugging mindset also transformed landscapes. The preserved countryside itself became an object of consumption, a backdrop to country passions, and a setting for the selective eulogisation of tradition and crafts. 'Rural fringes require farmland and forest protection to retain their attractive cultural landscapes', wrote urban historian Dolores Hayden.[57] Landscape preservation uneasily united farmers, incomers, penurban values, local politics and administrations. Farmer and Howard Agricultural Preservation Board member, Ridgeley Jones caught the essence of preservation in 1981: 'This land has served countless generations and once it goes into development, it will never be put back'. Agricultural preservation did not go uncontested when introduced in Howard in the 1980s.[58] Still, by 2007 Howard had preserved over 20,000 acres.[59] In Loudoun, preservation schemes introduced in 2000 now protect about 1% of the County.[60]

Criticism of preservation policies which purchased development rights (PDRs) came from farmers, taxpayers and some politicians, and covered inadequate compensation, exorbitant costs, 'snob' zoning favouring the already favoured, and the misuse of scarce resources. Leading farmers wondered if the PDR rules – keep the land in agriculture and forego the right to sell the land for development – could stand judicial challenge as development land values skyrocketed. Ironically, preservation cost most where it was most needed, and once preserved, neighbouring land rose in value – increasing development pressures. Other mechanisms employed for agricultural preservation included agricultural districting and right to farm rules. All three counties established agricultural districts that fixed land taxes to agricultural values to discourage farm sales due to taxes. Huge schools enrolments led to breathtaking development costs in Loudoun with increased tax burdens for all. To counter this, Loudoun dedicated 70,000 acres to the Agricultural and Forestal District Program (AFDP), beginning in 1979. The AFDP reduced the County's potential tax base, but also forestalled service-hungry development.

Howard introduced right-to-farm laws in 1978; Virginia created state-wide rules that affected Loudoun in 1981, and New York state rules applied to Niagara in 1971 – in response to pressure and compromise between farmers and political leaderships.[61] Right-to-farm regulations protected farming landscapes and farmers from potential nuisance suits. In their minds, incomers had split the rural landscape from its means of production, to then challenge the courts to rule against the irritations of farming. The need for right-to-farm ordinances provided hard evidence of the sometimes-frayed farmer-settler relationship. Simultaneously, preservation policies and ordinances underlined the status of agriculture as a worthy 'museum' repository of (redundant) rural values.

Some farmers repeatedly claimed that agricultural and residential uses were incompatible and that pockets of housing amid swathes of agricultural land disrupted farming by making the movement of equipment difficult. Farmers claimed that incomers trespassed, stole or destroyed crops and harassed livestock, whereas incomers retorted that noisy agricultural machinery held traffic up, loose animals destroyed gardens, and that muck spreading literally stank. Farmers and migrants together claimed that TDR policies preserved fragmented and low-grade countryside and that the money was better used elsewhere. Local and regional newspapers in all three counties repeatedly dedicated column inches to farmer-suburbanite conflicts.[62]

The setting of nature aside for leisure and sublime experiences has a long history in the U.S. George Catlin famously (1832) proposed that America protect 'pristine beauty and wilderness ...' for posterity, while Frederick Law Olmsted added utility to nature and wilderness in 1865, declaring, 'It is a scientific fact that the occasional contemplation of natural scenes ... is favourable to the health and vigour of men.' From around 1850 municipal and federal authorities established city parks and national parks that celebrated wilderness by constructing and stylising it.[63] This section looks at the development of park and preservation policy for amenity and aesthetic values.

Open spaces – parks, reserves, sanctuaries and recreational facilities – enlivened the city edge sensibility, as un-built and stylised natural environments differentiated country from the metropolis. Continuous belts of open land dividing the metropolis from countryside created valued settings. By establishing focal places beyond the city, open land made credible a penurban self-identification, even when such areas were deliberate reconstructions. Open spaces frequently surrounded historic houses and monuments, such as the Rust Sanctuary in

Loudoun that consisted of an imposing manor house and sixty acres and a protective barrier against growing Leesburg.[64] The Patapsco Female Institute Historic Park perched above Ellicott City connected visually with 32-mile-long riparian Patapsco Valley State Park, providing a country backdrop to the city and a rural exoskeleton to Howard County.[65] Howard, Loudoun and Niagara counties established recreational and open space areas from the late-1960s, partly in response to development. Other open spaces resulted from neighbourhood planning concepts, as places where suburbanites could conveniently spend leisure time. In 1990, Loudoun created the 357-acre Claude Moore Park which served the most densely populated areas of the county. The park combined wilderness, woods, sports and recreational areas, and housed the Loudoun Heritage Farm Museum in a nature-heritage-leisure complex.[66]

'For reasons not easily explained, most people seem to achieve a great deal of pleasure and satisfaction from being in natural surroundings', the Howard County 1960 General Plan argued, acknowledging the urgent need for preservation of open land. The plan proposed saving up to 25,000 acres.[67] Commenting on the disappearance of open space in 1961 (the year Jean Gottmann published *Megalopolis*), *Times, Ellicott City* ran the headline, 'Parks Needed: Merging Cities Threaten Open Space'.[68] Subsequent plans trumpeted open space as a primary objective. Patapsco and Patuxent Valley State Parks – 14,000 and 6,700 acres respectively – formed virtually continuous and effective riparian green belts protecting Howard County's interior mixing feral and stylised nature, old mill buildings and hewn stone. Maryland State funding and local planning helped in the creation of river parks, as concern over water pollution worried many people close to Chesapeake Bay's precarious ecology and rich fishing ground – especially after Rachel Carson's 1962 bestseller *Silent Spring*. Locally and nationally, the League of Women Voters was consistently a strident voice for such preservation.[69]

Loudoun County's 1969 plan remarked that the county had 'not ... felt the need for developed public recreational space ...' beyond that associated with schools and the new Sterling Park subdivision, due to the rural feel of the county. The plan proposed the creation of county and developer-financed public and private parks and recreation areas. Later plans recognised the essential necessity of maintaining open and recreational spaces for Loudoun's character and quality.[70] The emphasis on landscape and greenery protection in Howard and Loudoun matched the influence of resident opinion favouring open and natural space. Park regionalisation into green networks that joined separate areas together across jurisdictions became a goal of organisations like the American Farmland Trust and the Chesapeake Bay Foundation, and for regional organisations like the Metropolitan Washington Council of Governments.[71]

Frederick Law Olmsted had been a prime mover in the creation of the Niagara Reservation Park in the 1880s. Creating the Reservation led to the removal of energy-dependent and water-consuming industries from the Niagara Falls gorge and established parkland backdrops to the American Falls. 'Renaturing' the industrial landscape allowed Olmsted license. 1950s automotive mobility and the Robert Moses Parkway saw the city severed from the water again. In 2002, the Niagara Heritage Partnership campaigned successfully to close the road for a trial period.[72] Illustrating the deeply intertwined character of environment and imagination, environmentalists fêted the re-establishment of Olmsted's reconstruction.[73]

Sanctuaries and reserves embellished penurban countryside. They owed their existence in all three counties to private largesse, the philanthropy of prominent citizens, and vocal local interests. Partnerships between governments and various interests created places like Loudoun's Claude Moore Park or the Niagara Reservation restoration. Philanthropic and citizens' interests organised the Waterford Foundation in Loudoun and raised nearly $3.7 million for PDR's in 2003 to protect Waterford's achingly beautiful village vistas from development. Increasingly, private interests saw profits in preservation, such as in the 'South Riding' master built community in Loudoun that registered its land with the National Wildlife Federation's 'Backyard Wildlife Habitat Program'. Cluster-development regulations and developer self-interest converged to create storied open spaces complete with salamanders and rattlesnakes for potential buyers.[74]

The political compromises underlying the complex interests at the urban fringe showed the convergence of amenity and utility values. Without open land, the neo-rural dream would die, and without the direct and indirect financial support of the rest of the community, farming would expire. Between the two, scarce tax dollars were traded for limits on land-use freedom. Purchasing and maintaining parks cost money, underlining the compromise between the support of economic and aesthetic values. Governments knew that open, agricultural land drew people to the fringe and that keeping it needed their support. Indeed county demographers in Loudoun regularly and consistently measured how Loudouners conceived of their county. Beginning in the 1960s in Howard County, private corporations learned that access to open space sold real estate and could generate richer profits than traditional subdivisions, and interests showed that preservation motivated by profit or altruism could gain public and political support.[75]

CONCLUSION

On the urban fringe, beyond the gritty sprawl of the metropolis lies penurbia: a developing zone of imagining as much as transition, a place where ideas could be superimposed on the landscape. Here, the metropolitan mind – without the cookie-cutter subdivisions of metropolitan physicality – spilled across agricultural landscapes and created hybridised leisure countryside. One National Public Radio journalist accurately captured the atmosphere of hybrid farm country:

> Western Loudoun County, just minutes from downtown Washington, D.C., is still undeniably farm country, but you'll see more than the traditional fields of corn and dairy cows. Today, many of the local farmers are self-taught specialists raising water buffalo, llamas, goats, emus and bees. Others grow flowers and herbs, Christmas trees, organic vegetables and fruits, and grapes for wine.[76]

Blinding heterogeneity marked the landscape and ambience of the penurban fringe, not agricultural monoculture. The scenery created truly allowed the mind to wander and to consider the proposition of whether landscapes were degraded or improved by the interplay of rural and urban elements.

Academic and journalistic reports bemoaned the loss of agricultural land under development pressure, yet the leisured countryside which incomers laid over farmland was more 'Edenic' garden or park than empty vacuum. Although accurate quantitative data over time is hard to come by, Howard, Loudoun and Niagara probably housed more trees and bigger trees in 2008 than in 1945, and may well have housed greater overall biodiversity in the sections of the counties housing imagined countryside. Qualitative data is even more elusive, what type of trees, how big, or how native? With trees come wildlife; all three counties reported concern over the explosion in deer populations, especially over the increasing number of vehicle-animal collisions.[77] In recognition of the problem, Howard County created a 'Deer Task Force' in 1996.[78] Certainly, in the fall breeding season, road kill peppered roadsides and was often removed for game before transport cleanup officials arrived. Feral plots and gardens represented a veritable 'buffet for deer', as well as other fauna.[79] Beyond the damage to vehicles and gardens, disease motivated scrutiny of deer as (apparently) the prime vector of Lyme disease. Loudoun Lyme disease cases shot up after 1990, and accounted for fully half of Virginia totals, with strong increases observed in neighbours Fairfax and Montgomery counties. The interface between deer and humans was probably as much the result of habitat gain as a habitat encroachment through development. European aristocrats intentionally created deer parks for enjoyment, hunting and leisured restitution for centuries; American penurbanites created derivative landscapes almost by accident in their yearning for countryside. The anecdotal value of the return of large fauna – including deer, bears and coyotes – for the new country fringe ultimately seemed double edged, with pressure building to permit increased hunting.

Penurban landscapes emerged pragmatically as migrants from the city moved to the country to practice rural living, as they saw it. Incomers carried with them ideas of how countryside should look, sound and smell, ideas which resided deep in cultural appreciations of ideal landscapes. And they certainly also bore with them prejudices against certain kinds of landscape, including the highly specialised, productive and sanitised (yet still periodically smelly) agrarian vistas which emerged as viable farm sizes increased and mechanised. Ideas of countryside appropriateness probably also suffered a nostalgic idea of what a rural – or even rustic – landscape should look like. Granted the wherewithal from metropolitan incomes, jobs and house sales, incomers could literally take a vision from their mind's eye and project it across a plot of land, complete with the amenity care of horses, growing of wine, keeping of exotic animals and so on. In the process they supported a fine grained economy and visual culture which embellished landscapes through horse pasturage, riding schools, vineyards, vineries and the like. Moreover, the dispositions of incomers received timely support from county policy decisions such as land policy that had intended and unintended consequences. A five- or a ten-acre plot provided a substantial canvas for the penurban incomer to paint over, as well as soothing the needs of autonomy by providing exclusive domains. Protective policies such as agricultural zoning, districting, parks and preserves aided the creation of an imagined and then emplaced countryside in terms of an enduring backdrop and a greater textual cohesion.

The landscapes and ambiences of the urban fringe discussed in this paper are not 'natural', but contemporary cultural constructions superimposed on earlier agricultural landscapes and their underlying physical constructions. These hybrid constructions are the result of individual dispositions writ large, cultural ideals, economic opportunity and political support. They rest upon the cross pollination of ideas in mind and physical surroundings; envisaged, created and consumed. While few Americans live in small towns, villages or rural locations, most people express a preference for living in such places – despite their lack of first hand experience in living on the land or in small towns. Clearly the idyll of small scale and rural life has deep roots in the popular psyche, which some people can fulfil in part by buying a penurban home while others remain with their dreams in metropolitan surroundings.

While this paper rests on an examination of three eastern U.S. counties, preliminary research suggests that comparable patterns would emerge from close study of urban fringe counties elsewhere in the northern and Midwestern U.S. In other areas, water, climatic and regulatory concerns may force different manifestations of imagined countryside to emerge, such as the multi-acre 'ranchette' patterns in Colorado. Moreover, the creation of amenity landscapes in the countryside may also have a global reach, or at least reach into many western countries.[80] Post-1945 agricultural landscapes have transformed, to provide the imagined and hybridised countryside of contemporary penurbia. These new landscapes will probably evolve and prove transitory as development pressures increase, bringing more metropolitan and rural ideas in to dialogue.

NOTES

I would like to thank Dr. Georgina Endfield, and Dr. Peter Coates for their help in the preparation of this paper for publication, and for arranging blind-peer review. The reviewers' comments helped to improve the paper greatly. Thanks also go to Joseph B. Powell of Louisiana State University Press for his continuing help on the manuscript from which this article emerged. The University of Copenhagen, Department of English, Germanic, and Romance Studies has generously financed my research on the urban-rural fringe in the U.S. Lastly, thanks to my colleagues on the ongoing Contemporary America Project in Copenhagen for their continued support.

[1] Joel A. Tarr (2000) 'Urban History and Environmental History in the United States: Complementary and Overlapping Fields', in Historiography Series in Global Environmental History, H-Net. (http://www.h-net.org/~environ/historiography/historiography.html)

[2] See, for example, lifestyle magazines such as *Country Living* and *Country Home*, founded around 1980. These two magazines have over a million sales an issue, advertising revenues in the tens of millions, and with dedicated sections for capturing country style in the city.

[3] The conceptual divide between nature and culture ultimately fuels a cognitive incompatibility which at least partly lies between the relative comprehension of urban fringe phenomena by cultural geographers and environmental historians. See Judith Gerber, 'Beyond Dualism – the Social Construction of Nature and the natural and Social Construction of Human Beings', *Progress in Human Geography* 21, 1 (1997): 1–17.

[4] For more on hybrid socionatural landscapes, see Erik Swyngedouw 'Modernity and Hybridity: Nature Regeneracionismo, and the Production of Spanish Waterscape, 1890–1930', *Annals of the Association of American Geographers* 89, 3 (1999): 443–65.

[5] Amenity landscapes in a broader sense rely on differences in purchasing power between natives and incomers; made more extreme by a widening income gulf between winners and losers in an increasingly globalised economy and labour market. For more on the relationship between countryside, hybridity, and globalisation, see Michael Woods 'Engaging the Global Countryside: Globalization, Hybridity and the Reconstitution of Rural Place', *Progress in Human Geography*, 31, 4 (2007): 485–507. Woods sees countryside as being enacted upon, rather than an actor in its own right.

[6] By functional, I mean beyond the administrative and even occasionally statistical limits to urban areas. These limits vary according to the specific urban area studies, the history of the urban area, the region in which the urban area is located, and the size of the area.

[7] See Auguste Spectorsky, *The Exurbanites* (Philadelphia, PA: J.B. Lippincott Company, 1955); Albert LaFarge, *The Essential William H. Whyte* (New York: Fordham University Press, 2000); Jean Gottmann, *Megalopolis; The Urbanized Northeastern Seaboard of the United States* (New York: Twentieth Century Fund 1961); John Herber, *The New Heartland: America's Flight Beyond the Suburbs and How It Is Changing Our Future* (New York: Times Books, 1986 [first published in 1978]); Richard Louv, *America II* (New York: Tarcher, Inc., 1983); Joel Garreau, *Edge City: Life on the New Frontier* (New York: Anchor Books, 1991); Robert Lang and Jennifer LaFurgy, *Boomburbs: The Rise of America's Accidental Cities* (Washington, D.C: Brookings, 2007); Arthur Nelson and Thomas Sanchez, 'Lassoing Exurban Sprawl', (pre-publication draft, 2002); Arthur

Nelson and Thomas Sanchez, 'Debunking the Exurban Myth: A Comparison of Suburban Households', *Housing Policy Debate* 19, 2 (1999): 689–709; Arthur Nelson and Thomas Sanchez, 'Exurban and Suburban Households: A Departure from Traditional Location Theory?' *Journal of Housing Research* 8, (1997): 249–276.

[8] Defined in general terms by scholars working at Virginia Tech's Metropolitan Institute and elsewhere, including Arthur Nelson and Thomas Sanchez.

[9] 'Let's Look at Loudoun' – Loudoun County promotional brochure (1949).

[10] 2006 U.S. Census estimates. See http://quickfacts.census.gov/qfd/index.html

[11] Anne Sorensen, Richard Greene and Karen Russ, 'Farming on the Edge', co-published by *The American Farming Trust* and The Centre for Agriculture and Environment, North Illinois University (1997).

[12] Andres Duany, Elizabeth Plater-Zyberg and Jeff Speck, *Suburban Nation: The Rise of Sprawl*, (New York: North Point Press, 2002); James Howard Kunstler, *The Geography of Nowhere: The Rise and Decline of America's Man Made Landscape* (New York: Touchstone, 1993).

[13] Joe Surkiewicz, 'Greener Pastures: When Suburb Meets Country, Conflicts Can Arise', *Baltimore Sun*, 29 Jan. 1995.

[14] U.S. Agricultural Census figures are used throughout this paper except where otherwise stated.

For Howard: Department of Commerce (1972) 1969 Census of Agriculture, Vol. 1, Part 23 Maryland County Data; U.S. Department of Agriculture (1999) 1997 Census of Agriculture, Vol. 1, Part 20 Maryland State and County Data; and 2002 Census of Agriculture website, http://www.nass.usda.gov/census/ (for 1997 and 2002 data).

For Loudoun: Department of Commerce (1972) 1969 Census of Agriculture, Vol. 1, Part 24 Virginia, Section 2 County Data; U.S. Department of Agriculture (1999) 1997 Census of Agriculture, Vol. 1, Part 46, Virginia State and County Data; and 2002 Census of Agriculture website, http://www.nass.usda.gov/census/ (for 1997 and 2002 Data).

For Niagara County: U.S. Department of Commerce (1972) *1969 Census of Agriculture*, Part 7 New York, Section 2, County Data; U.S. Department of Agriculture (1999) *1997 Census of Agriculture*, Volume 1, Part 32, New York State and County Data; and 2002 Census of Agriculture website, http://www.nass.usda.gov/census/ (for 1997 and 2002 data).

[15] Missy Zane, 'Farmettes: New Way of Life', *Times, Ellicott City,* 16 Nov. (1974)

[16] Scott and Helen Nearing, *Living the Good Life: Being a Plain Practical Account of a Twenty Year Project in a Self-Subsistent Homestead in Vermont, Together with Remarks on How to Live Sanely & Simply in a Troubled World*, (Harborside, ME: Social Science Institute, 1954); Spectorsky, op cit; interview with Corey Childs, Director, Loudoun County Office, Virginia Cooperative Extension, 29 Oct. 2003.

[17] Michael Clark, 'Farming Withers Under Developer Pressure', *Baltimore Sun*, 18 Mar. 1979.

[18] Jamie Smith Hopkins, 'Farmer Wannabes Warned', *Baltimore Sun*, 11 Nov. 2001.

[19] Personal interviews with extension agents in all three counties were carried out in the fall of 2003.

[20] See the Cornell Cooperative Extension of Niagara County homepage, http://www.cce.cornell.edu/niagara/niagara.html#local-programs and the Virginia Agricultural

Extension Services Department of horticulture, http://www.hort.vt.edu/ for winemaking regionalism.

[21] All three were available in Loudoun County. For wine tours see Loudoun County Wine Trail, http://www.rural-loudoun.state.va.us/wine_trail.htm, Loudoun 2003 Farm Color Tour, http://www.rural-loudoun.state.va.us/fguid1.htm, and the Loudoun County Bed & Breakfast Guild webpage featuring many farm B&Bs, http://www.vabb.com/vabblist.asp.

[22] 'The 200,000 Acre Solution: Supporting and Enhancing a Rural Economy for Loudoun's 21st Century', Loudoun County Rural Development Task Force, 1998.

[23] See Judith Weinraub, 'New American Farmers', *Washington Post*, 15 Oct. 2003. Joan Thirsk, *Alternative Agriculture: a History from the Black Death to the Present Day* (Oxford: Oxford University Press 1997), agues historically that marginal farmers are often by necessity the most innovative.

[24] Emphasised in regular Loudoun County surveys that analyse the most important factors why people move to the County. See: Loudoun County Department of Economic Development, *Survey of Loudoun Residents*, Mar. 1990; *Choices and Changes Survey Results Summary*, Department of Planning Zoning and Community Development, Loudoun County, 1 May 1990 (4,000 respondents); *1997 Survey of Loudoun County Residents*, commissioned by the Office of County Administrator, Loudoun County, 1997 (1,000 respondents); *1999 Survey of Loudoun's Residents*, commissioned by the Office of County Administrator, Loudoun County, 1999 (1,000 respondents); 20*01 Survey of Loudoun's Residents,* Department of Economic Development, Loudoun County, 2001 (1,000 respondents);

2002 Survey of Loudoun's Residents, commissioned by the Department of Economic Development, Loudoun County, 2002 (1,000 respondents).

At a national level, see successive Gallup Polls asking on place of living preferences (city, suburb, small town, country), George H. Gallup, *The Gallup Poll: Public Opinion 1935–71(Vol. III)*, (New York: Random House, 1972), Volume III, 1996 & 2238; George H. Gallup, *The Gallup Poll: Public Opinion 1972–77 (Vol. I & II)*, (Wilmington, Delaware: Scholarly Resources Inc., 1978), 78 & 112, and Vol. II, 914; George H. Gallup, *The Gallup Poll: Public Opinion 1978*, (Wilmington, Delaware: Scholarly Resources, Inc., 1979), 83–86; George H. Gallup, 'Urban America: A Special Gallup Report', in *the Gallup Poll: Public Opinion 1978*, Wilmington, Delaware: Scholarly Resources, Inc., 83–86 Released March 2; George H. Gallup, 'Urban Problems Special Survey' in *the Gallup Poll: Public Opinion 1981*', (Wilmington, Delaware: Scholarly Resources, Inc., 1981), 82–83; George Gallup, JR., 'Ideal Place to Live' in *The Gallup Poll: Public Opinion 1985*, (Wilmington, Delaware: Scholarly Resources, Inc., 1986), 64–65; George Gallup, JR., 'America's Large Cities' in *The Gallup Poll: Public Opinion 1989*, (Wilmington, Delaware: Scholarly Resources, Inc., 1990), 207–9; George Gallup, JR., 'America's Large Cities', in *The Gallup Poll: Public Opinion 1998*, (Wilmington, Delaware: Scholarly Resources, Inc., 1999), 238.

[25] See Maryland Equine Census (2002) online, http://www.marylandhorseindustry.org/census2.htm, Virginia Equine Report (2001) online, http://www.nass.usda.gov/va/2001equinereport.pdf , and New York Equine Survey (2000) online, http://www.nass.usda.gov/ny/Equine2000/equine.htm.

[26] Interview with Caragh Fitzgerald and Martin Hamilton, Howard Cooperative Extension, 11 Nov. 2003 confirm underreporting. State organisations exhorted owners to report, see New York State Horse Council Newsletter, September 2007: http://www.nyshc.org/newsletters/SeptOct05.pdf (http://horsecouncil.org/about.html)

[27] U.S. Agricultural Census. See note 7.

[28] See Maryland Equine Census (2002) and Dawna Klosner-Wehner, 'Howard Farms Still a Growth Industry', *Baltimore Sun*, 'Howard County Hometown Guide', 21 Mar. 2004

[29] See Virginia Equine Report (2001). Louis Nicholls, Agricultural Development Officer at the Loudoun County Department of Economic Development confirmed the county's interest in equine industry research during an interview on 16 Oct. 2003.

[30] With the exception of Saratoga County. See New York Equine Survey (2000).

[31] U.S. Agricultural Census online:

[32] U.S. Agricultural Census, see note 7.

[33] Lockport Sources: *Lockport City Directory* (Buffalo, NY: R.L. Polk & Co., 1949); R.L. Polk & Co; and *Lockport City Directory* (Livonia, MI: R.L. Polk & Co., 2000); Loudoun Sources: *Leesburg, Middleburg, and Purcellville City Directory* (Richmond, VA: Hill Directory Company 1962); C & PTelephone, Bell Atlantic; and *Loudoun-Fauquier Yellow Pages* (Verizon, 2001). Loudoun Directories are on hand at the Thomas Balch Historical Library in Leesburg, VA. Howard Sources: *Columbia Directory 1972*; *Howard County Telephone Directory, 2003* (all lodged with the Columbia Archives, Columbia, MD); and *The Community Phone Book Columbia, Ellicott City, MD, 2004* (online).

[34] See Joseph Goddard, 'The Creation of Penurbia: A Geography of the Heart, 1945–2005', (Ph.D. diss., University of Copenhagen, 2005).

[35] See '58th Annual Howard County Fair', 2–9Aug., (2003 programme): 14 & 119. For the 2007 fair, see http://www.howardcountyfair.org/fair_schedule.htm . See '68th Annual Loudoun County Fair', 28July – 2 Aug., (2003) programme): 23 & 35. For the 2007 show see: http://loudounextra.washingtonpost.com/events/search/?category=100&q=&age=&cost=&start_date=2007-07-19&end_date=&x=35&y=13 . See the '2003 Niagara County Fair' July. 30–Aug. (press packet.) For the 2006 fair, see http://counties.cce.cornell.edu/niagara/2006%20fair%20events%20schedule.pdf

[36] 'First Annual Howard County Fair', 21–22 Aug. (1946 programme).

[37] '58th Annual Howard County Fair', 4-H Sheep-Lead, (2003 programme): 237, and '68th Annual Loudoun County Fair'. Department 3.1 Non-Ownership Sheep (2003 programme) p. 19.

[38] 'Maryland Sheep and Wool Festival' website, http://www.sheepandwool.org/index.htm.

[39] 'The 2003 Niagara County Fair' (2003 press packet).

[40] 'Maryland Wine: the Next Vintage', Maryland Wine and Grape Advisory Committee Report, 2004: 4. http://www.marylandwine.com/mwa/media/stories/wgacreport.shtml

[41] 'Economic Impact of New York Grapes, Grape Juice and Wine', 2005, MKF Research for the New York Wine and Grape Foundation: http://www.nywines.org/articles.root/804/Economic%20Impact%20of%20New%20York%20Grapes%20Grape%20Juice%20and%20Wine%202005.pdf

[42] 'Virginia 2006 Commercial Grape Report', Virginia Department of Agriculture and Consumer Services, online at: http://www.nass.usda.gov/Statistics_by_State/Virginia/Publications/Grape_Report/2006%20grape%20publication.pdf

[43] 'Maryland Wine: the Next Vintage', Maryland Wine and Grape Advisory Committee Report, 2004: 33.

[44] The 'County Wine Trail' was established in cooperation with the Loudoun Rural Economic Development Office, http://www.loudounfarms.org/Default.asp?Page=16

[45] See New York Orchard & and Vineyard Survey, 2001, online at: http://www.nass.usda.gov/ny/FruitTree/fruittree2002txt.pdf , and Thomas Prohaska, 'Niagara County Legislature Panel Won't Vote on Trucks-Only Bridge', *Buffalo News*, 18 Mar. 2004.

[46] The 'Niagara Wine Trail' is described on the Niagara USA website, http://www.niagara-usa.com/attractions/winetrail.html . The 'Wine in the Woods' festival webpage is recorded here: http://www.howardcounty.com/calendar/event_details.asp?ID=25466

[47] The role of women's' organisations as pioneers in local environmental struggles has been well documented elsewhere, not least by Richard Walker, *The Country in the City* (Seattle: University of Washington, 2007).

[48] Maximum zoning in Niagara measured around one acre in 2003, less than in Howard or Loudoun.

[49] Townships, not the County determined land use policy in Niagara County.

[50] See *Howard General Plan*, 1960: 63.

[51] See *Erie-Niagara Regional Plan Summary Report*, 1961: II-N-25.

[52] See Adam Rome, *The Bulldozer in the Countryside* (Cambridge: Cambridge University Press, 2000) for the adverse effects of self-servicing.

[53] Anne Keisman, 'Development Races the Court', *Loudoun Times Mirror*, 5 May 2004.

[54] Agricultural land could be assessed for reduced levels of tax in all three counties.

[55] Adrian Higgins, 'Teaching Woodlot Owners to See the Forest Beyond the Trees', *Washington Post*, 22 Jan 2004; Cornell Cooperative Extension, local programmes in Niagara: http://counties.cce.cornell.edu/niagara/#local-programs; Basics of farming short courses in Maryland, Howard Ag. Newsletter, 2: 2006 at: http://www.hceda.org/uploads/pdfs/HowardAg_2006_Issue_02.pdf .

[56] American Farmland Trust (AFT) and Chesapeake Bay Foundation 'Conserving the Washington-Baltimore Region's Green Network: The Time to Act is Now', report, released May 2004. http://www.farmland.org/greennetwork/Conserving%20a%20Green%20Network.pdf.

[57] Dolores Hayden, *Building Suburbia: Green Fields and Urban Growth*, (New York: Pantheon Books, 2003): 238.

[58] Gill Chamblin, 'Fighting for Their Land', *Howard County Times*, 29 Oct 1981.

[59] See Howard County Department of Zoning and Planning website: http://www.co.ho.md.us/DPZ/Agricultural/dpz_agricultural_preservation.htm

[60] See The Loudoun County Purchase of Development Rights Program webpage, http://www.co.loudoun.va.us/omagi/pdr/index.htm.

[61] Virginia Agricultural Protection Act, 1981, and New York's Agricultural Districts Law, 1971.

[62] Including the *Loudoun Times-Mirror*, *Howard County Times*, *Times, Ellicott City*, *Niagara Gazette*, the *New York Times*, the *Washington Post*, and the *Baltimore Sun*. Local historical societies in all three counties maintain clippings of conflicts in their archives.

[63] In Roderick Frazier Nash, ed., *American Environmentalism: Readings in Conservation History* (New York: McGraw-Hill, 1990), 33; and Carolyn Merchant, ed., *Major Problems in American Environmental History* (Lexington, MA: D.C. Heath, 1993), 383–384. See also Witold Rybczynski, *A Clearing in the Distance: Frederick Law Olmsted and America in the 19th Century* (New York: Touchstone, 1999).

[64] See Audubon Naturalist Society Rust Sanctuary website, http://www.audubonnaturalist.org/rustsanct.htm.

[65] See Patapsco Female Institute Historic Park website, http://www.patapscofemaleinstitute.org/friends.htm.

[66] See Claude Moore Park, Loudoun County Department of Parks, Recreation & Community Services website, http://www.loudoun.gov/prcs/parks/claude.htm . The National Wildlife Federation owned the park from 1975 to 1986.

[67] Howard County General Plan, Howard County Planning Commission. 1960: 39.

[68] Byline: 'Parks Needed: Merging Cities Threaten Open Space', *Times, Ellicott City*, 8 May 1963.

[69] Rachel Carson, *Silent Spring* (Boston, MA: Houghton Mifflin, 1962).

[70] Loudoun County, Loudoun County Choices and Changes General Plan, 1990–2010, 1991.

[71] Anne Sorensen et al., op cit.

[72] Bill Michelmore, 'The Parkway Problem', *Buffalo News*, 20 Feb. 2000.

[73] The Niagara Heritage Partnership maintains an extensive electronic campaign archive of articles and letters. See: http://niagaraheritage.org/index.html.

[74] See the National Wildlife Federation's 'Backyard Wildlife Habitat' website, http://www.nwf.org/backyardwildlifehabitat/southriding.cfm.

[75] Loudoun County Department of Economic Development surveyed local residents' attitudes regularly from 1990, as did Howard Research and Development – builders of Columbia new town. George Gallup polled nationally. Local newspapers in the counties also carried out irregular and relatively unscientific self-reported surveys.

[76] See Rudy Maxa, 'Western Loudoun's Rural Landscape – It's Not Your Father's Farm', June 2001,online, http://www.rudymaxa.com/article.php?ArticleID=45

[77] John Hanchette, 'Mountain Views: Exploding Deer Population Presents Problems for Officials and Motorists', the *Niagara Falls Reporter*, 28 June 2005.

[78] Howard County Department of Recreation and Parks, 'Deer Management', http://www.co.ho.md.us/RAP/RAP_Deermanagement.htm (accessed 25 Jan. 2008)

[79] Amy Gardner, 'Swelling Herds, A Growing Risk', in the *Washington Post*, 27 Mar. 2007.

[80] See Woods, 'Engaging the Global Countryside', 487.

Index

A

B

C

D

E

F

G

Index

Index

White Horse Press 'Themes in Environmental History' Series

We are pleased to announce a new series of environmental history readers, suitable for students. Comprising essays selected from our journals, Environment and History and Environmental Values, each inexpensive paperback volume will address an important theme in environmental history, combining underlying theory and specific case-studies.

The first volume, *Bio-invaders*, investigates the rhetoric and realities of exotic, introduced and 'alien' species. The book comprises a number of general essays, exploring and challenging common perceptions about such species, and a series of case studies of particular species in particular contexts. Its geographical coverage ranges from the United Kingdom to New Zealand by way of South Africa, India and Palestine; and the essays cover both historical and recent introductions.

ISBN 9781874267553 PB 280pp. £15/ $22.50 / €18.50 Halftones, black and white drawings, maps, graphs, tables.

CONTENTS

For ordering information please see our website, www.whpress.co.uk

www.ingramcontent.com/pod-product-compliance
Lightning Source LLC
LaVergne TN
LVHW091029080826
845145LV00002B/408
9781874267607